T0323672

Bavarian Tourism and the Modern World, 1800–1950

During the nineteenth and early twentieth centuries, the tourism industry of Bavaria consistently promoted an image of "grounded modernity." This romanticized version of the present reconciled continuity with change, tradition with progress, and nature with science. In an era of rapid and unprecedented change, simultaneously nostalgic and progressive grounded modernity produced an illusion of continuity. It helped make the experience of modernity more tangible by linking impersonal and abstract ideas, like national identity, with familiar experiences and concrete sights.

Bavarian Tourism and the Modern World, 1800–1950 examines the connections between Bavarian tourism and the turbulent experience of German modernity during this period. It gauges Germany's long and often unsettling journey to modernity using Bavarian tourism and travel as a lens. Closely examining guidebooks, brochures, postcards, and other tourist propaganda, Adam Rosenbaum argues that by pointing visitors to the past, tourism illuminated the present, and produced signposts to the future.

Adam T. Rosenbaum is an assistant professor of history at Colorado Mesa University, where he teaches courses on European and Asian history.

PUBLICATIONS OF THE GERMAN HISTORICAL INSTITUTE

Edited by
HARTMUT BERGHOFF
with the assistance of David Lazar

The German Historical Institute is a center for advanced study and research whose purpose is to provide a permanent basis for scholarly cooperation among historians from the Federal Republic of Germany and the United States. The Institute conducts, promotes, and supports research into both American and German political, social, economic, and cultural history; into transatlantic migration, especially during the nineteenth and twentieth centuries; and into the history of international relations, with special emphasis on the roles played by the United States and Germany.

Recent Books in the Series:

Gerald D. Feldman, *Austrian Banks in the Period of National Socialism*

Eric C. Steinhart, *The Holocaust and the Germanization of Ukraine*

Hartmut Berghoff and Uta Andrea Balbier, *The East German Economy, 1945–2010: Falling Behind or Catching Up?*

Thomas W. Maulucci, Jr., and Detlef Junker, editors, *GIs in Germany: The Social, Economic, Cultural, and Political History of the American Military Presence*

Alison Efford, *German Immigrants, Race, and Citizenship in the Civil War Era*

Lars Maischak, *German Merchants in the Nineteenth-Century Atlantic*

Ingo Köhler, *The Aryanization of Private Banks in the Third Reich*

Hartmut Berghoff, Jürgen Kocka, and Dieter Ziegler, editors, *Business in the Age of Extremes*

Yair Mintzker, *The Defortification of the German City, 1689–1866*

Astrid M. Eckert, *The Struggle for the Files: The Western Allies and the Return of German Archives after the Second World War*

Winson Chu, *The German Minority in Interwar Poland*

Christof Mauch and Kiran Klaus Patel, *The United States and Germany during the Twentieth Century*

Monica Black, *Death in Berlin: From Weimar to Divided Germany*

John R. McNeill and Corinna R. Unger, editors, *Environmental Histories of the Cold War*

Roger Chickering and Stig Förster, editors, *War in an Age of Revolution, 1775–1815*

Cathryn Carson, *Heisenberg in the Atomic Age: Science and the Public Sphere*

Michaela Hoenicke Moore, *Know Your Enemy: The American Debate on Nazism, 1933–1945*

Bavarian Tourism and the Modern World, 1800–1950

ADAM T. ROSENBAUM

Colorado Mesa University

CAMBRIDGE
UNIVERSITY PRESS

32 Avenue of the Americas, New York, NY 10013-2473, USA

Cambridge University Press is part of the University of Cambridge.

It furthers the University's mission by disseminating knowledge in the pursuit of education, learning, and research at the highest international levels of excellence.

www.cambridge.org
Information on this title: www.cambridge.org/9781107111950

© Adam T. Rosenbaum 2016

This publication is in copyright. Subject to statutory exception and to the provisions of relevant collective licensing agreements, no reproduction of any part may take place without the written permission of Cambridge University Press.

First published 2016

Printed in the United Kingdom by Clays, St Ives plc

A catalog record for this publication is available from the British Library.

ISBN 978-1-107-11195-0 Hardback

Cambridge University Press has no responsibility for the persistence or accuracy of URLS for external or third-party Internet Web sites referred to in this publication and does not guarantee that any content on such Web sites is, or will remain, accurate or appropriate.

Wem willst du klagen, Herz? Immer gemiedener
ringt sich dein Weg durch die unbegreiflichen
Menschen. Mehr noch vergebens vielleicht,
da er die Richtung behält,
Richtung zur Zukunft behält,
zu der verlorenen.

Rainer Maria Rilke, "Klage"

Contents

Figures

Acknowledgments

It is with great pleasure that I now thank the various individuals and institutions who have contributed to this project over the course of nearly a decade. I would like to begin with my adviser, Astrid M. Eckert, who has guided this project since its inception. Her impressive knowledge of modern Germany, her insightful and challenging feedback, and her dedication to my success have been invaluable assets throughout my career, before and after graduation. I am honored to call her a mentor, a colleague, and a friend.

I am also happy to thank a number of other professors associated with Emory University. I am particularly grateful to Walter Adamson and Brian Vick, whose close readings of early drafts helped to make the final product a more nuanced and thought-provoking work. Special thanks also go to Holger Afflerbach, Peter Höyng, Günther Kronenbitter, Jeffrey Lesser, James V.H. Melton, Judith Miller, Gyan Pandey, Matthew Payne, and Jonathan Prude.

For their stimulating questions and thoughtful comments about my research, I want to thank Shelley Baranowski, David Blackbourn, Alon Confino, Jürgen Kocka, Ferdinand Kramer, Thomas Lekan, Christof Mauch, Helmut Walser Smith, Hasso Spode, Fritz Stern, Richard Wetzell, Andreas Wirsching, and the individuals who attended presentations of my research in the United States and Germany. For their support and friendship at Colorado Mesa University, I also want to thank Doug O'Roark, Tim Casey, and Erika Jackson, among others.

Next, I must acknowledge my debt to the German Historical Institute in Washington, D.C. The GHI has been sponsoring my research since 2007, long before awarding my dissertation with the Fritz Stern Prize and supporting the publication of this book. I am also grateful to David Lazar and Brian Hart, along with the prize committees of the Fritz Stern and Parker-Schmitt Dissertation Prizes. Deborah Gershenowitz and the staff at Cambridge University Press deserve my thanks as well, as do the two anonymous readers of the manuscript.

For their generous financial and academic support, I want to recognize the American Historical Association, the German Academic Exchange Service, the Institute of European History in Mainz, the Rachel Carson Center for Environment and Society in Munich, and the administrations of Emory and Colorado Mesa Universities. For their expertise and assistance, I am grateful to the staffs of the Federal Archive in Berlin, the Historical Archive for Tourism at the Willy Scharnow Institute, the Bavarian Main State Archive, the Bavarian Economic Archive, the State Archives of Augsburg, Bamberg, Munich, and Nuremberg, the City Archives of Augsburg, Munich, and Nuremberg, the Bavarian State Library, the City and State Library of Augsburg, the City Library of Mainz, the institutional library of the IEG Mainz, the Robert W. Woodruff Library at Emory University, the Library of Congress in Washington, D.C., and the Tomlinson Library at Colorado Mesa University.

For their hospitality and good conversation in Munich and Berlin, I want to thank Frau Kern, Julius Dengler, and the Dudek family. I also have to thank the Rosenbaums. Without their steadfast support and patience, I would not have accomplished any of this. My parents demonstrated incredible conviction in me during every stage of this long process, and I cannot thank them enough. My brother Josh made the drive to Atlanta to support me during my prospectus defense, and has been a fan of this project ever since. Nevertheless, it is my wife who has truly lived with Bavarian tourism on an almost daily basis for years. For her ruthless review of drafts, her frequent flights to and from Germany, and her insistence on having fun in the midst of all these tasks, I dedicate this book to Ashley (who will certainly disapprove of this verbose sentence).

Portions of the Introduction and Chapters 2, 3, and 5 have appeared in print before, albeit in a rather different form. I am pleased to acknowledge the publishers and editors of the *Bulletin of the German Historical Institute* and *Central European History* for allowing me to use parts of the articles that appeared in their periodicals in this book.

Abbreviations

BArch	Federal Archive, Berlin
BayHStA	Bavarian Main State Archive, Munich
BDV	Federation of German Travel Associations
BWA	Bavarian Economic Archive, Munich
HAT	Historical Archive for Tourism, Free University Berlin
KdF	*Kraft durch Freude*, or "Strength through Joy" Program
RDV	Reich Central Office for German Tourism Promotion
SGSV	Administration of State Castles, Gardens, and Lakes
StAA	Augsburg State Archive
StAB	Bamberg State Archive
StadtAA	Augsburg City Archive
StadtAM	Munich City Archive
StadtAN	Nuremberg City Archive
StAM	Munich State Archive
StAN	Nuremberg State Archive
VVA	Augsburg Tourism Association

Introduction

Today, Bavaria is an internationally renowned travel destination, but this was not always the case. In fact, it was once overshadowed by other German destinations like the Rhineland and the Black Forest, conveniently situated along the meandering route of the aristocratic Grand Tour. It was the rise of the commercial tourism industry during the nineteenth century that first brought large numbers of visitors to the Kingdom of the Wittelsbachs. The region's appeal was truly multifaceted; from the rolling hills of the Franconian highlands to the snow-capped peaks of the Alps, from the medieval walls of former Imperial Free Cities to the galleries and beer halls of Munich, Bavaria had no shortage of sights worth seeing.

I first travelled to Bavaria not as a tourist or a historian, but as a high-school exchange student. Living in Munich for close to a year, I developed a passion for its history, culture, and cuisine, and found myself enamored with the so-called village of millions. Like a good urbanite, I was also drawn to the landscape outside the city, visiting various locales in the Alps and their foothills. I quickly realized that there was something remarkable about Upper Bavaria; it was so quintessentially German and yet so distinct from the other parts of the country that I toured that year. Furthermore, the people seemed proud of this otherness, and were eager to identify themselves as Bavarians first, and Germans second. Years later, as a graduate student at Emory University, I decided to examine Bavarian identity in more detail by considering how the region sold itself to domestic and foreign tourists.

In his influential book *The Tourist: A New Theory of the Leisure Class*, sociologist Dean MacCannell writes: "Entire cities and regions, decades and cultures have become aware of themselves as tourist attractions."[1] Tourism led to a massive remapping of Bavaria, raising the profile of some locations while rendering others invisible, but did it make Bavarians self-aware? Did tourism facilitate the creation of a distinctly Bavarian form of "Germanness"? These were my initial research questions, but the archive held more than a few surprises. I searched in vain for clues to the construction of a Bavarian regional identity, but what I ultimately uncovered was a complex relationship between the promises of tourism and the turbulent experience of modernity in central Europe. During the latter half of the nineteenth century, Germany quickly evolved from an assemblage of predominantly agrarian states into an industrial and military superpower. How did a growing tourism industry respond to industrialization, war, revolution, and widespread feelings of displacement and anomie? How did Germans decide to market their dynamic and volatile homeland to visitors from home and abroad? How did this constructed image reflect changing conceptions of nature, history, and modernity? These are the larger questions that the present work addresses, and the answers shed light on much more than Bavarian regional identity.

This is a book about leisure travel during a period of unprecedented transformations and dislocations. While travel has been a component of the human experience since ancient times, tourism is a distinctly modern phenomenon. As a cultural practice and a profitable business, tourism was pioneered by the nineteenth-century middle classes, who dedicated their limited free time to meaningful leisure activities. Although extended hikes and trips into the countryside were often sold as temporary flights from modern civilization, this was never simple escapism.[2] Modern leisure travel provided distance from the contemporary world, but it also provided perspective. In fact, tourism became an important feature of modern life itself; it was a form of therapy that allowed men and women to experiment with alternative possibilities. In a post-traditional world rendered unrecognizable by industrialization, urbanization, and the rise of the nation-state, the tourism industry promised to reconcile civilization and its discontents, anchoring contemporary urban society in the natural environment and a common past.

In Bavaria, the tourism industry consistently promoted an image of what I refer to as *grounded modernity*, a romanticized version of the

---

[1] Dean MacCannell, *The Tourist: A New Theory of the Leisure Class* (New York: Schocken Books, 1976), 16.

[2] For more on tourism as escapism, see Ursula A.J. Becher, *Geschichte des modernen Lebenstils. Essen-Wohnen-Freizeit-Reisen* (Munich: C.H. Beck, 1990), 197–198, 204–205.

present that reconciled tradition with progress, consistency with change, and nature with technology and science. This alternative vision provided the traveler with a taste of stability and a glimpse of authenticity, and it helped to make the modern world more comprehensible by linking impersonal and abstract ideas, like national identity, with familiar experiences and concrete sights. In an era of rapid and unprecedented change, grounded modernity produced the illusion of continuity. Though the two concepts may sound similar, "grounded modernity" is distinct from the discourse of "reactionary modernism" analyzed by historian Jeffrey Herf. The latter was limited to interwar intellectuals like Ernst Jünger and Martin Heidegger, who reconciled antimodern tendencies with technological modernization.[3] The language of grounded modernity, in contrast, was much more flexible, marketable, and widespread, and it was recognizable as early as the nineteenth century. Simultaneously nostalgic and progressive, it celebrated technology alongside several other aspects of modernity, including city planning, mass culture, and popular political movements.

While acknowledging the achievements of contemporary times, grounded modernity also glorified distance from everyday tedium. This was something that the Bavarian tourism industry ensured. Excursions into nature and vacations in health resorts provided visitors with a break from their hectic, dirty, and stressful urban existence. Trips to cities themselves provided access to historical milestones, in addition to granting new insight into the modern nation-state, defined by industrial progress and political triumph. In other words, tourism was always in the shadow of the present, even when it was seemingly fixated on the natural environment and the past. It could ground the individual traveler in search of meaning and perspective, but it also had the potential to ground the entire nation and the current political regime. The region of Bavaria offers numerous case studies that showcase how both visitors and the visited coped with modern life, and thus, paved the way for the future.

Bavaria, Modernity, and Tourism

By focusing on Bavaria, this book contributes to a growing body of scholarship that has employed the subnational "region" as a category of historical analysis. Decades ago, historians tended to dismiss the region as an anachronistic holdover from pre-modern times. Historians of Germany

---

[3] Jeffrey Herf, *Reactionary Modernism: Technology, Culture, and Politics in Weimar and the Third Reich* (New York: Cambridge University Press, 1984).

in particular rarely questioned nation-building as their "central theme," and according to James Sheehan, "even fewer questioned the role of the *nation* as the basic conceptual unit within which historical problems were to be defined."[4] Regions did not register as worthwhile topics, and when they did garner attention, it was only as sites of backwardness, or as bulwarks against modernization and the creation of a unified nation-state.[5] In recent decades, a new generation of historians has reversed this trend.[6] In the case of continental Europe, scholars have emancipated the region from the analytical framework of modernization theory, demonstrating that regional particularities are not always reactionary and antimodern, just as regionalism and nationalism are not always mutually exclusive.[7] These scholars have proven that regionalism is a worthwhile category of historical analysis, in addition to demonstrating that the paths of regionalism and the German *Heimat* movement in particular "do not always lead away from modernity, but rather to its very core."[8]

My work engages with this literature, but it does not concentrate on a uniform Bavarian identity as a "mediator" or "metaphor" for national identity. Instead, it deconstructs the notion of Bavarian regionalism by recasting the former kingdom and *Freistaat* as a region of localities. Divided by religion, culture, and history, Bavaria was a political and economic unit that only began to acquire its present shape in the early nineteenth century. Local tourism associations reflected these divisions by concentrating on a single town or city, or by promoting a smaller region

---

[4] James J. Sheehan, "What is German History? Reflections on the Role of the Nation in German History and Historiography," *The Journal of Modern History* 53, no. 1 (March 1981): 2.

[5] James Retallack, "Introduction: Locating Saxony in the Landscape of German Regional History," in *Saxony in German History: Culture, Society, and Politics, 1830–1933*, ed. James Retallack (Ann Arbor: University of Michigan Press, 2000), 18–19; David Blackbourn and James Retallack, "Introduction," in *Localism, Landscape, and the Ambiguities of Place: German-Speaking Central Europe, 1860–1930*, ed. David Blackbourn and James Retallack (Toronto: University of Toronto Press, 2007), 15–17.

[6] Celia Applegate, "A Europe of Regions," AHR Forum: "Bringing Regionalism back to History," *American Historical Review* 104, no. 4 (October 1999): 1164. See also Eric Storm, "Regionalism in History, 1890–1945: The Cultural Approach," *European History Quarterly* 33, no.2 (2003): 251–265.

[7] Caroline Ford, *Creating the Nation in Provincial France: Religion and Political Identity in Brittany* (Princeton: Princeton University Press, 1993); Celia Applegate, *A Nation of Provincials: The German Idea of Heimat* (Berkeley: University of California Press, 1990); Alon Confino, *The Nation as a Local Metaphor: Württemberg, Imperial Germany, and National Memory, 1871–1918* (Chapel Hill: University of North Carolina Press, 1997).

[8] Thomas Kühne, "Imagined Regions: The Construction of Traditional, Democratic, and Other Identities," in *Saxony in German History*, 51.

like "Northern Bavaria" or "Munich and the Bavarian Highlands." Consequently, this study does not focus on a single, Bavarian identity because that is rarely what the tourism industry chose to sell. In fact, it was not until the latter half of the twentieth century that tourist publications frequently presented the larger region of Bavaria as a collective tourist destination. Even then, the only thing "Bavarian" about many of these tourist destinations was their location.

This region of localities began as a duchy north of the Alps in the sixth century C.E. In 1180, Holy Roman Emperor Friedrich Barbarossa deposed the presiding Duke of Bavaria, and awarded the duchy to the Wittelsbach family, who ruled uninterrupted until 1918.[9] However, it was not until the Napoleonic Wars that Bavaria began to acquire its modern appearance, incorporating portions of largely Protestant Swabia and Franconia, including the cities of Augsburg and Nuremberg. With the support of Emperor Napoleon, Bavaria was also transformed into a kingdom, and on January 1, 1806, Duke Maximilian IV Josef became Maximilian I, King of Bavaria.[10] The region grew tremendously during this period, and its population nearly tripled, rising from 1.25 million in 1794, to 3.68 million in 1817.[11] The reign of Ludwig I (1825–1848) witnessed further growth, and was marked by the king's enthusiastic patronage of the arts, the gradual industrialization of Bavaria, and the construction of the first German railway between Nuremberg and Fürth in 1835.[12] In the midst of the 1848 revolutions, Ludwig I was succeeded by his son, Maximilian II, who became a patron of German intellectuals like Leopold von Ranke and Justus von Liebig.[13] After his death in 1864, the crown passed to eighteen-year-old Ludwig II. Later immortalized as the "Mad King" of Bavaria, he ruled for twenty-two years, a period during which central Europe experienced sweeping transformations.[14] During that time, Bavaria's ill-fated involvement in the 1866 Austro-Prussian

---

[9] For a helpful survey of Bavarian history, see Andreas Kraus, *Geschichte Bayerns: Von den Anfängen bis zur Gegenwart*, 3rd edn. (Munich: Beck, 2004).

[10] Manfred Treml, "Königreich Bayern (1806–1918)," in *Geschichte des modernen Bayern: Königreich und Freistaat*, ed. Manfred Treml, 3rd edn. (Munich: Bayerische Landeszentrale für Politische Bildungsarbeit, 2006), 19–26.

[11] W.R. Lee, *Population Growth, Economic Development and Social Change in Bavaria, 1750–1850* (New York: Arno Press, 1977), 12.

[12] See Golo Mann, *Ludwig I. von Bayern* (Frankfurt am Main: Fischer Taschenbuch Verlag, 1999).

[13] See Martin Schäfer, *Maximillian II.: König von Bayern* (Munich: W. Heyne, 1989).

[14] See Christopher McIntosh, *Ludwig II of Bavaria: The Swan King* (New York: I.B. Tauris, 1997).

FIGURE 1. Map of Bavaria with popular tourist destinations.

War on the side of the Austrian Empire and its reluctant alliance with Prussia in 1870 led to its incorporation into the German Empire after the defeat of Napoleon III's France.[15] Although the kingdom's sovereignty had been compromised, the Bavarian state continued to forge its own path, developing a separate system of taxation and even pursuing its own foreign policy.[16]

In spite of its special political status, Bavaria had a trajectory similar to those of other German regions, sharing the experiences of demographic

[15] For more on Ludwig II and the origins of the *Kaiserreich*, see Christof Botzenhart, *Die Regierungstätigkeit König Ludwig II. von Bayern: "ein Schattenkönig ohne Macht will ich nicht sein"* (Munich: C.H. Beck, 2004), 185–196.

[16] Allan Mitchell, "A Real Foreign Country: Bavarian Particularism in Imperial Germany, 1870–1918," *Francia* 7 (1979): 587–596.

growth, industrialization, war, and revolution. Nevertheless, some German historians have dismissed Bavaria as a provincial anomaly within the larger story of the modern nation-state. Others have been preoccupied with the growth of a Bavarian particularism that complicated the development of a broader German nationalism. Those who have taken Bavaria more seriously have analyzed how the Bavarian state promoted a separate identity throughout the nineteenth century, with tactics including the official codification of regional history, the promotion of a Wittelsbach cult of monarchy, and the display of regional costumes at royal events.[17] All of these efforts were designed to create allegiance to the dynasty and state, despite the fact that Bavaria was itself divided into older, regional units like Swabia and Franconia. At the same time, the development of a national infrastructure in the form of railways, postal service, legal statutes, and education also contributed to a broader regional consciousness in Bavaria.[18] This regional consciousness often coexisted with German patriotism. For example, the German imperial cult and the Bavarian cult of monarchy often overlapped and mutually reinforced one another in the same state-sponsored public spectacle in post-unification Bavaria.[19] Meanwhile, history lessons in Bavarian elementary school classrooms minimized Prussia's role in the German Empire while glorifying Bavarian contributions to both medieval and recent German history.[20] Though often absent from tourist propaganda, Bavarian particularism did exist within more official discourses, and was ultimately consistent with German nationalism.

Bavaria might have been officially part of the larger German nation-state, but certain features did distinguish it from other regions. Historian Abigail Green has emphasized the exceptional nature of Bavaria, arguing that the state's size, political significance, and predominantly Catholic population made it "atypical and far less representative of the Third

---

[17] Norbert Joseph Mayr, "Particularism in Bavaria: State Policy and the Public Sentiment, 1806–1906." Ph. D. diss., University of North Carolina, Chapel Hill, 1988, 96–187; Regina Bendix, "Moral Integrity in Costumed Identity: Negotiating 'National Costume' in 19th Century Bavaria," *The Journal of American Folklore* 111, no. 440 (Spring 1998): 133–145.

[18] Siegfried Weichlein, *Nation und Region: Integrationsprozesse in Bismarckreich* (Düsseldorf: Droste, 2004).

[19] Werner K. Blessing, "The Cult of Monarchy, Political Loyalty, and the Workers' Movement in Imperial Germany," *Journal of Contemporary History* 13, no. 2 (April 1978): 357–375.

[20] Katharine D. Kennedy, "Regionalism and Nationalism in South German History Lessons, 1871–1914," *German Studies Review* 12, no. 1 (February 1989): 11–33.

Germany" than Hanover, Saxony, or Württemberg.[21] Others have maintained that the region had "the strongest separate 'national' identification" in Germany, and that the differences between Bavarians, Swabians, and Franconians quickly faded away.[22] Historian Ute Planert has cast doubt upon such assumptions by arguing that Franconia's incorporation into the Bavarian state at the beginning of the nineteenth century actually produced a new Franconian identity that defined itself in opposition to the Catholic south.[23] My research builds upon this work by indicating that the notion of a uniform Bavarian identity is a historical myth that prevents us from appreciating the complexity of the Bavarian case. Furthermore, the tendency to brand Bavaria as exceptional has prevented us from considering its similarities with other German regions like Prussia and Baden, which were also internally divided, but lacked comparable reputations of regional particularism. In many regards, Bavaria was both exceptional and exemplary, and that is why it grants such valuable insight into the larger topics of collective identity and modernity.

Before proceeding further, it may be helpful to turn our attention to the latter concept. In his 1863 essay, "The Painter of Modern Life," art critic Charles Baudelaire used the term "modernity" to refer to "the transient, the fleeting, the contingent," an "indefinable something" that all artists should capture in their work. However, his subsequent assertion that every artistic epoch had its own "form of modernity" obscured the truly unique features of Baudelaire's day and age.[24] For many Europeans, the nineteenth and twentieth centuries represented an age of progress and divergence, defined by rationalization, industrialization, urbanization, "denaturalization," ongoing secularization, and the rise of the nation-state.[25] Collectively defined as modernization, these processes destroyed traditional relationships and networks, and uprooted large portions of

[21] Abigail Green, *Fatherlands: State-Building and Nationhood in Nineteenth Century Germany* (New York: Cambridge University Press, 2001), 10.

[22] Bendix, "Moral Integrity in Costumed Identity," 142–143; Mayr, "Particularism in Bavaria," 10.

[23] Ute Planert, "From Collaboration to Resistance: Politics, Experience, and Memory of the Revolutionary and Napoleonic Wars in Southern Germany," *Central European History* 39, no. 4 (December 2006): 689, 692. For more on the challenge of constructing a united Bavarian identity, see Manfred Hanisch, *"Für Fürst und Vaterland": Legitimationsstiftung in Bayern zwischen Revolution von 1848 und deutscher Einheit* (Munich: R. Oldenbourg, 1991).

[24] Charles Baudelaire, "The Painter of Modern Life," in *Selected Writings on Art and Literature*, trans. P.E. Charvet (New York: Penguin Books, 1992), 402–403.

[25] C.A. Bayly, *The Birth of the Modern World, 1780–1914* (Malden, MA: Blackwell, 2004), 11. For more on "denaturalization," see Wolfgang Schivelbusch, *The Railway*

society both literally and figuratively.[26] In 1848's "Communist Manifesto," Karl Marx and Friedrich Engels described the modern age as follows: "Constant revolutionizing of production, uninterrupted disturbance of all social conditions, everlasting uncertainty and agitation distinguish the bourgeois epoch from all earlier ones ... All that is solid melts into air, all that is holy is profaned ... "[27] This is modernity: the post-traditional condition wrought by modernization that began to define parts of Europe over the course of the long nineteenth century. Things had changed, and there was a widespread perception of living in a drastically altered world that was both inspiring and horrifying.[28] In the midst of such violent change and iconoclasm, some individuals sought more grounded and meaningful experiences. Their subjective visions became varieties of modernism: any attempt to deal with the disorienting experience of modernity by experimenting with alternative possibilities.[29]

Although historians continue to disagree about the nature of German modernity, with some still insisting on a "special path" of modernization, most agree that the late nineteenth century witnessed major breakthroughs and extraordinary complications.[30] In a matter of decades, Germany evolved from a loose alliance of agrarian states into a predominantly urban and industrial superpower.[31] *Gemeinschaft* gave way to *Gesellschaft*, or a "society in which every kind of social or political identity was suddenly disrupted and replaced by the anonymity and facelessness of modern life."[32] For many Germans, modernity represented a mixed bag of progress and loss, promise and despair. Still, they did

---

  Journey: The Industrialization of Time and Space in the Nineteenth Century (Berkeley: University of California Press, 1987), 1–15.

[26] Marshall Berman, *All That Is Solid Melts Into Air: The Experience of Modernity* (New York: Penguin Books, 1988), 17.

[27] Karl Marx and Friedrich Engels, "The Communist Manifesto," in *The Marx-Engels Reader*, ed. Robert Tucker (New York: Norton, 1972), 338.

[28] Bayly, *The Birth of the Modern World*, 10–11.

[29] Berman, *All That Is Solid Melts Into Air*, 5, 16.

[30] For more on the *Sonderweg* debate, see Jürgen Kocka, "German History Before Hitler: The Debate about the German Sonderweg," *Journal of Contemporary History* 23, no. 1 (January 1988): 3–16; Chris Lorenz, "Beyond Good and Evil? The German Empire of 1871 and Modern German Historiography," *Journal of Contemporary History* 30, no. 4 (October 1995): 729–765; William Hagen, "Master Narratives beyond Postmodernity: Germany's 'Separate Path' in Historiographical-Philosophical Light," *German Studies Review* 30, no. 1 (February 2007): 1–32.

[31] See Brett Fairbairn, "Economic and Social Developments," in *Imperial Germany, 1871–1918*, ed. James Retallack (New York: Oxford University Press, 2010), 61–82.

[32] Thomas W. Kniesche and Stephen Brockmann, "Introduction: Weimar Today," in *Dancing on the Volcano: Essays on the Culture of the Weimar Republic*, ed. Thomas

not think exclusively in terms of "modern" versus "antimodern," or "new" versus "old." Instead, they developed "blends and amalgams that are specific to particular times and social systems and must be thoroughly studied in their own right."[33] Thomas Lekan identifies one such amalgam in his work on German landscape preservation, in which he argues that middle-class environmentalists worked toward an "alternative modernity" by seeking "a harmonious balance between industrial technology and the natural environment in the countryside." For example, some environmental activists insisted that paper mills, mines, and even railways had become naturalized elements of the landscape, just as cities could remain connected to the past through the conservation of green spaces and medieval architecture.[34] More recently, Andrew Denning has examined the history of skiing in order to elucidate the concept of "Alpine modernism," an ideology that balanced neo-romantic "back to nature" impulses with a celebration of the more modern attributes of the new sport, including its rationality and its velocity. "By harmonizing modernity with the timeless Alps," Denning argues, "skiers generated a modern vision of paradise."[35] My research confirms that tourism served a similar function by allowing Germans (and foreigners) to temporarily inhabit a better version of modernity. Again, it was not an escape from the modern world, but rather a means of experimenting with alternative possibilities. However, like modernity in general, this experience was also ephemeral or "fleeting."

Scholars have not always been willing to acknowledge the broader significance of tourism, and it was once commonplace to dismiss tourism as an exercise in conformity, mediocrity, and superficiality.[36] Departing

---

W. Kniesche and Stephen Brockmann (Columbia, SC: Camden, 1994), 7. See also Ferdinand Tönnies, *Community and Society*, trans. Charles P. Loomis (New York: Dover Publications, 2002).

[33] Adelheid von Saldern, *The Challenges of Modernity: German Social and Cultural Studies, 1890–1960*, trans. Bruce Little (Ann Arbor: University of Michigan Press, 2002), 3.

[34] Thomas Lekan, *Imagining the Nation in Nature: Landscape Preservation and German Identity, 1885–1945* (Cambridge, MA: Harvard University Press, 2004), 63–67. See also Thomas Rohkrämer, *Eine andere Moderne? Zivilisationskritik, Natur und Technik in Deutschland, 1880–1930* (Paderborn: Schöningh, 1999).

[35] Andrew Denning, "Alpine Modern: Central European Skiing and the Vernacularization of Cultural Modernism, 1900–1939," *Central European History* 46, no. 4 (December 2013): 871. See also Denning, *Skiing into Modernity: A Cultural and Environmental History* (Oakland: University of California Press, 2015).

[36] See Paul Fussell, *The Norton Book of Travel*, ed. Paul Fussell (New York: Norton, 1987), 649.

from this older view, Dean MacCannell has argued that tourism is a means of overcoming the dreary monotony of modern life. "For moderns," writes MacCannell, "reality and authenticity are thought to be elsewhere: in other historical periods and other cultures, in purer, simpler lifestyles."[37] Tourism provides access to these supposedly more authentic worlds, allowing travelers to transcend modern life, while simultaneously making more sense of it. MacCannell's definition of tourism as a "search for authenticity" has drawn some criticism, with one scholar insisting that tourists favor the "extraordinary" over the "authentic."[38] Consequently, it is important to stress that authenticity is not synonymous with the "real" world, and the mundane routines and sights that tourists often seek to escape. Authenticity can also represent an idealized world that tourists may have never actually seen, an alternative reality that represents an improved version of the present. As a "component of the modern condition," even seemingly antimodern tourism functions as a modernism in its own right.[39]

Recent research has illustrated how nineteenth-century tourism in Scotland, Austria, and France reconnected visitors with a pre-industrial past, helping them to cope with the disorienting experience of modernity.[40] This suggests that similar discourses of grounded modernity resonated elsewhere in Europe. Equally valuable work has been published by several historians of modern Germany, who have identified connections between leisure travel and national identity.[41] The literature on the history of Bavarian tourism, on the other hand, is far from extensive, in spite of the region's contemporary status as a veritable tourist Mecca. Among the

---

[37] MacCannell, *The Tourist*, 3.

[38] John Urry, *The Tourist Gaze*, 2nd edn. (London: Sage Publications, 2002), 12.

[39] Anne E. Gorsuch and Diane P. Koenker, "Introduction," in *Turizm: The Russian and East European Tourist under Capitalism and Socialism*, ed. Anne E. Gorsuch and Diane P. Koenker (Ithaca, NY: Cornell University Press, 2006), 14.

[40] See Katherine Haldane Grenier, *Tourism and Identity in Scotland, 1770–1914: Creating Caledonia* (Burlington, VT: Ashgate, 2005); Jill Steward, "Tourism in the Late Imperial Austria: The Development of Tourist Cultures and Their Associated Images of Place," in *Being Elsewhere: Tourism, Consumer Culture, and Identity in Modern Europe and North America*, ed. Shelley Baranowksi and Ellen Furlough (Ann Arbor: University of Michigan Press, 2001), 108–134; Patrick Young, "Of Pardons, Loss, and Longing: The Tourist's Pursuit of Originality in Brittany, 1890–1935," *French Historical Studies* 30, no. 2 (2007): 269–304.

[41] See Hasso Spode, *Wie die Deutschen "Reiseweltmeister" wurden: Eine Einführung in die Tourismusgeschichte* (Erfurt: Landeszentrale für politische Bildung Thüringen, 2003); Rudy Koshar, *German Travel Cultures* (Oxford: Berg, 2000); Caitlin Murdock, "Tourist Landscapes and Regional Identities in Saxony, 1878–1938," *Central European History* 40, no. 4 (December 2007): 589–621.

few publications is a 1992 article by Helen Waddy Lepovitz, in which she argues that Bavarian tourism materialized over the course of the nineteenth century as a result of the constant flow of German pilgrims, patients, and painters. However, Lepovitz's emphasis on the singularity of the Bavarian tourist culture prevents us from considering the region's place in the larger history of tourism and the German nation-state. Furthermore, she confines her analysis to sites within Upper Bavaria, including Oberammergau and Murnau, offering a limited view of the tourist landscape.[42] In a more recent work, Joshua Hagen addresses the growth of tourism in Rothenburg ob der Tauber, a well-preserved medieval town in Middle Franconia. He argues that both local preservation efforts and the marketing of the town as a tourist destination turned Rothenburg into "a symbol of rootedness, community, and continuity with a bygone era."[43] Hagen's analysis of the relationship between tourism, memory, and imagining community is valuable, but his concentration on Rothenburg ob der Tauber does not allow for a broader investigation of the balancing of traditional and modern elements that was so common in tourist publications throughout Bavaria.

Organization and Overview

This study provides an overview of tourism in modern Bavaria, as well as a careful reading of the language used to market its diversity of attractions. Its cast of characters ranges from romantic poets and bourgeois physicians to tourism promoters and travelers from Germany and beyond. Its case studies are not exclusively from "Old Bavaria," but also from Swabia and Franconia, regions that were first incorporated into Bavaria at the beginning of the nineteenth century. Its time period, spanning from the early nineteenth century to the postwar period, allows for an analysis of the evolution of leisure travel and the growth of the tourism industry over the course of at least four distinct eras in modern German history.

In spite of this geographical diversity and extended time frame, this work offers several broader conclusions. The central argument is that the regional tourism industry consistently endorsed a vision of grounded modernity, combating the "consciousness of displacement" by inviting

---

[42] Helen Waddy Lepovitz, "Pilgrims, Patients, and Painters: The Formation of a Tourist Culture in Bavaria," *Historical Reflections/Réflexions Historiques* 18, no. 1 (1992): 121–145.

[43] Joshua Hagen, *Preservation, Tourism and Nationalism: The Jewel of the German Past* (Burlington: Ashgate, 2006), 1.

contemporary society to become reacquainted with nature, tradition, and history.[44] At the end of the nineteenth century, a trip to rural Bavaria was often advertised as a romantic flight from modern reality, during which guests could, ironically, anticipate modern accommodations and conveniences. Similarly, a trip to the spa allowed the tourist to reconnect with the natural environment while enjoying modern medical treatments and facilities. Bavaria therefore remained timeless, and yet decidedly of this time, or modern. The region was likewise marketed as quaint and rustic, but also as sophisticated and cosmopolitan. In order to attract visitors of various nationalities, and sometimes even faiths, the destination had to be both foreign *and* familiar. This cosmopolitan status became another indication of modernity. After World War I, the regional tourism industry began to advertise Bavaria as quintessentially German, but this was a product available to nearly all classes, creeds, and nationalities, with Jews representing a significant exception during the Third Reich. Furthermore, the popularity of Bavarian cities was not based on their historical record alone, but also on their contemporary relevance. Those that triumphed as tourist destinations did so because of their symbolic role within a new nation-state selectively grounded in German history and culture. These cities provided insight into the past and present, as well as hints of future greatness.

After an opening chapter that provides a historical overview of German travel, this study proceeds both chronologically and thematically. Each of the major chapters explores the language of grounded modernity in a different tourist locale during a distinct period of modern German history. These chapters also address topics that transcend the boundaries of the former Wittelsbach kingdom, including romanticism, class consciousness, modern medicine, industrialization, nationalism, and fascism. Chapter 2 addresses changing conceptions of nature and the development of middle-class leisure travel during the nineteenth century. Selecting the secluded region of "Franconian Switzerland" as the prototypical tourist destination visited by the German educated middle class, this chapter demonstrates how nineteenth-century tourism was predicated on a new appreciation of the natural environment fueled by romanticism and urbanization. While middle-class travelers sought a romantic respite in the mountainous landscape of Franconian Switzerland, they were not always willing to leave the city behind, and could anticipate modern accommodations

---

44 Koshar, *German Travel Cultures*, 8.

at the local inn, as well as telegraph machines and beer imported from Munich and Nuremberg.

Focusing on another destination defined by its natural surroundings, Chapter 3 examines the spa culture of Bad Reichenhall. In the late nineteenth century, the Bavarian tourism industry successfully recast this provincial town as an ideal urban space rooted in nature and frequented by an international clientele, marketing a grounded modernity with a cosmopolitan flair. In many regards, a stay in the spa was sold as an antidote to modern civilization, an experience that allowed guests to transcend their everyday lives and the mental horizons of the German nation. After 1914, the repercussions of total war undermined this carefully cultivated image. Converted into an inexpensive sick bay for German soldiers, Bad Reichenhall was cut off from its international clientele and most of its domestic visitors during World War I, when the language of nationalism abruptly replaced the language of cosmopolitanism.

Moving away from the natural environment and into the metropolis, Chapter 4 concentrates on the marketing of the historic city of Augsburg during the Weimar era. It reveals how the Augsburg Tourism Association, with the occasional support of the local municipal government, placed greater emphasis on the more modern dimensions of the city over the course of the 1920s. Their goal was not only to ground modernity, but also to modernize the city's historical ground, drawing connections between past and present. Marketing was part of this program, but the local tourism association was also responsible for refurbishing parts of the historic city and using new technology to reframe old attractions. In the end, they succeeded in promoting a more progressive and "German" vision of city. This selective vision of Augsburg ultimately diverted attention from its true civic identity, that of a politically charged and economically unstable city of workers.

The fifth chapter also focuses on the urban environment by examining Nazi tourism in Bavaria's two largest cities, Munich and Nuremberg. The local tourism industry of both cities transformed the sights associated with Hitler and the National Socialist movement, such as the Temples of Honor and the Party Rally Grounds, into the defining features of each city's contemporary identity. These sites also served as centers of the Nazi festival culture, which produced a pseudo-religious experience that blurred the lines between leisure travel and pilgrimage. In the meantime, traditional marketing themes never completely disappeared, and the tourism industry promoted new attractions against the backdrop

of the local and larger German past. In this manner, they helped to legitimize the Third Reich and its central concept of the *Volksgemeinschaft*,
a people's community united by history, culture, and, less obviously,
race. Although 1939 offers a logical ending point for this story, the book
concludes with an epilogue that describes the collapse of the German
tourism industry during World War II, as well as the obstacles faced by
the Bavarian tourism industry during the immediate postwar years.

Throughout these chapters, the source base consists primarily of
"tourist propaganda," a category including guidebooks, brochures, maps,
postcards, and posters. While recognizing the negative connotation of the
term "propaganda," as well as the fact that propaganda is usually associated with government agencies, I insist that the term provides us with
a useful way of thinking about these documents. While some of these
sources were intended for tourists who were already in Bavaria, others
were designed to convince potential vacationers that Bavaria was worthy
of a visit. The tourism industry defined all of these materials as propaganda because they were designed to influence the opinion of visitors,
before, during, and after the trip. Guidebooks, for example, were not
only "formulas for travel," indicating what "ought to be seen," but also
"distillations of the objects and routes of the tourist's cultural labor, and
of the possibilities and diversity of experience."[45] In other words, guidebooks helped to predetermine the practices and expectations of tourists,
ultimately standardizing the experience of travel. Another form of tourist
propaganda helped to standardize the memory of travel. Postcards, a
product of the modern travel industry, established the lasting images of
a particular destination by showcasing a "specific element of reality"
designed to find resonance.[46]

In addition to these examples of tourist propaganda produced predominantly in Bavaria itself, this work also engages with several other types
of historical documents. The files of various local and regional tourism
clubs and associations provide a behind-the-scenes glimpse into the operation of the tourism industry, and specifically, the decision-making process
behind the tourist propaganda. Articles from Bavarian newspapers allow
for similar insight, in addition to confirming the significance that tourism

---

[45] Ibid., 9. See also Rudy Koshar, "'What Ought to Be Seen': Tourists' Guidebooks and
National Identities in Modern Germany and Europe," *Journal of Contemporary History*
33, no. 3 (July 1998): 323–340.

[46] Helmut Beer, *Grüße aus Nürnberg 3, Nürnberg in Ansichtskarten um 1900 –
"Lebendige Altstadt"* (Nuremberg: W. Tümmels Buchdruckerei und Verlag GmbH,
1994), 12–13.

held for local communities. Statistics recording the number of visitors and overnight stays, typically assembled by local tourism associations and printed in local newspapers, help to demonstrate Bavaria's growing popularity as a tourist destination. Although the principal objective of the book is the analysis of a unique discourse cultivated by the tourism industry, it is also important to address the impact of these ideas and the actual experience of travel. With this goal in mind, I turn to a number of contemporaneous travel reports written by both German and foreign visitors.

The tourists who visited Bavaria between the French Revolution and World War II lived in a period of rapid social, economic, and political change. Whether departing from New York or London, Mainz or Munich, these travelers carried modernity with them, a form of baggage that influenced their expectations and determined their desires. Consequently, this book endeavors not only to showcase where people traveled and what they chose to see, but to determine why they traveled, and what their chosen destinations represented. Although it focuses on the cultural landscapes and historic cityscapes of Bavaria, it proposes a larger argument about how travel provides temporary access to the antecedents and foundations of the modern world. By pointing visitors to the past, tourism illuminated the present, and produced signposts to the future.

I

A Brief History of German Travel

First pioneered by the middle classes of Western Europe during the nineteenth century, tourism has become a global phenomenon. In 2000, tourism was the largest industry in the world, having earned an estimated 3.6 trillion dollars annually, or roughly 10.6 percent of the gross global product. The World Travel and Tourism Council, an industry lobby group, speculated that the tourism industry provided one in ten jobs globally, employing up to 255 million people.[1] Tourist organizations have predicted that by the year 2020, 1.6 billion of the world's 7.8 billion will travel internationally.[2]

Considering this rapid growth, it comes as no surprise that tourism has attracted the attention of geographers, economists, and sociologists for decades. And yet, these social scientists often fail to acknowledge that "tourism" is not some monolithic entity, but rather a set of processes, industries, and discourses that evolve over time in relation to the particular societies in which they are embedded.[3] Historians have only recently begun to give tourism the attention it deserves, demonstrating that the subject can grant insight into numerous dimensions of modern life, including the development of class consciousness, the construction

---

[1] Shelley Baranowski and Ellen Furlough, "Introduction," in *Being Elsewhere*, 1.

[2] Orvar Löfgren, *On Holiday: A History of Vacationing* (Berkeley: University of California Press, 1999), 6. See also Steven Wearing, Deborah Stevenson, and Tamara Young, *Tourist Cultures: Identity, Place and the Traveller* (London: Sage, 2010), 2–3.

[3] Andrea Leonardi and Hans Heiss, "Einleitung," in *Tourismus und Entwicklung im Alpenraum 18.–20. Jahrhundert*, ed. Andrea Leonardi and Hans Heiss (Innsbruck: Studien, 2003), 17.

of nations (and nationalism), economic growth at various levels, and the emergence of a global consumer culture.[4]

The following chapter engages with this scholarship in order to provide a historical overview of tourism in Germany, from its pre-modern roots to the eve of World War II. It begins with a concise history of European travel before the nineteenth century, identifying religious pilgrimages, spa visits, and the Grand Tour as important precursors to modern leisure travel. It then turns to the dawn of the modern tourism industry during the nineteenth century, detailing the expansion of the railway, the creation of the package tour, and the invention of the tourist guidebook. Finally, it addresses the roots of German mass tourism during the interwar period, identifying several commercial, industrial, and political developments that made travel a more viable option for a broader segment of the German population. This overview sets the stage for the case studies of the subsequent chapters, charting the broader history that shaped local and regional experiences. This exposition also introduces a number of themes that play a role throughout the book, including the relationship between class and culture, the nationalist implications of leisure travel, the dialectic between domestic and international tourism, and the expansion of the tourism industry itself.

From Travails to Tourism

In his influential 1958 article, "A Theory of Tourism," German author Hans Magnus Enzensberger writes: "Travel is one of the most ancient and common aspects of human life."[5] While many scholars agree that tourism is an essentially modern phenomenon, others have demonstrated that travel clearly is not.[6] Some have even gone so far as to argue that travel has acted as "central rather than a peripheral force in historical transformations," impacting the formation of territorial states, political units, and personal and collective identities throughout the ages.[7] Still,

---

4 Baranowski and Furlough, "Introduction," in *Being Elsewhere*, 21. See Hasso Spode, "Tourismusgeschichte als Forschungsgegenstand, Bilanz und Ausblick" in *Tourismus und Entwicklung im Alpenraum 18.–20. Jahrhundert*, 83–84.
5 Hans Magnus Enzensberger, "A Theory of Tourism," trans. Gerd Gemünden and Kenn Johnson, *New German Critique*, no. 68 (Spring–Summer 1996): 122.
6 See Lionel Casson, *Travel in the Ancient World* (Baltimore: Johns Hopkins University Press, 1994).
7 Eric J. Leed, *The Mind of the Traveler: From Gilgamesh to Global Tourism* (New York: Basic Books, 1991), 18.

people have not always traveled for the reasons that now motivate many of us to regularly take a trip. Before the advent of tourism, most travelers were involuntarily displaced by war, hunger, or poverty. These were hardly pleasure-seekers. In fact, the word "journey" was most often associated with the departure of a military force, just as the word "travel" derived from the French term for "tribulation" and "agony."[8]

Travel during the medieval and early modern periods was predominantly utilitarian (and in many cases, still is). Even those that relocated by choice often did so as a result of professional obligations or perceived religious duty. In a world without permanent academic institutions, both professors and students frequently wandered from town to town in search of fellow intellectuals and ancient texts.[9] Meanwhile, young men training for certain trades, such as carpentry or metal-working, were often expected to travel extensively in order to gain experience as journeymen. Similar to the itinerant intellectuals, journeymen moved from town to town, working in numerous workshops before acquiring the title of "master." The so-called *Walz* was an especially cherished tradition in the German-speaking lands of central Europe, where it was a mandatory rite of passage for craftsmen from the late medieval period through the nineteenth century.[10]

While a sense of professional obligation compelled intellectuals and aspiring craftsmen to leave home, a more divine motivation produced another category of travel. Pilgrimages, or the ritual of traveling to religious shrines, had a long tradition in Europe, even though the practice was neither an exclusively Christian nor an exclusively European custom. In fact, the pilgrimage is potentially "the oldest and most prevalent type of travel in human history."[11] In Europe, the tradition began with pre-Roman retreats to sacred locales allegedly possessing curative or prophetic properties. Beginning in the fourth century C.E., the acquisition of cherished relics, linked either to a Christian saint or Christ

---

[8] Larry Krotz, *Tourists: How Our Fastest Growing Industry Is Changing the World* (Boston: Faber and Faber, 1996), 4–5; Spode, *Wie die Deutschen "Reiseweltmeister" wurden*, 6.

[9] Fussell, ed., *The Norton Book of Travel*, 23; Leed, *The Mind of the Traveler*, 148–157.

[10] Rüdiger Hachtmann, *Tourismus-Geschichte* (Göttingen: Vandenhoeck & Ruprecht, 2007), 38–39; Rainer S. Elkar, "Auf der Walz – Handwerkerreisen," in *Reisekultur: Von der Pilgerfahrt zum modernen Tourismus*, ed. Hermann Bausinger, Klaus Beyrer, and Gottfried Korff (Munich: Oscar Beck, 1991), 57–61.

[11] Lutz Kaelber, "Paradigms of Travel: From Medieval Pilgrimage to the Postmodern Virtual Tour," in *Tourism, Religion and Spiritual Journeys*, ed. Dallen J. Timothy and Daniel H. Olsen (New York: Routledge, 2006), 49.

himself, raised the profile of certain pilgrimage sites, with Rome, Santiago de Compostela, Canterbury, and Cologne occupying the upper echelon of European shrines. The reputation of other pilgrimage sites rested upon reported miracles, including apparitions of the Virgin Mary or the apparent indestructibility of consecrated Eucharist wafers. Although the pilgrimage never became a "pillar" of the Christian faith, it became a common form of devotion during the medieval period, and the figure of the pilgrim took on a wider cultural significance, even being satirized in the works of Chaucer and Dante.[12]

Actual pilgrims tended to travel in groups and represented a surprising cross-section of medieval society that included both sexes, as well as members of the nobility, clergy, and merchant class. They embarked on these trips for a variety of reasons, among them penance, the cure of physical ailments, the desire to witness miracles, and the acquisition of indulgences.[13] However, by the late medieval period, not everyone who embarked upon a pilgrimage was motivated by such concerns. In an era when travel was limited to a very small portion of the overall population, the pilgrimage became a means of socializing and breaking from one's daily routine. For these reasons, some scholars have correctly identified the pilgrimage as form of "proto-tourism," or a precursor to modern leisure travel.[14] The commercialization of the practice definitely foreshadowed the future development of tourism. The opening of inns along important pilgrimage routes established the foundations of the hospitality industry, while the production and sale of pilgrimage badges was an early example of the souvenir business. Licensed shipmasters in Venice even offered a "pre-modern version of the package tour," arranging transportation and lodging for the more wealthy pilgrims.[15] The pilgrimage may have been an ostensibly religious matter, but it clearly had economic potential. Although the Protestant Reformation contributed to a decline in the practice, pilgrimages remained a common form of European travel well into the modern period, with Lourdes in particular still ranking as one of France's most popular destinations.[16]

[12] Diana Webb, *Medieval European Pilgrimage, c.700–c.1500* (New York: Palgrave, 2002), xi–xv, 4, 24–29. See also Jonathan Sumption, *The Age of Pilgrimage: The Medieval Journey to God* (Mahwah, NJ: Paulist Press, 2003).

[13] Webb, *Medieval European Pilgrimage*, 78–114.

[14] Hachtmann, *Tourismus-Geschichte*, 40–42.

[15] Kaelber, "Paradigms of Travel," 51; Klaus Herber, "Unterwegs zu heiligen Stätten – Pilgerfahrten," in *Reisekultur: Von der Pilgerfahrt zum modernen Tourismus*, 24.

[16] Suzanne K. Kaufman, "Selling Lourdes: Pilgrimage, Tourism, and the Mass-Marketing of the Sacred in Nineteenth-Century France," in *Being Elsewhere*, 63–88. See also Alison

The religious pilgrimage was closely related to another form of proto-tourism: visits to mineral springs and spas. The notion of "taking the waters" as a means of rejuvenation can be traced back to Classical Antiquity, when the ancient Greeks and Romans constructed public bathing facilities near mineral springs. Typically located within the forum, baths were popular gathering places where citizens could not only soak in warm and cold waters, but also eat, drink, and be merry.[17] The popularity of taking the waters diminished with the decline of the Roman Empire, as bathing facilities across Europe fell into disrepair and disrepute. During the Middle Ages, the Christian Church associated the practice with Roman depravity and infectious disease, and made efforts to eradicate the tradition. In spite of this, some Europeans continued to travel to mineral springs, which were now viewed in a somewhat different light. For a new generation of visitors, spring water promised both physical *and* spiritual rejuvenation, possessing sacred qualities and the ability to cure diseases and improve fertility.[18] Many mineral springs became religious shrines, and were often located near monasteries and convents. These religious institutions provided one of the few sources of health care available outside of medieval towns, and the use of mineral waters for both bathing and drinking became popular remedies. The pursuit of the cure overlapped with religious practice, and elements of the Christian faith developed new connections with water.[19]

While some mineral springs acquired religious connections, an urban bathing culture reemerged. As early as the thirteenth century, town-dwellers began to acknowledge the benefits of bathing. However, since not every person could afford a private bath, and little could be done with the remnants of Roman facilities in places like Wiesbaden, wealthy landowners opened public bathhouses in towns near thermal springs, such as Ems on the River Lahn. Within these facilities, guests could enjoy

Frank, "The Pleasant and the Useful: Pilgrimage and Tourism in Habsburg Mariazell," *Austrian History Yearbook* 40 (2009): 157–182.

[17] Margarita Dritsas, "Water, Culture and Leisure: From Spas to Beach Tourism in Greece during the Nineteenth and Twentieth Centuries," in *Water, Leisure and Culture: European Historical Perspectives*, ed. Susan C. Anderson and Bruce H. Tabb (New York: Berg, 2002), 194–195; Klaus Peter Goethert, "Badekultur, Badeorte, Bäderreisen in den gallischen Provinzen," in *Badeorte und Bäderreisen in Antike, Mittelalter und Neuzeit*, ed. Michael Matheus (Stuttgart: Steiner, 2001), 12; Casson, *Travel in the Ancient World*, 134, 209–210.

[18] Susan C. Anderson, "Introduction: The Pleasure of Taking the Waters," in *Water, Leisure and Culture*, 2.

[19] See Lepovitz, "Pilgrims, Patients, and Painters," 123–125, 131–133.

the services of a resident surgeon, as well as the pleasures of hot water and steam baths.[20] In the meantime, another distinct bathing culture emerged in the countryside. The appearance of so-called natural baths coincided with realization that the waters of saline and sulfuric springs also had restorative properties. In order to take advantage of this natural resource, entrepreneurs established bathing facilities and lodging outside of the safety of city walls, forcing guests to spend time in close proximity to the uncultivated natural environment. These natural baths became fashionable destinations in the Late Middle Ages, providing both physical rejuvenation and amusement for a clientele that can be accurately described as proto-tourists. The fact that political and religious authorities still linked urban bathing houses to the spread of disease and sin only contributed to the popularity of this novel travel culture.[21]

A third form of proto-tourism more exclusively associated with the early modern period is the Grand Tour. This was basically an educational rite of passage, "a sort of mobile finishing school" dominated by upper-class Englishmen during the seventeenth and eighteenth centuries.[22] It originated in the Elizabethan Age, when English nobles began sending their sons to the continent as a means of training them in diplomatic etiquette and cosmopolitan sociability.[23] Lasting anywhere from several months to several years, this extended tour of Europe followed a fairly standardized itinerary, including Paris, Florence, Venice, and Rome, with some variations featuring Hanover, Dresden, Vienna, and even St. Petersburg.[24] The Grand Tour consisted of a number of educational experiences, including language and fencing classes, trips to galleries, visits to court, and liaisons with women.[25] It was predicated on a new

---

[20] Matthias Bitz, *Badewesen in Südwestdeutschland 1550 bis 1840: Zum Wandel von Gesellschaft und Architektur* (Idstein: Schulz-Kirchner, 1989), 38–41; Hermann Sommer, *Zur Kur nach Ems: Ein Beitrag zur Geschichte der Badereise von 1830 bis 1914* (Stuttgart: Steiner, 1999), 11–12, 17.

[21] Bitz, *Badewesen in Südwestdeutschland*, 42–46; Birgit Studt, "Die Badenfahrt. Ein neues Muster der Badpraxis und Badegeselligkeit im deutschen Spätmittelalter," in *Badeorte und Bäderreisen in Antike, Mittelalter und Neuzeit*, 33–38.

[22] Lynne Withey, *Grand Tours and Cook's Tours: A History of Leisure Travel, 1750–1915* (New York: William Morrow and Company, 1997), 3.

[23] Michael G. Brennan, ed., *The Origins of the Grand Tour: The Travels of Robert Montagu, Lord Mandeville (1649–1654), William Hammond (1655–1658), Banaster Maynard (1660–1663)* (London: The Hakluyt Society, 2004), 16.

[24] Jeremy Black, *The British and the Grand Tour* (Dover, NH: Croom Helm, 1985), 10–15, 30–31.

[25] For more on sex during the Grand Tour, see Ian Littlewood, *Sultry Climates: Travel and Sex* (Cambridge, MA: Da Capo, 2002), 11–27.

devotion to systematic empiricism, or the idea that knowledge must be derived from first-hand experience and observation.[26] By touring the cities of Italy in particular, the "heart of the Grand Tour," the aspiring nobleman could see locations immortalized by Latin texts, establishing a connection between ancient and modern empires. In addition to providing this sense of historical continuity, the Grand Tour cultivated aristocratic camaraderie and a continent-wide class consciousness.[27]

The Grand Tour was an equally important tradition for the German aristocracy, who saw it as a mandatory rite of initiation. Like its British counterpart, the German *Kavaliersreise* featured the destinations of Paris, Rome, and Florence, but it also prioritized visits to the economic centers of London and Amsterdam. In general, the German variety tended to be a more explicitly educational affair. Accompanied by a "mentor" who doubled as both a tutor and tour guide, the young German nobleman visited some of the most well-known academies of Europe. There, he studied numerous subjects, among them law, history, mathematics, architecture, and military strategy.[28] Outside of the academies, edification remained the objective, and the list of sights worth seeing was predetermined by their perceived educational value. Alongside museums and historic buildings, mines and sites of industry were also highly recommended attractions. When the touring nobleman did manage to leave civilization behind for the countryside, it was only to observe and inventory flora and fauna. Again, the goal of this travel was not pleasure or reflection, but the acquisition of knowledge.[29] If modern leisure travel promises escape from everyday life, then the Grand Tour was designed to prepare the young European nobleman for the "complicated situations and rituals" of daily life at court.[30] It was a rehearsal, not a respite. Still, it was an important precursor to nineteenth-century tourism in that it popularized the idea

---

[26] James Buzard, "The Grand Tour and After (1660–1840)," in *The Cambridge Companion to Travel Writing*, ed. Peter Hulme and Ted Youngs (New York: Cambridge University Press, 2002), 37; Leed, *The Mind of the Traveler*, 184–189.

[27] James Buzard, *The Beaten Track: European Tourism, Literature, and the Ways to Culture, 1800–1918* (New York: Oxford University Press, 1993), 120.

[28] Thomas Freller, *Adlige auf Tour: Die Erfindung der Bildungsreise* (Ostfildern: Thorbecke, 2007), 7–10; Winfried Siebers, "Ungleiche Lehrfahrten – Kavaliere und Gelehrte," in *Reisekultur: Von der Pilgerfahrt zum modernen Tourismus*, 48–49. See also Mathis Leibetseder, *Die Kavalierstour. Adlige Erziehungsreisen im 17. und 18. Jahrhundert* (Cologne: Böhlau, 2004).

[29] Spode, *Wie die Deutschen "Reiseweltmeister" wurden*, 10–11.

[30] Hachtmann, *Tourismus-Geschichte*, 45.

of travel as a vehicle of edification, and an activity that confirmed class identity.

These lines of continuity between early modern travel and tourism have led some scholars to conflate the two phenomena. For example, in his masterly reconstruction of the lives of two sixteenth-century Swiss professionals, historian Emmanuel Le Roy Ladurie at one point refers to a group of people passing through Paris as "tourists."[31] Is this an accurate classification? Literary critic Paul Fussell draws a clear line between older and more modern forms of travel, arguing: "To constitute real travel, movement from one place to another should manifest some impulse of non-utilitarian pleasure."[32] Clearly, the guidebook-wielding tourists of contemporary Paris have little in common with the wandering collective discussed by Le Roy Ladurie. The latter certainly traveled, but they were not tourists, or "travelers," if we accept Fussell's distinction. Even if they were not fleeing persecution or famine, it is doubtful that their motivations were non-utilitarian. Conversely, both the religious pilgrimage and the Grand Tour had elements in common with modern leisure travel, but there were also crucial differences. Compelled by faith or regret, the pilgrim was rarely a pleasure-seeker. Compelled by social conventions and educational requirements, the young nobleman could not always consider the Grand Tour a vacation.

The dawn of tourism meant that travel was no longer the obligation of the faithful or the exclusive right of the privileged. This process began in the late eighteenth century, and was facilitated by the Romantic Movement and the Napoleonic Wars.[33] While the former inspired new attitudes toward history and the natural environment, the latter disrupted travel on a practical level while simultaneously producing a new category of tourist destination: the modern battlefield.[34] At the same time, the ramifications of revolution and reform shattered the cultural hegemony of the European nobility, thus opening a space for a new form of travel.[35] Steady economic growth in Western Europe after 1815 also meant that larger

---

[31] Emmanuel Le Roy Ladurie, *The Beggar and the Professor: A Sixteenth Century Family Saga*, trans. Arthur Goldhammer (Chicago: University of Chicago Press, 1997), 265.

[32] Fussell, ed., *The Norton Book of Travel*, 22.

[33] See Attilio Brilli, *Als Reisen eine Kunst war. Vom Beginn des modernen Tourismus: Die 'Grand Tour'*, trans. Annette Kopetzki (Berlin: Klaus Wagenbach, 2012), 49–69.

[34] See Stuart Semmel, "Reading the Tangible Past: British Tourism, Collecting, and Memory after Waterloo," *Representations*, no. 69 (Winter 2000): 9–37; Thomas Adam and Gisela Mettele, eds., *Two Boston Brahmins in Goethe's Germany: The Travel Journals of Anna and George Ticknor* (Lanham, MD: Lexington Books, 2009), 49–58.

[35] Buzard, *The Beaten Track*, 16–17.

segments of the population had the means to take a trip.[36] Still, the tourist only became a common sight during the late nineteenth century, when leisure travel became a popular pastime of the urban middle classes.[37] As Mark Twain sarcastically noted in *A Tramp Abroad*: "Seventy or eighty years ago Napoleon was the only man in Europe who could really be called a traveler . . . but now everybody goes everywhere."[38] Twain may be exaggerating here, as the type of tourist that he lampooned was decidedly bourgeois, but a new form of leisure travel was clearly on the rise after 1815. This development coincided with the growth of industrial civilization, and tourism was founded upon the promise of distance from the familiar urban environment and the workplace.[39] Stated differently, travel only became tourism when the affluent middle classes adopted the activity as a reprieve from city life and professional obligations. However, this escape was neither permanent nor compulsory. Unlike most pre-modern travelers, tourists relocated by choice.[40]

Another feature of tourism that distinguished it from earlier forms of travel was its commercial nature. Three developments in particular created the modern tourism industry: the expansion of the railway, the creation of the package tour, and the invention of the tourist guidebook. Of these three, the railway played perhaps the greatest role in revolutionizing travel. The railway was a direct product of industrialization, and England was accordingly the first country to embrace this new form of transportation. Nearly twenty years after the inaugural run of a steam locomotive outside of Leeds, the first intercity passenger line opened in 1830, connecting the industrial centers of Manchester and Liverpool, and cutting the travel time in half.[41] Five years later, the first German rail line opened in northern Bavaria, linking the cities of Nuremberg and Fürth. Soon enough, a growing network of tracks connected the major urban centers of central Europe, "leaving in the shadow all those possible destinations and sights which were not near the railway."[42] Previously daunting distances were dramatically shortened. The trip from Cologne

[36] Withey, *Grand Tours and Cook's Tours*, 62.
[37] Leonardi and Heiss, "Einleitung," 17.
[38] Mark Twain, *A Tramp Abroad* (New York: Oxford University Press, 1996), 345.
[39] Enzensberger, "A Theory of Tourism," 124–126; Buzard, *The Beaten Track*, 4.
[40] Taina Syrjämaa, "Tourism as a Typical Cultural Phenomenon of Urban Consumer Society," in *New Directions in Urban History: Aspects of European Art, Health, Tourism and Leisure since the Enlightenment*, ed. Peter Borsay, Gunther Hirschfelder, and Ruth E. Mohrmann (Münster: Waxmann, 2000), 177.
[41] Withey, *Grand Tours and Cook's Tours*, 96.
[42] Syrjämaa, "Tourism as a Typical Cultural Phenomenon," 185.

to Berlin, for instance, which had once required an entire week in a horse-drawn carriage, now only lasted fourteen hours.[43] By the late nineteenth century, the destination, and not the journey, became the focal point of travel. The new experience of rail travel also produced a unique mode of apprehending the environment as it flew by the window, what one scholar has referred to as "panoramic perception." Instead of concentrating on objects in the foreground, passengers were forced to grasp urban, industrial, and rural scenes as components of a larger, "aesthetically pleasing" landscape.[44] Thus, the railway journey ensured that travel was no longer an arduous travail, just as it promoted new visions of the environment.[45]

While the expansion of the railway expedited the process of traveling in the nineteenth century, the creation of the package tour standardized the experience. The English preacher Thomas Cook pioneered this innovation in 1841 when he chartered a train to transport 570 members of Leicester's "Anti-Alcohol Association" to a meeting in neighboring Loughborough. Four years later, Cook organized a pleasure trip to the seashore at Liverpool. This was followed by package tours to Scotland, which was quickly becoming a popular destination among the English middle classes.[46] Having enjoyed success in Britain, the preacher-turned-entrepreneur eventually set his sights on the continent. In 1855 he organized a tour to the French capital, hoping to capitalize on the Paris Exhibition. During the following decade, Cook expanded into Germany, Switzerland, and Italy, transporting customers to tourist attractions, booking rooms, and supplying valuable information. By the end of the 1870s, the Thomas Cook Company had sixty locations throughout Europe, as well as offices in the United States, Australia, India, and the Middle East.[47] Leisure travel had become a global industry.

Like the package tour, the tourist guidebook helped to standardize the process of travel, making it more predictable and routine. Loosely defined, travel literature dates back to the writings of Herodotus and Pausanias, but succinct works designed to "guide" travelers are a relatively recent invention. The first true tourist guidebooks did not appear until the early nineteenth century. These modern publications were recognizable by their

---

[43] Spode, *Wie die Deutschen "Reiseweltmeister" wurden*, 58.

[44] Schivelbusch, *The Railway Journey*, 52–69.

[45] John Towner, *An Historical Geography of Recreation and Tourism in the Western World, 1540–1940* (New York: John Wiley & Sons, 1996), 254.

[46] Withey, *Grand Tours and Cook's Tours*, 135–137. See also Grenier, *Tourism and Identity in Scotland*, 49–92.

[47] Withey, *Grand Tours and Cook's Tours*, 142, 159.

concise nature and manageable size, a noticeable improvement over earlier tomes like Ludwig Wilhelm Gilbert's three-volume *Handbook for
Travelers through Germany*, published in 1791.[48] It was the British John
Murray publishing empire that produced the archetypal tourist guidebook in 1836. *A Hand-Book for Travellers on the Continent*, based
on John Murray III's own notes from his tour of Europe, launched an
entire series of popular guidebooks, recognizable by their trademark red
covers.[49] These compact guides were designed to direct tourists to the
most important sights, identifying the best travel routes, and in general,
allowing the traveler to be independent of the services of on-site guides.

   In Germany, the "red books" of John Murray inspired Karl Baedeker,
whose name, like that of Thomas Cook, soon became synonymous with
tourism itself. Baedeker's career began in 1827, when he opened a small
bookstore in Koblenz, selling city maps, Rhine panoramas, and travelogues. After purchasing the Röhling publishing firm in 1832, Baedeker
took an interest in revising the late J.A. Klein's travel guide on the
Rhine. In order to ensure the accuracy of the new edition, Baedeker
traveled extensively, taking notes on hotels, restaurants, transportation
routes, and tourist sights. Published in 1839, the updated version of
the Rhineland guidebook was the first in a long series of internationally
renowned tourist guides.[50] These publications contained all the hallmarks
of the Murray handbooks, including a red cover, a table of contents,
detailed descriptions of routes, up-to-date information on prices and
schedules, and an index.[51] Baedeker, however, was the first to employ
a system of rating attractions and accommodations with stars, a practice later adopted by the Murray series.[52] Several other features of these
guidebooks ultimately distinguished them from their English competition, including their high-quality maps and affordable price.[53] Baedeker's
guides were also more streamlined, omitting even the brief commentary
that had characterized the Murray handbooks.[54] This proved to be a

---

48 Ulrich Pretzel, *Die Literaturform Reiseführer im 19. und 20. Jahrhundert: Untersuchun-
    gen am Beispiel des Rheins* (Frankfurt a.M.: Peter Lang Verlag, 1995), 61.
49 Withey, *Grand Tours and Cook's Tours*, 70.
50 Koshar, *German Travel Cultures*, 23.
51 Pretzel, *Die Literaturform Reiseführer*, 63–64.
52 Withey, *Grand Tours and Cook's Tours*, 72.
53 Jan Palmowski, "Travels with Baedeker – The Guidebook and the Middle Classes in
    Victorian and Edwardian England," in *Histories of Leisure*, ed. Rudy Koshar (Oxford:
    Berg, 2002), 120.
54 Koshar, "Tourists' Guidebooks and National Identities in Modern Germany and
    Europe," 330.

popular formula, and within several decades the Baedeker firm was publishing guidebooks in German, English, and French.[55] Baedeker's success
helped to establish the genre of the tourist guidebook, and publishing
houses across Germany would soon follow his example, producing a
deluge of "tourist guides," "guidebooks," and "handbooks" during the
second half of the nineteenth century.

The Educated Flight of the Middle Classes

Although the English are rightfully credited with pioneering the practice
of tourism, many historians have argued that the Germans had a certain
propensity for travel, demonstrating a tangible *Reiselust* that was evident
in the late eighteenth century.[56] In spite of poor travel conditions and
the lingering threat of bandits, educated, upper-class Germans traveled
like never before on the eve of the French Revolution. Inspired by the
Enlightenment, these men toured primarily for the sake of education,
and were eager to view architecture, inspect minerals and botanical specimens, and "examine collections of every imaginable kind." They also
traveled for the sake of conversation, trading ideas with fellow intellectuals in the learned societies and reading clubs surfacing around the Holy
Roman Empire. This *Reiselust* was apparent in such literary works as
Ludwig Tieck's *Franz Sternbald's Wanderings* (1798), a romantic novel
set in medieval times, and Johann Wolfgang von Goethe's *Italian Journey*,
based on a diary kept during his travels in Italy between 1786 and 1788.
Nevertheless, most travelers during this period had little in common with
modern tourists. On the eve of the long nineteenth century, as many as
one German in ten could be classified as itinerant. This mobile segment
of the population included peddlers, prostitutes, pilgrims, shepherds, and
journeymen; in other words, people in search of sustenance, professional
opportunities, and, both literally and figuratively, "greener pastures."[57]

After the French Revolution and the Napoleonic Wars, the touring
intellectuals and itinerant plebeians were joined by a new type of traveler:
the middle-class tourist. To broach the topic of the nineteenth-century
German middle classes, or *Bürgertum*, is to engage with a vast body
of literature. To summarize: over the past fifty years, historical debate

---

55 Withey, *Grand Tours and Cook's Tours*, 73.
56 Koshar, *German Travel Cultures*, 26; Spode, *Wie die Deutschen "Reiseweltmeister"
    wurden*, 6–7; David Blackbourn, *The Conquest of Nature: Water, Landscape, and the
    Making of Modern Germany* (London: Jonathan Cape, 2006), 24.
57 Blackbourn, *The Conquest of Nature*, 24–25, 54–55.

has shifted from a preoccupation with the "feudalization of the German bourgeoisie" to more nuanced discussions of the cultural dimensions of middle-class identity during what is now commonly referred to as the "bourgeois nineteenth century."[58] One of the most prolific authors on the subject, historian Jürgen Kocka, has cast doubt upon older conceptions of the German middle classes by arguing that this segment of the population constituted neither a unified class nor a social rank, and was only identifiable through its "external delimitations and shared culture."[59] Admittedly, this definition pertains by and large to the educated middle class, who did not always share their interests with the broader *Bürgertum*. Furthermore, the culture that defined them could not be indefinitely monopolized.[60] These issues have not dissuaded a new generation of German historians from shedding light on a distinctly middle-class culture, and the ways in which it could confirm identity on various levels.

If segments of the German middle classes were defined by a shared culture during the nineteenth century, then *Bildung* was the definitive feature of this culture. Once synonymous with education, the definition of *Bildung* expanded at the end of the eighteenth century, when it became synonymous with self-cultivation, or the elevation and transformation of the individual through cultural engagement and intellectual growth. The Prussian education reformer Wilhelm von Humboldt was instrumental in articulating this new ideal. In *The Limits of State Action*, written between 1791 and 1792, he asserted: "The true end of man, not that which his transient wishes suggest to him, but that which eternal immutable reason prescribes, is the highest possible development of his powers into a

---

[58] For a helpful summary of the literature addressing the nineteenth-century *Bürgertum*, see Jonathan Sperber, "Bürger, Bürgertum, Bürgerlichkeit, Bürgerliche Gesellschaft: Studies of the German (Upper) Middle Class and Its Sociocultural World," *Journal of Modern History* 69, no. 2 (June 1997): 271–297. Among the many important works on the subject are Ralf Dahrendorf, *Gesellschaft und Demokratie in Deutschland* (Munich: R. Piper, 1968); Hans-Ulrich Wehler, *The German Empire, 1871–1918*, trans. Kim Traynor (Dover, NH: Berg Publishers, 1985); David Blackbourn and Geoff Eley, *The Peculiarities of German History: Bourgeois Society and Politics in Nineteenth-Century Germany* (New York: Oxford University Press, 1984); Jürgen Kocka, ed. *Bürger und Bürgerlichkeit im 19. Jahrhundert* (Göttingen: Vandenhoeck & Ruprecht, 1987); Lothar Gall, *Bürgertum in Deutschland* (Berlin: Siedler, 1989).

[59] Jürgen Kocka, *Das lange 19. Jahrhundert. Arbeit, Nation und bürgerliche Gesellschaft* (Stuttgart: Klett-Cotta, 2001), 117–119.

[60] Jürgen Kocka, "Bürgertum und Bürgerlichkeit als Probleme der deutschen Geschichte von späten 18. zum frühen 20. Jahrhundert," in *Bürger und Bürgerlichkeit im 19. Jahrhundert*, 44–45.

well-proportioned whole. For culture of this kind freedom is the first and indispensable condition."[61] This quotation suggests that self-cultivation was not simply about the elevation of the individual; it also had political implications. By creating "responsible, enlightened, and virtuous citizens," self-cultivation would create a better society.[62] Distinctly German and grounded in religious and romantic notions of "inner growth," *Bildung* became the nation's "secular social ideal" during the nineteenth century.[63] It helped to transform leisure habits into cultural endeavors, confirming middle-class status in the process.[64] Tourism was one such habit, distinguishing the *Bürgertum* from the working classes who did not have the material means to travel, and the upper class who preferred an entirely different style of travel.[65]

Leisure travel occupied an important place in the lives of the educated middle class, even if men and women did not travel as extensively during every phase. As children, boys and girls often spent a few weeks each summer in the countryside with their mother, nursemaid, and occasionally their father. Leaving their sisters behind, adolescent boys later participated in extended hikes with friends, teachers, and their fathers. Higher education brought further travel opportunities for the young man, with the conclusion of studies often being celebrated with a continental tour, or *Bildungsreise*. With marriage, parenthood, and a career, middle-class men were less likely to travel, but did occasionally vacation in the countryside for several days during the summer. By middle age, the same men had usually established their professional reputation as doctors, lawyers, and professors, and could afford to travel more frequently. However, with the onset of old age and declining health, travel options became limited once again, with nearby health resorts and provincial getaways becoming the preferred destinations.[66]

In each of these cases, travel was an opportunity for members of the middle classes to step away from their everyday lives. For children and

---

[61] Quoted in W.H. Bruford, *The German Tradition of Self-Cultivation: 'Bildung' from Humboldt to Thomas Mann* (New York: Cambridge University Press, 1975), 16.

[62] Frederic C. Beiser, *The Romantic Imperative: The Concept of Early German Romanticism* (Cambridge, MA: Harvard University Press, 2003), 88–91.

[63] David Sorkin, "Wilhelm von Humboldt: The Theory and Practice of Self-Formation (Bildung), 1791–1810," *Journal of the History of Ideas* 44, no. 1 (Jan.–Mar. 1983): 66.

[64] Thomas Nipperdey, "'Bürgerlich' als Kultur," in *Bürger und Bürgerlichkeit im 19. Jahrhundert*, 147.

[65] See Pierre Bourdieu, *Distinction: A Social Critique of Taste*, trans. Richard Nice (Cambridge, MA: Harvard University Press, 1984), 68, 170–175.

[66] Philipp Prein, *Bürgerliches Reisen im 19. Jahrhundert: Freizeit, Kommunikation und soziale Grenzen* (Münster: Lit, 2005), 47–48.

their mothers, this meant traveling outside of the familiar world of the schoolhouse and the home. For young adults, this meant exposure to worlds that they had only read about during their studies. For the male heads of the household, this meant a break from work and professional responsibilities. Travel may have allowed for a change of pace and a break from the norm, but it could not exactly be defined as "non-utilitarian." In fact, the very notion of non-utilitarian leisure was at odds with the middle-class work ethic originally founded on the notion that "work is *the* end and purpose of life commanded by God."[67] Even in the midst of secularization, the bourgeoisie still subscribed to a "gospel of labor"; they praised productive work and dismissed idleness as "the worst vice."[68] Thus, "respectable leisure" existed somewhere between work and idleness.[69] As a form of respectable leisure, tourism provided distance from everyday life, but it did not free travelers from social expectations. It went hand-in-hand with *Bildung*; visiting historically significant sights, appreciating natural environments, and interacting with strangers were all forms of self-cultivation entailing the collection of knowledge, experiences, and emotions.[70] Traveling required valuable time and money, so there had to be a point to it all.[71]

The active pursuit of self-cultivation helped to distinguish tourism from the early modern varieties of travel, but during the early nineteenth century, the German middle classes tended to simply appropriate older forms of travel. The *Kavaliersreise*, for instance, was re-imagined as the middle-class *Bildungsreise*.[72] Although an extensive tour of Europe's urban and cultural centers remained the defining feature of the trip, emphasis in the nineteenth century shifted from the observation of academic, administrative, and economic systems to the appreciation of "historical monuments, aesthetic spectacles, and the folklore of foreign regions." The trip still constituted a rite of passage for young men, but these middle-class travelers began to distinguish themselves from the aristocracy by traveling for shorter periods of time, and actively pursuing individualized self-cultivation instead of the routine acquisition of

---

[67] Max Weber, *The Protestant Ethic and the "Spirit" of Capitalism and Other Writings*, trans. Peter Baehr and Gordon C. Wells (New York: Penguin Books, 2002), 107.

[68] Warren G. Breckman, "Disciplining Consumption: The Debate about Luxury in Wilhelmine Germany, 1890–1914," *Journal of Social History* 24, no. 3 (Spring 1991): 490.

[69] Prein, *Bürgerliches Reisen im 19. Jahrhundert*, 102.

[70] Ibid., 117–118, 256.

[71] Pretzel, *Die Literaturform Reiseführer*, 57.

[72] Paul Bernard, *The Rush to the Alps: The Evolution of Vacationing in Switzerland* (New York: Columbia University Press, 1978), 66.

knowledge.[73] The re-imagined continental tour also promoted a growing national consciousness among the German *Bürgertum*. Traveling over the Alps or beyond the Rhine allowed the young tourist to observe the political and cultural differences that made each country unique, and they theoretically returned with a greater appreciation for German institutions, as well as a clearer sense of German cultural identity.[74]

The German middle classes also adopted the practice of visiting spas. These destinations had experienced a renaissance during the eighteenth century, when towns located near mineral springs truly became spas, a term no longer limited to individual bathing facilities. In contrast to the relatively egalitarian bathing institutions of the Middle Ages, eighteenth-century spas were unequivocally aristocratic, standing in for the traditional summer residences of the European elite. In these temporary centers of upper-class culture, the significance of the waters and their curative properties was largely overshadowed by a new dedication to pleasure and the self-conscious exhibition of the aristocratic lifestyle.[75] Gambling, dancing, and target-shooting all became common forms of entertainment in spas, while bathing itself declined in popularity.[76] German spas also became centers of communication, uniting the upper class of diverse lands. The social transformation was mirrored by an architectural transformation, and fashionable spa towns like Bad Pyrmont became synonymous with their baroque facilities, including theatres, ballrooms, and casinos.[77] These structures demarcated a "cultural space" that was the elusive domain of the upper class.[78]

---

[73] Freller, *Adlige auf Tour*, 14; Prein, *Bürgerliches Reisen im 19. Jahrhundert*, 27, 88.

[74] Hachtmann, *Tourismus-Geschichte*, 49.

[75] Monika Steinhauser, "Das europäische Modebad des 19. Jahrhunderts: Baden-Baden – Eine Residenz des Glücks," in *Die deutsche Stadt im 19. Jahrhundert: Stadtplanung und Baugestaltung im industriellen Zeitalter*, ed. Ludwig Grote (Munich: Prestel, 1974), 96; David Blackbourn, "Fashionable Spa Towns in Nineteenth-Century Europe," in *Water, Leisure and Culture*, 16.

[76] Burkhard Fuhs, *Mondäne Orte einer vornehmen Gesellschaft. Kultur und Geschichte der Kurstädte, 1700–1900* (Hildesheim: Olms, 1992), 44–45.

[77] Reinhold Kühnert, "Badereisen im 18. Jahrhundert – Sozialleben zur Zeit der Aufklärung," *Journal für Geschichte* 1 (1987): 17–18. See also Reinhold Kühnert, *Urbanität auf dem Lande: Badereisen nach Pyrmont im 18. Jahrhundert* (Göttingen: Vandenhoeck & Ruprecht, 1984); William Bacon, "The Rise of the German and the Demise of the English Spa Industry: A Critical Analysis of Business Success and Failure," *Leisure Studies* 16 (1997): 173–187; Rolf Bothe, ed., *Kurstädte in Deutschland: Zur Geschichte einer Baugattung* (Berlin: Fröhlich & Kaufmann, 1984); Petra Simon and Margit Behren, *Badekur und Kurbad: Bauten in deutschen Bädern 1780–1920* (Munich: Diederichs, 1988).

[78] Fuhs, *Mondäne Orte einer vornehmen Gesellschaft*, 21–39.

The influx of middle-class visitors utterly transformed German spas during the nineteenth century, ensuring that these destinations were no longer the exclusive domain of royalty and nobility.[79] A desire for self-cultivation and physical and mental rejuvenation attracted this new demographic to places like Wiesbaden and Bad Ems, but once there, they engaged in the same activities enjoyed by the elite clientele, including dancing, gambling, and extended strolling.[80] The concentrated social environment and daily rituals of spa life promoted integration and communication across class barriers, leading one historian to argue that the nineteenth-century spa facilitated the development of a uniquely hybrid elite culture.[81] More accurately, a variety of spa guests enjoyed a variety of experiences that did not necessarily overlap, as noted in Chapter 3. Still, the fantasy of equality temporarily liberated the middle classes from their professional lives and the hierarchical class structure of the real world.[82] Consequently, the spa became a popular destination for a growing contingent of the wealthy middle classes eager to "be seen" rubbing shoulders with the international elite.[83]

While the German aristocracy and wealthy middle classes "took the waters" in the fashionable spa towns of central Europe, others members of the *Bürgertum* traveled to more provincial destinations. One example of this sort of destination was the climatic health resort, or *Luftkurort*, where fresh air was marketed as a viable remedy.[84] In such locations, the middle classes sought self-cultivation, but they also sought recovery and recreation. The two objectives were not necessarily opposed to one another, with mental and physical health serving as preconditions for self-cultivation, and *Bildung* justifying travel in the first place. Similar rationale compelled members of the middle classes to plan summer vacations in the German countryside away from designated health resorts. The

---

[79] Heikki Lempa, "The Spa: Emotional Economy and Social Classes in Nineteenth-Century Pyrmont," *Central European History* 35, no. 1 (2002): 41.

[80] Fuhs, *Mondäne Orte einer vornehmen Gesellschaft*, 465.

[81] Alexa Geisthövel, "Promenadenmischungen, Raum und Kommunikation in Hydropolen, 1830–1880," in *Ortsgespräche: Raum und Kommunikation im 19. und 20. Jahrhundert*, ed. Alexander C.T. Geppert, Uffa Jensen, and Jörn Weinhold (Bielefeld: Transcript, 2005), 207–209.

[82] Fuhs, *Mondäne Orte einer vornehmen Gesellschaft*, 227.

[83] Thomas Nipperdey, *Deutsche Geschichte, 1800–1866: Bürgerwelt und starker Staat* (Munich: C.H. Beck, 1983), 139; Wolfgang Kaschuba, "German Bürgerlichkeit After 1800: Culture as a Symbolic Praxis," in *Bourgeois Society in Nineteenth-Century Europe*, ed. Jürgen Kocka and Allan Mitchell (Providence: Berg, 1993), 416.

[84] Thomas Nipperdey, *Deutsche Geschichte, 1866–1918, Erster Band: Arbeitswelt und Bürgergeist* (Munich: C.H. Beck, 1990), 177.

latter half of the nineteenth century witnessed the growing popularity of the so-called *Sommerfrische*, a new category of destination that quickly became "a feature of the middle-class lifestyle."[85] Although this vague marketing term is often translated as "summer resort," the phrase "summer retreat" more effectively distinguishes this type of location from the health resorts mentioned above. In fact, a relative lack of tourism infrastructure was a defining feature of these summer retreats. Hotels, for example, were uncommon and visitors often rented rooms from locals. Similarly, the destination's principal attraction was its lack of attractions. The summer retreat was exactly that: a rural town or village near an urban center where the families of civil servants, clerks, and small businessmen could escape for a number of weeks each summer.

The *Sommerfrische* represents a noteworthy chapter in the larger development of German tourism for a number of reasons. First, as opposed to the *Bildungsreise* or the extended stay in a health resort, the summer retreat was a feasible travel option for the entire family, including women and children. In fact, female visitors often outnumbered men in these locales, as fathers could typically only escape their professional obligations for several days at a time. Second, the summer retreat helped to make the "vacation" an annual feature in the lives of middle-class families. Although recreational offerings were usually limited to children's festivals, bowling, and hiking, pleasure was the ostensible goal of these vacations, suggesting that in the latter half of the nineteenth century, the concept of "travel as education" was slowly being eclipsed by the desire for recovery and recreation.[86] Third, the summer retreat became the symbolic antithesis to the modern city, and an extended stay in the countryside allowed the middle-class traveler to leisurely re-connect with the rustic culture and inhabitants of their German *Heimat*.[87] This new variety of tourism also provided an agreeable proximity to the natural environment, which was now understood as a panacea for the ills of urban civilization.[88]

---

[85] Silke Götsch, "Sommerfrische: Zur Etablierung einer Gegenwelt am Ende des 19. Jahrhunderts," *Schweizerisches Archiv für Volkskunde* 98, no.1 (2002): 9.

[86] Spode, *Wie die Deutschen "Reiseweltmeister" wurden*, 97–99; Hachtmann, *Tourismus-Geschichte*, 93–97.

[87] See Applegate, *A Nation of Provincials*, 59–107; Confino, *The Nation as a Local Metaphor*, 99–207.

[88] Götsch, "Sommerfrische: Zur Etablierung einer Gegenwelt am Ende des 19. Jahrhunderts," 10–11.

For centuries, nature had been seen as the bane of mankind's existence, and a reminder of the limits of civilization.[89] The conception of nature as irrational and dangerous tended to keep visitors away from the sights that now attract so many tourists. The negative attitudes were also linked to the practical difficulties of traveling through mountainous regions or over tempestuous seas, an often tedious and dangerous undertaking in the ancient and early modern periods.[90] This all began to change in the late eighteenth century, when writers and artists started to re-conceptualize mountains, beaches, and rivers as places of sublime beauty, embodying a "wholeness supposedly lacking in commercial society."[91] One example: in his immensely popular novel, *Julie, or the New Heloise*, Jean-Jacques Rousseau extolled the virtues of isolated and pristine landscapes, writing: "Moreover, nature seems to want to veil from men's eyes her true attractions, to which they are too insensible, and which they disfigure when they can get their hands on them: she flees much-frequented places; it is on the tops of mountains, deep in the forests, on desert islands that she deploys her most stirring charms."[92] Once dismissed as wastelands or insurmountable obstacles, these mountains and forests now promised solace and deeper truths.

In Germany, the most striking manifestation of this mental shift was a new appreciation for the mountains and seashores, settings that provided the "starkest contrast" with cities and rural landscapes being "leveled and confined" in the name of progress.[93] While the discovery of natural attractions like the Alps can be traced to the eighteenth century, it was the romantics' rehabilitation of nature and the subsequent disenchantment wrought by urbanization that encouraged thousands of nineteenth-century tourists to follow scientists, poets, and painters into the wilderness.[94] Compared to the idealized German countryside, the Alps and Baltic and North Sea coastlines appeared even more "untouched,"

---

[89] Spode, *Wie die Deutschen "Reiseweltmeister" wurden*, 13.

[90] Withey, *Grand Tours and Cook's Tours*, 21; Casson, *Travel in the Ancient World*, 231.

[91] Koshar, *German Travel Cultures*, 24. See also Christof Mauch, "Introduction: Nature and Nation in Transatlantic Perspective," in *Nature in German History*, ed. Christof Mauch (New York: Berghahn, 2004), 5.

[92] Jean-Jacques Rousseau, *Julie, or the New Heloise: Letters of Two Lovers Who Live in a Small Town at the Foot of the Alps*, trans. Philip Stewart and Jean Vaché (Hanover, NH: University Press of New England, 1997), 394.

[93] Blackbourn, *The Conquest of Nature*, 71.

[94] Bernard, *Rush to the Alps*, 9, 24–25; Mary L. Barker, "Traditional Landscape and Mass Tourism in the Alps," *Geographical Review* 72, no. 4 (October 1982): 396.

allowing for real detachment from the outside world. Such locations also possessed a sublime beauty, a "delicious terror" that poets and philosophers associated with moral and political virtue.[95] Furthermore, the air and water of these locations supposedly possessed curative properties, and seawater in particular was linked to the prevention of multiple illnesses and debilities.[96] Swimming and mountain-climbing thus became popular means of recovery, as well as recreation. This was an important development in the larger story of tourism: physical activity became a regular feature of the vacation, thereby expanding the expectations of the middle-class tourist.[97] These activities were also decidedly non-aristocratic, solidifying a middle-class culture based not only on status symbols, but on leisure patterns as well.[98]

Alongside the Alps and the northern beaches, the Rhine River also became a popular middle-class tourist destination during the nineteenth century. The romantic poets Friedrich Schlegel, Clemens Brentano, and Ludwig Achim von Arnim toured the Rhine in 1802, recording their impressions and collecting local legends and songs for a reading public interested in re-connecting with a "national past."[99] After the Napoleonic Wars, the Rhine became a symbol of German identity, with authors like Ernst Moritz Arndt characterizing it as the "crucible of German nationhood."[100] Thus, romanticization occurred in tandem with nationalization, and the Rhine became the quintessential German tourist destination during the nineteenth century, popular among both domestic and international tourists. The portion of the river between Mainz and Cologne, often referred to as the Rhine Gorge or the Middle Rhine, was the most striking stretch of the river, prompting one American tourist to proclaim: "This glorious river is perfectly studded with beauty and historic recollections."[101] More than any other German destination, the Middle Rhine offered the complete package: evidence of nature's infinite power and scope in the river itself; dark forests, rolling mountains, and

[95] Edward Dickinson, "Altitude and Whiteness: Germanizing the Alps and Alpinizing the Germans, 1875–1935," *German Studies Review* 33, no. 3 (October 2010): 581. See also Löfgren, *On Holiday*, 26–28.

[96] Spode, *Wie die Deutschen "Reiseweltmeister" wurden*, 17–19.

[97] Bernard, *Rush to the Alps*, 77.

[98] Peter H. Hansen, "Albert Smith, the Alpine Club, and the Invention of Mountaineering in Mid-Victorian Britain," *Journal of British Studies* 34, no. 3 (July 1995): 309.

[99] Pretzel, *Die Literaturform Reiseführer*, 28–29.

[100] Thomas Lekan, "A 'Noble Prospect': Tourism, Heimat, and Conservation on the Rhine, 1880–1914," *The Journal of Modern History* 81, no. 4 (December 2009): 832.

[101] Adam and Mettele, eds., *Two Boston Brahmins in Goethe's Germany*, 164–165.

stark cliffs along its banks; scenes of pastoral life in the terraced vine-yards and rural communities in its vicinity; and picturesque reminders of the medieval past in the numerous ruins adorning its course. The Middle Rhine boasted attractions both timeless and historical, made accessible with the help of the package tour and steamship travel. These modern innovations brought a deluge of visitors to this tourist destina-tion, and after 1871, the Rhine became an integral part of the German *Bildungsreise*.[102] This destination, once seen as a sanctuary from the modern world of commodities, eventually became a commodity itself.[103]

Nineteenth-century tourism in natural settings exemplified several important trends: the romanticization and commodification of nature; the significance of travel as a marker of middle-class identity; and the increas-ingly common balancing of self-cultivation, physical revitalization, and recreation in the vacation experience. By emphasizing the importance of this variety of leisure travel, I do not mean to insinuate that the German tourism industry relied exclusively on natural attractions during the decades before the Great War. On the contrary, cities like Berlin, Dresden, and Munich had reputations as tourist hubs long before the mass tourism of the twentieth century, even if many of them had been overlooked by the Grand Tourists of the seventeenth and eighteenth centuries. These cities were not only tourist attractions in their own right, but also centers of an expanding tourism industry. Munich, for example, served as the headquarters for several organizations that supported regional tourism, including the Association for the Promotion of Tourism in Munich and the Bavarian Highlands (founded in 1869), the State Association for the Expansion of Bavarian Tourism (founded in 1890), and the State Tourism Council of Bavaria (founded in 1910). The third organization, subsidized by the royal government, actively promoted Bavarian attractions not only to tourists, but also to locals. In 1912, they passed a resolution to have oversized posters of Bavarian tourist attractions displayed in train stations throughout the region, encouraging residents to share the "tourist gaze" with their out-of-town visitors.[104] Later that year, the same organization decided that Munich primary school teachers should instruct students on how to interact with tourists, not only in order to encourage future visits,

---

[102] Lekan, "Tourism, *Heimat*, and Conservation on the Rhine," 834, 844.
[103] Enzensberger, "A Theory of Tourism," 129; Pretzel, *Die Literaturform Reiseführer*, 36–38. See also Thilo Nowack, "Rhein, Romantik, Reisen. Der Ausflugs- und Erhol-ungsreiseverkehr im Mittelrheintal im Kontext gesellschaftlichen Wandels (1890 bis 1970)" (Ph.D. diss., Rheinische Friedrich-Wilhelms-Universität, Bonn, 2006), 12–51.
[104] See Urry, *The Tourist Gaze*, 1–4.

but also to convey the importance of regional tourism.[105] The outbreak of World War I prevented the implementation of these plans, but their very existence confirms that tourism was becoming a big business, with undeniably high stakes.

The Origins of Mass Tourism

The Great War was a turning point in the broader history of tourism on several levels. It devastated the tourism industry of countless destinations, as the commitment to "total war" led to a marked decrease in consumption in general, and leisure travel in particular. Although some spa towns managed to stay in business as a result of the influx of wounded soldiers, most tourist locales witnessed the disappearance of both their clientele and their male labor force. On the other hand, the experience of the war itself dramatically expanded the realm of possibilities as far as travel was concerned. The sheer scale of the conflict led to the deployment of millions of soldiers across Europe, exposing peasants and workers to completely new worlds.[106] For these members of the lower classes, the experiences of traveling to the front, viewing unfamiliar landscapes, and encountering foreign cultures produced a new desire to experience the extraordinary. German soldiers in particular were especially interested in touring new lands, traveling throughout the occupied areas of war-torn Belgium, France, and the Russian and Austro-Hungarian Empires.[107] These wartime experiences foreshadowed a new stage in the history of leisure travel: mass tourism.

Mass tourism represented the culmination of several trends discussed in the previous section, among them the commercialization and streamlining of the travel experience. In her pioneering work on the subject, historian Christine Keitz identifies four additional features of this twentieth-century phenomenon. First, mass tourism was ostensibly egalitarian and transcended social barriers. What was once the obligation of the aristocracy and later the privilege of the middle classes effectively became a viable option for the largest demographic of industrial society: the workers. Second, mass tourism was easily and routinely planned, something guaranteed by travel bureaus offering all-inclusive, package

[105] StadtAM, Fremdenverkehrsamt, 12: "Landesfremdenverkehrsrat, Bayerischer: Berichte, 1911–1920."

[106] Koshar, *German Travel Cultures*, 67.

[107] David W. Lloyd, *Battlefield Tourism: Pilgrimage and the Commemoration of the Great War in Britain, Australia, and Canada, 1919–1939* (New York: Berg, 1998), 23.

vacations in the tradition of Thomas Cook. Third, mass tourism was a direct product of socioeconomic change, most obviously, the promise of paid vacation days. Fourth, mass tourism relied on the existence of a "mass tourism infrastructure" built on the transportation and hospitality industries. Simply stated, sights worth seeing and locales worth visiting could not be enjoyed unless the means existed to relocate and accommodate those who were eager to tour.[108]

While Keitz insists that German mass tourism began during the Weimar era, others maintain that mass tourism did not emerge until after the Nazi seizure of power.[109] If we define mass tourism as a truly egalitarian enterprise, then periodization becomes even more challenging, as tourism is *still* not a realistic option for many individuals around the world. That being said, the point worth emphasizing is that the German tourism industry and its clientele began to grow dramatically during the interwar period. A number of structural preconditions paved the way for this development, including the rationalization of labor, the increased amount of leisure time enjoyed by German workers, and the period of relative economic stability between the hyperinflation and the Great Depression.[110] After 1924, the stabilization of the German currency and the renegotiation of reparations "made industrial restructuring not only politically possible, but also economically essential."[111] Adoption of assembly-line manufacturing techniques led to an "intensification of the labor process," and numerous official holidays were sacrificed in the process. In exchange, the eight-hour work day became standard practice, giving laborers an unprecedented amount of daily free time. Furthermore, many employers sought to ensure prolonged productivity by granting their employees annual, paid vacation days, even though no nationwide legislation mandated this policy.[112] This did not become common practice throughout Western Europe until the 1930s, when the annual vacation became a

---

[108] Christine Keitz, *Reisen als Leitbild: Die Entstehung des modernen Massentourismus in Deutschland* (Munich: Deutscher Taschenbuch Verlag, 1997), 13–15.

[109] Hasso Spode, "Fordism, Mass Tourism and the Third Reich: The 'Strength through Joy' Seaside Resort as an Index Fossil," *Journal of Social History* 38, no. 1 (Autumn 2004): 132–134.

[110] Eric Weitz, *Weimar Germany: Promise and Tragedy* (Princeton: Princeton University Press, 2007), 167.

[111] Mary Nolan, *Visions of Modernity: American Business and the Modernization of Germany* (New York: Oxford University Press, 1994), 131–132.

[112] Keitz, *Reisen als Leitbild*, 24, 29, 33; Jürgen Reulecke, "Vom blauen Montag zum Arbeiterurlaub: Vorgeschichte und Entstehung des Erholungsurlaubs für Arbeiter vor dem Ersten Weltkrieg," *Archiv für Sozialgeschichte* 16 (1976): 205.

form of "long overdue compensation for increasing strain" on industrial workers.[113]

Still, paid vacation days did not necessarily guarantee a trip elsewhere, and most Germans lacked the financial means to travel during the early years of the Weimar Republic.[114] Again, it was not until the economy stabilized in the mid 1920s that leisure travel became a more realistic prospect for a broader spectrum of the population. With job stability and money to spare, office workers and retail employees, members of the so-called salaried masses, adopted the practice of leisure travel.[115] Meanwhile, the expansion of the German welfare state coincided with the broadening of the expectations of civil servants. For this demographic, an annual vacation would acquire the status of an entitlement, just as the popular rhetoric of egalitarianism and democracy compelled other segments of the population to expect similar opportunities.[116] By the second half of the 1920s, the middle-class multitude that had monopolized tourism since the late nineteenth century was joined by salaried employees, civil servants, and a growing number of industrial laborers.

Various statistics confirm that tourism was expanding during the Weimar era. At the turn of the century, less than 1 percent of the entire German workforce enjoyed an annual vacation, even though some civil servants and office employees had been granted annual vacation leave during the late nineteenth century.[117] By 1914, 10 percent of German manual laborers had a legal claim to vacation days, compared to the over 60 percent of white-collar workers who enjoyed similar rewards.[118] These numbers increased significantly by 1928, when it was reported that 95.3 percent of the entire workforce now had a right to vacation guaranteed by their employers.[119] This was a larger percentage than in France and England, even though German workers generally received fewer vacation days.[120] Two-thirds were ensured a paid vacation of three days or less,

---

[113] Kaspar Maase, *Grenzenloses Vergnügen: Der Aufstieg der Massenkultur, 1850–1970* (Frankfurt am Main: Fischer, 1997), 189.

[114] Gerald D. Feldman, "Welcome to Germany? The 'Fremdenplage' in the Weimar Inflation," in *Geschichte als Aufgabe. Festschrift für Otto Büsch*, ed. Wilhelm Treue (Berlin: Colloquium, 1988), 637.

[115] See Siegfried Kracauer, *The Salaried Masses: Duty and Distraction in Weimar German*, trans. Quinton Hoare (New York: Verso, 1998).

[116] Keitz, *Reisen als Leitbild*, 29, 32.

[117] Reulecke, "Vom blauen Montag zum Arbeiterurlaub," 221–226.

[118] Keitz, *Reisen als Leitbild*, 33–34.

[119] Hachtmann, *Tourismus-Geschichte*, 101.

[120] Spode, *Wie die Deutschen "Reiseweltmeister" wurden*, 110.

while only 12 percent of workers could anticipate a vacation of twelve days or more.[121] While many workers remained financially incapable of taking advantage of their newly guaranteed vacation time, the number of overnight stays by domestic tourists in western Germany rose by approximately 40 percent between 1924 and 1929, climbing from 233 million to 322 million.[122] During roughly the same period, the number of overnight stays in German youth hostels skyrocketed from 60,000 in 1919, to over 4,000,000 in 1932, confirming the popularity of this affordable vacation option.[123] Alongside the growing number of youth hostels, the number of vacation homes catering to the limited financial means of German workers rose to 300 by the end of the Weimar era, with over 25,000 beds available at reasonable rates.[124] A 1931 report issued by the Munich Chamber of Industry and Commerce announced the arrival of a "new type of tourist," noting that laborers had joined office workers, senior citizens, and members of the middle classes in their search for reasonably priced activities and affordable accommodations.[125]

This growth coincided with a mental shift concerning leisure travel and what it represented. During the 1920s, tourism became part of a rapidly developing "mass culture," taking its place alongside cinema, radio, and spectator sports as standard features of modern life.[126] As an activity no longer defined by class, tourism also became a symbol of social cohesion "beyond the control of the market and the state."[127] Not only did leisure travel open up new worlds to those in the position to afford them, it also promised deliverance from the hustle and bustle of the city, the office, the factory, and even the home, if only for a matter of days at a time. In the midst of ongoing industrialization, urbanization, and rationalization, tourism allowed wider segments of society to escape the monotony of daily existence.[128] In a 1925 essay entitled "Travel and Dance," German journalist Siegfried Kracauer argued that leisure travel allowed people

---

[121] Koshar, *German Travel Cultures*, 71.
[122] Becher, *Geschichte des modernen Lebensstils*, 219; Keitz, *Reisen als Leitbild*, 41; Günter Menges, *Wachstum und Konjunktur des deutschen Fremdenverkehrs 1913 bis 1956* (Frankfurt am Main: Kommissionsverlag Waldemar Kramer, 1959), 23.
[123] Koshar, *German Travel Cultures*, 73.
[124] Spode, *Wie die Deutschen "Reiseweltmeister" wurden*, 108.
[125] StadtAA, 25, 105: "Förderung des Fremdenverkehrs, VII. Band, 1931."
[126] Eberhard Kolb, *The Weimar Republic*, 2nd edn., trans. P.S. Falla and R.J. Park (New York: Routledge, 2005), 95–98.
[127] Gary Cross, *Time and Money: The Making of Consumer Culture* (London: Routledge, 1993), 8.
[128] Urry, *The Tourist Gaze*, 3–4.

to distance themselves from the "deadeningly familiar" limits of their daily affairs, reminding themselves that there was, simply put, something more to life. He characterized travel as a means of emancipation and transcendence, possessing an almost spiritual character as it replaced the experience of the "here and now" with tangible evidence of "the Beyond." The passion for travel evident during the Weimar era was noteworthy not in the details of how or where one traveled, but simply in the fact that one could travel at all, and remove one's self from a "habitual location."[129] Tourism was not just a product of modernity; it was a therapy for it.

This therapeutic modernism was available to workers, as well as women and children. While young people "pioneered modern tourism" by popularizing weekend excursions and extended hikes into the country-side, women began to constitute the majority of visitors at many tourist destinations during the 1920s.[130] Many had worked outside of the home during World War I, becoming accustomed to a certain degree of inde-pendence and mobility that the tourism industry sought to provide.[131] In a period during which the Comedian Harmonists famously extolled the virtues of "*Wochenend und Sonnenschein*," more Germans were travel-ing more frequently, but they were also traveling more frugally than the wealthy travelers that had preceded them.[132] According to calculations by the contemporaneous economist Artur Bormann, the domestic tourist spent, on average, 10 marks per day, with the 80–90 percent of travelers comprising the so-called middle classes averaging 7–8 marks per day. This is significantly less than the 20 marks per day spent by domestic tourists in Bavaria in 1914, a figure cited by Maximilian Krauss, the General Director of the National Railway Office for German Travel.[133]

The growth and diversification of the transportation industry ensured that these new tourists would not only require less money to enjoy a vacation, but also less time. The railway had been instrumental in the early expansion of tourism, but the nearly eighty-year, uninterrupted expansion of the German rail network came to an abrupt halt at the

---

[129] Siegfried Kracauer, "Travel and Dance," in *The Mass Ornament: Weimar Essays*, trans. Thomas Y. Levin (Cambridge, MA: Harvard University Press, 1995), 66, 70–71, 73.

[130] Detlev Peukert, *The Weimar Republic: The Crisis of Classical Modernity*, trans. Richard Deveson (New York: Hill and Wang, 1992), 176.

[131] Syrjämaa, "Tourism as a Typical Cultural Phenomenon," 181.

[132] Spode, *Wie die Deutschen "Reiseweltmeister" wurden*, 112, 105.

[133] Keitz, *Reisen als Leitbild*, 44–45. See also Maximilian Krauss, "Die Grundlagen des Fremdenverkehrs in München und im Bayerischen Hochland," in *Fünfundzwanzig Jahre Fremdenverkehr: Werkstatterinnerungen und Grundlagen*, ed. Maximilian Krauss (Munich: Gerber, 1929).

beginning of the Weimar era.[134] The path was now clear for other forms of transportation utilizing the internal combustion engine, which presented some serious competition for the railway. The motor bus, a new form of transportation that was relatively flexible compared to the railway, became especially popular during the 1920s. Soon enough, previously isolated vacation destinations were made accessible by bus lines catering specifically to tourists, one example being the popular *Luft Hansa* "Spa Service." The nationwide network of private and post bus lines grew exponentially between 1913 and 1928, expanding from 3,000 to 56,000 kilometers. At the same time, more wealthy tourists could reach new destinations with their own motor vehicles, and automobiles and motorcycles became a common sight in resort areas.[135] The popularity of motor vehicles forced the newly founded German Reich Railway (*Deutsche Reichsbahn*) to re-evaluate its pricing system as well as the condition of the trains themselves.[136] In order to compete with tourist bus lines in particular, the National Railway began offering package deals, which included sight-seeing tours, meals, and even overnight accommodations within the ticket price. This initiative proved to be a great success, and in 1927, the German Reich Railway triumphantly announced that 835,000 customers had traveled with these special tourism trains, or *Sonderzüge*.[137]

Another important feature of mass tourism in the Weimar Republic was the creation of literally hundreds of local tourism associations, as well as several important national organizations. Although many popular destinations, like Bad Reichenhall and Munich, had been represented by a local organization long before 1920, the interwar period witnessed the emergence of local tourism associations and offices across the nation. By the beginning of 1928, the number of private tourism associations (*Vereine*) in Germany numbered approximately 700. These organizations often assumed the responsibilities of the "Beautification Societies" of earlier decades, in addition to overseeing the creation and quality of

---

[134] Keitz, *Reisen als Leitbild*, 78.

[135] Spode, *Wie die Deutschen "Reiseweltmeister" wurden*, 106. See also Rudy Koshar, "Germans at the Wheel: Cars and Leisure Travel in Interwar Germany," in *Histories of Leisure*, 216; Alon Confino and Rudy Koshar, "Régimes of Consumer Culture: New Narratives in Twentieth-Century German History," *German History* 19, no. 2 (June 2001): 156.

[136] For more on the financial troubles of the German National Railway Company, see Alfred C. Mierzejewski, "The German National Railway Company, 1924–1932: Between Private and Public Enterprise," *The Business History Review* 67, no. 3 (Autumn 1993): 406–438.

[137] Keitz, *Reisen als Leitbild*, 25–26, 78–86.

the local tourism infrastructure, as well as the production and distribution of tourist propaganda. Before World War I, these local associations were loosely organized into the Federation of German Travel Associations (BDV), an organization that provided a forum for local tourism associations to meet and discuss common issues and international marketing. In 1918, the BDV was joined by the Central European Travel Bureau (MER), whose shareholders eventually included various state governments, the German Reich Railway, and the shipping companies of the Hamburg America Line and North German Lloyd. As the only organization authorized to sell German train tickets at their original prices outside of train stations, the MER enjoyed great success. By the end of the 1920s, it operated offices in four major cities and kiosks around the nation, selling inexpensive package tours to popular German getaways.[138] In the intervening time, another organization was established with the explicit goal of attracting foreign tourists to Germany. Founded in 1920, the Reich Central Office for German Tourism Promotion (RDV) saw it as their "cultural duty" to re-establish communication between foreigners and Germans, and thereby improve their nation's image after World War I. Subsidized by the German Reich Railway after 1928, the RDV had offices in twelve different countries and distributed propaganda around the world.[139]

A new appreciation for the economic potential of tourism helps to explain this new corporate interest. After the war, governments at various levels recognized tourism as a vital and independent sector of the German economy.[140] In destinations like Rothenburg ob der Tauber, tourism associations claimed that leisure travel would help to "reacquaint Germans with their cultural roots," while also injecting the local economy with "desperately needed cash."[141] A 1927 study commissioned by the Tourism Association of Munich and the Bavarian Alps reached similar conclusions, insisting that tourism-generated revenue could benefit local communities by funding the construction of new buildings, the improvement of schools, and the maintenance of "hygienic and social facilities," thereby contributing to the "education and health" of the local community.[142] Admittedly, some locals may have had the occasional

---

[138] Hachtmann, *Tourismus-Geschichte*, 114–115.
[139] Keitz, *Reisen als Leitbild*, 59–61.
[140] Ibid., 57.
[141] Hagen, *Preservation, Tourism and Nationalism*, 150.
[142] Adolf Moser, *Die wirtschaftliche und finanzielle Bedeutung des bayerischen Fremdenverkehrs für Land und Gemeinden* (Munich: Fremdenverkehrsverband München und bayrische Alpen, 1927), 21.

complaint about tourism and its repercussions, but even the most vehement criticisms could not refute the economic significance of this new industry. Moreover, the study reported that out of 555 communities that participated in a 1925 survey, only 15 noted "irrelevant complaints" about tourism.[143]

The economic value of leisure travel was seemingly indisputable, and the German tourism industry viewed international tourism in particular as an important means of achieving a favorable balance of credit while the national economy was heavily burdened by reparation payments and the foreign occupation of the Ruhr.[144] In this context, foreign currency became one of the nation's most important imports, and the primary objective behind the cultivation of international tourism.[145] RDV marketing targeted citizens of the United States in particular, employing the straightforward slogan: "Germany wants to see You!"[146] American travel to Germany did grow briefly after 1918, but declined again in the early 1920s, when inflation produced unpredictable exchange rates and an explosive political climate. In the meantime, visitors from bordering countries descended upon Germany, eager to take advantage of the beneficial exchange rate not only by traveling for less, but also by purchasing consumer goods at shockingly low prices. This "plague of foreigners" drained local resources and eventually led to the further destabilization of the German mark.[147]

While the German tourism industry pursued both foreign tourists and their currency, Germans traveling to foreign destinations became a subject of debate between the national government and various tourism organizations. Just as international tourists were enthusiastically encouraged to visit Germany, nationals themselves were urged to "See Germany First."[148] Similar financial concerns motivated the two marketing campaigns; one was aimed at acquiring foreign currency in order to re-invigorate the national economy, while the other sought to keep German currency within the country. Spending a vacation within one's own nation was characterized as a "duty to the fatherland," a

[143] Ibid., 12.
[144] Spode, *Wie die Deutschen "Reiseweltmeister" wurden,* 107.
[145] Keitz, *Reisen als Leitbild,* 55.
[146] Hachtmann, *Tourismus-Geschichte,* 117–118.
[147] Feldman, "The 'Fremdenplage' in the Weimar Inflation," 636–649. See also Bernd Widdig, *Culture and Inflation in Weimar Germany* (Berkeley: University of California Press, 2001), 46; David Clay Large, *Berlin* (New York: Basic Books, 2000), 176–178.
[148] StAM, Kurverwaltung Bad Reichenhall, 32: "Bund deutscher Verkehrsvereine und Reichszentrale für deutsche Verkehrswerbung, 1913–1931."

common marketing strategy with roots in the prewar period.[149] In Germany, the national government even went so far as to impose relatively high fees on citizens who decided to spend their vacation abroad, a measure that sparked protests in 1924 and 1931.[150] During this volatile period, domestic tourism had the potential to do more than bolster the economy; it could also enhance loyalty to the nation-state by forging a connection between citizens and the land itself. The creation of profit therefore went hand-in-hand with the creation of the patriotic citizen, now exposed to "authoritative representations of 'ourselves,' 'our landscape,' and 'our cultural ways and traditions'."[151]

If Germans demonstrated an unquenchable taste for travel during the peak years of the Weimar Republic, then the worldwide Great Depression forced many to consider a diet. Between 1929 and 1933, the number of overnight stays in Germany fell by 29 percent, reaching a figure below that of the prewar years.[152] However, this statistic does not necessarily imply that fewer people were traveling; many were simply traveling for less time. As the result of dramatically reduced incomes, some vacation options were no longer feasible, but this did not mean people abandoned their annual vacation altogether. In general, the German tourist sought out shorter and cheaper alternatives, and the travel industry responded to these demands. For example, starting in 1932, the German Reich Railway began offering 50 percent reduced fares to summer retreats outside urban centers, a program so popular that it was continued until 1938.[153] Tourism had become a feature and symbol of modern life that society would not quickly abandon.

The expansion of tourism continued during the Nazi period, when leisure travel acquired even more explicitly nationalist and political overtones. Shortly after the so-called seizure of power in 1933, the National Socialist dictatorship commenced with an extensive mobilization of German society in the name of nation and race. All other forms of allegiance, including class, religion, and region, were to be relegated by a new

---

[149] Spode, *Wie die Deutschen "Reiseweltmeister" wurden*, 107; Orvar Löfgren, "Know Your Country: A Comparative Perspective on Tourism and Nation Building in Sweden," in *Being Elsewhere*, 137; Pieter M. Judson, *Guardians of the Nation: Activists on the Language Frontiers of Imperial Austria* (Cambridge, MA: Harvard University Press, 2006), 141–176.

[150] Keitz, *Reisen als Leitbild*, 67.

[151] Baranowski and Furlough, "Introduction," in *Being Elsewhere*, 7–8.

[152] Spode, *Wie die Deutschen "Reiseweltmeister" wurden*, 105.

[153] Hachtmann, *Tourismus-Geschichte*, 118–119.

devotion to the people's community (*Volksgemeinschaft*) and the regime itself. However, before the regime could transform attitudes and values, they first had to transform institutions. In the early months of 1933, the new government embarked upon an ambitious "coordination" (*Gleichschaltung*) of all local organizations, purging members, reorganizing executive committees, fusing groups together, and abolishing others altogether. Autonomous associations, a dominant feature of German social life since the nineteenth century, were no more, and tourism associations were no exception. On June 23, 1933, Adolf Hitler signed the Law for the Reich Committee for Tourism, a move applauded by many representatives of the nation's travel industry. This Reich Committee for Tourism fell under the jurisdiction of the Ministry of Propaganda and Joseph Goebbels, but the man who made many of the most important decisions regarding tourism was Hermann Esser, a native Bavarian who had been a committed Nazi since the early 1920s. The coordination of German tourism streamlined the industry and transformed leisure travel into a political and ideological matter. In addition to forcing local *Vereine* to join newly formed state tourism associations supervised by the Reich Committee for Tourism, Esser forced local tourism associations to carry out "Aryanization" by expelling their Jewish members and employees.[154]

Centralization of the tourism industry continued on March 23, 1936, when the Law for the Reich Tourism Association modified the legal status of the national tourism organization and awarded it greater control over its members. This legislation also established the legal definition of "tourism communities," which were forced to join the regional state tourism associations.[155] The Reich Tourism Association was now, in effect, a "corporate body of public law," situated atop a chain of command that went all the way down to the local tourism communities. The national organization selected the chairmen of the regional associations, authorized their annual budgets, and reviewed copies of official souvenirs, guidebooks, brochures, and posters. However, the preexisting local tourism industry rarely received specific orders on what to publish, and retained control over the language employed to sell its sights to potential visitors. The Reich Tourism Association did issue guidelines on correct content and formatting in 1936, but the instructions only applied to state

---

[154] Kristin Semmens, *Seeing Hitler's Germany: Tourism in the Third Reich* (New York: Palgrave Macmillan, 2005), 16–20, 24–25.
[155] A "tourism community" was defined as any locale in which the annual figure of overnight stays was greater than 25 percent of the population.

tourism publications, and tended to focus almost exclusively on questions of style, in addition to displaying concern over "exaggerated epithets and allusions to foreign destinations."[156] However, in a few cases the new government did actively influence the marketing of certain attractions by ordering the local tourism industry to follow a pre-approved script. Such was the case with the famous Böttcherstrasse, a popular thoroughfare in Bremen renowned for its expressionist architecture. After years of Nazi condemnation, Hitler officially recognized the street "as a protected monument, albeit a negative example of degenerate art and architecture."[157] The Nazis could not stop tourists from visiting the Böttcherstrasse, but they did ensure that tour guides and promotion materials echoed the party line.

The sweeping coordination of the German tourism industry confirms that the National Socialist dictatorship took an unprecedented interest in leisure travel. Why? In the wake of the Great Depression, there was an obvious economic advantage to a healthy tourism industry. Furthermore, tourism could be an effective means of showcasing the new Germany and repairing its international reputation, especially during the 1936 Olympics.[158] A 1938 memo from Goebbels confirmed that "the accommodation of foreigners was of the utmost significance for international propaganda," but that these visitors, unless they expressed interest, should not be inundated with information about the National Socialist Movement.[159] The regime seemed especially interested in appealing to the tourists of Great Britain, who were to be presented with a revitalized and hospitable nation.[160] American tourists were targets as well, and an April 1934 edition of *The Chicago Tribune* announced that the German Railway Administration was offering a 60 percent fare reduction for Americans traveling that summer.[161] These American tourists proved

---

[156] Semmens, *Seeing Hitler's Germany*, 21–24, 45, 85.

[157] S. Jonathan Wiesen, *Creating the Nazi Marketplace: Commerce and Consumption in the Third Reich* (New York: Cambridge University Press, 2011), 111–112.

[158] See David Clay Large, *Nazi Games: The Olympics of 1936* (New York: W.W. Norton & Company, 2007).

[159] StAN, Regierung von Mittelfranken (Abgabe 1978), 3699: "Landesfremdenverkehrsrat, 1933–1952."

[160] Angela Schwarz, "British Visitors to National Socialist Germany: In a Familiar or in a Foreign Country?" *Journal of Contemporary History* 28, no. 3 (July 1993): 487–488. See also Angela Schwarz, *Die Reise ins Dritte Reich: Britische Augenzeugen im nationalsozialistischen Deutschland (1933–39)* (Göttingen: Vandenhoeck & Ruprecht, 1993).

[161] *The Chicago Tribune* (Chicago), April 15, 1934.

to be "easy prey" for Nazi propaganda, and they often returned with simplistic but positive impressions of the Third Reich, thus contradicting the negative reports of journalists and diplomats.[162]

Foreigners aside, the National Socialist dictatorship was also intent upon displaying a positive image of the new nation to Germans themselves. The tourism industry invited domestic travelers to reacquaint themselves with their fatherland, with propaganda once again compelling Germans to "See Germany First." At the same time, an increasingly egalitarian conception of tourism implied that every member of the people's community should enjoy the privilege of travel.[163] The automobile was set to play an important role in this new vision of tourism, with Hitler prophesying about a "nation on wheels" in which reasonably priced cars were not simply for commuting, but also for vacations.[164] Just as the railroad had served as a symbol of modernity and an instrument of national unification in the previous century, the automobile was set to play the same role in the twentieth century.[165]

In addition to promoting a positive image of modern Germany, the National Socialist dictatorship hoped that vacations would improve the quality of the German workers' life, theoretically increasing production, and creating a greater sense of working class solidarity (as long as it was in line with Nazi objectives).[166] With these goals in mind, the German Labor Front founded its own leisure agency in 1933. The "Strength through Joy" program, or *Kraft durch Freude* (KdF), offered discounted leisure activities and vacations to working-class Germans, even if many workers could never hope to afford them. Initially referred to as "After

---

[162] Michaela Hoenicke Moore, *Know Your Enemy: The American Debate on Nazism, 1933–1945* (New York: Cambridge University Press, 2010), 71–72.

[163] Fascist nations were not the only ones to actively encourage mass tourism during the Great Depression. See Ellen Furlough, "Making Mass Vacations: Tourism and Consumer Culture in France, 1930s to 1970s," *Comparative Studies in Society and History* 40, no. 2 (April 1998): 247–260; Michael Berkowitz, "A 'New Deal' for Leisure: Making Mass Tourism during the Great Depression," in *Being Elsewhere*, 185–212.

[164] Koshar, *German Travel Cultures*, 117. For more on the origins of the *Autobahn* during the Nazi period, see Thomas Zeller, *Driving Germany: The Landscape of the German Autobahn, 1930–1970*, trans. Thomas Dunlap (New York: Berghahn, 2007), 47–78.

[165] Anthony McElligott, *The German Urban Experience, 1900–1945* (New York: Routledge, 2001), 166.

[166] Hasso Spode, "Arbeiterurlaub im Dritten Reich," in *Angst, Belohnung, Zucht und Ordnung: Herrschaftsmechanismen im Nationalsocialismus*, ed. Carole Sachse, Tilla Siegel, Hasso Spode, and Wolfgang Spohn (Opladen: Westdeutscher Verlag, 1982), 286–287. See also Keitz, *Reisen als Leitbild*, 215–223.

Work," Strength through Joy was modeled after the Italian *Dopolavoro* program and was essentially an elaborate diversion technique, designed to compensate workers for the loss of their unions, insufficient wage increases, and "the increasing regimentation of life."[167] This was accomplished with reasonably priced concerts, day-trips, and package vacations to the German countryside and historic locales like Rothenburg ob der Tauber.[168] The program quickly became the largest travel agency in Germany, prominently represented by its massive cruise ships carrying thousands of working-class Germans to Italy, Portugal, Yugoslavia, and Norway.[169] Domestic group vacations became the program's "crowning effort," helping to convince the public that the new regime could substantially enhance the quality of their lives, while also ensuring a certain amount of complicity and preparing the populace for the work ahead.[170] Such efforts ultimately contributed to the "taming" of the German working classes.[171] Strength through Joy tourism also allowed the regime to chart a third path between socialism and Fordism by developing a "modest and disciplined form of consumption in accord with its ethic of self-sacrifice and common purpose."[172] The results were impressive. Writing in 1940, American journalist Lothrop Stoddard claimed: "There seems to be no doubt that *Kraft durch Freude* is generally popular and that it is prized as the outstanding benefit which the industrial masses have gained from the Nazi regime."[173]

Besides the placation of the "industrial masses," another objective behind Strength through Joy tourism was the integration of Germany's various "tribes" into a racially pure *Volksgemeinschaft*. The central planning of KdF excursions revealed a "solidarist agenda," as tour groups

---

[167] David Welch, *The Third Reich: Politics and Propaganda*, 2nd edn. (New York: Routledge, 2007), 61, 69–70. See also Victoria De Grazia, *The Culture of Consent: Mass Organization of Leisure in Fascist Italy* (New York: Cambridge University Press, 1981).

[168] Hagen, *Preservation, Tourism and Nationalism*, 188–222.

[169] Koshar, *German Travel Cultures*, 123.

[170] Hagen, *Preservation, Tourism and Nationalism*, 190; Hachtmann, *Tourismus-Geschichte*, 121–124. For more on the KdF program within Nazi propaganda, see Sascha Howind, *Die Illusion eines guten Lebens: Kraft durch Freude und nationalsozialistische Sozialpropaganda* (Frankfurt am Main: Peter Lang, 2013).

[171] See Tim Mason, "Die Bändigung der Arbeiterklasse im nationalsozialistischen Deutschland," in *Angst, Belohnung, Zucht und Ordnung*, 11–53.

[172] Shelly Baranowski, *Strength Through Joy: Consumerism and Mass Tourism in the Third Reich* (New York: Cambridge University Press, 2004), 147. For more on Nazi consumerism, see Wiesen, *Creating the Nazi Marketplace*.

[173] Lothrop Stoddard, *Into the Darkness: Nazi Germany Today* (New York: Duell, Sloan & Pearce, 1940), 138.

were often sent from one region to another in the hopes of eradicating various forms of particularism.[174] By forcing the culturally diverse citizens of the Third Reich to socialize with one another, state-sponsored travel would foster unity. A 1940 official publication on "Strength through Joy" tourism praised the manner in which the program brought together people from different parts of Germany, allowing them to forge relationships and "draw connections with friends."[175] In reality, the goal of dismantling regional particularism often failed as a result of the tourists' unwillingness to interact with their hosts or fellow travelers from other parts of the Reich, and the "different German tribes" often "remained segregated."[176]

Although its success remains debatable, the Strength through Joy program has more or less monopolized the attention of scholars addressing tourism in Nazi Germany, overshadowing the fact that "individual or familial travel" remained the norm throughout the period.[177] Even at its peak, KdF tourism was responsible for a mere 10.2 percent of the overnight stays in Germany by Germans.[178] In her monograph on tourism in the Third Reich, historian Kristin Semmens argues that Strength through Joy tourism coexisted with two other distinct varieties, defined as the "normal tourist culture" and the "Nazi tourist culture." While the former was merely a continuation of pre-1933 commercial tourism, the latter was a direct product of the rise of National Socialism. Important sites in the history of the movement, such as the Temples of Honor in Munich or the Reich Party Rally Grounds in Nuremberg, became popular tourist attractions, and were often incorporated into important mass events during the Nazi festival calendar.[179] The popularity of these new sights serves as further evidence of the Nazi impact on the German tourism industry.

By the 1930s, tourism had become a prominent feature of modern German society. No longer limited to the aristocracy and middle classes, it was now theoretically available to the multitudes (as long as they were members of the so-called people's community). However, during this explosive period of German history, tourism provided much more than an escape from everyday life; it was an important means of gaining

---

[174] Baranowski, *Strength Through Joy,* 120.
[175] Werner Kahl, *Der deutsche Arbeiter reist!* (Berlin: Deutscher Verlag, 1940), 16.
[176] Spode, "Arbeiterurlaub im Dritten Reich," 311.
[177] Koshar, *German Travel Cultures,* 125.
[178] Semmens, *Seeing Hitler's Germany,* 4.
[179] Ibid., 42–43.

perspective on the modern German nation. The middle-class tourists of the long nineteenth century pursued similar objectives, inspired by romantic visions of self-cultivation and the natural environment. We can now turn to these issues in more detail, using the case study of Franconian Switzerland to grant new insight into the early development of tourism in Bavaria and Germany at large.

2

Landscape Tourism in Franconian Switzerland

"Franconian Switzerland is a wonderfully charming mountain landscape; with its magnificent treks, secluded spaces, and idyllic spots of an exceptional nature, it occupies a portion of Upper and Middle Franconia, and is rightfully deserving of the name derived from common parlance."[1]

Friedrich Ende's *Practical Guide through Franconian Switzerland* (1894)

Nestled between the cities of Erlangen, Bamberg, and Bayreuth, Franconian Switzerland was often overlooked on nineteenth-century political maps of the Kingdom of Bavaria. The secluded region was, however, a prominent feature on tourist maps, and it was an established attraction long before the dawn of modern transportation or package tours. It was one of many "little Switzerlands" in central Europe, despite the fact that its highest peak measured a mere 627 meters, and its rolling and verdant landscape seemed more Appalachian than Alpine. In this particular case, the Swiss label implied much more than mountains; it invoked an entirely different world.

For nineteenth-century poets, artists, and middle-class tourists, Franconian Switzerland represented an isolated landscape that seemed relatively untouched by its few human inhabitants. This was a place where time had effectively stood still, a sanctuary where the traveler was distant and safe from the noise, traffic, and stress of urban life that was beginning to define German society. Modernization, entailing the interrelated

---

[1] Friedrich Ende, *Praktischer Führer durch die Fränkische Schweiz (mit ausführlicher Orientierungs-Karte)* (Nuremberg: Selbstverlag von Friedr. Ende and Erh. Kolb, 1894), 1.

processes of industrialization and urbanization, contributed to a growing distance between society and the natural environment. It led mankind to seek respite from civilization in unspoiled nature, just as it generated the technology that made such an escape possible. Nineteenth-century tourism was therefore both a manifestation of modernity *and* a therapy for it. Its practitioners were treated to the best of both worlds: distance coupled with convenience, and a foreign landscape furnished with some of the familiar features of the city. Nature may have been the primary attraction in places like Franconian Switzerland, but visitors could also anticipate modern accommodations at the local inn, as well as telegraph machines and beer imported from Munich and Nuremberg. Far from home, they still had the option to reconnect.

Middle-class travelers sought a romantic respite in Franconian Switzerland, but they also desired a vacation that was rationalized and action-packed, and therefore worthy of their valuable time and money. Late nineteenth-century guidebooks catered to these desires by guaranteeing a standardized and unforgettable tourist experience, a synthesis of distance and comfort that temporarily grounded travelers in search of solace. I define this type of leisure travel as "landscape tourism" because the landscape was the defining feature of a vacation in Franconian Switzerland. This does not, however, preclude the fact that landscape tourism did coexist and even overlap with other forms of tourism (scientific, medical, historical) that feature throughout the book. Although some of these forms displayed nostalgic tendencies, every one of them was a product of modernity. Even seemingly antimodern travel had modern roots.

Romanticism, Urbanization, and the Return to Nature

It is a common argument that the German people have a unique relationship with the natural environment. In his ethnographic work, *Germania*, ancient Roman historian Tacitus identified a virtuous life in the forest as one of the defining characteristics of the Germanic tribes. Centuries later, central European scholars and landscape painters glorified the indigenous German wilderness, even as thousands of trees fell victim to deforestation.[2] In his 1797 novella, *The Fair Eckbert*, the romantic author Ludwig Tieck coined the term *Waldeinsamkeit* to express the pseudo-spiritual connection between the German people and the

---

[2]   Simon Schama, *Landscape and Memory* (New York: Vintage Books, 1996), 81–100.

"untamed wilderness" which had allegedly existed for centuries.[3] In recent years, historians have documented how both the German natural environment and attitudes toward it shifted during the modern period.[4] While one preeminent scholar has identified some of the ways in which the Germans set out to "conquer" nature during the last three centuries, others have examined the origins of the German environmental movement during the late nineteenth and early twentieth centuries, demonstrating that middle-class activists often worked toward a "better modernity" by protecting the environment and transforming it into a unifying symbol for society at large.[5]

In regions like Franconian Switzerland, nature was not strictly an adversary to be conquered; it was also a vehicle of self-cultivation, a source of healing, and a marketable commodity. However, it should be stressed that this natural environment bore the marks of civilization. There was no "unspoiled" nature or "wilderness" in central Europe, only landscapes exploited by humans for their own varying needs.[6] These landscapes were also products of the mind, "constructs of the imagination projected onto wood and water and rock," as historian Simon Schama has claimed.[7] In other words, humans mobilized landscapes both physically and discursively for a number of ends, ranging from the creation of shipping lanes to the construction of the regional *Heimat*. Thus, the study of the German natural environment requires attention not only to the land itself, but also to the cultural landscapes constructed by society. Nineteenth-century tourism in Germany revolved around such settings, from the Luneburg Heath to the Harz Mountains, from the Middle Rhine to Franconian Switzerland.[8] Visiting these destinations was a means of

---

[3] Eric Schwartz, "Waldeinsamkeit: Subjective Ambivalence in German Romanticism," *International Journal of the Humanities* 5, no. 4 (November 2007): 208.

[4] See Mark Cioc, *The Rhine: An Eco-Biography, 1815–2000* (Seattle: University of Washington Press, 2002); Hans-Werner Frohn and Friedmann Schmoll, *Natur und Staat: Staatlicher Naturschutz in Deutschland 1906–2006*, ed. Hans-Werner Frohn and Friedmann Schmoll (Münster: Landwirtschaftsverlag, 2006); Mauch, *Nature in German History*.

[5] Blackbourn, *The Conquest of Nature*; Lekan, *Imagining the Nation in Nature*; William Rollins, *A Greener Vision of Home: Cultural Politics and Environmental Reform in the German Heimatschutz Movement, 1904–1918* (Ann Arbor: University of Michigan Press, 1997), 33.

[6] Blackbourn, *The Conquest of Nature*, 187.

[7] Schama, *Landscape and Memory*, 61.

[8] See Hansjörg Küster, "Die Entdeckung der Lüneburger Heide als 'schöne Natur,'" *Themenportal Europäische Geschichte* (2010), www.europa.clio-online.de/2010/Article=429 (accessed October 20, 2010).

"turning to nature," but like other examples of this practice, it was neither antimodern nor irrational.[9] Instead, landscape tourism was a manifestation of modernity itself, fueled by romanticism and urbanization.

German romanticism was a complex literary, artistic, philosophical, and ultimately political movement, inspired by "the painful and melancholic conviction that in modern reality something precious has been lost... "[10] It created a new perception of the natural environment that prefigured both tourism and the organized environmentalism of the early twentieth century.[11] Romanticism was ideologically related to the Enlightenment and the work of Rousseau in particular, but it was historically connected to the French Revolution, which had helped to produce a modern society defined by materialism and egoism. Its core principles, including imagination, introspection, and revelation, emerged in several important literary works of the late eighteenth century, most notably *Heartfelt Effusions of an Art-Loving Friar*, published anonymously by Ludwig Tieck and Wilhelm Heinrich Wackenroder in 1796.[12] In these works and others, Tieck and his contemporaries advocated the middle-class principle of *Bildung*, which implied both personal cultivation and the education of the public. *Bildung* was the "fundamental ethical ideal" of German romanticism, and the key to social and political reform that would reestablish a sense of community. It entailed cultivating not only reason, but also sensibility, sensitivity, and love.[13] In pursuit of this holistic ideal, a generation of young intellectuals and artists turned their attention to all that was intrinsically organic and time-honored in Germany, glorifying isolated landscapes and medieval ruins. In the process, they diverged from the Enlightenment and its preoccupation with reason.[14]

The revolutionary ideas of the German romantics quickly spread beyond the intellectual circles of Berlin and Jena. Although romanticism

---

9   See John Alexander Williams, *Turning to Nature in Germany: Hiking, Nudism, and Conservation, 1900–1940* (Stanford: Stanford University Press, 2007).
10 Michael Löwy and Robert Sayre, *Romanticism Against the Tide of Modernity*, trans. Catherine Porter (Durham: Duke University Press, 2001), 21.
11 Richard Hölzl, "Nature Preservation in the Age of Classical Modernity: The Landesausschuss für Naturpflege and the Bund Naturschutz in Bavaria, 1905–1933," *Bulletin of the German Historical Institute, Washington D.C.*, Supplement 3: "From Heimat to Umwelt: New Perspectives on German Environmental History" (2006): 31.
12 See Theodore Ziolkowski, *Vorboten der Moderne: Eine Kulturgeschichte der Frühromantik* (Stuttgart: Klett-Cotta, 2006).
13 Beiser, *The Romantic Imperative*, 25–27, 49.
14 Marsha Morton, "German Romanticism: The Search for 'A Quiet Place,'" *Art Institute of Chicago Museum Studies* 28, no. 1 (2002): 9.

was essentially a literary movement with a visual arts element, its impact was apparent in the disciplines of music and science as well. Romanticism also renewed interest in historical research, which was no longer dismissed as mere "Enlightenment pragmatism," but instead understood as a means of helping humanity "find sense in the past and . . . a niche for themselves and their existence in the flow of universal development."[15] Even though German romanticism often directed attention to an idealized past, its disciples wanted to construct a better modernity, not flee from it altogether. By reconnecting contemporary society with nature, tradition, and history, romantics hoped to make modernity more agreeable.[16] Embracing the natural environment and a simpler way of life was the route to true freedom, and not just the theoretical independence championed by the *philosophes*, or the *liberté* delivered by the French armies.

Early romantics supported a synthesis between nature and society in the spirit of the ancient Greeks, arguing that this reorientation would counteract the materialism and egoism of modern life. They were also among the first to express concern that the natural environment was being compromised by "rationalization, economic self-interest, and a purely instrumental view of nature."[17] In response, the romantics sought to protect and "reenchant" the natural environment, which they viewed as a spiritual domain and an idealistic embodiment of a better world.[18] Artists like Caspar David Friedrich used their work to promote a new faith in *Waldeinsamkeit*, glorifying the sacred and redemptive qualities of nature.[19] Such visions helped to rehabilitate nature in the eyes of many, and romantic sentiments fueled the growth of nineteenth-century tourism, in Germany and elsewhere.[20]

If romanticism rehabilitated the natural environment, then urbanization guaranteed its veneration. In 1815, Germany was still predominantly rural, and only Berlin and Hamburg could register more than 100,000 residents. This changed during the second half of the nineteenth century, when the growth of rural populations more or less stopped while

---

[15] Dietrich von Engelhardt, "Romanticism in Germany," in *Romanticism in National Context*, ed. Roy Porter and Mikuláš Teich (New York: Cambridge University Press, 1988), 109, 112, 115–116.

[16] Beiser, *The Romantic Imperative*, 102.

[17] Max Blechman, "The Revolutionary Dream of Early Romanticism," in *Revolutionary Romanticism*, ed. Max Blechman (San Francisco: City Light Books, 1999), 3.

[18] Löwy and Sayre, *Romanticism Against the Tide of Modernity*, 32.

[19] Morton, "German Romanticism," 12.

[20] Buzard, *The Beaten Track*, 19; Enzensberger, "A Theory of Tourism," 125.

urban populations swelled. Urbanization proceeded the most rapidly in the Rhineland, the Ruhr, and Saxony, but cities grew throughout the future German Empire, a process stimulated by the constant influx of rural migrants.[21] In 1850 there were six German cities with a population of over 100,000 residents. By 1870, there were eleven.[22] In Bavaria, the populations of both Munich and Nuremberg increased by over 200 percent between 1875 and 1910.[23]

These statistics reflect the rapid growth of urban populations in Germany during the long nineteenth century, but the term urbanization also referred to "fundamental changes of urban life styles" involving social structures, communications, human relations, and living conditions.[24] As centers of politics, industry, and culture, cities signified progress on several levels, but they were not necessarily pleasant places in which to live, as Rousseau suggested when he referred to them as "the abyss of the human species."[25] Nineteenth-century cities were synonymous with pollution and disease, and even affluent middle-class residents were not entirely immune from the drawbacks of urban life.[26] The *Bürgertum* inhaled air pollution created by the burning of coal, just as they were forced to reckon with the manure that covered city streets before the dawn of trams and subways. By the end of the century, new standards of cleanliness were fueling a growing fear of sewage gas and the general filth associated with the living conditions of working families.[27] Such fears were vindicated by the frequent epidemics that devastated urban populations throughout the nineteenth century.[28]

In addition to posing these physical risks, the modern city had an impact on the behavior of its inhabitants. Moralists charged urban life

---

[21] James Jackson, *Migration and Urbanization in the Ruhr Valley, 1821–1914* (Atlantic Highlands, NJ: Humanities Press, 1997), 1–2; See also Friedrich Lenger, "Building and Perceiving the City: Germany around 1900," in *Towards an Urban Nation: Germany since 1780*, ed. Friedrich Lenger (New York: Berg, 2002), 90–92.

[22] David Blackbourn, *The Long Nineteenth Century: A History of Germany, 1780–1918* (New York: Oxford University Press, 1998), 199.

[23] Nipperdey, *Deutsche Geschichte, 1866–1918, Erster Band*, 35–37.

[24] Klaus Tenfelde, "Urbanization and the Spread of an Urban Culture in the Nineteenth and Twentieth Centuries," in *Towards an Urban Nation*, 24.

[25] Jean-Jacques Rousseau, *Emile, or On Education*, trans. Allan Bloom (New York: Basic Books, 1979), 59.

[26] For more on nineteenth-century Hamburg in particular, see Richard Evans, *Death in Hamburg: Society and Politics in the Cholera Years* (New York: Oxford University Press, 1987), 109–179.

[27] Andrew Lees and Lynn Hollen Lees, *Cities and the Making of Modern Europe, 1750–1914* (New York: Cambridge University Press, 2007), 60–62.

[28] Evans, *Death in Hamburg*, 183–196, 226–256.

with the degradation of the lower classes, whose members were turning away from religion and embracing crime as a means of survival.[29] Pundits linked the modern city to a variety of social problems, ranging from alcoholism and prostitution, to revolutionary unrest and the breakdown of the family.[30] In his 1887 study, *Community and Society*, German sociologist Ferdinand Tönnies argued that urbanization had helped to replace an organic community governed by tradition and "natural will" with an anonymous society defined by competition, hostility, fear, and "rational will." With some nostalgia, he writes: "In the village the household is independent and strong, also in the town the household is preserved and has a certain beauty; only in the city does the household become sterile, narrow, empty, and debased to fit the conception of a mere living place which can be obtained everywhere in equal form for money."[31]

In the eyes of many nineteenth-century critics, the city was to blame for everything that was wrong with modern society.[32] One of the earliest and most influential anti-urban writers was the Bavarian journalist Wilhelm August Riehl, who associated urbanization with "the loss of national character, the growth of social, psychological, and political instability, and numerous cultural ills."[33] Like a later generation of German romantics, Riehl advocated flight from the cities and a return to the natural environment, which he depicted as the basis of German socio-political identity, the last refuge of medieval virtue, and the antidote to modern materialism and disenchantment.[34] Numerous authors echoed the ideas of Riehl in the following decades, denouncing the physically and spiritually detrimental effects of the city, and idealizing the "unspoiled" and "pure" countryside.[35] This new view of nature was undeniably linked to the denigration of the modern city, but it was also a product of the growing distance between the urban world and the natural environment. The

---

[29] Lees and Lees, *Cities and the Making of Modern Europe*, 147. See also Eric A. Johnson, *Urbanization and Crime: Germany 1871–1914* (New York: Cambridge University Press, 1995).

[30] See Andrew Lees, *Cities, Sin, and Social Reform in Imperial Germany* (Ann Arbor: University of Michigan Press, 2002).

[31] Tönnies, *Community and Society*, 162.

[32] Jürgen Reulecke, *Geschichte der Urbanisierung in Deutschland* (Frankfurt am Main: Suhrkamp, 1985), 139–146.

[33] Andrew Lees, "Critics of Urban Society in Germany, 1854–1914," *Journal of the History of Ideas* 40, no. 1 (January-March 1979): 62–64.

[34] Wilhelm Heinrich Riehl, *Die Naturgeschichte des Volkes als Grundlage einer deutschen Sozial-Politik*, vol. I, Land und Leute, 2nd edn. (Stuttgart: J.G. Cotta, 1861), 43–59, 83–122.

[35] See Raymond Williams, *The Country and the City* (New York: Oxford University Press, 1973).

rapid urbanization of the late nineteenth century produced a longing for more natural settings, but this world was only desirable because it was no longer "oppressively close."[36] Describing the appeal of Alpine slopes to city-dwellers in *The Magic Mountain*, German author Thomas Mann clarified: "Born a stranger to remote, wild nature, the child of civilization is much more open to her grandeur than are her own coarse sons, who have been at her mercy from infancy ... They know next to nothing of the religious awe with which the novice approaches her ... "[37] This "remote, wild nature" proved attractive to the educated bourgeoisie because it no longer held them captive, and instead promised a host of benefits.

Just as romanticism and urbanization contributed to a "back to nature" mentality that fueled leisure travel in Germany, the growth of the tourism industry itself began to endanger the natural environment. In 1880, music professor Ernst Rudorff wrote an article condemning a proposed funicular railway up the Drachenfels Mountain outside of Bonn, one of the tourist highlights on the Middle Rhine. Rudorff, the founder of the German Homeland Protection movement, indicted the German people for standing by while entrepreneurs and technocrats attempted to bend nature to their own will, spoiling "untouched" landscapes in the process. He lashed out against the modern figure of the "tourist" in particular, describing his primary characteristic as an obsession with seeking out "every possible beauty and singularity" for the sake of personal amusement. The tourist may "celebrate nature," wrote Rudorff, "but he celebrates it just as he prostitutes it."[38] This article was the symbolic first strike in the German conservation movement, even though the attempt to stop the construction of the railway itself was ultimately unsuccessful.[39] Still, this criticism of tourism's reliance on modern technology and its violation of the natural environment foreshadowed subsequent complaints in locales like Franconian Switzerland and Bad Reichenhall.

Urbanization and romanticism compelled members of the educated middle class to turn their vacations into quests for authenticity and self-cultivation in "untouched" natural settings. However, the realities

---

[36] Bernard, *The Rush to the Alps*, 14, 64–65. See also Joachim Radkau, *Nature and Power: A Global History of the Environment*, trans. Thomas Dunlap (New York: Cambridge University Press, 2008), 26.

[37] Thomas Mann, *The Magic Mountain*, trans. John E. Woods (New York: *Vintage International*, 1995), 467.

[38] Ernst Rudorff, "Ueber das Verhältniss des modernen Lebens zur Natur," *Preussische Jahrbücher* 45 (1880): 261–276.

[39] Blackbourn, *The Conquest of Nature*, 184.

of travel during the late nineteenth century did not necessarily facilitate these goals, and tourists had little time for the romantic ideals of imagination, introspection, and revelation.[40] With only a limited amount of vacation days per year, the majority of middle-class tourists could not be too philosophical while enjoying the natural environment, and many appeared obsessed with consuming as much as possible in a short space of time. Guidebooks covering Franconian Switzerland encouraged this behavior by supplying only the most essential information, as well as action-packed, day-by-day itineraries, practically ensuring that the tourist received his or her fill. These guidebooks also saved time by arming the tourist with the necessary emotional vocabulary, indicating the proper responses to the most important sights and vistas. In the process, these publications helped to construct a distinctly bourgeois tourist gaze that echoed romantic sentiments and anti-urban inclinations. Before discussing these themes in greater detail, we must first turn to the discovery of Franconian Switzerland.

The Discovery of the Tourist Idyll

Although largely overlooked by eighteenth-century Grand Tourists, Bavaria became a popular destination during the nineteenth century. One of the earliest stars of the regional tourism industry was the area eventually known as Franconian Switzerland, located in the heart of the Franconian Jura highlands. The Franks first settled this region around the Wiesent River in the early eighth century, with various branches of prominent noble families exercising control over small, autonomous territories. Many of these loosely defined political entities were absorbed into the Diocese of Bamberg in 1007. Over the next four centuries, the area ruled from Bamberg continued to grow, just as the threat of military encroachment led to the construction of new fortifications throughout the region, among them, the fortresses of Gößweinstein and Pottenstein. During the early modern period, the mountainous region east of Bamberg was the site of regular warfare, with the German Peasants' War and Thirty Years War leaving eighty-six of the region's fortresses in ruins.[41]

---

[40] Pretzel, *Die Literaturform Reiseführer*, 59–60.

[41] Gustave Voit, Brigitte Kaulich, and Walter Rüfer, *Vom Land im Gebirg zur Fränkischen Schweiz: Eine Landschaft wird entdeckt* (Erlangen: Palm & Enke, 1992), 11–20. See also Anton Sterzl and Emil Bauer, *Fränkische Schweiz: Gesichter und Kräfte einer Landschaft* (Bamberg: St. Otto Verlag, 1969), 8–20.

For centuries, soldiers were among the only visitors to this secluded area between the cities of Erlangen, Bamberg, and Bayreuth, commonly referred to as "the land in the mountains." Its residents were poor farmers tilling a rocky and unrewarding soil, and even the local nobility struggled to make ends meet. Two major roads crossed portions of the region, but other thoroughfares were poorly maintained and dangerous. Untamed rivers and steep inclines ensured that travel along local routes could only be accomplished with the help of local guides, an occupation that ensured some meager income for impoverished nobles. All of this began to change in 1774, when the minister and aspiring natural scientist Johann Friedrich Esper published a "detailed report" on the caves near Muggendorf, a small village on the Wiesent.[42] The wooded peaks of the Franconian Jura contained hundreds of caves, some of them stretching nearly 500 meters into the earth. After several years of intensive research in this subterranean world, Esper produced a dense guidebook that detailed a remarkable variety of rock formations and prehistoric life-forms, including the newly-discovered "cave bear," or *Ursus spelaeus*. Written during the final years of the Enlightenment and quickly translated into French, this publication inaugurated an era of scientific exploration in Franconia. Soon, hundreds of legitimate and amateur scientists flocked to secluded destinations like the Rosenmüller Cave, eager to make their own discoveries, or at least walk away with some prehistoric souvenirs.[43]

The discovery of the caves was only the first chapter in the larger discovery of the destination eventually known as Franconian Switzerland. The amateur scientists were followed by the romantics, who were enthralled with the region's rolling mountains and medieval ruins. In June 1793, a young Ludwig Tieck and Wilhelm Heinrich Wackenroder embarked upon an eleven-day tour of the region around Bayreuth. Berliners by birth, the two law students were eager to explore the territory recently annexed by Prussia in 1791, and their subsequent travel reports foreshadowed their trademark infatuation with medieval history and the natural environment. Departing from Erlangen, the two began by stopping in Ebermannstadt and Streitberg, two small towns along the banks of the Wiesent. While both commented on the hospitality of

---

[42] See Johann Friedrich Esper, *Ausführliche Nachricht von neuentdeckten Zoolithen unbekannter vierfüssiger Thiere und denen sie enthaltenden, so wie verschiedenen andern denkwürdigen Grüften der Obergebürgischen Lande der Marggrafthums Bayreuth* (Nuremberg: G.W. Knorrs Erben, 1774).

[43] Voit, Kaulich, and Rüfer, *Vom Land im Gebirg zur Fränkischen Schweiz*, 30–32, 182–189.

Ebermannstadt's inhabitants, they wrote even more glowingly of the land-scape around Streitberg, with Tieck proclaiming in a letter: "Oh, nature is truly inexhaustible in its beauty! Here is genuine pleasure, for a pic-turesque terrain purifies men..."[44] Tieck and Wackenroder were espe-cially enamored with the ruins of the Neideck fortress, which stood atop a precipice outside of Streitberg. Wackenroder described their ascent to the sight: "We carried ourselves over the broken rocks and through the thick woods that cover the slopes of the mountain, and admired the vast rubble. I have never seen greater or more beautiful ruins."[45] Eventually standing within the remains of the medieval fortress, both men gazed through the medieval windows at the mountain views, which Wackenroder compared to "canvases in a frame."[46]

The travel reports of Tieck and Wackenroder displayed a reverence toward historical sites that was increasingly common in early nineteenth-century Germany. More than just a scenic stop during a hike, medieval ruins were symbols of a past slipping into obscurity, as well as physical reservoirs of historical consciousness itself. In a secularized world, both historical monuments and timeless natural settings provided transient sources of divine inspiration, evoking what one historian has referred to as the "historical sublime."[47] Tieck and Wackenroder had been startled by the beauty of the area around Streitberg and Muggendorf, and they were compelled to reproduce the sentiment and impart it to others. Their travel reports sparked the imagination of their literary contemporaries, with men like Jean Paul and Ernst Moritz Arndt following in their footsteps around the turn of the century. The latter stopped in Muggendorf in 1798, and was equally impressed by the remains of the Neideck, which he characterized as the "greatest and most romantic ruins" located on German soil.[48]

Just as the poets had followed the scientists, the painters now fol-lowed the poets. Like their literary predecessors, these artists were capti-vated by the romantic landscapes of the region around Muggendorf. Early

44 Ludwig Tieck and Wilhelm Heinrich Wackenroder, *Die Pfingstreise von 1793 durch die Fränkische Schweiz, den Frankenwald and das Fichtelgebirge* (Helmbrechts: Wilhelm Saalfrank, 1970), 16.
45 Ibid., 17, 44–45.
46 Ibid., 45.
47 Susan Crane, *Collecting and Historical Consciousness in Early Nineteenth-Century Germany* (Ithaca: Cornell University Press, 2000), 18, 24–27, 44–45.
48 Quoted in Voit, Kaulich, and Rüfer, *Vom Land im Gebirg zur Fränkischen Schweiz*, 36, 40.

FIGURE 2. Ludwig Richter's drawing of the Neideck Ruins in Gustav von Heeringen, *Wanderungen durch Franken* (Leipzig, 1840).

publications on the region included copper etchings and lithographs of the natural landscape, helping to establish the region's status as "picturesque," a late eighteenth-century neologism used to refer to landscapes that were idyllic, varied, and ultimately "paintable."[49] During the early nineteenth century, Munich artist Domenico Quaglio completed several drawings of the region's medieval ruins that were reproduced in tourist publications. Even more influential in creating the visual iconography of Franconian Switzerland was German painter Ludwig Richter, who was commissioned by a Leipzig publisher to illustrate the multivolume series *Picturesque and Romantic Germany*.[50] Traveling through the region in 1837, Richter made five engravings that established the image of a secluded and idyllic retreat, where smiling peasants toiled in the midst of rolling mountains and towering ruins.[51]

The region certainly had its admirers, but it still lacked a marketable name. Although the area was widely referred to as the "Muggendorfer Mountains" for decades to come, Esper foreshadowed future developments in 1774 when he commented: "The entire landscape looks

[49] Löfgren, *On Holiday*, 19–21.
[50] Among the titles in this series was Gustav von Heeringen, *Wanderungen durch Franken* (Leipzig: G. Wigand, 1840).
[51] Voit, Kaulich, and Rüfer, *Vom Land im Gebirg zur Fränkischen Schweiz*, 47–51.

Swiss."[52] Over thirty years later Johann Christian Fick went a step further in his *Historical, Topographical, and Statistical Description of Erlangen and its Environs.* In reference to the mountainous region surrounding the Wiesent River, a land with "unrestrained natural beauty," Fick pioneered the label "Franconian Switzerland," a designation that was buried one hundred pages into the text.[53] Why Switzerland? The Alpine nation was the original romantic destination, a site of spiritual transcendence glorified by authors like Rousseau and Lord Byron. It became continental Europe's foremost travel destination during the early nineteenth century, and it established the criteria by which other destinations would be judged.[54] The very name of Switzerland became synonymous with tourism, and *"die Schweiz"* was pragmatically adopted as a label for German regions characterized by their mountainous (or at least hilly) landscapes. The first was "Saxon Switzerland" outside of Dresden, a landscape of rocky peaks, valleys, and caves that attracted painters like Caspar David Friedrich and Ludwig Richter.[55] The discovery of Saxon Switzerland was followed by the discoveries of Franconian Switzerland in northern Bavaria, "Kroppach Switzerland" in the Taunus Mountains, "Holstein Switzerland" between Kiel and Lübeck, and even "Hersbruck Switzerland," also located in Franconia.[56]

Johann Christian Fick was the first author to label the Muggendorfer Mountains as "Franconian Switzerland," but later travel writers incorporated Switzerland into the titles of their works. The first to do so was local poet Jakob Reiselsberger, author of the 1820 publication, *Little Switzerland, or Invitation to Travel in Streitberg, Muggendorf, Weischenfeld, and their Environs.* In the preface of this self-published work, Reiselsberger justified his use of the label by insisting that the natural environment of the Franconian region, now part of Bavaria, also featured "many sublimely beautiful and admirable curiosities," but that they were available in a "reduced degree."[57] In other words, a vacation there was

---

[52] Esper, *Ausführliche Nachricht von neuentdeckten Zoolithen,* 7.

[53] Johann Christian Fick, *Historisch-topographisch-statistische Beschreibung von Erlangen und dessen Gegend mit Anweisungen und Regeln für Studirende* (Erlangen: J.J. Palm, 1812), 109.

[54] See Bernard, *The Rush to the Alps;* Withey, *Grand Tours and Cook's Tours,* 196–219.

[55] Hansjörg Küster, *Schöne Aussichten. Kleine Geschichte der Landschaft* (Munich: C.H. Beck, 2009), 82; Sterzl and Bauer, *Fränkische Schweiz,* 29.

[56] Spode, *Wie die Deutschen "Reiseweltmeister" wurden,* 18; Prein, *Bürgerliches Reisen im 19. Jahrhundert,* 145–146.

[57] Jakob Reiselsberger, *Die Kleine Schweiz, oder Einladung zur Reise nach Streiberg, Muggendorf, Weischenfeld und deren Umgebungen* (Weischenfeld: Selbstverlag des Verfassers, 1820), 1.

more reasonable than a trip to the real Switzerland. The "Invitation" itself consisted of an extended poem praising the virtues of the mountainous region, including the colorful medieval past exemplified in ruins, the mysterious character of the prehistoric caves, the hospitality of the local population, and even the quality of local food, especially the trout that filled the Wiesent. However, the dominant theme of this publication, and practically all that followed, was the abundance of natural attractions in the region. From its unique plant life and stalactites, to its river valleys and mountains, Franconian Switzerland was advertised as a place where one could breathe easily, and enjoy the spectacles of nature. Reiselsberger began the poem with a simple request:

> Leave the town behind, visit the open fields,
> Come to Little Switzerland,
> For every friend of nature
> It provides an appeal so refreshing.[58]

The first two lines of this stanza recurred as a motif throughout the extended poem, confirming that such natural landscapes were viewed as the symbolic antithesis to the urban environment as early as 1820. Indeed, Reiselsberger's work did more than launch the Swiss label; it established the marketing formulas used for decades to come.

Reiselsberger's invitation was echoed by Joseph Heller, a Bamberg historian and travel writer who published the first "tourist handbook" on Franconian Switzerland in 1829. This work abandoned the poetics of Reiselsberger in favor of the practical prose of Murray and Baedeker, even a few years before their respective debuts. Heller's handbook was directed at middle-class hikers, supplying these visitors with an overview of travel routes, a series of practical tips, an alphabetical inventory of sights, a map, and two illustrations. Like Reiselsberger, Heller insisted that Franconian Switzerland boasted all that the real Switzerland possessed in abundance, but here it was available "on a condensed scale, and therefore more pleasant to behold, as it was possible to look across it and grasp it as a single image."[59] Furthermore, if the Swiss Alps were the quintessential "sublime" landscape, possessing a sort of terrifying beauty, then the rolling mountains of Franconian Switzerland were more of a picturesque landscape, idyllic and peaceful, and therefore less intimidating to potential visitors. This "romantic land" contained a diversity of

---

[58] Ibid., 1.
[59] Joseph Heller, *Muggendorf und seine Umgebungen oder die fränkische Schweiz: Ein Handbuch* (Bamberg: J.C. Dresch, 1829), V.

attractions, leading Heller to guarantee: "Nature offers at least something for everyone."[60] While naturalists could marvel at every mountain and cave, "friends of history and romanticism" would be impressed with the fortresses of Streitberg, Neideck, and Gößweinstein, whose bloody histories yielded a new appreciation for the "peace of contemporary times." Additionally, those in search of a rural retreat would be charmed by the region's "picturesque villages" and the customs of the "simple and hardworking" people.[61] In other words, Heller endorsed both the landscape and the community that it supported.

The vision of Franconian Switzerland promoted by Reiselsberger and Heller was intrinsically nostalgic, idealizing the natural and pastoral character of the region as an antidote to modern life. The prehistoric caves, the medieval ruins, and the timeless landscape were the defining attractions of the region, but a more contemporary feature emerged in the mid nineteenth century. In 1841, entrepreneurs in the village of Streitberg established the foundations of a modern health resort with the opening of a "whey cure facility" (*Molkekuranstalt*), a simple establishment where visitors could drink the nutrient-filled dairy by-product. In 1852, Dr. Theodor Weber opened a modest Streitberg inn and began marketing "fresh mountain air" as a natural remedy. Weber also contributed to the middle-class colonization of the surrounding landscape by developing a network of trails through rocky alcoves and deposits of prehistoric shells. The primary walkway, the *Dr.-Weber-Kurpromenade*, was the first of its kind in Franconian Switzerland, leading both tourists and patients to an overlook with views of the Wiesent river valley, the surrounding mountains, and the Streitberg and Neideck fortress ruins.[62] Equipped with this new infrastructure, the village acquired a reputation as a climatic health resort, celebrated for "the purity of its air and the beauty of its surroundings." It was also a place where the urban bourgeoisie could distinguish themselves from aristocratic travelers by dressing simply and mingling with peasants.[63] A vacation there provided a reprieve from the city, but it allowed middle-class tourists to return reinvigorated, with clean air in their lungs and new insight into the attractive simplicity of rural life.

Streitberg's early transformation into a climatic health resort added a new dimension to the tourist experience, suggesting that Franconian

---

[60] Ibid., VIII.
[61] Ibid., VI–X.
[62] Voit, Kauflich, and Rüfer, *Vom Land im Gebirg zur Fränkischen Schweiz*, 355.
[63] Bernard, *Rush to the Alps*, 88–89.

Switzerland did not have to rely exclusively on landscape tourism. Some travel writers refused to endorse this new direction. In 1858's *Illustrated Visitors' Guide to Franconian Switzerland and the Fichtel Mountains*, Philipp von Körber claimed that Streitberg, once an "idyllic village," had been transformed into "a health resort, occupied by fashionable society from April through October." He reported that "the innkeepers and locals have quickly learned to raise the prices of provisions and accommodations to the level anticipated by those in the popular spas."[64] In other words, Streitberg's new status as a health resort was corrupting the character of the rural people. Even worse, it was encouraging visitors to overlook the real attractions of the region, which were to be found outside of the village. In retrospect, Körber's appeals seem unwarranted, as medical tourism was not nearly as popular in Franconian Switzerland as it proved to be in Bad Reichenhall, the subject of the next chapter. In fact, it was limited to the villages of Muggendorf and Streitberg, and only played a supporting role in tourist publications.

Like most nineteenth-century publications on Franconian Switzerland, Körber's 1858 guidebook was directed primarily at middle-class hikers and nature enthusiasts. This source affords an invaluable glimpse into mid-century landscape tourism, a physical undertaking that was available to all those who had the energy, time, and money. Körber began his guide with a scientific overview of the region, covering its geological composition and its flora and fauna, past and present. He then moved on to more practical tips for hikers, recommending routes and particular attractions. At the time, Franconian Switzerland was a region that could only be enjoyed on foot, and many of the most rewarding spots were only accessible via arduous paths. While Körber did not directly discourage "delicate women and older people" from participating in these excursions, he did recommend that they familiarize themselves with their options and ultimately choose more moderate hikes. He also encouraged visitors to employ the services of an experienced guide, not only to ensure that they take relatively straightforward and safe routes, but also in order to carry "some refreshments and the hand luggage of the travelers."[65] This was literally travel off the beaten path, but it was also carefully organized and mapped for middle-class beginners.

---

[64] Philipp von Körber, *Illustrirter Fremdenführer durch die fränkische Schweiz und das Fichtelgebirg, Bamberg, Bayreuth, Erlangen und Coburg* (Bamberg: Verlag der Buchner'schen Buchhandlung, 1858), 23.

[65] Ibid., 1, 20–22.

This more practical and less intimidating version of Switzerland attracted German and international tourists. In his 1839 travelogue, German writer Gustav von Heeringen noted that English and French researchers were increasingly common among the visitors descending upon the region's caves.[66] In 1852, one of these visitors published an account of his "historical tour" of Franconia. Englishman Charles Taylor devoted two of seventeen chapters to the mountainous region around Muggendorf, which he praised for its scientific wonders and its "picturesque and beautiful scenery." Like so many other travelers of the early nineteenth century, Taylor was interested primarily in the region's extensive caves, and reported that they were filled with stalactites and the bones of prehistoric beasts. He also noted the plethora of living species in the region, including rare specimens of insects and plants. "To all those who pursue Nature in all or any of these, her varied and delightful paths," claimed Taylor, "this region will yield an abundant store of enjoyment."[67] Fellow Englishman Sir John Forbes traveled through Franconian Switzerland in 1855, and was likewise impressed by the "picturesque" and "placid beauty" of the Wiesent valley. However, this aristocratic traveler was disappointed with both the Rosenmüller Cave and the Gößweinstein castle, the latter supposedly "devoid of beauty." Forbes also described local accommodations as "sufficient, though rude," indicating that the local tourism industry still had improvements to make if it wanted to appeal to a more refined, cosmopolitan crowd.[68]

In 1861, *Harper's New Monthly Magazine* published a piece on Franconian Switzerland by the American writer Bayard Taylor, who was already well-known for his travel accounts of Africa and Asia.[69] Taylor had journeyed to Germany in pursuit of restitution and "moderate daily exercise," and having already visited the landscapes of Saxony, Thuringia, and the Black Forest, he set out for Franconian Switzerland, and specifically the drinking, bathing, and walking cures of Streitberg. Although he was less than impressed with the local *Kurhaus*, which was reportedly filled with "sallow, peevish, irritable, unhappy persons,"

[66] Heeringen, *Wanderungen durch Franken*, 175.

[67] Charles Taylor, *A Historical Tour in Franconia, in the Summer of 1852* (London: Longman &. Co., 1852), 151, 160.

[68] John Forbes, *Sight-Seeing in Germany and the Tyrol in the Autumn of 1855* (London: Smith, Elder, and Co., Cornhill, 1856), 315–318.

[69] This piece was later reprinted in collections of Taylor's work as "A Walk through the Franconian Switzerland." See Bayard Taylor, *At Home and Abroad: A Sketchbook of Life, Scenery, and Men* (New York: G.N. Putnam, 1862), 286–318.

the American tourist was moved by the surrounding landscape. His accounts of hikes through the region correspond well with the romantic idealization of the countryside that was so prevalent in Germany. For example, he recounted his walk between Streitberg and Muggendorf as follows:

> The dew lay thick on the meadows, and the peasants were everywhere at work shaking out the hay, so that the air was sweet with grass-odors. Above me on either side, the immense gray horns and towers of rock rose out of the steep fir-woods, clearly, yet not too sharply defined against the warm blue sky. The Wiesent, swift and beryl-green, winding in many curves through the hay-fields, made a cheerful music in his bed.[70]

In this passage, the author drew upon both picturesque and sublime conceptions of nature, juxtaposing the diligent human population with the gigantic rock forms that disrupted the otherwise rolling mountain landscape. In addition to these sights, Taylor was also enthralled with the standard attractions of Franconian Switzerland, including the ruins of the Neideck fortress, the castle of Gößweinstein, and the "wonderfully picturesque" village of Pottenstein. Foreshadowing the direction of later guidebooks, he supplied little information on the background of these sites, concluding that Franconian Switzerland was "less interesting in a historical point of view than on the account of its remarkable scenery and its curious deposits of fossil remains."[71] Like future visitors and guidebook authors, Taylor was interested in sentiment, not historical specifics. Still, his travel report confirms that Franconian Switzerland could function as a romantic respite for non-Germans as well, especially for those fleeing a war-torn country.

Just a few years after this article appeared, Franconian Switzerland found itself at the heart of a war-torn country. In 1866, the Kingdom of Bavaria sided with the Austrian Empire in its losing effort against Prussia in what amounted to the German version of the Civil War, with several skirmishes taking place in Franconia itself. Four years after the defeat of the Habsburg Empire and its allies, Bavaria joined the northern German states in their campaign against Napoleon III's France. With the subsequent unification of the German Empire, Bavaria was integrated into the new federalist system. Unification certainly had an impact on the nascent tourism industry, with the disappearance of boundaries across the empire eliminating one of the greatest impediments to travel. Meanwhile,

---

[70] Bayard Taylor, "The Franconian Switzerland," *Harper's New Monthly Magazine*, January 1862, 147.

[71] Ibid., 146–150.

some guidebook publishers began to endorse a unified German identity, with Baedeker in particular promoting the "impressive cultural tradition" and "modern technologies" of the new nation-state.[72] Grieben's 1876 guidebook on *The Fichtel Mountains and Franconian Switzerland* reflected this trend, but without the emphasis on modernity evident in the Baedeker guides. A passage from the guidebook's conclusion exemplified this nationalized line of marketing:

Whoever has at one time picked up his hiking staff in order to behold the natural wonders of our German Fatherland, should direct his course to the Fichtel Mountains, and to Franconian Switzerland. He will return home delighted and refreshed, armed with the conviction that we possess precious pearls in our German *Heimat*, treasures that are insufficiently known, classified, and praised.[73]

For over seventy years poets and travel writers had advertised Franconian Switzerland as romantic and idyllic; the Grieben's guidebook complicated the equation by adding the word "German," describing the trip as a patriotic duty. This is especially remarkable because it appears to be the only publication that did so. Local publications typically avoided such jingoism, and the tourism industry seemed reluctant to engage with these broader identities. Franconian Switzerland may have been one of the birthplaces of the Bavarian tourism industry, but its marketing did little to construct a Bavarian regional identity, let alone a German national identity.

The Pleasant Feeling of Distance

By the final decades of the nineteenth century, Franconian Switzerland was attracting more than amateur scientists and poets. Economic growth, increased wages, and legislation guaranteeing paid vacations for civil servants all contributed to an increase in middle-class tourism after German unification.[74] Still, the growing number of visitors did little to improve economic conditions in Franconian Switzerland, and the region remained relatively impoverished. Although villages like Muggendorf, Streitberg, Gößweinstein, and Pottenstein acquired a reputation for their comfortable inns and multitudes of guests, the short tourist season

---

[72] Koshar, *German Travel Cultures*, 64.
[73] Grieben's Reise-Bibliothek (Firm), *Das Fichtelgebirge und die Fränkische Schweiz. Mit besonderer Berücksichtigung von Bamberg und Bayreuth*, 5th edn. (Berlin: Verlag von Alber Goldschmidt, 1876), 131.
[74] Götsch, "Sommerfrische: Zur Etablierung einer Gegenwelt am Ende des 19. Jahrhunderts," 8.

effectively limited the amount of capital to be earned. Franconian Switzerland was a *Sommerfrische*; the inns were largely empty between October and May, and the hospitality industry was forced to rely on the occasional traveling artisan or farmer, who tended to be more frugal than the average, middle-class tourist.[75]

On the other hand, between May and October, Franconian Switzerland received a regular stream of tourists, both male and female. An 1871 issue of the American religious magazine, *The Ladies' Repository*, introduced Franconian Switzerland to middle-class women, describing the region as a picturesque district that was "geographically as unlike Switzerland as it is possible . . . to be." The author also noted that the destination was popular among German tourists, but aside from the occasional geologist or day-tripper, there were "few foreigners."[76] However, the destination's inclusion in various English-language travelogues since the early nineteenth century suggests that American and English tourists were no strangers to Franconian Switzerland.[77] One 1887 travelogue is especially illuminating. The author, R. Milner Barry, was a wealthy English woman who traveled across Franconian Switzerland with two female companions after making a pilgrimage to nearby Bayreuth.[78] Like many British tourists, she organized much of her vacation with the Thomas Cook Company beforehand, and carried her guidebook with her wherever she went. She was genteel, but she was also interested in an authentic tourist experience, and was determined to mingle with natives and improve her German language skills. What is unique about Milner's account is that she perpetuates romantic clichés about Franconian Switzerland while simultaneously offering candid commentary on the quality of accommodations and the behavior of the local population. Her first-hand account actually corresponds well with the work of local travel writers, who reached out

---

[75] Sterzl and Bauer, *Fränkische Schweiz*, 31.

[76] T.D. Ansted, "From Alsace to the Hartz," *The Ladies' Repository: A Monthly Periodical Devoted to Literature and Religion*, January–June 1871, 21–22.

[77] In addition to previously cited travelogues by Charles Taylor and John Forbes, see Edmund Spencer, *Sketches of Germany and the Germans, With a Glance at Poland, Hungary, and Switzerland in 1834, 1835, and 1836*, Vol. I (London: Whitaker & Co., 1836), 301–309; Henry John Whitling, *Pictures of Nuremberg and Rambles in the Hills and Valleys of Franconia* (London: R. Bentley, 1850), 191–193; Thomas Sopwith, *Three Weeks in Central Europe. Notes of an Excursion, Including the Cities of Treves, Nuremberg, Leipzig, Dresden, Freiberg, and Berlin* (London: Willis, Sotheran, and Co., 1869), 42–45.

[78] R. Milner Barry, *Bayreuth and Franconian Switzerland* (London: S. Sonnenschein, Lowrey & Co., 1887).

to middle-class tourists by promoting the region as a romantic respite that was accessible and unforgettable.

Like earlier publications, guidebooks published in Franconia between 1885 and 1900 employed the motifs of natural beauty, pastoral simplicity, and medieval mystery; what distinguished them was a new emphasis on practicality and efficiency, reflecting the changing nature of leisure travel during the late nineteenth century. The primary objective of these publications was not to muse or indoctrinate, but to accommodate, equipping visitors with information that was "necessary and worth-knowing." This was done so in a "quick and clear" manner, as guaranteed by an 1891 guidebook published by the Bläsing University Bookstore of Erlangen.[79] As most of these examples of tourist propaganda focused exclusively on Franconian Switzerland, a tourist region renowned for its compact size, these guides were much briefer than the larger Baedeker, Grieben, or Meyer handbooks. Alternately labeled as "small," "practical," and sometimes "complete" guides, they were organized concisely and logically, concentrating more on functional knowledge rather than descriptive exposition. For example, Friedrich Ende's 1895 *Complete Guide through the Entire Franconian Switzerland*, only sixty-four pages long, began with a short introduction ("Brief Notes Instead of a Long Preface"), followed by an alphabetical list of tours through the region, and a concentrated description of each route. The publication then concluded with advertisements for local accommodations, an index of destinations and attractions, and a detailed map identifying various sights worth seeing, including castles, mills, caves, and specific panoramas.[80]

Streamlined and functional, these guidebooks allowed middle-class tourists to conquer an unfamiliar landscape quickly and enjoyably. Armed with their trustworthy guide, the individual tourist would not be met with surprises, nor would he or she be inconvenienced with decision-making, as all the important accommodations and attractions were already classified and pre-evaluated.[81] In fact, most guidebooks on Franconian Switzerland offered explicit recommendations for travelers. For example, an 1895 Bläsing guidebook identified the top ten sights, including Streitberg and the ruins, Muggendorf and the caves, the castle and pilgrimage church of

---

[79] *Kleiner Führer durch die Fränkische Schweiz, sowie Wegweiser durch das Schwabachtal von Erlangen nach Gräfenberg und die sogenannte Herbrucker Schweiz* (Erlangen: Th. Bläsings Universitäts-Buchhandlung, 1891), "Foreword."

[80] Friedrich Ende, *Vollständiger Führer durch die ganze Fränkische Schweiz und Teile der Oberpfalz* (Nuremberg: Selbstverlag von Friedrich Ende, 1895).

[81] Pretzel, *Die Literaturform Reiseführer*, 16, 76–79.

Gößweinstein, and the village of Pottenstein.[82] These publications also recognized that most nineteenth-century tourists were not representatives of the "leisure class," and their time and money remained limited. Consequently, the guidebooks not only provided accurate information on prices, but also took time restraints into account. Tourist guidebooks rarely recommended more than five days of hiking in the region, unlike earlier publications.[83] The Bläsing guide suggested three days in Franconian Switzerland, but in case of emergency, most tourists could "at least briefly acquaint themselves with the highlights" in one-and-a-half days.[84] An 1887 guidebook advised travelers with a single day in the region to head straight for Muggendorf, visiting the Rosenmüller Cave first, and then the Neideck ruins outside of Streitberg on the return trip.[85] The authors of these guidebooks assumed that tourists were determined to make the most of their time away from work and home. For example, Anton Schuster's *Small Guide through Franconian Switzerland*, published in 1891, worked under the assumption that tourists would take one of the morning trains to Forchheim, on the western fringe of Franconian Switzerland, either leaving Nuremberg at 5:00, or Bamberg at 4:22.[86]

Why were middle-class tourists in such a rush to behold the various attractions of Franconian Switzerland? Guidebooks covering the region published between 1885 and 1900 were unanimous in designating the mountainous region as "romantic," thus appealing to bourgeois society's desire for solace and respite in natural settings.[87] Although some scholars have claimed that romanticism was only influential in Germany for roughly forty years, from the 1790s through the 1830s, the concept itself clearly retained cultural significance and informed the worldview of the educated middle class.[88] However, when these guidebooks employed the term "romantic," it suggested a somewhat simpler understanding of

[82] *Die Fränkische Schweiz, das Schwabachthal und die Gräfenberger Umgebung* (Erlangen: Th. Bläsings Universitäts-Buchhandlung, 1895), 7–8.

[83] Heeringen, *Wanderungen durch Franken*, 175; Taylor, *A Historical Tour in Franconia*, 160.

[84] *Die Fränkische Schweiz, das Schwabachthal und die Gräfenberger Umgebung*, 7–8.

[85] *Führer durch die Fränkische Schweiz, Mit Wegweiser durch das Schwabachthal von Erlangen nach Gräfenberg und die sog. Hersbrucker Schweiz* (Erlangen: Verlag von Andreas Deichert, 1887), 1.

[86] Anton Schuster, *Kleiner Führer durch die Fränkische Schweiz* (Bamberg: Reindl, 1891), 1.

[87] For example, Anton Schuster employed the word "romantic" at least four times in the first five pages of his short guidebook. Ibid., 1–5.

[88] Engelhardt, "Romanticism in Germany," 109.

the word that did not reflect the ideological sophistication of turn-of-the century intellectuals. In this case, authors used the term to characterize the landscape, villages, and medieval architecture of Franconian Switzerland as idyllic, secluded, and evocative of a bygone era that was more attractive in the shadow of industrialization and urbanization. This was a simplified romanticism, colored by vague notions of *Bildung* and spiritual redemption, but ultimately more focused on achieving distance from the undesirable aspects of the modern city, including the pollution and the working class.[89] As the majority of nineteenth-century tourists were bourgeois urbanites, this compulsion is not surprising.[90]

Among the many "romantic" features of Franconian Switzerland, it was the natural landscape that received the most attention and praise from late nineteenth-century guidebooks. Most guidebook authors identified their audience as "friends of beautiful nature," easily enchanted with the region's "beautiful wooded valleys, its clear mountain water, and the numerous caves with their stunning stalactites and stalagmites, and the fossils of pre-historic animals."[91] The definitive qualities of this environment were not only its beauty, but its purity and tranquility, even more remarkable in juxtaposition to the filth and noise of the modern city. In 1890's *Romanticism of Franconian Switzerland*, Adam Koch-Neuses described the region as "a little piece of earthly paradise" that managed to remain sheltered from the "rational and practical achievements" of modern civilization.[92] An 1889 guidebook published by Andreas Deichert painted an even more striking picture:

> Whenever long shadows stretch out from the wooded slopes of the mountains in the east, whenever the stunning rock formations stand before the splendor of the sunset, whenever we see the pure water of the river winding between beautiful meadows and the diligently-cultivated fields of the peasant, then the region gives us a vision of peace and rural tranquility, and we begin to enjoy the pleasant feeling of distance from the consuming life of crowded cities.[93]

---

[89] See Morton, "German Romanticism," 11.

[90] Syrjämaa, "Tourism as a Typical Cultural Phenomenon," 180, 182.

[91] *Kleiner Führer durch die Fränkische Schweiz, sowie Wegweiser durch das Schwabachtal von Erlangen nach Gräfenberg und die sogenannte Herbrucker Schweiz; Die Fränkische Schweiz, das Schwabachthal und die Gräfenberger Umgebung,* 5.

[92] Adam Koch-Neuses, *Die Romantik der Fränkischen Schweiz* (Forchheim: F.A. Streit, 1890), 3.

[93] *Die Fränkische Schweiz und die Kur-Anstalt zur Streitberg: Ein treuer Führer für Reisende und ärztlicher Rathgeber für Kurgäste nebst Naturgeschichte der Fränkischen Schweiz* (Erlangen: Verlag von Andreas Deichert, 1889), 6.

Guidebooks cast Franconian Switzerland as an idyllic retreat and a refuge from urban life, but it was not exactly a "wilderness." This environment was neither completely natural nor timeless, consisting of "items of nature" as well as "human artifacts."[94] The region's mountains and forests, for instance, were dotted with medieval ruins and rustic mills, which guidebooks celebrated as reminders of a romanticized past and a simpler way of life. In contrast, the actual residents of the region were nearly invisible in the tourist propaganda. Although earlier guidebook writers like Joseph Heller had called attention to the customs of the "simple and hard-working" natives, most guidebook writers of the late nineteenth century overlooked the local population. For example, the 1889 Deichert guidebook called the tourist's attention to "diligently-cultivated fields," while failing to identify the peasants responsible for this work.[95] Actually paying attention to these commoners could evoke memories of the urban working class, a feature of the city that middle-class tourists sought to escape. In general, these guidebooks were more preoccupied with the natural wonders of the tourist region, a common phenomenon in late nineteenth-century tourist propaganda.[96] When the local inhabitants did appear, guidebooks cast them as hospitable hosts or as idyllic representations of rural life, not unlike those featured in the well-known engravings by Ludwig Richter. Leo Woerl's 1890 guidebook portrayed the region's inhabitants as "friendly and obliging, and not to mention hospitable," listing them alongside an agreeable climate and fresh air as the destination's greatest amenities. The same guidebook also featured a full-page picture of the landscape around Gößweinstein, with a number of peasant children playing in the foreground.[97] In this case, the human inhabitants of the region were incorporated into the natural landscape itself, becoming part of the holistic representation of the romanticized region.[98] These were not real people, but symbols of an alternate way of life that was quickly disappearing.

---

94 Eeva Jokinen and Soile Veijola, "Mountains and Landscapes: Towards Embodied Visualities," in *Visual Culture and Tourism*, ed. David Crouch and Nina Lübbren (New York: Berg, 2003), 259.

95 *Die Fränkische Schweiz und die Kur-Anstalt zur Streitberg*, 6.

96 Palmowski, "Travels with Baedeker," 121.

97 Leo Woerl (Firm), *Führer durch Mittelfranken, die Hersbrücker und Fränkische Schweiz* (Würzburg: Verlag von Leo Woerl, 1890), 45–46. The Woerl guidebook on Upper Franconia contained the same text and illustrations for its section of Franconian Switzerland. See Leo Woerl (Firm), *Führer durch Oberfranken* (Würzburg: Verlag von Leo Woerl, 1891), 72–85.

98 Buzard, *The Beaten Track*, 188.

Unlike the guidebooks, first-person travelogues usually afforded more attention to the human inhabitants of Franconian Switzerland, although the authors inevitably reduced the locals to caricatures. In his 1890 travelogue on the region, Koch-Neuses devoted a brief section to the rural Volk, describing them as firmly attached to the natural environment and their "traditional customs and festivals," which appealed to the "romantic longing for the good, old days and the blissfully simple and innocent era of the past."[99] This author depicted the local population in terms of simplicity and authenticity, distinguishing them from the masses of urban society. In her 1887 travelogue, R. Milner Barry offered a more candid account of the local residents. She praised their honesty and hospitality, and observed that the inhabitants of Pottenstein in particular seemed to take "a pride and pleasure in the lovely and romantic scenery which surrounds them." In a subsequent passage Barry recounted her conversation with a local girl who seemed to lack this enthusiasm for the "romantic scenery." After asking where a certain road led, Barry received this uncommitted response: "Nowhere in particular . . . but there is a rock called the Pfaffenstein near, and a great many strangers go up to see the view, which they say is very grand."[100] While tourist publications displayed little interest in "authentic natives," this local displayed little interest in the landscape itself.

For late nineteenth-century tourists, the most popular method of enjoying the landscape of Franconian Switzerland was hiking, which was still a relatively recent phenomenon. At the end of the early modern period, traveling by foot had a rather unglamorous reputation, and was understood primarily as a burden by those professional and social groups who were regularly on the move. For these wanderers, the natural environment was a hazardous domain of obstacles, and something to be traversed quickly, not leisurely.[101] Recreational walking, or hiking, only became an established practice during the late eighteenth and early nineteenth centuries, after the rehabilitation of the natural environment.[102] This new pastime ultimately became a celebrated vehicle of self-cultivation, in addition to creating a sense of community among the middle classes by distinguishing

---

[99] Koch-Neuses, *Die Romantik der Fränkischen Schweiz*, 23.

[100] Barry, *Bayreuth and Franconian Switzerland*, 117, 126.

[101] Wolfgang Kaschuba, "Die Fußreise – Von der Arbeitswanderung zur bürgerlichen Bildungswesen," in *Reisekultur: Von der Pilgerfahrt zum modernen Tourismus*, 165–166.

[102] Rebecca Solnit, *Wanderlust: A History of Walking* (New York: Viking, 2000), 14, 17–22; Löfgren, On Holiday, 48–51.

them from the aristocracy, who preferred to travel by coach.[103] The fact that it was a relatively inexpensive activity did not hurt.[104]

Hiking was not only the most popular and economical method for enjoying the natural landscape of Franconian Switzerland at the end of the nineteenth century; it was practically the only one. Due to the poor conditions of local roads and the remote location of many of the attractions, traveling by coach was not always practical. An 1887 guidebook noted that a horse-drawn omnibus was the preferable way of reaching Streitberg, but that upon arrival, the hiking commenced. Although this publication also included several recommendations for visitors traveling by coach, it was clear that this form of transportation was only helpful in conveying the tourists to centralized locations. Consequently, this guide functioned essentially as a sort of pathfinder, offering concise descriptions of hiking routes, and indicating clearly what sights and natural wonders should be enjoyed along the way.[105] Another guidebook stressed that visitors must follow certain hiking routes during a vacation in the region. One in particular, the nine-kilometer road from Muggendorf to Behringersmühle, was marked with an asterisk and characterized as "indisputably the scenically most beautiful stretch in Franconian Switzerland."[106] According to such publications, there was no better way to experience the natural wonders of Franconian Switzerland than to leisurely hike through the very heart of the region. Like other forms of leisure travel, one of the defining characteristics of this variety of tourism was movement itself, and the middle-class vacationers consumed kilometers as well as landscapes. Such open-air mobility stood in stark contrast to the rigid routines of city life.

Movement aside, hiking in the Franconian Switzerland was ultimately a means of arriving at spots where the tourist could enjoy views of the mountainous landscape. At this point, the merit of a particular trek had little to do with physical activity, but depended instead on the quality of the views encountered along the way. For example, an 1889 guidebook described the route from Muggendorf to Gößweinstein as a series of

---

[103] Denise Phillips, "Friends of Nature: Urban Sociability and Regional Natural History in Dresden, 1800–1850," *Osiris* 18 (2003): 45–46; Kaschuba, "Die Fußreise," 170. See also Heikki Lempa, *Beyond the Gymnasium: Educating the Middle-Class Bodies in Classical Germany* (Lanham, MD: Lexington Books, 2007), 163–193.

[104] Lekan, "Tourism, Heimat, and Conservation on the Rhine," 839.

[105] *Führer durch die Fränkische Schweiz, Mit Wegweiser durch das Schwabachthal von Erlangen nach Gräfenberg und die sog. Hersbrucker Schweiz*, 1–3.

[106] *Die Fränkische Schweiz, das Schwabachthal und die Gräfenberger Umgebung*, 20.

"picturesque views," during which one could "joyfully survey...the lovely charms of nature." The same guidebook advised travelers to slow their pace between Gößweinstein and Pottenstein, where they might overcome the fleeting experience of modernity by leisurely enjoying the panoramas of this "romantic landscape."[107] Friedrich Ende's 1894 guidebook praised the "wild and romantic" scenery around the village of Pottenstein, which did not possess any specific tourist attractions other than "an impressive view" of the "grotesque rock formations" that surrounded the community.[108] R. Milner Barry was likewise impressed by the landscape outside of Pottenstein, which she characterized as "some of the wildest and most remarkable scenery of the *Fränkische Schweiz.*"[109]

Many views in Franconian Switzerland were defined by their proximity to medieval ruins. An 1891 guidebook promoted the views from Streitberg, where the river valley between the mountains began to narrow and take on "a more romantic form." On one side of the Wiesent, the fortress of Streitberg cast its shadow over the village from its location on a rocky precipice. Just across the river, the ruins of Neideck fortress stood atop a steep cliff-side.[110] Like the region's rural inhabitants, the ruins were part of the larger mountainous landscape, existing as pleasant reminders of a bygone era that neither detracted from the splendor of nature, nor threatened the idealized image of the Middle Ages popularized by the romantics. Admittedly, these sites had been a popular subject of travel writers since the late eighteenth century. However, what was noteworthy about the late nineteenth-century guidebooks was the lack of historical exposition. Commentary on the castles and ruins was brief, and often transitioned into a description of the views that could be achieved from their elevated positions. For example, the 1890 Woerl guidebook advised travelers to take the path from Muggendorf up to the Neideck ruins, described simply as "extensive and imposing." The mountain-top ruins did, however, promise "nice views in all directions."[111] Apparently, it was not necessary that the tourist actually follow in the footsteps of the romantics by touring the medieval fortresses themselves.

This obsession with the natural environment was a distinctly modern sentiment linked to urbanization. As noted earlier, nature only became

[107] *Die Fränkische Schweiz und die Kur-Anstalt zur Streitberg*, 38, 41–42.
[108] Ende, *Praktischer Führer durch die Fränkische Schweiz*, 13–14.
[109] Barry, *Bayreuth and Franconian Switzerland*, 108.
[110] *Kleiner Führer durch die Fränkische Schweiz, sowie Wegweiser durch das Schwabachtal von Erlangen nach Gräfenberg und die sogenannte Herbrucker Schweiz*, 9.
[111] Woerl, *Führer durch Mittelfranken, die Hersbrucker und Fränkische Schweiz*, 57.

a marketable commodity when it was removed from the realm of the ordinary.[112] Distance allowed for the nineteenth-century idealization of natural landscapes, but distance was also the definitive feature of most of the views endorsed in guidebooks on Franconian Switzerland. Practically, this meant being far enough away to get a good view. In discussing the best views of the region's medieval ruins, R. Milner Barry concluded: "All these castles require to be seen from a distance, as it is only thus one can realize the height of the rocks on which they stand."[113] In other cases, it was not just distance from the landscape itself that was important, but distance from civilization. For instance, the castle of Gößweinstein was supposedly most striking when it suddenly appeared on the horizon after the tourist rounded a bend following the Wiesent River from Muggendorf. Upon arriving in the village of Gößweinstein itself, the visitor was typically not invited to tour the fortress or even the historical pilgrimage church, but instead compelled to climb the nearby "*Wagnershöhe*" and enjoy the "magnificent view" of the Wiesent, Püttlach, and Eschbach river valleys, as well as a "gorgeous panorama" of the Upper Pfalz, the Fichtel Mountains, and the cities of Bayreuth and Kulmbach in the distance.[114] Even local communities acknowledged that attractive vistas were central to the tourist experience in Franconian Switzerland. In 1891, the official organ of the "State Association for the Promotion of Tourism in Bavaria" reported that the local beautification society of Gößweinstein had established a new overlook known as the "*Fischersruhe.*" This new spot was accessible via a "comfortable ascent," and supposedly afforded a "superb view" of the region.[115] This elevated perspective allowed the tourist to consume several sights simultaneously, conserving time and mastering the scenic topography. In many regards, landscape tourism allowed middle-class travelers to develop "a sense of ownership, entitlement and familiarity" with a world that was temporally far away.[116]

[112] Stephen C. Bourassa, *The Aesthetics of Landscape* (London: Belhaven Press, 1991), 3–4.

[113] Barry, *Bayreuth and Franconian Switzerland*, 136.

[114] Ende, *Praktischer Führer durch die Fränkische Schweiz*, 16–17.

[115] StAB, Regierung von Oberfranken, 1978: "Fremdenwesen, Hebung des Fremdenverkehrs, Nordbayerischer Verkehrsverein, 1891–1920." "Thätigkeit bayer. Verschönerungs- und Kur-Vereine," *Bayerisch Land und Volk: Offizielles Organ des Landesverbandes zur Hebung des Fremdenverkehrs in Bayern* 2, no. 2 (1891/92). This report was included in an insert, without page numbers.

[116] Mary Louise Pratt, *Imperial Eyes: Travel Writing and Transculturation*, 2nd edn. (New York: Routledge, 2008), 3, 12.

THE CASTLE OF GÖSSWEINSTEIN.

FIGURE 3. Illustration of Castle Gößweinstein from *Harper's New Monthly Magazine*, 1862. Note the toiling peasants in the foreground. From the author's collection.

Enjoying views of the mountainous landscape was the primary justification for hiking in Franconian Switzerland, but it was not the only one. Hiking was also a means of observing nature up close, and appreciating it on a scientific as well as on an aesthetic level. Romanticism may have shaped the dominant perceptions of the tourist region, but the enthusiasm for natural history that was so characteristic of the latter half of the nineteenth century shaped the behavior of many visitors. In central Europe, the empirical observation of "local nature" actually dated back to the early modern period. By the time of the Enlightenment, natural history was understood as part of the larger discipline of *Vaterlandskunde*, a distinct form of cultural geography. The nineteenth century witnessed the emergence of civic natural history societies across German-speaking lands. These organizations consisted primarily of educated middle-class urbanites who dedicated much of their free time to observing and collecting plant and animal life in the nearby countryside.[117] Like the gardening movement of the late nineteenth century, this practice provided access to nature, but it did so as part of a distinctly urban culture.[118]

An appreciation for natural history was not at odds with romanticism, and the latter certainly contributed to both the idealization and historicization of nature.[119] While a certain "culture of progress" led many Germans to idealize the natural landscape and the obscure medieval past, it also drew thousands of amateur natural scientists into the countryside, "on the lookout for living species as well as fossils."[120] In any case, it was a devotion to self-cultivation that led travelers to take an active interest in the flora and fauna, past and present, of regions like Franconian Switzerland. Guidebooks may have committed more space to praising particular views, but they accommodated "friends of natural history" as well, supplying overviews of sinkholes, springs, and the extensive plant and animal life of the "lovely, romantic region."[121] Guidebooks also directed this category of visitor to the unique fossilized remains found in Franconian Switzerland. Ammonites and prehistoric clams could easily be observed and catalogued during hikes through the mountainous landscape, while others could be viewed in private collections, like the one assembled by Limmer am Markt of Muggendorf.[122]

Both "friends of nature" and "friends of natural history" were treated to a host of attractions during their stay in Franconian Switzerland, but some of the most spectacular attractions were contained within the mountains themselves. Esper's 1774 work was responsible for directing the attention of the scientific community to this secluded region of Franconia, but nearly a century of touring, observing, and plundering ensured that the larger caves of Franconian Switzerland no longer contained the "hundreds of cart-loads of bony remains" observed by earlier tourists like Charles Taylor.[123] Nevertheless, even visitors who were primarily interested in the larger romantic landscape were advised to include at least

[117] Phillips, "Friends of Nature," 44–45.
[118] Tomomi Hotaka, "Contact with Nature as Urban Culture in the Modern Age: The Gardening Movement in the Second Imperial Age in Germany," in *New Directions in Urban History*, 127–146.
[119] Engelhardt, "Romanticism in Germany," 112, 115.
[120] Blackbourn, *The Conquest of Nature*, 178, 181.
[121] For example, see the section entitled "Natural History of Franconian Switzerland" in *Die Fränkische Schweiz und die Kur-Anstalt zur Streitberg*, 73–122.
[122] Ende, *Vollständiger Führer durch die ganze Fränkische Schweiz*, 12.
[123] Taylor, *A Historical Tour in Franconia*, 154; Voit, Kauflich, and Rüfer, *Vom Land im Gebirg zur Fränkischen Schweiz*, 175–202.

one cave in their tourist itinerary, and guidebooks continued to advertise these natural wonders as one of the defining features of the region. The 1890 Woerl guidebook described the caves of Franconian Switzerland as "internationally-renowned," and recommended the Rosenmüller Cave in particular. The text insisted that "no tourist should miss out" on this particular attraction, which required little time to visit, and even boasted a worthy view of the Wiesent valley from its entrance.[124] Other guidebooks noted that some of these caves still contained a few fossils, a feature which secured their place among the most interesting caves "in the entire world."[125] The authors of guidebooks joined natural scientists in speculating as to how so many animals, including species of bears, lions, hyenas, and wolverines, ended up in these subterranean chambers.[126] This mystery may have eluded scientific explanation, but it fueled the romantic imagination of the educated middle class.

Descriptions of the caves generally highlighted their enigmatic and "prehistoric" qualities, reflecting romantic notions of natural history, as well as an interest in scientific empiricism, albeit abbreviated for tourist consumption. However, visiting many of the larger caves required more than enthusiasm, and guidebooks recommended warm clothing as well as the services of a local guide. In Muggendorf, the residence of the local guide to the Rosenmüller Cave was clearly marked with a sign for tourists.[127] In addition to an escort, some caves also required that visitors bring their own light along with them, while others were illuminated by more progressive means. By 1890, the interior of the Rosenmüller Cave was lit up by "Bengal light," first used for photography in 1854. Elsewhere, individual sections of the Sophien Cave near Rabenstein could be illuminated by burning strips of magnesium, a service that cost half of a mark, but came highly recommended by Ende's 1895 guidebook.[128] Franconian Switzerland's numerous caves represented a subterranean world of mystery that had existed long before the dawn of the industrial age. Paradoxically, it was contemporary attitudes toward nature and science that filled these caves with visitors. Moreover, modern techniques literally

---

[124] Woerl, *Führer durch Mittelfranken, die Hersbrücker und Fränkische Schweiz,* 46, 52–53.
[125] Ende, *Praktischer Führer durch die Fränkische Schweiz,* 1.
[126] *Die Fränkische Schweiz, das Schwabachthal und die Gräfenberger Umgebung,* 7.
[127] Ende, *Praktischer Führer durch die Fränkische Schweiz,* 17.
[128] Woerl, *Führer durch Mittelfranken, die Hersbrücker und Fränkische Schweiz,* 52–53; Ende, *Vollständiger Führer durch die Fränkische Schweiz,* 16.

illuminated this pre-modern realm, creating a stage on which middle-class tourists could showcase their scientific knowledge and romantic curiosity. Tourism in Franconian Switzerland promised distance from modern civilization, but it was also a distinctly modern activity. Eager to vacation in a region evocative of a bygone era, the middle-class travelers also anticipated modern standards of cleanliness, comfort, and convenience at local accommodations. This is one of the central paradoxes of nineteenth-century tourism identified by Hans Magnus Enzensberger: "The destination has to be both: accessible and inaccessible, distant from civilization and yet comfortable."[129] Guidebooks through Franconian Switzerland catered to this predisposition, including advertisements of inns and restaurants promising *gemütlich* and *bürgerlich* accommodations, as well as some of the modern conveniences of the city.[130] Local inns like the "Gasthof zur Terrasse" in Pinzberg pointed to a list of inviting features, including: "Beautiful, shaded garden. Lovely view into the Regnitz and Wiesent valleys. Recognized quality kitchen with an extensive selection for every time of the day. Specialty: Fish. Good beer from the Reifschen Brewery of Erlangen. Pure wines. Guest rooms with good beds.[131] Johann Distler's Gasthof in Pottenstein similarly advertised a large veranda with views and "numerous and friendly guest rooms," as well as "Munich beer (in bottles)," reaching out to residents of the Bavarian capital and international visitors accustomed to Munich beer.[132] Other inns promised beer from Munich, Nuremberg, and Bamberg.[133]

Every inn presented itself as comfortable and accommodating, but publications often noted that the quality could vary. The 1895 Bläsing guidebook informed visitors that inns in the larger communities tended to be satisfactory, while those in smaller villages left "something to be desired."[134] R. Milner Barry reported that the local population was always warm and hospitable, but she did not hesitate to complain about

[129] Enzensberger, "A Theory of Tourism," 127. For a similar dynamic in France, see Patrick Young, "La Vieille France as Object of Bourgeois Desire: The Touring Club de France and the French Regions, 1890–1918," in *Histories of Leisure*, 182–183.

[130] The terms "gemütlich" and "Gemütlichkeit" remain somewhat difficult to translate. They can refer to hospitality, friendliness, and coziness, or a generally pleasant, good-natured, and easy-going nature.

[131] Schuster, *Kleiner Führer durch die Fränkische Schweiz*, 5.

[132] Ende, *Praktischer Führer durch die Fränkische Schweiz*, 25.

[133] *Kleiner Führer durch die Fränkische Schweiz, sowie Wegweiser durch das Schwabachtal von Erlangen nach Gräfenberg und die sogenannte Herbrucker Schweiz*. Page numbers are not used for the advertisements at the end of this particular guidebook.

[134] *Die Fränkische Schweiz, das Schwabachthal und die Gräfenberger Umgebung*, 12.

the "monstrous eider-downs" in her Pottenstein room, or the "decidedly offensive smell" outside of the inn. She concluded that most inns in the region were "primitive," "crowded," and lacking "sufficient elements of comfort for the English traveler."[135] Attempting to accommodate the demanding tastes of such visitors, several locations in Franconian Switzerland emphasized a somewhat more refined character. Pottenstein's "Gasthaus zum Goldenen Anker," for example, marketed itself not only with "lovely views and good beds," but also a *bürgerliche* kitchen" and "real service," indirectly ensuring the satisfaction of its middle-class clientele.[136] In some cases, visitors could even receive mail and telegrams within the inns themselves, as was the case at Behringersmühle's "Gasthof zur Post."[137] Middle-class visitors may have sought a romantic respite in the Franconian Switzerland, but they were not completely willing to leave their modern life behind. Like many contemporary travelers, they ultimately realized that the modern world was "inescapable."[138]

As a sanctuary from the modern world *and* an explicitly modern travel destination, Franconian Switzerland was ideal for both brief and extended stays, either resting in a designated health resort or actively hiking through its "most beautiful valleys."[139] The region was a venue of self-cultivation and rejuvenation, and it managed to attract "tourists, day-trippers, and summer vacationers," categories alternately employed by local guidebooks.[140] These categories did not refer to men alone, and guidebooks often marketed Franconian Switzerland as a travel destination for the entire family. Franz Dittmar's 1897 guidebook classified Streitberg as both a health resort and a summer retreat, noting that the so-called cure tax was only five marks for an entire family.[141] In another guidebook, the "Gasthof und Restauration zur Eisenbahn" of Ebermannstadt guaranteed an "excellent stay for families and tourists,"

---

[135] Barry, *Bayreuth and Franconian Switzerland*, 121, 111–112, 117–118, 141–142.

[136] Ende, *Vollständiger Führer durch die ganze Fränkische Schweiz*, 8, 63.

[137] *Kleiner Führer durch die Fränkische Schweiz, sowie Wegweiser durch das Schwabachtal von Erlangen nach Gräfenberg und die sogenannte Herbrucker Schweiz*. Other guidebooks noted that post offices and telegraph stations were available in both Streitberg and Muggendorf. See Ende, *Praktischer Führer durch die Fränkische Schweiz*, 18; Franz Dittmar, *400 Ausflüge in die Umgegend von Nürnberg und Fürth, in das Pegnitztal, in die Altdorfer Gegend, in das Rednitz- und Altmühlgebiet und in die Fränkische Schweiz* (Nuremberg: Tümmel, 1897), 100–101.

[138] Leed, *The Mind of the Traveler*, 44.

[139] *Die Fränkische Schweiz, das Schwabachthal und die Gräfenberger Umgebung*, 7.

[140] Ende, *Praktischer Führer durch die Fränkische Schweiz*, 1.

[141] Dittmar, *400 Ausflüge in die Umgegend von Nürnberg und Fürth*, 100.

distinguishing between the two varieties of clientele.[142] Women belonged to both categories of traveler, and guidebooks urged them to be just as adventurous as their male counterparts. Woerl's 1890 guidebook, for example, offered some explicit advice for women visiting the Rosenmüller Cave, recommending brushes for those that sought to clean the fringes of their apparel upon leaving the damp caverns.[143]

In Franconian Switzerland, the entire middle-class family could enjoy a break from the modern world that they knew. These visitors helped to create a new industry that stimulated the local economy and modified the landscape itself. Consisting of the interrelated sectors of propaganda, hospitality, and transportation, the tourism industry aimed at making the experience of travel more practical, comfortable, and predictable. These were attractive qualities to the middle-class traveler with limited time and money. In Franconian Switzerland, there was clearly a hospitality industry in place by 1890, while scientists, poets, and travel writers had celebrated the region in various publications for over a century. In spite of this, some representatives of the tourism industry remained unsatisfied. An article printed in an 1891 issue of *Bavarian Land and Folk*, the official journal of the State Association for the Expansion of Bavarian Tourism, reported that residents of Nuremberg, Bamberg, and Bayreuth, regularly visited Franconian Switzerland, but that "a further increase of tourism was possible as well as desirable." Suggested targets included the residents of Bavaria's neighboring states, as well as the "visitors from all lands" that regularly flocked to Nuremberg, a city with a growing reputation as "a focal point of international tourism."[144]

The biggest obstacle standing between non-Bavarian tourists and Franconian Switzerland was the region's relative inaccessibility via modern means of transportation. While the German rail network had expanded to 24,000 miles by 1873, this particular tourist destination remained off the grid.[145] Tourist propaganda confirmed this state of affairs, with the 1876 Grieben's guidebook reporting that Franconian Switzerland did not possess a railway, and it was "unlikely" that they would receive one "in the near future."[146] Visitors could travel by rail to Forchheim, the

[142] *Die Fränkische Schweiz, das Schwabachthal und die Gräfenberger Umgebung*, 33.

[143] Woerl, *Führer durch Mittelfranken, die Hersbrücker und Fränkische Schweiz*, 53.

[144] StAB, Regierung von Oberfranken, 1978. "Einige Worte über Hebung des Fremdenverkehrs in Bayern," *Bayerisch Land und Volk: Offizielles Organ des Landesverbandes zur Hebung des Fremdenverkehrs in Bayern* 2, no. 2 (1891/92): 13.

[145] Blackbourn, *The Long Nineteenth Century*, 180.

[146] Grieben, *Das Fichtelgebirge und die Fränkische Schweiz*, 96.

"gateway to Franconian Switzerland," but their options were then limited to traveling by foot or by coach. While most guidebook authors praised the virtues of leisurely hiking through the mountainous landscape, others hoped that the region would be spared the "granite gates" and "iron tracks" of modern transportation.[147]

In spite of these concerns, modernity traversed the boundaries of Franconian Switzerland once again in the summer of 1891, when the railway line between Forchheim and Ebermannstadt opened. The new line transported visitors from the former location to the new "gateway to Franconian Switzerland" in roughly one hour, an important breakthrough that was heralded by the Woerl guidebook in 1890, months before the railway was even launched.[148] The town of Ebermannstadt celebrated the opening of the railway on May 23, 1891, hosting an extravagant ceremony featuring a parade, music, and the decoration of the new train station.[149] The 1891 issue of *Bavarian Land and People* subsequently reported that the new railway was greeted with "festive jubilation" by the locals of Franconian Switzerland, and especially the inhabitants of Ebermannstadt. Some more "conservative citizens," on the other hand, were reluctant to see the railway extend further into the region, a plan that was already in the works. Still, they did not reject this modern technology outright; they were pleased with the new line, and simply supported a more gradual modernization of Franconian Switzerland.[150] Similar concerns about the pace of modernization led to a 1907 Ebermannstadt resolution banning automobiles and their "exaggerated speed" from the narrow roads of the region.[151] Like attempts to delay the expansion of the railway, this attempt was ultimately unsuccessful.

---

[147] Koch-Neuses, *Die Romantik der Fränkischen Schweiz*, 3.
[148] Woerl, *Führer durch Mittelfranken, die Hersbrücker und Fränkische Schweiz*, 45.
[149] *Amts-Blatt für die kgl. Bezirksämter Forchheim & Ebermannstadt sowie für die kgl. Stadt Forchheim* (Forchheim), May 23, 1891.
[150] StAB, Regierung von Oberfranken, 1978. "Eine Neue Verkehrslinie für die Fränkische Schweiz," *Bayerisch Land und Volk: Offizielles Organ des Landesverbandes zur Hebung des Fremdenverkehrs in Bayern* 2, no. 2 (1891/92): 18–19. The railway was not the only new form of transportation that debuted in Franconian Switzerland during this period. An 1898 guidebook published by the Bläsing company offered a ten-page section entitled "Tours for Bike-Riders," outlining ten different biking routes through the region. See *Die Fränkische Schweiz, das Schwabachthal und die Gräfenberger Umgebung, Unter besonderer Berücksichtigung der Radfahrtouren* (Erlangen: Th. Bläsings Universitäts-Buchhandlung, 1898).
[151] Lilly Schottky, *Geschichte des Fränkische-Schweiz-Vereins, und andere heimatkundliche Beiträge* (Erlangen: Palm & Enke, 1989), 48.

While the opening of the Forchheim–Ebermannstadt railway line improved the region's accessibility, some members of the local community took additional measures to cultivate tourism. In 1901, August Deppisch, a physician from Pottenstein, and Johannes Tremel, a priest from a village outside Bayreuth, founded the "Franconian Switzerland Association." This association assumed responsibility over the local tourism industry, and publicly declared its goals as: "making visits to Franconian Switzerland possible for strangers, enhancing the experiences of local friends of nature, and providing the current population with the benefits of an enhanced and better-regulated tourism."[152] Echoing the statutes of both local beautification societies and *Heimat-Vereine*, the association was dedicated to improving the physical and spiritual well-being of visitors and local residents alike. These objectives were achieved through a number of actions, including the preservation of "natural wonders," the creation of trails, the improvement of accommodations, the funding of research into local history and geography, and even the promotion of hiking among the local youth (again, the region's residents apparently did not possess the same enthusiasm for the landscape as the middle-class urbanites). These activities reveal an ideological commitment to the middle-class ideal of *Bildung*, as well as a practical commitment to the broad improvement of tourism, which promised benefits for the entire local community. By 1908, the Franconian Switzerland Association counted 600 members, a figure that included locals as well as middle-class residents of Nuremberg, Bamberg, and Bayreuth.[153]

* * *

In 1906, a group of middle-school students from Nuremberg toured Franconian Switzerland for several days. Their teacher, Viktor Wolfinger, subsequently published a book about the experience that utilized reports submitted by students. In one of these papers, a student praised the "romantic and beautiful" landscape around Gößweinstein, stating that the "holy and heavenly quiet" of that place had touched her very soul. In another paper, a student proclaimed that the experience of hiking over the mountains and valleys of Franconian Switzerland had changed her, and the thought of returning to the "narrow streets" of Nuremberg "broke her heart."[154] Tourism transformed Franconian Switzerland over the course

[152] Quoted in Ibid., 99.
[153] Ibid., 37–43, 99–101.
[154] Viktor Wolfinger, *Ergebnisse einer Schulreise durch die Fränkische Schweiz. Festgestellt aus freien Schüleraufsätzen* (Nuremberg: Verlag der Friedrich Kornschen Buchhandlung, 1908), 20, 83.

Fränk. Schweiz. Streitberg. Blick in das Wiesent Tal.

FIGURE 4. Postcard featuring Streitberg and environs, 1920s. From the author's collection.

of the nineteenth century, inviting modernity into a once secluded region. However, the colonization and commodification of the landscape did not seem to detract from its overall power, as several visitors testified. Although the majority of records of the Franconian Switzerland Association were destroyed in the Second World War, surviving statistics suggest that the popularity of the region grew significantly during the early twentieth century, with rapid growth during the Weimar era. For example, the number of visitors to spend at least one night in Gößweinstein increased from 9,870 during the 1913–1914 season, to 28,590 in 1925–1926, and finally 43,425 in 1930–1931.[155] The character of leisure travel in Germany certainly changed during this period, as larger segments of society were attracted by new forms of propaganda and the allure of the package tour. Yet the underlying justification of tourism remained the flight from everyday life, and in many cases, respite from modern civilization.

This longing for a sanctuary from modern civilization was first evident among the middle-class tourists of the nineteenth century, who pioneered a new style of leisure travel that distinguished them from early modern pilgrims and aristocratic Grand Tourists. For the *Bürgertum*, tourism constituted not only a break from their day-to-day life, but also a means of developing individual personality, enhancing body and mind,

[155] Philip Schwartz, *Bayern im Lichte seiner hundertjährigen Statistik*, ed. Philip Schwartz (Munich: J. Lindauersche Universitäts-Buchhandlung, 1933), 75.

acquiring culture, defining collective identity, and even asserting status. This was not a uniquely German phenomenon, but central Europe did possess a multitude of venues where these goals could be achieved, including the Harz Mountains, the Thuringian Forest, and the various "little Switzerlands."[156] Among them, Franconian Switzerland serves as an excellent example of the tourist destinations celebrated by the educated middle class. This region in northern Bavaria boasted attractions similar to those in the Alps or the Middle Rhine, including mountains, medieval ruins, and rustic villages. The difference was that its attractions were less intimidating and more manageable. Romantic self-cultivation was readily available in Franconian Switzerland, but its acquisition was expedited and rationalized for middle-class tourists who were pressed for time and money.

In addition to shedding light on a distinctly bourgeois tourist gaze, this case study of Franconian Switzerland has also demonstrated that the early Bavarian tourism industry did not emerge exclusively in Upper Bavaria, nor did it evolve independently of outside influences, as has been suggested.[157] The ideological predispositions and behavior that shaped landscape tourism within Franconian Switzerland were not indigenous to Bavaria, even if many of its visitors were. Furthermore, this case study has shown that tourists did not only import new attitudes and leisure habits into Franconian Switzerland; they were likewise responsible for the partial modernization of the mountainous region, with telegraph machines and the railway following on their heels. Tourism provided a reprieve from modern civilization, but it was also a harbinger and reflection of modernity. In search of some grounding in a rapidly changing world, bourgeois travelers altered the very nature that they came to venerate.[158] The following chapter expands upon these themes by considering how tourism transformed the Upper Bavarian community of Reichenhall into a modern and cosmopolitan health resort, where the Alpine landscape was not only a scenic backdrop, but the basis of many of the spa's progressive treatments. Surrounded by nature and cosmopolitan company, guests enjoyed an alternative modernity in which they could temporarily transcend both their everyday lives and the mental horizons of the German nation.

---

[156] For similar arguments, see Hansen, "Albert Smith, the Alpine Club, and the Invention of Mountaineering in Mid-Victorian Britain"; Young, "La Vieille France as Object of Bourgeois Desire."

[157] Lepovitz, "Pilgrims, Patients, and Painters."

[158] Buzard, *The Beaten Track*, 28.

3

Nature, Modernity, and the Spa Culture of Bad Reichenhall

"Positioned between the southern German capitals of Munich and Vienna, Reichenhall combines the picturesque setting of an Alpine summer retreat and Bavarian and Austrian *Gemütlichkeit* with the infrastructure of a first-class health resort. It promises a sojourn that will provide the ill with a wealth of remedies, the convalescent with the quiet and comfortable pleasure of nature, and the summer visitor and tourist with a diversity of pleasurable distractions, to the point that it will be difficult to tackle all of them in the space of a single vacation."[1]

Bad Reichenhall: Illustrated Brochure, 1904
(Distributed by the Bad Reichenhall Spa Association)

Located on the Alpine frontier between Bavaria and Austria, Reichenhall was once a secluded town, historically defined by its salt industry. Its reputation began to change in the mid nineteenth century, after a number of enterprising locals opened "cure facilities," thereby establishing the foundations of a modern health resort. By the end of the century, the spa town drew over 10,000 guests per season. The local community accommodated these visitors with an expanding hospitality industry and a growing number of pleasurable activities. By 1900, the recently renamed Bad Reichenhall had become more than a spa: it was a multifaceted and modern tourist destination, offering progressive medical treatment and cosmopolitan entertainment, along with easy access to the Alpine environment.

While the marketing of some German resorts relied on their international clientele and luxurious accommodations, other resorts depended

[1] Kurverein e.V. Bad Reichenhall, *Bad Reichenhall: Illustrierter Badprospekt des Kurortes* (Munich: Alphons Bruckmann, 1904), 98.

91

on the reputation of their medical treatments and natural surroundings. Bad Reichenhall stood out among spas like Baden-Baden and Wiesbaden in that its marketing regularly stressed *all* of these themes. In fact, tourist publications struggled to summarize the destination in a single sentence. Bad Reichenhall was an Alpine oasis of urban culture visited by members of the European royalty and nobility, but it was also "a first-class health resort" with progressive medical treatments. Conversely, the natural environment itself was the source of the resort's most popular treatments, and the basis of an identity that transcended both temporal and national boundaries. Balancing these disparate elements, the local tourism industry did not merely promote Bad Reichenhall, they marketed a vision of grounded modernity, demonstrating how Germans could reconcile neo-romantic "back to nature" sentiments with seemingly contradictory attitudes toward technological modernity and urbanity, as well as competing local, national, and international identities.

In order to illuminate the relationship between leisure travel and broader conceptions of nature and modernity in the early twentieth century, the following chapter recounts the rise and fall of the tourism industry of Bad Reichenhall, paying special attention to its marketing during the fifteen years before World War I. At the turn of the twentieth century, the local tourism industry depicted a vacation in the Alpine spa as a cure for the disorienting experience of modernity described by Max Nordau, Georg Simmel, and other contemporary social scientists. Still, guests could expect modern treatments, amenities, accommodations, and transportation. The newness of it all was undeniable. In other words, the Reichenhall spa culture did not provide an escape from modernity; it provided a more acceptable version of it. When rooted in nature and *Gemütlichkeit*, modernity proved much easier to sell. After 1914, the repercussions of total war undermined this carefully cultivated image. Converted into an inexpensive sick bay for German soldiers, Bad Reichenhall was isolated from its international clientele and many of its domestic visitors during World War I. The language of nationalism abruptly replaced the language of cosmopolitanism, and the once thriving tourism industry was on the verge of collapse by 1918. The success story of the prewar decades had come to an end.

Nature, Medicine, and the Nineteenth-Century Spa

In 1838's *Handbook for Travellers to the Continent*, John Murray reported: "With the Germans an excursion to a watering-place in the summer is essential to existence, and the necessity of such a visit is confined to no one class in particular, but pervades all . . . "[2] While the pioneer of the modern guidebook overestimated the egalitarian character of German spas, which remained segregated in some regards, it is true that the clientele of these destinations was becoming more diverse over the course of the nineteenth century. The rise of middle-class tourism forever changed the social dynamic of German spas, leading to a greater variety of attractions and activities. Meanwhile, a new appreciation for the natural environment and a growing health consciousness created unique expectations among the expanded clientele. Many guests now justified their visit to the spa as a form of physical and mental recovery, a "necessity" in an increasingly hectic and demanding urban world. Recovery was available in many forms. In resorts like Baden-Baden and Wiesbaden, nature became central to the notion of the *Kur*, with local tourism industries transforming the environment into a popular selling point not only for patients, but also for tourists, day-trippers, and sports enthusiasts.

Nature had not always been a defining feature of the spa experience. During the eighteenth century, upper-class spa guests displayed little interest in the natural landscape. Although many resorts included formal French-style gardens, this green space was hardly "natural." Instead, the heavily manicured and symmetrical gardens underscored the power of the local elites by symbolizing mankind's triumph over the natural environment. Nature was supposed to bow to man, and not the other way around. The self-contained world of the spa represented a certain vision of civilization, and local authorities kept it aesthetically pleasing by banishing all vestiges of uncultivated wilderness and rustic culture to the outskirts of the town. This changed during the era of urbanization, when middle-class spa guests sought to reconnect with a simpler world deserted in pursuit of progress.[3] Although the social nucleus of the spa remained within the resort itself, the nineteenth century witnessed a gradual colonization of the surrounding environs with pathways, benches, and marked vistas.[4] Extended walks and excursions into the countryside became a popular pastime among both middle-class visitors and the international elite. After visiting Baden-Baden in the mid 1830s, Englishman Edmund Spencer remarked: "The walks and rides in the vicinity are diversified and

---

[2] John Murray, *A Handbook for Travellers to the Continent*, 2nd edn. (London: John Murray and Son, 1838), 200.
[3] Fuhs, *Mondäne Orte einer vornehmen Gesellschaft*, 30–31, 83, 89.
[4] Lempa, "The Spa: Emotional Economy and Social Classes in Nineteenth-Century Pyrmont," 48.

pleasant; affording more resources to the visitor than the amusements of the town."[5] By the latter half of the nineteenth century, excursions into the natural environment had become a standard feature of the German spa experience, just as "nature" became an integral component of the "cure."

A new dedication to the healing power of nature was just one manifestation of the increased attention to medicine in German spas during the late nineteenth century. The process had begun several decades beforehand, when some watering places began to deliberately market themselves not as "luxury spas," but as "respectable health resorts." Incapable of directly competing with internationally renowned destinations like Bad Ems and Karlsbad, smaller spas targeted a growing demographic that traveled in search of medical cures.[6] This strategy may have attracted new customers, but it also disappointed those expecting a more refined spa experience. Visiting the Bavarian spa Bad Kissingen in 1842, Mary Shelley wrote: "I am in the midst of my *cur*, and we are all in the midst of a general cure of a regiment of sick people. It is odd enough to seek amusement by being surrounded by the rheumatic, the gouty, the afflicted of all sorts. I do not think I shall be tempted to a German bath again, unless I am seriously ill."[7]

The medicalization of German spas proceeded more rapidly after gambling was banned in the German Empire in 1872. The casino had been a central institution in spas like Baden-Baden, where Fyodor Dostoyevsky was inspired to write the 1866 short story, *The Gambler*.[8] Attracting the middle-class residents of nearby cities as well as members of the wealthy, international elite, the allure of high stakes helped to distinguish German spas from the health resorts of France, where gambling was forbidden.[9] Casinos also helped to subsidize the expansion of German spas. During

[5] Edmund Spencer, *Sketches of Germany and the Germans: With a Glance at Poland, Hungary, and Switzerland in 1834, 1835, and 1836*, Vol. II (London: Whitaker & Co., 1836), 49–50.

[6] Fuhs, *Mondäne Orte einer vornehmen Gesellschaft*, 65; Simone Grün, "Kuren und Erholung im stadtfernen Gebiet," in *Strukturwandel einer Region: Der Odenwald im Zeitalter der Industrialisierung*, ed. Christof Dipper (Darmstadt: Technische Universität Darmstadt, 2000): 235–239.

[7] Mary Wollencraft Shelley, *Rambles in Germany and Italy in 1840, 1842, and 1843* (London: Edward Morton, 1844), 184.

[8] Fyodor Dostoyevsky, *The Gambler*, trans. Constance Garnett (New York: Dover Publications, 1996).

[9] Sommer, *Zur Kur nach Ems*, 76–77.

his stay in Baden-Baden, American diplomat Henry Ruggles observed that the "[m]oney lost by the venturesome players has been spent by millions in adorning the town and converting the country far and near into a magnificent park."[10] Without the casino, fashionable spas faced not only a minor identity crisis, but a potentially major financial crisis. In response, many local administrations decided to remarket their spas as comfortable but refined health resorts. They strategically invested in elaborate medical facilities and the newest spa technology. The medical benefits of a trip to the spa were central once again, and for many visitors, a visit to the spa became a ritualistic experience revolving around health.[11] While eighteenth-century spa guests periodically took the waters in order to preserve good health, nineteenth-century spa guests deliberately took the waters in order to improve their health. The visitor in pursuit of physical and mental rejuvenation was joined by the patient in pursuit of a tangible cure.[12]

The increasing medicalization of German spas reflected larger changes in the way medicine was practiced and health care was provided. Philosopher Michel Foucault argues that the rise of modern medicine and "the birth of the clinic" were founded upon new ways of viewing and discussing the body, as doctors "described what for centuries had remained below the threshold of the visible and the expressible."[13] With French doctors leading the way, clinical medicine became an observational rather than an experimental science, "learned at the bedside and in the morgue by recording and interpreting facts."[14] The "medical gaze" allowed for the systematic classification of symptoms, diseases, and their causes, giving physicians the potential to do more than just ease the suffering of their patients. The cure was more probable than ever. In Germany, the rise of medicine as a legitimate science during the late nineteenth

---

[10] Henry Ruggles, *Germany Seen Without Spectacles, or Random Sketches of Various Subjects Penned from Different Standpoints in the Empire* (Boston: Lee and Shepard, 1883), 57.

[11] Geisthövel, "Promenadenmischungen, Raum und Kommunikation in Hydropolen," 212. For more on an earlier but similar transformation in French spas, see Douglas Mackaman, *Leisure Settings: Bourgeois Culture, Medicine, and the Spa in Modern France* (Chicago: University of Chicago Press, 1998), 96–100.

[12] Blackbourn, "Fashionable Spa Towns in Nineteenth-Century Europe," 10.

[13] Michel Foucault, *The Birth of the Clinic: An Archaeology of Medical Perception*, trans. A.M. Sheridan (New York: Routledge, 2003), xii.

[14] Roy Porter, "Medical Science," in *The Cambridge History of Medicine*, ed. Roy Porter (New York: Cambridge University Press, 2006), 152–156.

century coincided with major discoveries that helped to establish the country as "the world's most powerful scientific culture."[15] German physicians pioneered new treatments and technology like x-rays, while state-funded researchers in Berlin identified the bacterial culprits behind pneumonia and tuberculosis, helping to confirm that modern cities were "breeding grounds" for infectious diseases.[16]

Cities were the source of many health concerns during the late nineteenth century, and the expansion of the urban environment coincided with the rise of medicine as a legitimate science. In his 1892 work, *Degeneration*, physician and social critic Max Nordau wrote about the urban environment's negative impact on mental health: "The inhabitant of a large town, even the richest, who is surrounded by great luxury, is continually exposed to unfavourable influences which diminish his vital powers far more than what is inevitable. He breathes an atmosphere charged with organic detritus; he eats stale, contaminated, adulterated food; he feels himself in a state of constant nervous excitement . . . "[17] According to Nordau, these "unfavourable influences," along with the fatigue produced by the velocity of modern life, were responsible for the diseases of degeneration and hysteria that were allegedly rampant at the end of the nineteenth century.[18] While not everyone agreed with Nordau's prognosis, a milder form of hysteria did approach epidemic status before World War I. First identified by the American physician George Miller Beard in the late 1860s, the condition known as neurasthenia produced the symptoms of fatigue, anxiety, depression, and impotence. Medical literature described it as "a disorder of weak nerves or nervous irritability," allegedly caused by mental overexertion and overwork, as well as excessive alcohol and sexual indulgence.[19] In his 1903 essay, *The Metropolis and Mental Life*, German sociologist Georg Simmel connected nervousness with the urban experience, arguing: "The psychological basis of the metropolitan type of individuality is the intensification of nervous stimulation that results from the swift and uninterrupted change of outer

---

[15] Robert Proctor, *The Nazi War on Cancer* (Princeton: Princeton University Press, 1999), 15.

[16] Reinhard Spree, *Soziale Ungleichheit vor Krankheit und Tod: Zur Sozialgeschichte des Gesundheitsbereichs im Deutschen Kaiserreich* (Göttingen: Vandenhoeck & Ruprecht, 1981), 107; McElligott, *The German Urban Experience*, 97, 99.

[17] Max Nordau, *Degeneration* (Lincoln: University of Nebraska Press, 1968), 35.

[18] Ibid., 1–44.

[19] Michael Hau, *The Cult of Health and Beauty in Germany: A Social History, 1890–1930* (Chicago: University of Chicago Press, 2003), 15–17.

and inner stimuli... With each crossing of the street, with the tempo and multiplicity of economic, occupational and social life, the city sets up a deep contrast with small town and rural life... "[20] Taking their lead from Nordau, Simmel, and Walter Benjamin, historians have linked neurasthenia to industrialization, rapid economic growth, and the "over-stimulation" produced by the speed, technology, and excitement of the modern metropolis.[21] In other words, modernity had diminished fin-de-siècle society, and the new science of medicine could provide both the diagnosis and the cure.[22]

The transformation of medicine into a clinical science meant that doctors were no longer forced to rely on natural remedies and speculative techniques, and as members of a recently professionalized medical guild, they tended to disparage those practitioners who did. These changes in the medical profession coincided with vast improvements in public health in Germany. Between 1876 and 1913, the number of doctors in the German Empire more than doubled, from 14,000 to 34,000, surpassing the overall population increase of approximately 40 to 65 million. This period also witnessed a rapid decline in mortality rates and a sharp increase in life expectancy, advances which can be attributed not only to a greater number of health care providers, but also to improved diets and standards of hygiene, as well as a new health consciousness that led people to see disease as something that was often treatable, if not avoidable altogether.[23] Another breakthrough occurred in 1884, when Otto von Bismarck introduced national insurance legislation, effectively creating the medical profession by guaranteeing government funds for the treatment of illness, disability, and accidents among industrial workers.[24] After 1900, insurance was extended to almost all trades, increasing the "tangible benefits" for working-class patients, as well as doctors.[25] This legislation helped to

---

[20] Georg Simmel, "The Metropolis and Mental Life," in *The Urban Sociology Reader*, ed. Jan Lin and Christopher Mele (New York: Routledge, 2013), 25.

[21] Andreas Killen, *Berlin Electropolis: Shock, Nerves, and German Modernity* (Berkeley: University of California Press, 2006), 42–43; Joachim Radkau, *Das Zeitalter der Nervosität: Deutschland zwischen Bismarck und Hitler* (Munich: Hanser, 1998); Michael Cowan, *Cult of the Will: Nervousness and German Modernity* (University Park, PA: Pennsylvania State University Press, 2008), 8, 30. See also Walter Benjamin, *Illuminations* (New York: Schocken Books, 1969), 174–175.

[22] See Jennifer M. Kapczynski, *The German Patient: Crisis and Recovery in Postwar Culture* (Ann Arbor: University of Michigan Press, 2008), 9–10.

[23] Nipperdey, *Deutsche Geschichte, 1866–1918, Erster Band*, 150–157, 165.

[24] Paul Weindling, *Health, Race, and German Politics between National Unification and Nazism, 1870–1945* (New York: Cambridge University Press, 1989), 20.

[25] Killen, *Berlin Electropolis*, 82, 88–90.

make spa treatments available to a greater percentage of the population, even if an extended stay at a distant health resort remained unrealistic for most day laborers.[26]

During the final decades of the long nineteenth century, the German state also took a more active role in supervising the practice of medicine in health resorts. It began to license and regulate spa doctors, who, like general practitioners, now studied at state universities, where spa medicine was a legitimate subject. This institutional recognition strengthened the reputation of the German spa industry, helping to validate it in the eyes of the scientific community and the general public.[27] The reputation of individual resorts became linked to the competency of the increasingly influential spa doctors.[28] Still, spa medicine occupied a sort of middle ground, appealing to those in pursuit of legitimate, scientific treatment, as well as those favoring alternative forms of medicine revolving around so-called natural cures. On one hand, scientific research continued to corroborate the therapeutic properties of mineral water, which had become popular treatments for heart conditions and rheumatism. On the other hand, the healing power of fresh air and sunshine that attracted so many spa guests could not be easily verified, even though it was a common assumption among members of the popular "life reform movement."[29]

The term "life reform" first gained currency during the 1880s, and refers to "a broad spectrum of movements seeking alternative modernities."[30] The predominantly middle-class advocates of life reform were generally suspicious of the regular medical profession and developed their own strategies for the achievement of good health, including vegetarianism, nudism, and therapeutic baths.[31] This was a direct response to the nineteenth-century transformation of medicine into a clinical science, a development that had led many Germans to reject modern, "mechanistic scientific thinking" in favor of a more holistic and natural

---

[26] Fuhs, *Mondäne Orte einer vornehmen Gesellschaft*, 354.

[27] Bacon, "The Rise of the German and the Demise of the English Spa Industry," 181–182.

[28] Sommer, *Zur Kur nach Ems*, 603–612.

[29] Nipperdey, *Deutsche Geschichte, 1866–1918, Erster Band*, 162–165.

[30] Kevin Repp, *Reformers, Critics, and the Paths of German Modernity: Anti-Politics and the Search for Alternatives, 1890–1914* (Cambridge, MA: Harvard University Press, 2000), 266, 269–270.

[31] See Eva Barlösius, *Naturgemässe Lebensführung: Zur Geschichte der Lebensreform um die Jahrhundertwende* (Frankfurt am Main: Campus Verlag, 1997); Chad Ross, *Naked Germany: Health, Race, and the Nation* (New York: Berg, 2005); Williams, *Turning to Nature in Germany*, 23–66.

approach to medicine.[32] The German life reform movement was also a response to the larger process of modernization, which had allegedly "alienated" modern society from its natural state.[33] Thus, natural therapies promised both physical and mental rejuvenation, as well as a form of solace in uncertain times. More importantly, they allowed for a sense of agency. Whether plagued by genuine ailments or just a general feeling of inadequacy, individuals could take control of their lives by devoting themselves to natural therapies that improved the health of both body and mind.[34] Although the life reform movement was critical of modern civilization, it was not explicitly antimodern. Instead of advocating a retreat to an idealized past, they hoped that their ideas would guide modern society to a better future. In other words: the movement was not just about medicine, it was about self-cultivation and the improvement of society at large.[35] With these goals in mind, many of the movement's followers sought to reconcile nature with modern civilization by seeking "recuperative and alternative treatments in picturesque rural surroundings."[36]

With their diverse treatments, picturesque surroundings, and refined sociability, German spas provided both welcome distractions and necessary rejuvenation. They promised respite from professional pressures, and the possibility of returning to the outside world refreshed and motivated.[37] Spas like Bad Reichenhall were therefore more than just the newest spin on the age-old tradition of taking the waters; they grounded the experience of modernity, providing an invaluable remedy for the growing pains of industrial society. Furthermore, this was a "cure" that was available to an international clientele, and not just Bavarians or Germans. In general, this was a much more expansive vision of grounded modernity than that promoted in Franconian Switzerland; not only did it reacquaint contemporary society with the natural environment while simultaneously glorifying elements of technological modernity and urbanity, it also united tourists across regional and national boundaries.

---

32 Anne Harrington, *Reenchanted Science: Holism in German Culture from Wilhelm II to Hitler* (Princeton: Princeton University Press, 1996), xv.

33 Hau, *The Cult of Health and Beauty in Germany*, 1.

34 Ibid., 17.

35 Barlösius, *Naturgemässe Lebensführung*, 19, 224, 230.

36 Jill Steward, "The Spa Towns of the Austro-Hungarian Empire and the Growth of Tourist Culture: 1860–1914," in *New Directions in Urban History*, 96–97.

37 Fuhs, *Mondäne Orte einer vornehmen Gesellschaft*, 469–470; Sommer, *Zur Kur nach Ems*, 28.

The Construction of a Spa Town

The history of Reichenhall is extensive, and has always been connected with its primary natural resource: salt.[38] The salt industry originated as early as 400 B.C.E., when the area's Celtic inhabitants began employing the local saline springs to produce the so-called white gold.[39] The extraction of this valuable commodity continued into Roman times, when the small settlement in the province of Noricum, Ad Salinas, became the focal point of salt production in the Alps. During the Middle Ages, the saline wealth of the town now known as Reichenhall ("rich in salt") became a source of contention between the local inhabitants, the Duke of Bavaria, and the Archbishop of Salzburg, located a mere fourteen kilometers away. Reichenhall entered a period of relative stability after the fifteenth century, when Georg the Rich, Duke of Bavaria, created a state monopoly over salt production, establishing the foundations of an economic monoculture.[40] The transformation of the Duchy of Bavaria into a centralized kingdom at the beginning of the nineteenth century brought several important changes to Reichenhall, including the further consolidation of the salt industry.[41] However, in spite of some improvements in the channeling of brine waters, production declined, just as the regional saline industry began to face new competition from salt-producing towns in Baden and Württemberg.[42]

In the meantime, local saline became significant in another regard. At the end of the eighteenth century, salt water became a commonly prescribed *Kur*. In Germany, this treatment was available at seaside resorts along the Baltic and North Sea coastlines, or in specifically designed saline baths, which were available in Bad Pyrmont as early as 1790.[43] In

---

[38] Bruno Alexander, *Bad Reichenhall als klimatischer Kurort* (Munich: Verlag der Ärztlichen Rundschau Otto Gmelin, 1911), 5; Johannes Lang, *Geschichte von Bad Reichenhall* (Neustadt an der Aisch: Verlag PH.C.W. Schmidt, 2009), 12. For a more concise overview of Reichenhall's history, see Herbert Pfisterer, *Bad Reichenhall in seiner bayerischen Geschichte*, 2nd edn. (Munich: Motor + Touristik-Verlag, 1988).

[39] For more on the Celtic mining of salt, see Mark Kurlansky, *Salt: A World History* (New York: Penguin Books, 2003), 52–60.

[40] Lang, *Geschichte von Bad Reichenhall*, 296–300.

[41] Herbert Pfisterer, "Reichenhalls Umbruchjahre im frühen 19. Jahrhundert," in *Das Heilbad Bad Reichenhall im 19. und 20. Jahrhundert: Festschrift anläßlich des 100-jährigen Jubiläums der Baderhebung 1890–1990*, ed. Hans-Wolfgang Städtler (Bad Reichenhall: Staatliche Kurverwaltung Bad Reichenhall, 1990), 13–15.

[42] Josef Wysocki, *Leben im Berchtesgadener Land, 1800–1990* (Bad Reichenhall: Sparkasse Berchtesgadener Land, 1991), 63–64; Lang, *Geschichte von Bad Reichenhall*, 566.

[43] Lang, *Geschichte von Bad Reichenhall*, 576.

southeastern Bavaria, the utilization of local saline as a therapeutic remedy began in Kirchberg, just across the Saalach River from Reichenhall. A
Salzburg physician first documented the medicinal properties of the community's spring waters in 1713. Over one hundred years later, a Kircherg
doctor opened a saline bath, but the modest facility only managed to
attract locals.[44]

On the other side of the river, two events paved the way for Reichenhall's transformation into "the Queen of German Alpine Baths," a common designation in tourist publications.[45] The first occurred during a
November evening in 1834, when a massive fire engulfed Reichenhall,
leaving 75 percent of the town in ruins.[46] Bavarian king Ludwig I allo-
cated a sum of 10,000 gulden for the rebuilding of Reichenhall, but he
insisted on the modernization of the town through the widening of the
medieval streets and the rational alignment of new buildings. Reichenhall's citizens consented, demolishing most of the medieval wall and
replacing the town's winding alleyways and narrow squares with open
avenues and centrally located plazas.[47] The centerpiece of the new town
was the Royal Saline Works, which reflected the neo-baroque sensibilities of Ludwig's court architects.[48] Confronted with disaster, Reichenhall transformed itself into one of Bavaria's most modern urban centers, "newly constructed and crisscrossed with wide streets and land-
scaped squares."[49] The reconstruction and modern look of Reichenhall
became common topics in the tourist propaganda of the turn of the
century.

The second event that paved the way for Reichenhall's transformation was the opening of the Kuranstalt Axelmannstein on May 15, 1846.
Attempts to launch a spa industry in Reichenhall had begun in 1837,
when the municipal government appealed to the Bavarian state for financial assistance in the construction of a saline bath. The state government declined this request on three separate occasions during subsequent

[44] Herbert Pfisterer, "Die Frühe Entwicklung der Kurortmedizin und der Balneotherapie in Reichenhall," *Das Heilbad Bad Reichenhall im 19. und 20. Jahrhundert*, 145–
146.
[45] StAM, Kurverwaltung Bad Reichenhall, 269: "Bücher, Zeitschriften, Reklame, 1910–
1956"; Kurverein e.V. Bad Reichenhall, *Bad Reichenhall: Illustrierter Badprospekt des
Kurortes* (Bad Reichenhall: M. Zugschwerdts Nachf., 1911), 13.
[46] Lang, *Geschichte von Bad Reichenhall*, 558–563.
[47] Pfisterer, *Bad Reichenhall in seiner bayerischen Geschichte*, 288–291, 293.
[48] Lang, *Geschichte von Bad Reichenhall*, 564–565.
[49] Adolf Bühler, *Führer durch Bad Reichenhall, Salzburg & Berchtesgaden*, 21st edn. (Bad
Reichenhall: H. Bühler, 1900), 9.

years, repeatedly advising Reichenhall to utilize its own resources.[50] Local efforts intensified after 1844, when Mathias Mack, a pharmacist recently arrived from Kelheim, was elected mayor. During his first term in office, Mack made the construction of a bathing facility his chief priority, and he mobilized limited resources in pursuit of this goal. He also cultivated a business relationship with two of Reichenhall's most influential residents, district court judge Wilhelm Freiherr von Pechmann and Royal Saxon tax inspector Ernst Rinck. In league with Mack, these two men provided much of the capital necessary for the construction of Reichenhall's first spa facility.[51]

The Kuranstalt Axelmannstein was located in the lavish home of the late Kaspar von Reiner, the father-in-law of both Rinck and von Pechmann. It was a saline and whey cure facility, where guests could bathe in one of fifteen heated salt water baths and drink beverages produced from mountain herbs and the whey of local goat milk. Before its opening, Rinck had secured a deal with the municipal government, exchanging the right to levy a so-called cure tax for the inexpensive supply of salt water for bathing.[52] The natural resource that had been synonymous with the local economy for centuries was now utilized in a completely new fashion, promising tangible benefits for both local residents and out-of-town visitors. Since the inception of the Reichenhall spa culture, nature was an integral part of the cure.

Nevertheless, even the early Reichenhall spa culture was not limited to its medical treatments. The fact that other Bavarian health resorts like Bad Kissingen and Rosenheim already offered saline baths meant that Reichenhall had to provide additional attractions.[53] Alongside its bathing chambers and comfortably furnished rooms, the Kuranstalt Axelmannstein (or the *Kurhaus*, as it was initially known) contained an elegantly decorated dining hall and a billiard room, where guests could congregate and socialize. The Axelmannstein also featured its own English-style park, where guests could promenade and inhale the salt-infused air, thus catering to a middle class increasingly obsessed with nature. The combined package of medical treatments, social diversions, and Alpine views proved popular, and by the end of the first season, Reichenhall's first spa facility had registered ninety-two guests.[54]

[50] Hubert Vogel, *Geschichte von Bad Reichenhall* (Munich: Verlag des Historischen Vereins von Oberbayern, 1971), 76.
[51] Lang, *Geschichte von Bad Reichenhall*, 580–582.
[52] Ibid., 580–582.
[53] Wysocki, *Leben im Berchtesgadener Land*, 116–117.
[54] Pfisterer, *Bad Reichenhall in seiner bayerischen Geschichte*, 312–314.

Reichenhall's popularity soared after the summer of 1848, when Bavaria's new king, Maximilian II, sojourned in Reichenhall for several months with his family and entourage.[55] Local historian Johannes Lang describes this single vacation as "the moment when Reichenhall tourism was born."[56] The king's visit secured the reputation of the new spa, with 164 guests following his example the following season.[57] Maximilian's visit also encouraged other European royals to visit the Bavarian spa, and during the following decades, members of the Russian, Swedish, Portuguese, Austrian, and Prussian royal families vacationed in Reichenhall, contributing to the town's growing reputation as a cosmopolitan resort.[58] Although Reichenhall never played an important role in European politics and diplomacy along the lines of Bad Ems or Karlsbad, royal patronage did become an important element of the spa's image, and was proudly promoted by local tourist propaganda. The presence of such celebrities, a category that included kings, queens, and even Otto von Bismarck, served as a powerful advertisement for the town, encouraging members of the upper class to confirm their status by following in the footsteps of the most elite.[59]

By 1855, Reichenhall was attracting 1,000 guests per season, but the local community initially proved ill-equipped for the increase in numbers.[60] While the Kuranstalt Axelmannstein struggled to accommodate its patrons, unlucky visitors were forced to seek lodgings outside of the town in nearby Kirchberg and St. Zeno. The municipal government responded in 1850 by encouraging the locals to offer accommodations to guests during the summer season. Soon dozens of citizens posted notices advertising single rooms or entire apartments to out-of-town visitors.[61] In the years that followed, other enterprising locals followed the example of Ernst Rinck and tried their hand at the cure business itself. The sons of local politician and pharmacist Mathias Mack opened a whey drinking hall in 1857, and an inhalation and respiration facility in 1863. Eventually known as the Dianabad, this facility featured the town's first pneumatic

55 Ibid., 314–315.
56 Lang, *Geschichte von Bad Reichenhall*, 587.
57 Herbert Pfisterer, "Eine kleine Geschichte der Kurstadt Reichenhall (1850–1990)," in *Das Heilbad Bad Reichenhall im 19. und 20. Jahrhundert*, 23.
58 StAM, Kurverwaltung Bad Reichenhall, 7: "Amtsgeschäfte des Badeskommisars, 1861–1937."
59 Kurverein e.V. Bad Reichenhall, *Bad Reichenhall: Illustrierter Badprospekt des Kurortes* (1911), 5–6. See also Sommer, *Zur Kur nach Ems*, 72–74; Steward, "The Spa Towns of the Austro-Hungarian Empire and the Growth of Tourist Culture," 110.
60 Vogel, *Geschichte von Bad Reichenhall*, 76.
61 Pfisterer, "Eine kleine Geschichte der Kurstadt Reichenhall (1850–1990)," 23–24.

chambers, a novel form of therapy in German spas first introduced in Bad Ems.[62] The Marienbad opened in 1868, followed by the Louisenbad, the Maximiliansbad, the Ludwigsbad, and the Wilhelmsbad, among others. In the meantime, publications by prominent German physicians helped to establish the reputation of Reichenhall's modern medical treatments and facilities, leading to further expansion.[63]

For middle-class tourists who struggled to reconcile their work ethic with the very notion of leisure travel, spa medicine offered the ideal justification for an extended vacation.[64] In Bad Reichenhall, these visitors had access to a growing number of practicing physicians, a figure that rose from nine to thirty-one between 1870 and 1906. Dr. Georg Liebig, an associate of Mathias Mack and the spa's most influential physician during the latter half of the nineteenth century, was the first to catalog the various medical disorders that could be successfully treated in Bad Reichenhall, among them catarrhal inflammation of the lungs, chronic rheumatic disorders, and various skin infections.[65] By the end of the nineteenth century, the Bavarian spa was also known for the treatment of heart disease, nervous conditions, and gynecological complaints, a popular subject in spa medicine literature.[66] However, it was respiratory disorders that remained Bad Reichenhall's primary specialty, and tourist publications promised relief for those suffering from chronic pneumonia, emphysema, and asthma.[67] Such claims helped to attract both upper-class and middle-class travelers to the Bavarian spa town during the latter half of the nineteenth century.

Still, new spa facilities and modern treatments were just a few of the attractions that Reichenhall had to offer. Members of the community established a lending library in 1853 and a small *Heimat* museum in 1854, where visitors could take a break from modern medical treatments by familiarizing themselves with regional customs and history. Locals also opened businesses catering to the spa's affluent clientele, including hair salons, tobacco stores, jewelry shops, and banks. Other residents offered

[62] Sommer, *Zur Kur nach Ems*, 47.
[63] Pfisterer, "Die Frühe Entwicklung der Kurortmedizin und der Balneotherapie in Reichenhall," 148–149, 156–157.
[64] See Mackaman, *Leisure Settings*, 6.
[65] Lang, *Geschichte von Bad Reichenhall*, 596–599; Pfisterer, "Die Frühe Entwicklung der Kurortmedizin und der Balneotherapie in Reichenhall," 155–159.
[66] Fuhs, *Mondäne Orte einer vornehmen Gesellschaft*, 249.
[67] StAM, Kurverwaltung Bad Reichenhall, 23: "Landesverein zur Hebung des Fremdenverkehrs, 1890–1896."

boat and raft rides on the nearby *Thumsee*, converting this feature of the natural environment into a profitable tourist attraction.[68] This swift economic reorientation led Munich travel writer Ludwig Steub to criticize the Reichenhall natives for their hasty abandonment of the traditional mountain lifestyle in favor of "service and slavery to the spa crowd."[69] Modernity manifested itself in many ways in the Alpine community, but the new, capitalist orientation of Reichenhall left some Bavarians with doubts. Still, it is noteworthy that this particular complaint came from an outsider, and not from a member of the local community that was profiting from increased tourism.

In addition to reconfiguring the economic orientation of the locals, tourism had implications for the town's physical appearance. A mere three weeks after the opening of the Kuranstalt Axelmannstein, middle-class citizens founded a Beautification Society. This group was responsible for improving the sanitary conditions of the town, paving new walkways, planting trees, designating particularly rewarding views with markers, and providing coaches for excursions to nearby scenic locales. In general, they promoted a picturesque view of Reichenhall, blurring the boundaries between the modern town and its Alpine surroundings. Their efforts helped to establish the foundations of the local tourism industry, confirming that the spa's success was not fortuitous, but the direct product of a concerted, local strategy.[70] The Beautification Society existed in several incarnations through 1908, when it was reorganized as the Spa Association, or *Kurverein*, an organization that supported economic growth through the development of tourism infrastructure and the distribution of propaganda.[71]

The Bavarian Ministry of the Interior also played an active role in Reichenhall's transformation by appointing a state spa commissioner in 1856. This official was responsible for utilizing cure tax dividends to organize activities for the resort's visitors, leading to the emergence of a new social life centered on the Kuranstalt Axelmannstein and its grounds. The Kurhaus hosted "soirées musicales," chamber music concerts, and extravagant balls, while the adjacent park became the scene of festive

---

[68] Lang, *Geschichte von Bad Reichenhall*, 588, 590.
[69] Ludwig Steub, *Wanderungen im bayerischen Gebirge* (Munich: G.A. Fleischmann's Buchhandlung, 1862), 42.
[70] Lang, *Geschichte von Bad Reichenhall*, 584–585.
[71] Herbert Pfisterer, "140 Jahre im Dienste des Fremdenverkehrs: Aus der Geschichte des Kur- und Verkehrvereins e.V. Bad Reichenhall," in *Das Heilbad Bad Reichenhall im 19. und 20. Jahrhundert*, 183–185.

illuminations and the firework displays of so-called Italian nights.[72] In 1868, the spa commissioner signed an agreement with the Munich conductor, Joseph Gungl, who assembled a twenty-one man orchestra to perform open-air concerts every morning and evening during the summer season, in addition to playing at the weekly balls.[73] Such orchestras were common in nineteenth-century spas, where they provided "diversion and distraction during the long periods of enforced inactivity that made up a large part of the *curistes*' day."[74] In spas like Reichenhall, live music also accompanied the post-drinking cure promenade, providing rhythm to therapy, from 6:00 to 8:00 each morning.[75] The *Kurmusik* became part of the daily regimen in Reichenhall, helping to distinguish it from existence at a lower altitude. Such new routines also slowed the passage of time. As Thomas Mann explained in *The Magic Mountain*, "the insertion of new habits or the changing of old ones is the only way to preserve life, to renew our sense of time, to rejuvenate, intensify, and retard our experience of time – and thereby to renew our sense of life itself."[76] New routines made the days count.

While measures taken by the Reichenhall Beautification Society and the spa commissioner contributed to the overall experience of guests, the number of visitors remained limited due to the resort's isolated location in the Bavarian Alps. As late as the 1850s, the coach ride from Munich to Reichenhall still required two full days of travel. In 1860, a railway line between Munich and Vienna finally opened, decreasing the travel time between the Bavarian capital and Reichenhall to approximately seven hours. During the following season, Reichenhall registered over 2,000 guests for the first time.[77] This did not satisfy some representatives of the local tourism industry, who demanded a separate rail connection for the growing resort.[78] Other residents voiced reservations about the expansion of the railway into Reichenhall, worrying that trains would tarnish the idyllic quality of the resort and potentially bring more guests than the

72 Pfisterer, *Bad Reichenhall in seiner bayerischen Geschichte*, 323–324.
73 Pfisterer, "Eine kleine Geschichte der Kurstadt Reichenhall (1850–1990)," 25–27.
74 Ian Bradley, *Water Music: Music Making in the Spas of Europe and North America* (New York: Oxford University Press, 2010), 12.
75 Wysocki, *Leben im Berchtesgadener Land*, 159; Christoph-Hellmut Mahling, "'Residenzen des Glücks'. Konzert – Theater – Unterhaltung im Kurorten des 19. und frühen 20. Jahrhunderts," in *Badeorte und Bäderreisen in Antike, Mittelalter und Neuzeit*, 89.
76 Mann, *The Magic Mountain*, 102.
77 Wysocki, *Leben im Berchtesgadener Land*, 121.
78 Steub, *Wanderungen in bayerischen Gebirg*, 42.

community could accommodate.[79] Several locals clearly had reservations about the rapid modernization of their Alpine community, but they did not necessarily disapprove of tourism itself. Furthermore, they were in the minority, and could not stop Reichenhall from receiving its own train station on a line with Freilassing in 1865. The spa town was now indirectly connected with every major city on the continent, a feature that helped to establish its "European reputation."[80] An 1893 Beautification Society flyer, printed in German, French, and Russian versions, confirmed the rail connections to the resort, as well as the exceptional views from the train:

[Reichenhall] is connected through a secondary line to the Munich-Salzburg route, on which twenty trains run daily, while from Reichenhall itself, twelve trains per day depart along the mountain line to Berchtesgaden, which travels through extremely interesting and wonderful views of the Alpine landscape. The majority of Germany's larger train stations provide direct tickets to Reichenhall.[81]

Situated along "one of the most exquisite tracts ever traversed by a railway," as noted by one travel writer, Reichenhall was now accessible to anyone who could afford a ticket.[82] Moreover, the resort became even further integrated into its scenic surroundings through the experiences of rail travel and panoramic perception.

By the final decade of the nineteenth century, Reichenhall had secured its reputation as an "internationally renowned and frequently visited spa and health resort," as noted in an 1892 guidebook published in Zurich.[83] The transformation of Reichenhall, like so many other Alpine destinations, was a "reciprocal" process, fueled by both outside interest in the curative power of nature and local interest in the economic potential of tourism.[84] It was also a product of state intervention. In 1890, Reichenhall officially became Bad Reichenhall, when the government of Prince

---

[79] Lang, *Geschichte von Bad Reichenhall,* 620–621.
[80] Steub, *Wanderungen im bayerischen Gebirg,* 36; Julius Bernard, *Reisehandbuch für das Königreich Bayern und die angrenzenden Länderstriche, besonders Tyrol und Salzkammergut mit besonderer Rücksicht auf Geschichte, Topographie, Handel und Gewerbe* (Stuttgart: Paul Gauger, 1868), 150.
[81] StAM, Kurverwaltung Bad Reichenhall, 273: "Badeprospekte, 1901–1934."
[82] Lisbeth Gooch Séguin Strahan, *Walks in Bavaria: An Autumn in the Country of the Passion-Play* (London: Alexander Strahan, 1884), 281.
[83] Caesar Schmidt, *Illustrirtes Wanderbuch für Südbayern und Salzkammergut* (Zurich: Verlag von Caesar Schimdt, 1892), 175.
[84] Alison F. Frank, "The Air Cure Town: Commodifying Mountain Air in Alpine Central Europe," *Central European History* 45, no. 2 (June 2012): 200.

Regent Luitpold formally renamed the town.[85] Still, its transformation into a modern spa had come with a price. The abolition of the Bavarian state's monopoly over the salt trade in 1868 and the subsequent decline of the local saline industry had made Reichenhall's residents increasingly dependent on tourism as a means of income.[86] This reflects a general trend among smaller tourist locales: the demise of one economic monoculture based on extraction led to the adoption of a new one based on hospitality. While the latter promised prosperity, it could also yield new forms of cultural anxiety and economic vulnerability.[87] In Bad Reichenhall, the expansion of the local tourism infrastructure contributed to a municipal debt that had reached 1.3 million marks by 1896.[88] Hoping to achieve financial stability, the local government appealed to Munich to be included in the ranks of the "Royal Baths." The state government granted this request in 1899, and Bad Reichenhall became an official Bavarian *Staatsbad*. Its growing financial problems became the concerns of the state, and the Bavarian Ministry of Finances was involved in decisions relating to local taxes, building projects, and the management of all spa institutions utilizing saline.

Bad Reichenhall's new status almost immediately bore fruit in the form of the Royal Cure House, or *Königliche Kurhaus*.[89] This impressive neo-baroque structure, a product of government investment, first opened its doors in May 1900.[90] Unlike the older spa facilities, this building was explicitly dedicated to recreation. It contained a large ballroom that could accommodate 1,500 guests, as well as a café-restaurant and various reading, music, billiard, and conversation rooms, all "tastefully-decorated," according to a local guidebook.[91] A memorandum published in Munich proudly detailed the amenities of the 450,000 mark building, including its electricity and plumbing.[92] The social center of Bad Reichenhall

[85] Stefan Kantsperger, "Die Entwicklung Reichenhalls zwischen 1890 und 1899: Der Weg vom Bad zum Staatsbad," in *Das Heilbad Bad Reichenhall im 19. und 20. Jahrhundert*, 60–61.

[86] Wysocki, *Leben im Berchtesgadener Land*, 65; Vogel, *Geschichte von Bad Reichenhall*, 75.

[87] Hal K. Rothman, *Devil's Bargains: Tourism in the Twentieth-Century American West* (Lawrence, KS: University Press of Kansas, 1998), 26–27. See also Krotz, *Tourists*, 177.

[88] Vogel, *Geschichte von Bad Reichenhall*, 71.

[89] Kantsperger, "Die Entwicklung Reichenhalls zwischen 1890 und 1899," 61–69.

[90] Thomas Fühl, "Von Klassizimus bis Neubarock," in *Kurstädte in Deutschland*, 84.

[91] Fritz Wiedemann, *Führer durch Bad Reichenhall und Umgebung mit Berchtesgaden und Salzburg* (Bad Reichenhall: M. Zugschwerdts Nachfolger, 1915), 40.

[92] *Das Königliche Kurhaus in Bad Reichenhall: Denkschrift zur Feier der Eröffnung* (Munich: Baugeschäft Heilmann & Littman, 1900), 1–2, 25.

subsequently shifted from Kuranstalt Axelmannstein to the new and emphatically modern Kurhaus, where members of elite society could indulge in pleasurable distractions, and distinguish themselves from those visitors focused on the cure.[93]

A Wealth of Remedies and Distractions

At the turn of the century, the Reichenhall spa culture was a combination of "the pleasant and the useful," a unique blend of Alpine views, urbane entertainment, and modern medicine that catered to both middle-class and elite tastes.[94] However, the Bavarian spa town faced serious competition not only from international health resorts like Vichy and Marienbad, but also from a number of fashionable resorts within the German Empire itself, including Baden-Baden, Wiesbaden, and Bad Kissingen. Each of these German spas had a particular claim to fame at the beginning of the twentieth century. For example, a 1903 guidebook for Baden-Baden emphasized the resort's picturesque environs, describing them as "one of the most beautiful and lovely spots on the planet, blessed by nature with lavish splendor."[95] Conversely, the self-promotion of Wiesbaden focused on the spa's natural environment *and* its cosmopolitan character. A local guidebook published in 1913 praised the resort's mild climate, its charming scenery and hiking opportunities, and finally, its secluded but vibrant urban character.[96] Elsewhere, the marketing of Bad Kissingen concentrated on its cosmopolitan clientele and its diverse social offerings. A 1905 Meyer's guidebook spoke of the Bavarian resort's "elegant amenities" and international clientele, who could enjoy billiards, concerts, promenades, and refined company in the resort's stylish facilities.[97]

Bad Reichenhall may have been a latecomer to the spa business, but its appeal was complex. Its claim to fame could not be reduced to a simple formula, and its marketing stressed nearly all of the elements

93 Pfisterer, *Bad Reichenhall in seiner bayerischen Geschichte*, 335; Lang, *Geschichte von Bad Reichenhall*, 638–639.
94 Frank, "The Pleasant and the Useful."
95 Carl Wilhelm Schnars, *Wild's Führer durch Baden-Baden und Umgebung* (Baden-Baden: Verlag der C. WILD'schen Hof-Buchhandlung, 1903), 1.
96 *Der Neue Fremdenführer durch Wiesbaden, Langenschwalbach, Schlangenbad und Umgebungen* (Wiesbaden: A. Menne Nachfolger, 1913), 7–8.
97 Meyers Reisebücher (Firm), *Süd-Deutschland* (Leipzig: Bibliographisches Institut, 1905), 82–83.

found in other German spas, but with a greater emphasis on the resort's modern and progressive character. Tourist propaganda in the early twentieth century epitomized this balanced marketing, promoting Bad Reichenhall's progressive treatments and medical facilities, while also appealing to luxury-seeking tourists and middle-class day-trippers in pursuit of a peaceful summer retreat. By offering a detailed analysis of the tourist propaganda between the turn of the century and World War I, this section provides a profile of Bad Reichenhall at the pinnacle of its success, before the upheaval of the early twentieth century changed it forever.

In describing the balanced medical and social cure of Bad Reichenhall, local tourist propaganda revolved around three central motifs: nature, modernness, and cosmopolitanism. Perhaps the most prominent of these three motifs was the spa's close relationship with the natural environment, which was the basis of multiple cures. For example, locals used mountain herbs like brooklime, watercress, and dandelions to produce an "herbal juice" (*Kräutersaft*), a novel treatment popularized by Mathias Mack.[98] Similarly, local dairy products were the basis of many popular drinking cures, including whey and kefir, a fermented milk drink. Even more important was the local saline, which patients could imbibe in a diluted or concentrated form, while a purgative solution produced from the former was available for both local consumption and exportation.[99] Saline was central to bathing cures as well, including diluted saline and carbonic acid baths, which were supposedly beneficial for those suffering from heart conditions and neurasthenia.[100]

Bad Reichenhall's saline springs also made the air itself a valuable remedy, producing a marine-like climate at an already advantageous, high altitude.[101] The spa enjoyed a reputation as "Germany's largest climatic health resort," where fresh mountain air helped to make the treatment of pulmonary disorders a specialty.[102] Tourist propaganda described the

---

[98] Wysocki, *Leben im Berchtesgadener Land*, 120; Lang, *Geschichte von Bad Reichenhall*, 600.

[99] Kurverein e.V. Bad Reichenhall, *Bad Reichenhall: Illustrierter Badprospekt des Kurortes* (1904), 62–63.

[100] Kurverein e.V. Bad Reichenhall, *Bad Reichenhall: Illustrierter Badprospekt des Kurortes* (1911), 19.

[101] See Frank, "The Air Cure Town."

[102] Wiedemann, *Führer durch Bad Reichenhall und Umgebung*, 5; HAT, Prospekte, D061/09/00//-45: *Bayerisches Verkehrsbuch: Bayern Rechts des Rheins* (Munich: Selbstverlag des Vereins zur Hebung des Fremdenverkehrs in München und im bayerischen Hochlande (e.V.), 1904), 79–80.

local air as the spa's "sovereign cure," most effectively administered in the *Gradierhaus*, a 170-meter long, open-ended wooden structure in the spa's large park, the *Kurgarten*. Within this structure, saline flowed through a densely stacked pile of twigs, facilitating an accelerated evaporation that simultaneously reduced the temperature and infused the air with beneficial saline particles, small quantities of iodine and bromine, and a considerable amount of ozone.[103] This simple technique, once used for concentrating the salt solution, was an effective means of commodifying Bad Reichenhall's most precious natural resource, and it caught the attention of the international and local press. A June 1901 issue of the British tourism magazine *The Traveller* declared: "Verily, the idea was a good one, and its practical application at Reichenhall has deservedly done much to give to the place that fame which it now enjoys ... providing the atmosphere of mid-Atlantic in an Alpine valley."[104] Even foreign publications emphasized the uniqueness of the Bavarian resort, helping to attract international guests in the process.

Nature had bestowed many gifts upon Bad Reichenhall, investing both water and air with alleged curative properties. Salt aside, the surrounding landscape itself possessed therapeutic potential. During the final decades of the nineteenth century, physicians speculated that bathing and inhalation treatments were insufficient means of restoring the health of many patients. They began to prescribe hiking, which if conducted properly, could contribute to the strengthening of heart muscles. This was the logic behind Dr. Max Joseph Oertel's "terrain cure," which entailed physical exercise, carefully prescribed walks, and the ascent of progressively steeper mountain trails. The Bad Reichenhall valley proved ideal for the program, as it featured long, flat stretches and a range of ascents.[105] In accordance with Oertel's guidelines, locals charted a special network of trails through the town's environs in 1886, with the steepest path providing an incline of 10 percent.[106] The terrain cure became a popular addition to the resort's growing lists of treatments, helping to blur the lines between Bad Reichenhall and the surrounding landscape.

[103] Kurverein e.V. Bad Reichenhall, *Bad Reichenhall: Illustrierter Badprospekt des Kurortes* (1904), 57, 59.

[104] StAM, Kurverwaltung Bad Reichenhall, 242: "Literatur und Pressestimmen, 1884–1908."

[105] Alexander, *Bad Reichenhall als klimatischer Kurort*, 8; Kurverein e.V. Bad Reichenhall, *Bad Reichenhall: Illustrierter Badprospekt des Kurortes* (1904), 67.

[106] Pfisterer, "Die frühe Entwicklung der Kurortmedizin und der Balneotherapie in Reichenhall," 163.

Historically, a stroll in the spa meant following the carefully manicured promenades of the town itself. Mathias Mack was the first to lead
guests into the mountainous surroundings of Reichenhall, inviting both
patients and tourists into the uncultivated wilderness and providing them
with information on local flora and fauna.[107] By the turn of the twentieth century, the natural environs of the spa were no longer simply a
"tamed and decorative" backdrop; they were the site of physical activity
that was central to the very notion of the cure.[108] Tourist propaganda
emphasized that there were over 200 kilometers of trails in the spa town
and its environs, while the local section of the German Alpine Association posted large-scale maps of these routes in the *Kurgarten* and at
the train station.[109] In his 1900 guidebook, Adolf Bühler pointed out
that the resort's numerous trails not only provided the opportunity to
enjoy the scenic landscape, but also constituted an essential component
of the larger cure experience, allowing the guest to comfortably exercise
out in the open, while methodically increasing the amount of physical
exertion.[110] This was a decidedly pragmatic understanding of the natural
environment that valued proximity to nature but ultimately lacked the
romantic sensibility of the earlier nineteenth century.

Still, Bad Reichenhall's close relationship with nature helped to ground
the health resort, offering an important balance to its more modern
dimensions. A 1904 Spa Association brochure reminded visitors: "One
must not remain in his or her room in Reichenhall; out into God's magnificent and beautiful nature!"[111] Nature was an essential element of the spa's
identity, from its surrounding mountains and valleys, to the green spaces
of the "grand garden city" itself.[112] Although it was not a planned organic
community like Hellerau in Dresden, Bad Reichenhall reflected the ultimate goal of the international garden city movement: "to enrich urban
life with the positive psycho-social characteristics attributed to living in

---

[107] Lang, *Geschichte von Bad Reichenhall*, 600.
[108] Geisthövel, "Promenadenmischungen, Raum und Kommunikation in Hydropolen,"
214.
[109] HAT, Prospekte, D061/09/00/l-45: *Bayerisches Verkehrsbuch: Bayern Rechts des
Rheins*, 80; Friedemann, *Führer durch Bad Reichenhall und Umgebung*, 141.
[110] Bühler, *Führer durch Bad Reichenhall, Salzburg & Berchtesgaden*, 14.
[111] Kurverein e.V. Bad Reichenhall, *Bad Reichenhall: Illustrierter Badprospekt des
Kurortes* (1904), 91.
[112] Guidebooks often highlighted Bad Reichenhall's parks and gardens as one of the
town's distinctive features. See HAT, Sachkatalog, BRU-65/BAYERN-12 . . . D061/09:
August Schupp, *Bayerisches Hochland mit Salzburg und angrenzendem Tirol*, 12th edn.
(Munich: A. Bruckmann's Verlag, 1907), 198–199; Kurverein e.V. Bad Reichenhall,
Bad Reichenhall: Illustrierter Badprospekt des Kurortes (1911), 13.

FIGURE 5. Postcard featuring Bad Reichenhall and its Alpine surroundings, undated. From the author's collection.

close contact with nature."[113] Postcards tended to picture Bad Reichenhall completely dominated by its natural surroundings, with the town engulfed in green and overshadowed by towering mountains.[114] These views were similar to nineteenth-century images of Franconian Switzerland: nature dwarfed civilization, but did not obscure it altogether. A 1904 guidebook published by a regional tourism association suggested that nature sheltered the spa town, as it was "pleasantly surrounded by marvelous mountains" providing "a lush perimeter" of "wild beauty."[115] Sublimely timeless, this wild perimeter stood beyond the "disenchanted" and "demystified" world of capitalism described by Max Weber, Siegfried Kracauer, and others.[116]

In Bad Reichenhall, the Alpine landscape became an attraction for both convalescents and tourists alike. A 1911 brochure in English published by the Spa Association declared:

[113] Maiken Umbach, *German Cities and Bourgeois Modernism, 1890–1924* (New York: Oxford University Press, 2009), 112–113.

[114] Author's Collection: "BAD REICHENHALL – Blick von der Villa Hessing auf Zwiesel und Staufen." The origins of this postcard are unknown, but it was dated June 28, 1911.

[115] HAT, Prospekte, D061/09/00//-45: *Bayerisches Verkehrsbuch: Bayern Rechts des Rheins*, 79.

[116] Weber, *The Protestant Ethic and the "Spirit" of Capitalism and Other Writings*, 13. See also Kracauer, "The Mass Ornament," in *The Mass Ornament*, 80–81.

Bad Reichenhall with its incomparable natural beauties offers a profusion of variety for excursions which no other spa in Germany can equal. For the bathing guests and tourists more than 250 kilometers of carefully kept promenades and forest walks have been laid out which are specially adapted for terrain cures. The roads around Bad Reichenhall for carriages and motor cars are the most beautiful in the Bavarian Highlands.[117]

Incomparable and unparalleled, the "natural beauties" around Reichenhall represented much more than just another category of cure. Paradoxically, it was modern technology in the form of the automobile that provided access to this pre-modern world. In addition to the scenic promenades and drives, the Spa Association advertised a number of outdoor sporting activities. "Carefully-trimmed" courts were open to visitors interested in playing tennis, while an equestrian path along the Saalach came highly recommended to guests who were fond of horseback riding. The 1911 guidebook also noted that local streams were perfect for trout-fishing, just as the nearby forests contained a variety of wild game for hunters.[118] Similarly, a 1904 example of the popular Woerl guidebook series noted that experienced mountain climbers had the opportunity to practice their craft in this beautiful locale, referred to as a "piece of paradise."[119] For this category of tourist, nature was central to the Bad Reichenhall experience.

The resort managed to draw even more visitors when it started to market itself as a winter travel destination shortly before World War I. Debate on this issue began in 1904, when the Association for the Promotion of Tourism in Munich and the Bavarian Highlands urged the local tourism industry to consider turning the resort into a venue for winter sports.[120] Five years later, a locally distributed brochure entitled "Is Bad Reichenhall Suited to be a Year-Round Tourist Destination?" concisely outlined the changes that would have to be implemented in order to extend the tourist season through the harsh Bavarian winter.[121] With blueprint in hand, several members of the local community built a new

---

[117] StAM, Kurverwaltung Bad Reichenhall, 269.

[118] Kurverein e.V. Bad Reichenhall, *Bad Reichenhall: Illustrierter Badprospekt des Kurortes* (1911), 39.

[119] Leo Woerl, *Führer durch Bad Reichenhall und Umgebung* (Leipzig: Woerl's Reise-bücherverlag, 1904), 5–6.

[120] StAM, Kurverwaltung Bad Reichenhall, 24: "Münchner Fremdenverkehrsverein, 1903–1928."

[121] StAM, Kurverwaltung Bad Reichenhall, 256: "Allgemeiner Charakter des Kurortes, 1890–1936."

level of infrastructure for another class of tourist.[122] A 1911 publication issued by the Spa Association proudly announced Bad Reichenhall's new identity as a "pleasant winter destination," where guests could enjoy the new sports of bobsledding and skiing before returning to their hotels with central heating.[123] The publication also advertised wildlife feeding areas, once more redirecting attention to the spa's natural surroundings, now covered with snow.[124] Bühler's 1915 guidebook likewise endorsed the resort's new season, asserting: "During the winter, Reichenhall is not only a recommended spot for those in need of rest and recovery, but also a rich source of stimulus for sports enthusiasts."[125]

Bad Reichenhall's special relationship with the natural environment was a central motif of early twentieth-century tourist propaganda, but it was connected to a second group of marketing claims that revolved around modernness in various incarnations. In one sense, the town that had burned to the ground in 1834 was inevitably modern. Rebuilt in line with nineteenth-century tastes, it was a model for city-planning, and guidebooks commonly referred to its "modern look."[126] Tourist maps showed a town that was not only dotted with "green" spots, but also crisscrossed with wide avenues and perpendicular intersections.[127] Other developments around the turn of the century helped to secure Bad Reichenhall's identity as a modern urban space. In 1890, an electric power plant opened in Kirchberg, allowing for the illumination of Reichenhall's streets. Two years later, Reichenhall acquired its first telephone. In 1898, the town opened its first movie theater and welcomed its first automobile, a 6-PS-Benzinwagen owned by a local physician, Karl von Heinleth. Four years later, tourists had the opportunity to rent a ten-seat, motor bus for daytrips into the mountains. Echoing older reservations about the railway, some locals expressed concern about the potentially dangerous effects of automobiles. In order to appease these locals, the government declared in 1905 that spa guests who wished to bring their car on vacation must first secure their permission.[128] Eight

[122]   Pfisterer, "Eine kleine Geschichte der Kurstadt Reichenhall (1850–1990)," 49.

[123]   For more on skiing as a modern sport, see Denning, "Alpine Modernism," 857–872.

[124]   StAM, Kurverwaltung Bad Reichenhall, 265: "Bücher, Zeitschriften, Reklame, 1900–1955."

[125]   Adolf Bühler, *Fremden-Führer durch Bad Reichenhall, Berchtesgaden, Salzburg und Lofer* (Bad Reichenhall: H. Bühler, 1915), 48.

[126]   HAT, Sachkatalog, BRU-65/BAYERN-12 . . . D061/09: Schupp, *Bayerisches Hochland mit Salzburg und angrenzendem Tirol*, 198–199.

[127]   Wiedemann, *Führer durch Bad Reichenhall und Umgebung*, 38.

[128]   Pfisterer, "Eine kleine Geschichte der Kurstadt Reichenhall (1850–1990)," 48–49.

years later, an article in the *Official Register of Guests* complained about the number of automobiles and bicycles in Bad Reichenhall, insisting that these modern inventions spread dust and the smell of gasoline, in addition to preventing people from enjoying the physical benefits of walking.[129] Once again, modern technology was compromising the appreciation of nature. Notwithstanding such complaints, the local community generally insisted on providing urban amenities to its cosmopolitan clientele, thus explaining the relatively early adoption of these forms of technology. As was the case in other Bavarian tourist locales, the rise of tourism in Bad Reichenhall fueled a unique form of modernization, and it did so in spite of antimodern sentiments.[130]

Tourist publications highlighted the many modern features of the idealized urban space of Bad Reichenhall, from the recently opened Royal Cure House, to the exquisitely clean asphalt roads illuminated by electric light.[131] While the 1904 Woerl guidebook called attention to the town's two power plants, which supplied most hotels with electric lighting, the *Illustrated Brochure* of 1904 directed attention to the town's waste management program and its new sewage system, created in line with "the most modern principles."[132] Another publication issued by the Spa Association in 1912 described the town's saline works as an impressive example of modern engineering, as well as a noteworthy tourist attraction. The brochure reported that the saline works pumped 400,000 liters of salt water to the *Gradierhaus* each day, in addition to noting that the interior of the spring building was "fabulously lit" in multi-colored electric light for all to see.[133] In his 1906 travelogue, American tourist Frank Roy Fraprie dedicated the majority of the Bad Reichenhall chapter to the saline works, augmenting his description with facts about the springs, their varying degrees of saltiness, and the engineering involved in their exploitation, including the construction of "an underground canal half a mile long and big enough to float a boat."[134] Like the rustic mills

[129] *Amtliche Fremdenliste für Bad Reichenhall* (Bad Reichenhall), May 27, 1913.

[130] Helena Waddy, *Oberammergau in the Nazi Era: The Fate of a Catholic Village in Hitler's Germany* (New York: Oxford University Press, 2010), 27–29; Hagen, *Preservation, Tourism and Nationalism*, 116, 145.

[131] StadtAM, Zeitgeschichtliche Sammlung, 117/1: "Fremdenverkehr Oberbayern, vor 1945."

[132] Woerl, *Führer durch Bad-Reichenhall und Umgebung*, 11; Kurverein e.V. Bad Reichenhall, *Bad Reichenhall: Illustrierter Badprospekt des Kurortes* (1904), 46.

[133] StAM, Kurverwaltung Bad Reichenhall, 265. See also Karl Baedeker, *Südbayern, Tirol, Salzburg, usw.* (Leipzig: Karl Baedeker, 1908), 101.

[134] Frank Roy Fraprie, *Little Pilgrimages Among Bavarian Inns* (Boston: L.C. Page & Company, 1906), 164.

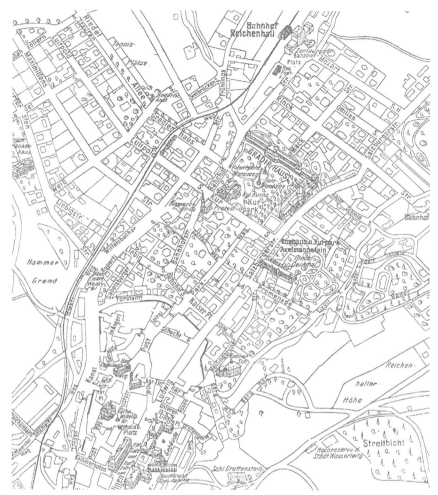

FIGURE 6. Map of Bad Reichenhall from Fritz Wiedemann's guidebook, 1915. From the author's collection.

of Franconian Switzerland, the saline works of Bad Reichenhall were a symbol of the local community's symbiosis with the natural environment. Like the factories of Augsburg discussed in the next chapter, the saline works were also an indication of progress. Simultaneously old and new, this Bad Reichenhall institution was a marketable example of grounded modernity, as it demonstrated how nature and technology could coexist.

Tourist propaganda similarly portrayed Bad Reichenhall's treatments as unequivocally modern. This emphasis distinguished the resort from nearby Alpine destinations like Berchtesgaden, which tended to rely more on their rustic character and sporting opportunities.[135] Physician Bruno Alexander portrayed the Bavarian resort's cure regimen as "truly in tune with the time," while the previously cited article in *The Traveller* depicted the spa as a "very progressive place," noting the simple ingenuity of the *Gradierhaus*, as well as the "fine needle-baths, steam and Russian vapor baths, douches, inhalations, gymnastics, massage and last, but not least, pneumatic rooms for treatment by compressed air."[136] The hermetically-sealed pneumatic chambers constructed by the Mack family, advertised as "the largest in the world," became a particularly popular selling point for the tourism industry.[137] Tourist publications explained how the technology functioned and identified the benefits that these chambers held for both the respiratory and cardiac systems.[138] A 1911 issue of *The Boston Medical and Surgical Journal* praised the new technology at Bad Reichenhall, declaring: "Patients suffering from asthma and chronic bronchitis claim great relief from daily treatments of this kind of one to two hours' duration."[139] Bühler's 1915 guidebook claimed that when it came to modern medicine, Bad Reichenhall "did not hold back," and was the first spa destination to recognize the curative potential of radium-heavy spring water.[140] In this case, Bad Reichenhall demonstrated how modern society might utilize natural resources in new ways. Other publications, like the 1904 *Illustrated Brochure*, underscored the novelty of the spa's electric baths, which allowed patients to subject portions of their bodies to controlled doses of electric light and elevated temperatures, a reportedly effective treatment for those suffering from rheumatism and neurasthenia.[141] The treatment of the latter became one of Bad Reichenhall's specialties during the early twentieth century.[142] As previously noted, this modernity-induced condition essentially paralyzed

[135] Wysocki, *Leben im Berchtesgadener Land*, 127.
[136] Alexander, *Bad Reichenhall als klimatischer Ort*, 8; StAM, Kurverwaltung Bad Reichenhall, 242.
[137] Ernst Platz, *Unser Bayerland*, hrsg. Vom Verein zur Förderung des Fremdenverkehrs in München und im bayerischen Hochland (Munich: Gerber, 1907), 14.
[138] Alexander, *Bad Reichenhall als klimatischer Ort*, 7.
[139] Horace Packard, "Bad Reichenhall: A Health Resort of Southern Germany," *The Boston Medical and Surgical Journal* 165, no. 1 (September 1911): 488.
[140] Bühler, *Fremden-Führer durch Bad Reichenhall, Berchtesgaden, Salzburg und Lofer*, 16, 19.
[141] Kurverein e.V. Bad Reichenhall, *Bad Reichenhall: Illustrierter Badprospekt des Kurortes* (1904), 65.
[142] Wiedemann, *Führer durch Bad Reichenhall und Umgebung*, 18; Packard, "Bad Reichenhall," 488.

FIGURE 7. Photo of a pneumatic chamber in Bad Reichenhall's official guidebook, 1912. From the author's collection.

its victims, making them incapable of coping with the pressures of the external world. Bad Reichenhall's electric baths promised to rejuvenate those suffering from neurasthenia, "shocking" them out of their powerlessness. This was a distinctly modern treatment for a distinctly modern ailment.

"Modern," "progressive," and "highly-developed"; these were phrases that defined Bad Reichenhall's cityscape, infrastructure, spa facilities, and treatments. By stressing these attributes within the tourist propaganda of the period, these authors indirectly made larger claims about the modernness of not only Bavaria, but Germany at large. In 1900, Bad Reichenhall was a small town, situated on the edge of a provincial region, within a nation-state that had existed for barely three decades. Consequently, claims to be modern could be seen as claims of equality with or even superiority over other regions and nations of Europe. Bad Reichenhall had grown dramatically over the course of a few decades, and its recent ability to compete with well-established resorts like Vichy or Marienbad symbolized the potential of both the German Empire and the Kingdom of Bavaria. Natural resources and impressive landscapes established a deeper identity that transcended the present day, but they coexisted with an architectural, technological, and scientific modernity that implied progress for town, region, and nation alike. Tourist publications corroborated this image by praising the extraordinary features of the Bavarian resort, and explicitly comparing them to those found in other resorts. For example, Wiedemann's 1915 guidebook contended that no other spa, in Germany or elsewhere, could compete with Bad Reichenhall's exceptional diversity of medical treatments and facilities.[143]

Since such claims could be construed as declarations of regional or national exceptionalism, it is important to note that overtly patriotic sentiments were virtually nonexistent within the prewar tourist propaganda. One reason for this was the fact that Bad Reichenhall lay only a few kilometers away from the Austro-Hungarian Empire. In fact, a short hike over the wooded Kirchholz east of town led vistors to the Bavarian village of Bayerich Gmain, separated by a narrow stream from the Austrian town of Großgmain. Such close proximity to the Habsburg lands demonstrated the somewhat arbitrary nature of national boundaries, in addition to ensuring that tourist propaganda rarely advertised the health resort as exclusively Bavarian or German. In fact, guidebooks usually incorporated Bad Reichenhall into a larger tourist region that included destinations on both sides of the border. For example, guidebooks on the Austrian Tirol and Salzburg, such as the 1907 Geuther guide to the Salzkammergut, regularly featured information on the Bavarian spa.[144] Similarly, guidebooks published in Bavaria and even Bad Reichenhall itself often covered nearby Austrian tourist attractions.[145] These publications confirmed that the Bavarian spa was neither a distinctly German destination, nor a destination visited exclusively by Germans (or German speakers).

Its inclusion in a unified Alpine tourist region certainly contributed to the spa's international character, but it was ultimately the clientele, and not the geography, that secured Bad Reichenhall's cosmopolitan reputation. By the late nineteenth century, international visitors had become

---

[143] Wiedemann, *Führer durch Bad Reichenhall und Umgebung*, 17.

[144] HAT, Sachkatalog, GEU-207/SALZKAMMERGUT-6...A26: Geuthers Reiseführer (Firm), *Salzkammergut und Salzburg*, 6th edn. (Leipzig: Karl P. Geuthers Reiseführerverlag, 1913), 165.

[145] See Theodor Trautwein, *Das Bairische Hochland mit dem Allgäu, das angrenzende Tirol und Salzburg nebst Salzkammergut*, 6th edn. (Augsburg: Lampart, 1893); Adolf Bühler, *Führer durch Bad Reichenhall, Salzburg & Berchtesgaden*, 21st edn. (Bad Reichenhall, 1900); August Schupp, *Bayerisches Hochland mit Salzburg und angrenzendem Tirol*, 12th edn. (Munich, 1907); Wiedemann, *Führer durch Bad Reichenhall und Umgebung* (Bad Reichenhall, 1915); Adolf Bühler, *Fremden-Führer durch Bad Reichenhall, Berchtesgaden, Salzburg und Lofer* (Bad Reichenhall, 1915).

a fixture of many modern spas, even if "international" simply implied European.[146] This was the case in Bad Reichenhall, where Russian, Hungarian, and even American guests became part of the spa's larger profile. In addition to targeting international visitors by issuing publications in English, French, and Russian translations, the Bad Reichenhall tourism industry used this clientele as part of its marketing strategy.[147] A 1907 guidebook published by the Association for the Promotion of Tourism in Munich and the Bavarian Highland underscored this cosmopolitanism in its description of Bad Reichenhall:

[W]henever the lavish splendor and wealth of the elegant world is displayed among the sounds of the *Kurmusik*, whenever members of the international community go strolling along carefully-groomed paths under tall trees, whenever our ears detect conversation in multiple languages, then we realize anew that we are vacationing in a world spa.[148]

The visible affluence of the international elite and the melody of up to ten different languages became tangible symbols of Bad Reichenhall's cosmopolitan character.[149] A 1904 publication described the "colorful and captivating image" of evenings in the Royal Cure House, where international guests possessing "exotic beauty" and "famous names" socialized under the glow of electric light.[150] An August 1908 article in the *Neues Münchener Tagblatt* echoed this marketing, reporting that "the most beautifully-situated spa destination in Germany" annually served as a "playground" for countless guests from all over Europe and numerous exotic locales.[151] While amusing themselves under the tall trees and electric light of Bad Reichenhall, these foreign guests came into contact with an idealized version of the present, a grounded modernity available for their consumption.

What did a status as a cosmopolitan resort mean for the town of Bad Reichenhall itself? In short, diversity implied independence from local, regional, and national affiliations. With the help of its international

---

[146] Sommer, *Zur Kur nach Ems*, 221–223. See also Geisthövel, "Promenadenmischungen, Raum und Kommunikation in Hydropolen," 206, 226; Lempa, "Emotional Economy and Social Classes in Nineteenth-Century Pyrmont," 41; Mann, *The Magic Mountain*, 68–72.

[147] StAM, Kurverwaltung Bad Reichenhall, 273: "Badeprospekte, 1901–1934."

[148] Platz, *Unser Bayerland*, 14.

[149] Lang, *Geschichte von Bad Reichenhall*, 649.

[150] Kurverein e.V. Bad Reichenhall, *Bad Reichenhall: Illustrierter Badprospekt des Kurortes* (1904), 79.

[151] *Neues Münchener Tagblatt* (Munich), August 25, 1908.

patrons, Bad Reichenhall transcended Upper Bavarian and German identities. It was an idyllic destination that now "belonged to the world,"
as Ludwig Steub noted in 1862, but it was not the only German location to embrace a cosmopolitan identity.[152] As historian Glenn Penny
has noted in his work on Leipzig's ethnographic museum, "local interests
and cosmopolitan visions continued to play dominant roles in the ways
Germans conceived of themselves right into the twentieth century."[153] In
Bad Reichenhall, a cosmopolitan and "world-famous" status served as
evidence of progress and a cornerstone of its modern status.[154]

Bad Reichenhall's international clientele was an integral part of its
larger image, and tourist publications encouraged the cosmopolitan clientele to settle for nothing less than "excellent" accommodations in Bad
Reichenhall. Hans Scheurer's guidebook offered an especially flattering
endorsement of the facilities, insisting that guests from all countries would
find themselves in a "distinguished, but comfortable" establishment.[155]
While some publications stressed the first-class nature of Bad Reichenhall's accommodations, a 1914 article in a local newspaper warned
against characterizing the town's facilities as luxurious, emphasizing
that these institutions existed first and foremost for "genuinely sick
people."[156] Similarly, advertisements in the back pages of the *Register
of Guests* seemed to appeal to at least two different types of guest. For
instance, the Restaurant in the Hotel Luisenbad advertised "first-class
service" and "all of the delicacies of the season," including lobster and
caviar, while the management of the Hotel Forst announced the availabil-
ity of an "elegant automobile" for tours within the country and beyond
its borders. On the other hand, the Kuranstalt Viktoriabad limited its
advertisement to a list of medical treatments, ranging from more traditional bathing and inhalation regimens to pneumatic chambers and a
"Radium-Emanatorium."[157]

---

[152] Steub, *Wanderungen in bayerischen Gebirg*, 201.

[153] Glenn Penny, "Fashioning Local Identities in an Age of Nation-Building: Museums,
Cosmopolitan Visions, and Intra-German Competition," *German History* 17, no. 4
(October 1999): 490.

[154] In his 1908 guidebook on Bad Reichenhall, Scheurer uses the phrase "world famous"
three times in six pages, referring to the town itself, the pneumatic chambers, and the
local saline springs. Scheurer, *Führer durch den Chiemgau*, 160–166.

[155] Ibid., 165–166.

[156] StAM, Kurverwaltung Bad Reichenhall, 276: "Das Wochenblatt 'Der Untersberg,'
1914." *Der Untersberg: Bad Reichenhaller Wochenblatt* (Bad Reichenhall), May 16,
1914.

[157] *Amtliche Fremdenliste für Bad Reichenhall* (Bad Reichenhall), August 30, 1913, June
17, 1913, May 31, 1913.

From the international elite to the nervous and incurable, Bad Reichenhall catered to a variety of guests whose experiences did not necessarily overlap. It had the amenities of a luxury spa and a Spartan health resort, but it also appealed to those in search of a *Sommerfrische*. A 1913 local advertisement for excursions to the Schafberg in Salzkammergut promised the "cheapest and most worthwhile" day trip, thus appealing to middle-class tourists in search of more frugal activities.[158] A letter published in a 1908 edition of the *Wiener Hausfrau-Zeitung* celebrated the simplicity and unpretentiousness of Bad Reichenhall, which was "in fact not a spa, but a *Sommerfrische*, made up of beautiful walkways interspersed with villas, while the 'cure' seems to exist only as a justification for rest between these strolls."[159] In addition to confirming the resort's status as a *Sommerfrische*, this letter suggests that physical activity had become such a prominent feature of the spa experience that guests now needed medical treatment as a "justification for rest." Sarcasm aside, Bad Reichenhall offered its guests a variety of activities and experiences, and some were clearly more provincial than those found in larger urban centers. For example, locals organized exhibitions of Upper Bavarian customs and costumes, thus preserving and commodifying regional identity for their cosmopolitan guests.[160] After learning something about this identity, tourists could literally buy it in the form of souvenirs and regional costumes, or *Tracht*, available at a local shop owned by K.F. Eckhardt.[161] The commodification of peasant culture continued with the 1912 opening of the "Reichenhall Country Theater," a group that regularly performed classic folk comedies, dramas, and tragedies.[162] This was all part and parcel of Bad Reichenhall's vision of grounded modernity, a heterogeneous world in which small-town traditions coexisted with big-city innovations, and *Lederhosen* coexisted with lobster.

Bad Reichenhall could appeal to the elite, the ill, and the economical. By the beginning of the twentieth century, Bad Reichenhall could even appeal to visitors of different faiths. Although Upper Bavaria was a traditionally Catholic region, the local community worked to ensure that religion did not impede tourism. A local government publication in 1893 confirmed that it was in the best interests of the tourism industry to propagate a cosmopolitan identity; the nationality and the religious affiliation

---

[158] Ibid. September 7, 1913.
[159] *Wiener Hausfrau-Zeitung: Organ für hauswirtschaftliche Interessen* (Vienna), July 19, 1908.
[160] Wysocki, *Leben im Berchtesgadener Land*, 163–164.
[161] *Amtliche Fremdenliste für Bad Reichenhall* (Bad Reichenhall), August 2, 1913.
[162] Lang, *Geschichte von Bad Reichenhall*, 649.

of the guest should never be an issue. Not only did the Bad Reichenhall community refuse to discriminate against non-Catholic guests, they even invited them to continue their religious practices during their extended stays. Although the town contained only two Protestant residents in 1846, Prussian and Franconian travelers were increasingly common, and at least one-third of all visitors were Lutheran. With the help of Ernst Rinck and local doctor Adolf Schmid, Protestant guests contributed to the construction of a neo-gothic church in 1881, creating a space for weekly services during the tourist season.[163] Flyers printed by the Beautification Society around the turn of the century confirmed the existence of the Protestant church, providing guests with information on its location and services.[164]

Religious tolerance for the sake of tourism did not make Bad Reichenhall unique, and the construction of churches for foreign guests was fairly common in larger health resorts, even in predominantly Catholic regions.[165] More noteworthy is the fact that the Reichenhall tourism industry accommodated its many Jewish guests during this period. Woerl's 1904 guidebook publicized two restaurants offering kosher food, as well as weekly religious services in their respective "prayer rooms."[166] The 1904 *Illustrated Brochure* contained separate advertisements for both the *Israelitisches Restaurant Bermann* and the *Israelitisches Hotel und Pension National*, one of the town's oldest and largest restaurants.[167] Bad Reichenhall even featured a Jewish slaughterhouse, and in 1877, the émigré Jewish community began plans for the construction of their own cemetery.[168] This émigré community featured some of Bad Reichenhall's most prominent citizens, including several practicing physicians, as well as the owners of the Louisenbad and the town's largest department store.[169]

---

[163] Vogel, *Geschichte von Bad Reichenhall*, 72–73; Lang, *Geschichte von Bad Reichenhall*, 612; StAM, Kurverwaltung Bad Reichenhall, 8: "Kirchen- und Religionssachen, 1873–1938."

[164] StAM, Kurverwaltung Bad Reichenhall, 273.

[165] Steinhauser, "Das europäische Modebad des 19. Jahrhunderts," 106.

[166] Woerl, *Führer durch Bad-Reichenhall und Umgebung*, 12, 16.

[167] Kurverein e.V. Bad Reichenhall, *Bad Reichenhall: Illustrierter Badprospekt des Kurortes* (1904), 29, 43.

[168] Lang, *Geschichte von Bad Reichenhall*, 614, 618. For more on the Jewish spa experience, see Sommer, *Zur Kur nach Ems*, 328; Frank Bajohr, *"Unser Hotel ist judenfrei": Bäder-Antisemitismus im 19. und 20. Jahrhundert* (Frankfurt am Main: Fischer, 2003), 11–52; Miriam Triendl-Zadoff, *Nächstes Jahr in Marienbad. Gegenwelten jüdischer Kulturen der Moderne* (Göttingen: Vandenhoeck & Ruprecht, 2007).

[169] Johannes Lang, "Vom 'Judenbad' zum 'judenfreien' Staatsbad: Jüdische Kurtradition und Bäderantisemitismus in Bad Reichenhall," *Jahrbuch des Nürnberger Instituts für NS-Forschung und jüdische Geschichte des 20. Jahrhunderts* (2014): 137, 144.

Clearly, the Catholic identity of Upper Bavaria did not preclude the spa's cosmopolitan status, and on the eve of World War I, the spa even welcomed several Muslim princes.[170] Tourism appeared to promote a brand of tolerance that was especially remarkable in the early twentieth century.

Nature, modernness, cosmopolitanism; the three motifs which dominated the tourist propaganda on Bad Reichenhall were all part of this tourist attraction's larger character. By blending these appeals, the local tourism industry responded to the disorienting experience of modernity with a vision of what could be. While it is difficult to assess the reception of these messages among the tourists themselves, the success of Bad Reichenhall's marketing can be verified on another level. Simply put, tourists voted with their feet, and statistics assembled by the spa commissioner confirm that thousands of visitors chose Bad Reichenhall during the years before the Great War. While numbers did not rise every year, being somewhat susceptible to international crises, they increased by over 35 percent between 1900 and 1913, from 11,350 to 15,447.[171] Furthermore, in 1913, only 2,479 of 15,447 guests were Bavarian, and only 5,076 were from other parts of Germany; 5,799 had traveled from Austria-Hungary, 1,473 from Russia, and 137 from America. The resort registered 7,892 foreign guests during the year before the war, over half of the total figure.[172] In 1914, the town's identity as an international spa was undeniable, even though some locals did voice concerns that the tourism industry was relying too heavily on visitors from Eastern and Southern Europe.[173] The Great War vindicated these concerns, exposing Bad Reichenhall to a much more destructive side of modernity.

Total War and the Nationalized Cure

On the eve of World War I, the community of Bad Reichenhall could proudly advertise itself as a success story. In a matter of decades, the sleepy saline town had developed into a modern and cosmopolitan tourist destination, widely renowned as the "Queen of the German Alpine Baths" and "Germany's largest climatic resort." However, this success had come

---

[170] Lang, *Geschichte von Bad Reichenhall,* 618.
[171] The season, or "year," ran from April 1 to March 31. It should also be noted that these figures only reflect those guests who stayed overnight, and not the number of overnight stays themselves, or the number of those who stayed for less than a day, visitors known as *Passanten.*
[172] StAM, Kurverwaltung Bad Reichenhall, 286: "Fremdenverkehr, 1854–1936."
[173] Lang, *Geschichte von Bad Reichenhall,* 657.

with a price. The rapid expansion of the spa and hospitality industries had made the local community dependent on tourism as a source of income. This left them vulnerable when tourism declined as a result of recession or international crisis, like when the number of guests dropped by 55 percent during the Austro-Prussian War of 1866.[174] Four decades later, Fritz Söllner, mayor of Bad Reichenhall from 1900–1926, was forced to admit: "Without the spa, we are a poor mountain town, without trade, without change, without traffic, without a hinterland."[175] In spite of this realization, the municipal government remained fixated on the tourism industry. Their extensive investment in urban infrastructure, including the improvement of roadways and sanitation, contributed to a debt that had reached 2.6 million marks by 1909.[176] Many Bad Reichenhall inhabitants began to realize that tourism was a "devil's bargain"; it had promised economic vitality, but had led to a number of "unanticipated and irreversible consequences."[177]

The Great War revealed the depth of these problems. In addition to exacerbating the city's financial predicament, the war cut the destination off from its international clientele, just as nationalist jargon was employed to convert the town's modern facilities into cheap sick bays for German soldiers. The medicalization that had gained momentum during the previous century was essentially completed. Ironically, it was the presence of these wounded soldiers that kept the community afloat, a development ominously foreshadowed by the opening of a military convalescence home in 1913.[178] In the meantime, Bad Reichenhall became even more secluded. Like wartime Franconian Switzerland, it also became a quieter place, abandoned by both tourists and a large portion of its male population.[179]

A dearth of reliable sources makes it difficult to ascertain how the citizens of Bad Reichenhall initially reacted to the outbreak of war. Local

---

[174] Ibid., 622, 626.

[175] Quoted in Ibid., 644.

[176] Karl Leinberger, *Der Fremdenverkehr in Bad Reichenhall, seine Grundlagen, seine Entwicklung und seine Wirkungen* (Bad Reichenhall, 1923), 99–100; Vogel, *Geschichte von Bad Reichenhall*, 71.

[177] Rothman, *Devil's Bargains*, 10–11.

[178] Pfisterer, *Bad Reichenhall in seiner bayerischen Geschichte*, 340; StAM, Kurverwaltung Bad Reichenhall, 836: "Errichtung und Betrieb eines Militär-Erholungsheimes in Bad Reichenhall, 1911–1932."

[179] Schottky, *Geschichte des Fränkische-Schweiz-Vereins*, 58. For a similar situation in Freiburg, see Roger Chickering, *Great War and Urban Life in Germany: Freiburg, 1914–1918* (New York: Cambridge University Press, 2007), 68–69, 112–113.

historian Herbert Pfisterer claims that the August 1914 declaration of war unleashed an "abundance of national sentiment and an inexplicable outburst of excitement" in Bad Reichenhall.[180] Additional research casts doubt upon such a conclusion, with one historian in particular arguing that news of mobilization was greeted with "despondency and pessimism" in rural Bavaria.[181] Reactions in Bad Reichenhall probably varied, but one thing is certain: the impact on the tourism industry was profound. As tensions escalated between Austria-Hungary and Serbia in July 1914, foreign guests began to flee the Bavarian resort by the hundreds. Those that remained desperately tried to stay in touch with family and friends at home, and the local post office struggled to process thousands of telegrams. Once the war officially began, many tourists and locals reacted with panic, stocking up on provisions and rushing to the local bank in order to exchange paper currencies for gold coins. Communications via telephone and telegram quickly broke down as a result of overwhelming demand and inadequate manpower. While many panicked, others paraded. On August 4, a crowd of Bad Reichenhall residents demonstrated their support for the war effort by accompanying the first 200 local recruits to the train station.[182] Thus began the exodus of the community's young, male workforce, leaving women behind to manage the various hotels, inns, and bathing facilities.

In spite of the initial hysteria, Bad Reichenhall still hosted over 200 Russian citizens and several Serbians in late August, 1914.[183] However, the government no longer viewed these foreign nationals as "vacationers," but instead as "heteronomous objects of the German bureaucracy," liable to be interned in special camps for "enemy aliens."[184] Although the tourism industry took measures to ensure that international guests were accommodated until they could be safely transported home, a climate of suspicion and apprehension quickly took hold. Fear of espionage led to fights between locals and foreigners, increased surveillance of

---

[180] Pfisterer, *Bad Reichenhall in seiner bayerischen Geschichte*, 341.

[181] Jeffrey Verhey, *The Spirit of 1914: Militarism, Myth, and Mobilization in Germany* (New York: Cambridge University Press, 2000), 38–71; Benjamin Ziemann, *War Experiences in Rural Germany, 1914–1923*, trans. Alex Skinner (New York: Berg, 2007), 19.

[182] Lang, *Geschichte von Bad Reichenhall*, 661–669.

[183] StAM, Kurverwaltung Bad Reichenhall, 248: "1. Weltkrieg 1914–1918, 1914–1920."

[184] Christoph Jahr, "Keine Feriengäste 'Feindstaatenausländer' im südlichen Bayern während des Ersten Weltkriegs," in *Der Erste Welkrieg im Alpenraum. Erfahrung, Deutung, Erinnerung,* ed. Hermann J.W. Kuprian and Oswald Uberegger (Innsbruck: Wagner, 2006), 233.

international guests, and the mandate that telephone conversations could only be held in German. Russian guests in particular were treated with open contempt: they were not allowed to receive mail or money transfers, and were forced to rely on massively devalued rubles to pay their hotel and medical bills. Any display of wealth or Russian identity in general aroused hostility among the locals. This new hatred was so profound that the proprietor of the local hotel, the "Russian Court," promptly changed the name of the Reichenhall institution to the "German Court." The guests who had until so recently defined the resort were no longer welcome, as aggressive nationalism eclipsed long-established habits of hospitality. Before conditions could deteriorate further, the vast majority of Russian guests were transported to neutral Switzerland in mid August.[185]

In spite of the departure of foreign guests, local authorities sought to ensure that the tourism industry remained in operation. On August 26, 1914, the state spa commissioner contacted the various spa institutions to confirm their operation during the war. Some replied promptly that they remained fully operational, while others promised to stay open until October and provide their patients with the "entire cure." Others, like the Dianabad, admitted that they would be forced to close as soon as their last guest left, since so many of their male workers had been called to the front. This regrettable turn of events, however, did not stop the last institution from ensuring that its facilities would be made available to convalescing soldiers. Similarly, on September 11, the Bad Reichenhall Sanatorium announced that it would provide medical treatment and accommodations to recovering army officers for five marks per day (not including beverages). Just over a week later, the Josef Mack Firm, Reichenhall's leading manufacturer of saline by-products and spa paraphernalia, announced that it would provide saline bath tablets at reduced rates to the military hospital in Munich.[186]

During the early months of the war, charity became a means of uniting local communities in support of both the soldiers and the nation itself.[187] In both Franconian Switzerland and Bad Reichenhall, various organizations appealed to the "spirit of 1914" in order to secure accommodations for members of the German military and their families.[188] In Bad

[185] Lang, *Geschichte von Bad Reichenhall*, 670–674.
[186] StAM, Kurverwaltung Bad Reichenhall, 248.
[187] Verhey, *The Spirit of 1914*, 105–106.
[188] Schottky, *Geschichte des Fränkische-Schweiz-Vereins*, 58–59.

Reichenhall, a December 1914 issue of the local newspaper announced the imminent return of "thousands and thousands" of German sons, fathers, cousins, and brothers, whose suffering on the battlefield was a direct consequence of their commitment to the "fatherland." An appeal for sympathy then transitioned into a demand for unity: "The call of the fatherland falls on those of us in the German health resorts, endowed with invaluable sources of recuperation and rejuvenation in their effervescent medicinal springs, their mild air, their green forests, and sunny heights. It is our duty to assist in the providing of care."[189] "Love of the fatherland," the "most fundamental and transcendent of civic virtues," ensured that it was the obligation of spa proprietors to provide for their countrymen.[190] Similar language was employed by regional organizations. A 1916 communiqué distributed by the Association for the Promotion of Tourism in Munich and the Bavarian Highlands announced the creation of the Organization for Spa Treatment, noting: "The cooperation of the local organizations as well as individuals in the realization of the organization...is a patriotic duty."[191] Participation in this new organization, established to ensure suitable and reasonable accommodations for "cure-worthy" soldiers in Bavarian spa destinations, became representative of a deeper commitment to a collective, national victory.

Jingoist language was only one factor pushing Bad Reichenhall down this road; government policy was another. Although various organizations had compelled the local tourism industry to offer reduced rates to German soldiers, it was not initially mandatory. In fact, in December 1914 the spa commissioner informed the Imperial Ministry of Finance that it was doubtful that Bad Reichenhall's hotel and spa proprietors would be able to offer reduced rates to all members of the German military, especially since most of these establishments were privately owned. On the eve of the 1915 season, the commissioner contacted the management of other German spa resorts in order to ascertain what measures they had taken to accommodate soldiers. The administrations of Bad Homburg and Bad Kreuznach responded that they had suspended the cure tax for convalescing soldiers and officers and reduced prices for treatments by up to 50 percent, while the management of Bad Ems and Bad Oeynhausen reported that they were offering spa treatments at absolutely no

---

[189] StAM, Kurverwaltung Bad Reichenhall, 248.

[190] Chickering, *The Great War and Urban Life in Germany*, 352.

[191] StAM, Kurverwaltung Bad Reichenhall, 247: "Fonds zur Errichtung eines Sänger-heimes in Bad Reichenhall, 1911–1919."

cost. Before Bad Reichenhall could follow these examples, the Bavarian government took the initiative and instituted a policy. In April 1915, the Royal Ministry of Finance proclaimed that all members of the German armed forces (as well as the Austro-Hungarian military) were no longer obligated to pay cure taxes, in addition to being entitled to a standard 40 percent reduction in the price of spa treatments.[192] That summer, a flyer distributed throughout Bad Reichenhall confirmed the new policies, announcing that the owners of the spa facilities had agreed on a standard reduced rate for soldiers, while "combatants are not obliged to pay the cure tax... family members and others enjoy the same privilege, if they are in the company of a sick or wounded soldier there for treatment."[193] Compelled by both a sense of patriotic duty and the dictates of the state, the Bad Reichenhall community followed a course of action that ultimately kept the tourism industry alive, while significantly limiting the amount of profit earned.

Indeed, much of the profit the tourism industry was accustomed to earning had disappeared along with most of its clientele in the fall of 1914, when the war closed borders across Europe. The Spa Association had anticipated this in September, when they appealed to the Bavarian government for subsidies to complete Bad Reichenhall's transformation into a year-round tourist destination.[194] One year later, Mayor Fritz Söllner confirmed that the town's economic well-being was in serious jeopardy, largely because of its location on the border of the empire. As noted before, a significant percentage of the spa's clientele regularly visited from Austria-Hungary, Russia, and the Balkan states, parts of Europe that were now cut off from Germany as a result of official bans on travel and other ramifications of war.[195] Statistics gathered between 1914 and 1918 confirm an initial decrease in visitors followed by a phase of partial recovery. Between April 1, 1914 and March 31, 1915, 11,514 guests were registered in Reichenhall's hotels and inns, a noticeable decrease

---

[192] StAM, Kurverwaltung Bad Reichenhall, 249: "Vergünstigungen für Kriegsteilnehmer des 1. Weltkriegs, 1914–1922."

[193] StAM, Kurverwaltung Bad Reichenhall, 248. A 1915 publication issued by the Association for the Promotion of Tourism in Munich and the Bavarian Highland listed Bad Reichenhall among the many resorts where special rates were available for soldiers. HAT, Sachkatalog, D061/09/01/915/VER: *München, Die Kurorte, Sommerfrischen und Gaststätten im Bayerischen Hochland. Kriegsausgabe*, 3rd edn. (Munich: Verein zur Förderung des Fremdenverkehrs in München und im Bayrischen Hochland (e.V.), 1915), 108–111.

[194] Lang, *Geschichte von Bad Reichenhall*, 674.

[195] StAM, Kurverwaltung Bad Reichenhall, 248.

from the previous season's 15,447. Numbers dropped to 6,570 in 1915 before rising to 8,726 in 1916, and leveling off at 8,398 in 1917. As might be expected, most guests during this period were German soldiers suffering from both physical wounds and shattered nerves.[196] The number of visitors from Austria-Hungary decreased from 4,140 in 1914, to 928 in 1918, while visitors from America, England, France, and Belgium were virtually non-existent. Surprisingly, the Russian Empire was represented with an impressive three visitors per season in 1916 and 1917. This figure does not include Russian prisoners of war interned in Bad Reichenhall during the war, "visitors" that reportedly enjoyed considerable freedom and were particularly fond of the *Kurmusik*.[197]

As the number of guests fluctuated during the course of the war, the face of the clientele shifted dramatically from the prewar norm. The cosmopolitan elite were now replaced by the convalescing, uniformed masses of the German army, who were promised the same amenities as the earlier clientele, including progressive treatments and facilities, as well as "all the comforts of an international spa."[198] As early as 1915, the German Spa Association acknowledged the potentially awkward pairing of patrons in many of the nation's spas by appealing to the patriotic sensibilities of the remaining normal guests:

We appeal to you all, German men and women, who are able to sojourn in peace and comfort in German spas, because your German brothers stand before hardship and death ... in order to watch over you. Open your hearts and hands, so that these men can hopefully be privy to the blessing of convalescence among us. God will reward you, for what you have done for your brothers![199]

Potential tension between the new and old clientele in Bad Reichenhall was a minor problem in the larger scheme of things; providing sustenance for guests proved to be a much more serious issue as the war progressed. Although southern Bavaria was a "classical farming region" where agriculture occupied over half of the working population outside of Munich, its urban communities were especially hard hit by food shortages after 1914. Disruptions in the supply of animal feed and artificial fertilizers caused by the Allied blockade caused crop yields to plummet, and the

---

[196] See Paul Frederick Lerner, *Hysterical Men: War, Psychiatry, and the Politics of Trauma in Germany, 1890–1930* (New York: Cornell University Press, 2003): 40–60.
[197] *Münchner Neueste Nachrichten* (Munich), May 7, 1915.
[198] HAT, Sachkatalog, D061/09/01/915/VER: *München, Die Kurorte, Sommerfrischen und Gaststätten im Bayerischen Hochland. Kriegsausgabe*, 108.
[199] StAM, Kurverwaltung Bad Reichenhall, 838: "Bäderfürsorge für Kriegsteilnehmer, 1915–1919."

situation only worsened during the "turnip winter" of 1916–1917.[200] While residents and visitors in rural communities like Rothenburg ob der Tauber managed to remain relatively well-fed, city-dwellers faced the most severe food crisis in close to a hundred years.[201] Daily scarcities of basic foodstuffs became an omnipresent reminder of the Great War, and ultimately contributed to the collapse of the German war effort.[202]

In Bad Reichenhall, these widespread shortages became a huge obstacle for the tourism industry on two levels: the local community now had to provide for its remaining guests *and* deal with the repercussions of bad press. For example, the *Dresdner Anzeiger* reported during the summer of 1915 that German visitors to Bavaria should consider importing food from home, as local communities were having difficulties procuring sufficient amounts.[203] Subsequent reports from Franconian Switzerland confirmed that the local authorities were refusing to issue ration cards to tourists, who were advised to bring their own bread.[204] In an effort to improve the region's image, the Association for the Promotion of Tourism in Munich and the Bavarian Highlands posted a notice in newspapers across Germany assuring potential visitors that the supply of bread in Bavaria was regulated along the same lines as it was in other regions of the country.[205] The situation seemed more serious a year later, when a June 1916 issue of the *Bayerische Staatszeitung* declared: "In Bavaria, the distribution of important food stuffs, most notably meat and butter, is carefully regulated and severely limited in every local municipality." Fresh milk was only obtainable with the appropriate documentation, while butter was only available to guests during "meat-less" Tuesdays and Fridays. Meat was only provided to tourists in limited amounts, just as watered-down beer (*Dünnbier*) was only obtainable during specific hours at restaurants.[206] In Bad Reichenhall, the local government took costly measures to provide for both locals and visitors, securing cheap

---

[200] Ziemann, *War Experiences in Rural Germany*, 15–16, 166–168.

[201] Hagen, *Preservation, Tourism and Nationalism*, 147.

[202] Chickering, *The Great War and Urban Life in Germany*, 217; Thierry Bonzon and Belinda Davis, "Feeding the Cities," in *Capital Cities at War: Paris, London, Berlin 1914–1919*, ed. Jay Winter and Jean-Louis Robert (New York: Cambridge University Press, 1997), 308, 311.

[203] *Dresdner Anzeiger* (Dresden), June 16, 1915.

[204] Schottky, *Geschichte des Fränkische-Schweiz-Vereins*, 59.

[205] HAT, ZSF, 072: "Mitteilungen des Vereins zur Förderung des Fremdenverkehrs in München und im bayrischen Hochland (e.V.), 1907–1920."

[206] StAM, Kurverwaltung Bad Reichenhall, 248. *Bayerische Staatszeitung. Kgl. Bayerischer Staatsanzeiger* (Munich), July 3, 1916. For a similar account of wartime rationing and its effects on diets, see Chickering, *The Great War and Urban Life in Germany*, 165–179, 263–275.

provisions for the former, and expensive imported goods for the latter.[207] In spite of these efforts, the shortage of food became more alarming as the war continued, and many residents were forced to rely on a rapidly-expanding black market.[208] In 1917 locals came up with a provisional solution: transforming the *Kurgarten* into a large vegetable garden that would help feed both Bad Reichenhall and Berchtesgaden.[209]

The rationing of basic staples adversely affected the quality of any visit to Bad Reichenhall, but another government decree effectively limited the length of the visit itself. In November 1917 the Bavarian Ministry of War announced that beginning in December, spa and winter sport destinations with populations of less than 6,000 were not permitted to accommodate guests for more than one week at a time, that is, unless the guest was a member of the military that had been granted permission for an extended spa visit, or a civilian that was in possession of a doctor's note. This legislation was a desperate means of preserving precious resources, but it only did further damage to the fragile tourism industry of destinations like Bad Reichenhall.[210] In the intervening time, the resort became more isolated as a result of the increasing strain on the German railways, the primary means of transportation and communication during the war. Travel that was deemed "unnecessary" was either eliminated altogether, or made less desirable through increased fares. At the same time, fuel shortages ensured that passenger trains were forced to travel more slowly, without internal lighting, and often without heat during the winter months.[211] These were hardly ideal travel conditions.

Cut off from its international clientele, compelled to cater to guests who were not expected to pay their way, and plagued with shortages of the most essential provisions, the tourism industry of Bad Reichenhall and the entire community that it supported was on the verge of collapse by 1918. While some Germans expressed optimism in the wake of the Russian capitulation and the new offensive on the Western Front, the residents of Bad Reichenhall remained inconsolable. An article in a February 1918 issue of the *Reichenhaller Grenzbote* pronounced: "Today Reichenhall is the poorest and most economically-stunted town in Bavaria."[212] That

---

[207] Leinberger, *Der Fremdenverkehr in Bad Reichenhall*, 100.
[208] Lang, *Geschichte von Bad Reichenhall*, 678.
[209] StAM, Kurverwaltung Bad Reichenhall 251: "Gemüseanbau im Kurgarten während des 1. Weltkriegs, 1917–1918."
[210] StAM, Kurverwaltung Bad Reichenhall, 248.
[211] Chickering, *The Great War and Urban Life in Germany*, 289–290.
[212] *Reichenhaller Grenzbote: Tagsblatt für den Kurort Bad Reichenhall/Amtsblatt der Behörden des Grenzbezirks* (Bad Reichenhall), February 5, 1918.

very same month, a massive public meeting took place in Bad Reichenhall's Hotel Deutscher Kaiser, where nearly 1,000 citizens met to discuss
the emergency situation, and to draft a statement of grievances. Instead of
blaming the war itself, the community targeted the Bavarian government,
accusing them of having abandoned the spa in 1914. On February 21,
1918, Bad Reichenhall's representative to the Munich Chamber of Commerce, Karl Schiffman, elaborated upon the committee's complaints. He
confirmed that the number of international visitors had dropped dramatically since the outbreak of the war, leading the tourism industry to rely on
German visitors. Legislation making a physician's note mandatory for an
extended stay in a Bavarian spa not only barred entire categories of visitors, it ensured that many Germans were less likely to visit, as genuinely
sick individuals tended to trust their own doctors and visit nearby spas.
On the subject of insufficient provisions, Schiffman made his case simply:
"One cannot live on good air alone." Guarantees of rations had not been
kept, even though spa destinations in northern Germany, like Bad Oyn-
hausen and Bad Kreuznach, could sufficiently provide for their guests, and
even turn it into a selling point. Furthermore, while Bad Reichenhall's
annual number of visitors plummeted, Bad Kreuznach's figures reportedly rose from 10,000 to 19,000 between 1914 and 1916. In conclusion,
Schiffman reprimanded the Bavarian government for their inability to
maintain regular rail connections to Alpine tourist destinations, noting
that during the previous winter, various delays and transfers had turned
the trip from Munich to Bad Reichenhall into an odyssey lasting up to
twenty-four hours. The solutions recommended by Schiffman in Munich
were simple: eliminate the need for required documentation, guarantee
the regular delivery of provisions, and take measures to standardize and
expedite rail travel.[213]

While the Chamber of Commerce did make some attempts to improve
rail connections between Munich and Bad Reichenhall during the summer of 1918, the Bavarian government failed to address the other two
grievances. The legislation making official documentation a prerequi-
site to a spa visit was not overturned until after the war, while the
Bavarian government received complaints about insufficient provisions
in Bad Reichenhall for months to come.[214] Community leaders declared
in May 1919 that a full-scale reopening of spa facilities was unthinkable
at that point.[215] Several months earlier, the state spa commissioner had

[213] BWA, Industrie- und Handelskammer, 343: "Fremdenverkehr in Bayern, 1917."
[214] HAT, ZSF, 072.
[215] BWA, Industrie- und Handelskammer, 343.

predicted that Bad Reichenhall would not be able to recover anytime soon, and subsequently requested that the resort be allowed to maintain its status as a sick bay for German soldiers, because then at least a portion of the "victimized" community could remain employed.[216] The number of visitors to Bad Reichenhall subsequently dropped to 7,516 during the 1919 season, the second lowest figure since the outbreak of the war, but rose again to 11,675 during the 1920 season, the highest figure since 1914. Over 10,000 of these visitors were German, but the international guests appeared to be returning slowly as well: 646 Austrians, 345 Czechoslovakians, 116 Hungarians, 32 Rumanians, and even 10 Belgians.[217]

These figures appeared promising, but comparative statistics confirm that the tourism industry of Bad Reichenhall never regained the momentum that had characterized the prewar period. During the season of 1913–1914, Bad Reichenhall could boast of 542,000 overnight stays, far more than two other spa destinations in southern Bavaria, Bad Tölz and Oberstdorf, which only registered 146,000 and 227,000 nights respectively. However, Bad Reichenhall's numbers dropped dramatically during the following decade, and remained low. Only 445,000 overnight stays were registered during the 1925–1926 season, and only 473,000 during 1930–1931. Bad Tölz, on the other hand, registered 235,000 during 1925–1926, and 265,000 during 1930–1931. Oberstdorf fared even better, with a recorded 280,000 nights in 1925–1926, and an impressive 483,000 during 1930–1931. While the number of overnight stays is not synonymous with the number of guests, it is nevertheless striking that business in the spa towns of Bad Tölz and Oberstdorf nearly doubled over the course of seventeen tumultuous years, reflecting both the growth of mass tourism and the decline of the elite tourism associated with destinations like Bad Reichenhall.[218] As one local historian notes: "After the war, Bad Reichenhall was confronted with a completely different market situation. The world and its political map had changed, and large segments of the former clientele (from the Dual Monarchy, for instance) were lost."[219] In 1911, approximately 55 percent of the spa's clientele were foreign; in 1925, international guests constituted less than 15 percent.[220] Bad Reichenhall could still boast of many of the same attractions that had

[216] StAM, Kurverwaltung Bad Reichenhall, 248.
[217] StAM, Kurverwaltung Bad Reichenhall, 288: "Fremdenverkehr, 1898–1937, 1951."
[218] Schwartz, *Bayern im Lichte seiner hundertjährigen Statistik*, 75, Tabelle 18.
[219] Pfisterer, "Eine kleine Geschichte der Kurstadt Reichenhall (1850–1990), 51.
[220] Vogel, *Geschichte von Bad Reichenhall*, 77.

made it a prestigious destination in the first place, but the cosmopolitan elite that helped to define the spa were gone forever.

* * *

As a scenic summer retreat, a progressive health resort, and a modish tourist destination, prewar Bad Reichenhall exemplified several trends in Imperial Germany. Its development into a popular tourist destination during the nineteenth century can be linked to the widespread glorification of the natural environment and the rise of middle-class tourism in Germany, both consequences of modernization discussed in the previous chapters. Similarly, Bad Reichenhall's status as a *Kurort* reflected a new health consciousness, as well as the state-endorsed rise of the medical profession. However, the fact that not all visitors were technically patients confirms that the spa promised both medical and social rewards, and that middle-class tourism was becoming more than just a utilitarian exercise built around the concept of *Bildung*. While some travelers sought a tangible cure, and others engaged in pleasurable distractions, the town itself embraced change; rebuilding to achieve a modern look, refinancing to ensure further progress, and even re-conceptualizing to attract an international clientele.

Tourist propaganda cultivated Bad Reichenhall's image as a peaceful destination that was equally progressive and sophisticated, but also grounded. By connecting the spa's natural surroundings with its modern character and facilities, contemporaneous publications established the image of a forward-looking community rooted in nature and tradition. Many a visitor may have left behind the commotion of city life for the secluded community of Bad Reichenhall, but what they found there was essentially an alternative reality, a grounded modernity that provided temporary stability and authenticity. The cosmopolitan clientele was a central feature of this alternate urban culture, allowing the resort to transcend regional and national identities and claim parity with the international luxury spas with which it competed.

After 1914, this carefully balanced image was upset by the implications of total war. National solidarity overshadowed cosmopolitan harmony, and the local community turned to its fellow Germans as their principal clientele. While the Great War may not have destroyed Bad Reichenhall's reputation as a progressive spa with idyllic natural surroundings, it did effectively curb international tourism. This remained a problem after 1918, as the Bavarian tourism industry actively targeted fellow Germans in the hopes of revitalizing the economy, while simultaneously reaching out to foreigners in order to repair the nation's damaged reputation.

The next chapter addresses these issues by examining the tourism industry of Augsburg during the Weimar era. During uncertain political and economic times, the local tourism association, struggled to sell the 2,000-year-old city as a viable tourist attraction to both domestic and international visitors. The tourist propaganda that they sanctioned attempted a careful balance between a colorful past and an industrial present, producing a rather different vision of grounded modernity than that found in the Alpine world of Bad Reichenhall.

4

The Augsburg Tourism Industry and the German Past

"As a result of fortunate circumstances, Augsburg has remained unusually protected from the barbarism of modern times; internally united, today's city stands as an illustration of the past, and a living example not only of how an old German city appeared, but how a new German city should appear." [1]

Augsburg Official Guidebook 1924
(Distributed by the Augsburg Tourism Association)

Before the devastation of World War I, the tourism industries of Franconian Switzerland and Bad Reichenhall reinvented natural settings as modern attractions. During the 1920s, the tourism industry of Augsburg tried something similar, attempting to redefine a historically significant location as a progressive metropolis. After three decades of relying almost exclusively on Augsburg's historical credentials, the local tourism association began to call attention to the more contemporary features of the urban environment, suggesting that the 2,000-year-old city may not have been completely "protected" from the modern world. As a metropolis of over 100,000 inhabitants and the second most important industrial center in Bavaria, "The City of the German Renaissance" was also the "German Manchester," defined by its factories and contemporary culture as well as by its well-preserved monuments and museums.

Still, history remained central to Augsburg's contemporary identity throughout the interwar period. The sheer weight of that history helped to

---

[1] StadtAA, 20, Nr. 585: "Förderung des Fremdenverkehrs, I. Band, 1917–1925." *Augsburg Amtlicher Führer (Mit einem Stadtplan und 30 Abbildungen)* (Augsburg: Selbstverlag des Fremden-verkehrs-Vereins Augsburg, 1924), 5–6.

ground the German nation, providing it with an epic tale of achievement and progress, stretching from the city's Roman roots to its modern-day industrialization. In other words, it was all connected; historical Augsburg and modern Augsburg were synonymous, and the city's living presence complemented its illustrious past. The local tourism industry sold Augsburg as a metaphor for the larger German nation, combining historical significance with contemporary relevance in a new spin on grounded modernity. By advertising the city as quintessentially "German," the Augsburg tourism industry bypassed local and regional particularisms, providing an accessible vision of the nation to both domestic and foreign visitors.

For various reasons identified in this chapter, efforts to transform modern Augsburg into a tourist hub were not entirely successful, confirming that the cultivation of tourism was not always a smooth process. Nevertheless, the story of the Augsburg tourism industry demonstrates the various ways in which leisure travel was evolving during the interwar period. For example, throughout the 1920s the tourism industry of Augsburg selectively embraced modern technology and spotlighted new attractions in order to attract a broader demographic, thus moving beyond the *Bildung*-oriented travel of the nineteenth-century bourgeoisie. On the other hand, its discursive attempts to connect past and present while framing the entire history of Augsburg with German patriotism reveal the broader nationalist impulses of the interwar tourism industry. As noted earlier, tourism was no longer an exclusively economic enterprise; it was a means of creating loyalty to the modern nation-state during extremely volatile times. Interwar tourism was also a means of healing, and not just for the nervous middle classes, but for the entire German nation. In the wake of recent traumas, the Augsburg tourism industry developed a vision of German identity that revolved around a long and colorful past, a robust and world-renowned industry, and various cultural achievements, both old and new. However, this version of grounded modernity, like all others, was selective. The local tourism industry advertised Augsburg as a historically rooted modern metropolis, thereby diverting attention from the other Augsburg, a politically charged and economically unstable city of workers.

Marketing Modern Germany

An increase in paid vacation days and the diversification of the transportation industry helped to lay the foundations of mass tourism during the Weimar era, but the expanded marketing of leisure travel was equally important. At a time when tourism was widely associated with both economic vitality and patriotic resolve, marketing made the nationalist impulses of travel explicit. Marketing also helped to demystify the notion of the vacation elsewhere, making it seem like a real possibility for segments of society that had never had the opportunity to travel. Tourist propaganda no longer spoke to the middles classes alone; it now targeted the masses, promoting tourism as an affordable and central component of modern life.

As a "common denominator of modern industrial life," marketing became both a rational science and a powerful form of "national self-promotion" in early twentieth-century Germany.[2] Prior to World War I, the standard genres of tourist propaganda, including brochures, posters, and postcards, tended to be one-dimensional, promoting a single attraction or even hotel. After 1918, the tourism industry recognized the limits of this traditional marketing, and acknowledged that propaganda should not just encourage tourism, it should produce it. They updated the more traditional forms of tourist propaganda, employing shorter slogans and glossy photography to attract a wider demographic. They also began to utilize the mass media, and by the end of the 1920s, slide shows, neon signs, and radio broadcasts were all advertising tourism. Cinema also became a popular means of promotion during this period, and short tourism films regularly preceded feature films.[3] Tourist propaganda became an everyday sight during the interwar period, ubiquitous in store windows, train stations, and movie theaters.[4] As a "visually present" component of modern life, the very idea of travel became a commodity, even if a vacation remained unrealistic for many.[5]

While the German tourism industry incorporated new techniques and technology into its arsenal, the marketing itself began to glorify the experience of modernity. This meant that propaganda dedicated more and more space to urban centers, which radiated with "the excitement, power and vitality of the new nation-state."[6] Especially radiant was Berlin, a frantic

[2] Janet Ward, *Weimar Surfaces: Urban Visual Culture in 1920s Germany* (Berkeley: University of California Press, 2001), 92–93. See also Pamela E. Swett, S. Jonathan Wiesen, and Jonathan R. Zatlin, "Introduction," in *Selling Modernity: Advertising in Twentieth-Century Germany*, ed. Pamela E. Swett, S. Jonathan Wiesen, and Jonathan R. Zatlin (Durham: Duke University Press, 2007), 8; Wiesen, *Creating the Nazi Marketplace*, 156–157.

[3] Keitz, *Reisen als Leitbild*, 95–111.

[4] Syrjämaa, "Tourism as a Typical Cultural Phenomenon," 188–189.

[5] Hachtmann, *Tourismus-Geschichte*, 117.

[6] McElligott, *The German Urban Experience*, 150.

city pulsating with industry, culture, and traffic, immortalized in Walter Ruttman's 1927 film, *Berlin: Symphony of a Metropolis*.[7] A brochure issued by the Trade-Fair and Tourism Office of the City of Berlin in the late 1920s characterized the city as the center of the German government, as well as "the nerve system of the German economy," with "the large banks, central offices of the cartels and syndicates, the economic associations, and the labor unions." The publication celebrated modernity in various forms, featuring black-and-white photographs of the West Harbor, the Radio Tower, the Berlin Airport, and even a stream of cars on the brochure's cover.[8]

The marketing of other German cities also took a more modern turn. The reputation of Cologne, for example, no longer relied on its cathedral and art galleries alone. A Weimar-era guidebook on the Rhineland issued by the Reich Central Office for German Tourism Promotion (RDV) described the city, in English, as:

... the venerable Rhenish metropolis, the leading trading city in the Rhineland, the seat of the Fairs of Rhineland and Westphalia, the center of a world-famous industry, the important Rhenish port, where a large new harbor is now in the course of construction, one of the main European railway and airway junctions, the favorite resort of visitors and meeting place of congresses...[9]

As a tourist attraction, Cologne offered evidence of the nation's cultural achievements and its contemporary economic significance. Similarly, a 1926 RDV brochure covering the region of Württemberg emphasized the modern features of both Ulm and Stuttgart. Depicting Ulm as "[o]ne of the most important industrial and trading towns in Württemberg," the brochure also offered a more balanced description of Stuttgart, combining an emphasis on contemporary significance with praise for the city's scenic location and cultural offerings. Still, the list of Stuttgart attractions included the following highlights: "Perfect sanitary conditions. Excellent Schools. Technical Academy. Libraries, museums, valuable collections. Six railway stations. Aerodrome in Böblingen."[10] Even the marketing of the popular tourist destination of Dresden, the "Florence of the Elbe," changed noticeably during this period. A guidebook published during the

---

[7] Large, *Berlin*, 205–209.
[8] BayHStA, Sammlung Varia, 267: "Deutsche Verkehrs- (Fremdenverkehrs-) Vereine."
[9] HAT, Prospekte, D060/00/-33/RDV/-33/RDV/3/Verkehrsbücher: *Germany, The Rhine* (Berlin: Reichsbahnzentrale für Deutsche Verkehrswerbung, undated), 75.
[10] HAT, Prospekte, D060/00/-33/RDV/-33/RDV/3/Verkehrsbücher: *Germany, Württemberg: Black Forest and the Lake of Constance* (Berlin: Reichsbahnzentrale für Deutsche Verkehrswerbung, 1926), 26, 48.

late 1920s defined the cultural center as an "industrial city," with over 7,900 factories and 172,000 workers engaged in the production of chocolate, cigarettes, machinery, and photography equipment.[11] This was not the same Dresden that nineteenth-century tourists had admired.

The marketing of German cities in the Weimar Republic reaffirmed the modernity of the nation-state, manifested in various achievements in industry, transportation, education, and even hygiene. It was undeniably present-minded, and it drew the tourist's attention to contemporary Germany.[12] Unlike the transcendental travel described by Siegfried Kracauer, this sort of tourism was in fact focused on the "here and now," and its meaning was not "exhausted in the mere fact of changing locations."[13] However, this modern travel culture was just one of many, and past and present coexisted within the Weimar tourist experience, as they did throughout German society at large. While many tourists immersed themselves in urban mass culture, others sought solace in a more reassuring set of national memories. These impulses were not necessarily incompatible, and in places like Augsburg, the tourist could indulge in both.

So why was history so attractive to many Germans? In the Weimar Republic, the past became more precious because recent events had created a rupture in the continuum of German history. According to historian Peter Fritzsche, something similar happened when the French Revolution and the Napoleonic Wars separated regular people from "their remembered pasts."[14] As a result, a new historical consciousness emerged, a distinctly romantic understanding of the past colored by a melancholic sense of loss, but also a desire to rediscover things left behind. The German nation experienced a similar rupture with the past after World War I, when mobilization, combat, and defeat drew millions of citizens into the relentless flow of history, depositing them in unfamiliar territory.[15] Further political and economic upheaval after the armistice only heightened this sense of discontinuity and "bewilderment," and a prevailing mood of disenchantment characterized the period.[16] As the present became synonymous with crisis, the remote past offered potential solace.[17]

---

[11] BayHStA, Sammlung Varia, 267.
[12] See Koshar, *German Travel Cultures*, 112.
[13] Kracauer, "Travel and Dance," in *The Mass Ornament*, 71.
[14] Peter Fritzsche, *Stranded in the Present: Modern Time and the Melancholy of History* (New York: Harvard University Press, 2004), 33.
[15] See Anton Kaes, *Shell Shock Cinema: Weimar Culture and the Wounds of War* (Princeton: Princeton University Press, 2009), 2.
[16] Peukert, *The Weimar Republic*, 83.
[17] Peter Fritzsche, "Landscape of Danger, Landscape of Design: Crisis and Modernism in Weimar Germany," in *Dancing on the Volcano*, 30. See also Rudy Koshar, *Germany's*

Reconnecting with the past was also a means of cultivating national-ism. In an 1882 lecture at the Sorbonne, French scholar Ernest Renan asserted that the "nation, like the individual, is the culmination of a long past of endeavors, sacrifice, and devotion." Renan was one of the first scholars to argue that nationalism rested upon the foundation of the past, but he also suggested that forgetting was just as important as remembering.[18] In the late twentieth century, scholars of nationalism called our attention to "imagined communities" and "invented tradi-tions," arguing that the absence of real bonds among members of the nation-state necessitates acts of fabrication.[19] In opposition to such views, one scholar insists that "nationhood" rests on real ethnic bonds, as well as older cultural practices and ideological concepts.[20] All would agree that the "past" is an essential component of nationalism, but it is impor-tant to emphasize that the past is inherently flexible and open to poten-tially divisive and destructive uses. In an 1874 essay, German philosopher Friedrich Nietzsche claimed that modern society needed history, but that excessive, uncritical "valorization" of the past could promote compla-cency and misguided patriotism. In medical terms prefiguring those of Nordau, Nietzsche argued that this "historical sickness" could lead to the "atrophy and degeneration of life."[21]

Interwar German society did not heed Nietzsche's warning. They cel-ebrated a distant past defined by victory and progress that obscured the more recent memories of defeat and decline. Foreign visitors were also in search of the historical Germany. In the 1927 publication, *Motor Ram-bles in Central Europe*, English travel writer Frank Rimington wrote of the "necessity of establishing international goodwill," and insisted that travel would help the world "to substitute memories of a Germany which was once congenial – the Germany which gave to the world a Goethe, a Schiller, a Beethoven, a Wagner, a Humboldt, and so many other out-standing benefactors in Literature, in Art, and in Science – in place of

Transient Pasts: Preservation and National Memory in the Twentieth Century (Chapel Hill: University of North Carolina Press, 1998), 110.

[18] Ernest Renan, "What is a Nation?," in *Nation and Narration*, ed. Homi K. Bhabha (New York: Routledge, 1990), 8–22.

[19] Benedict Anderson, *Imagined Communities: Reflections on the Origin and Spread of Nationalism* (New York: Verso, 1991); Eric Hobsbawm, "Introduction: Inventing Tra-ditions," in *The Invention of Tradition*, ed. Eric Hobsbawm and Terence Ranger (New York: Cambridge University Press, 1983), 1–14.

[20] Anthony D. Smith, *The Cultural Foundations of Nations: Hierarchy, Covenant and Republic* (Oxford: John Wiley & Sons, 2008).

[21] Friedrich Nietzsche, *Unfashionable Observations*, trans. Richard T. Gray (Stanford: Stanford University Press, 1995), 85, 165.

a Germany that became so rightfully hateful."[22] In the 1930 travelogue, *Come With Me Through Germany*, American author Frank Schoonmaker noted that there were still some unanswered questions about postwar Germany: "Has the Reich still time for the old and the beautiful? Is a new America rising between the Vistula and the Rhine? Did the friendliness, the indefinable *bonhomie* of the German people entirely disappear during four years of war?"[23] A desire to answer these questions led many travelers to the defeated Reich. In search of authentic Germany, Schoonmaker and Rimington even set their sights on Augsburg, the "City of the German Renaissance."

Historically significant, Augsburg could provide a more appealing set of memories to both international visitors and the disillusioned German people. The city's 2,000-year-old history was one of political prominence, cultural affluence, and international prestige. The cityscape itself presented physical evidence of greatness, and its architecture imparted a tangible "sense of the past."[24] In the wake of war and revolution, and in the midst of depression and political upheaval, the historic city was a model of endurance, providing a "constant in a changing world."[25] However, over the course of the 1920s, the local tourism industry of Augsburg began to market modern vitality alongside historical relevance. They innovatively cast contemporary achievements as the extension of earlier glory, helping to cultivate a modern German identity defined by the themes of historical continuity, industry, and culture.

Trials, Tribulations, and Tourism

Augsburg's illustrious past was clear for all to see. In perpetual contention with the citizens of Mainz, Trier, and Cologne, Augsburg's residents claimed that their city was the oldest in the German nation, pointing to a history that stretched nearly 2,000 years into the remote past. Originally known as Augusta Vindelicorum, Augsburg began as a Roman garrison

---

[22] Frank C. Rimington, *Motor Rambles in Central Europe: Some Descriptions and Some Reflections* (New York: Houghton Mifflin Company, 1927), 2–3.
[23] Frank Schoonmaker, *Come With Me Through Germany* (New York: Robert M. McBride & Company, 1930), 4–5.
[24] Maiken Umbach, "Memory and Historicism: Reading between the Lines of the Built Environment, Germany c. 1900," *Representations*, 88, no. 1 (Fall 2004): 28.
[25] Cara Aitchison, Nicole E. Macleod, and Stephen J. Shaw, *Leisure and Tourism Landscapes: Social and Cultural Geographies* (New York: Routledge, 2000), 141.

camp at the convergence of the Rivers Lech and Wertach, fifteen years before the birth of Christ. When Munich was no more than a settlement of monks along the River Isar, Augsburg was already flourishing as a provincial capital and trading post. On more than one occasion, invaders had levelled the city to the ground, but Augsburg always rose again.[26]

As the former capital of Emperor Friedrich Barbarossa and an Imperial Free City, Augsburg reached its prime in the fifteenth and sixteenth centuries, when it became a center of international commerce rivaling Venice and Antwerp. Its name became synonymous with the Fugger and Welser banking familes, whose collective wealth transformed the city's appearance and secured Augsburg's international reputation during the Renaissance. Augsburg also played a prominent role in the German Reformation, hosting Martin Luther at the Imperial Diet of 1518, and serving as the venue for the *Confessio Augustana* (1530) and the Peace of Augsburg (1555). After the latter technically ended religious strife in the Holy Roman Empire, Augsburg was divided between Protestant and Catholic citizens, with Lutherans constituting roughly two-thirds of the population. This confessional divide was epitomized by Augsburg's Basilica of Saint Ulrich and Saint Afra, which actually consisted of both Catholic and Protestant churches.

The Thirty Years War of 1618–1648 inaugurated two centuries of decline for Augsburg, but the city's incorporation into the Kingdom of Bavaria in 1805 heralded an era of rebirth.[27] Augsburg became the capital of the Bavarian province of Swabia and Neuburg, the base of a large garrison, and one of the most important industrial centers of southern Germany, fueled by the hydropower of the Lech and Wertach Rivers. After the opening of rail connections with Munich and Nuremberg during the 1840s, several large-scale textile and machinery factories arose around Augsburg's historic center, among them, the Sanderschen Maschinenfabrik, forerunner to the Maschinenfabrik Augsburg-Nürnberg (MAN). These factories initially relied on local workers, but eventually drew impoverished residents of rural Bavaria, Württemberg, Austria-Hungary, and Switzerland, thus expanding the city's Catholic and

---

[26] See Wolfgang Zorn, *Augsburg: Geschichte einer deutschen Stadt* (Augsburg: Mühlberger, 1972); Gunther Gottlieb, *Geschichte der Stadt Augsburg: Von der Römerzeit bis zur Gegenwart*, ed. Gunther Gottlieb (Stuttgart: Konrad Theiss Verlag, 1984); Bernd Roeck, *Geschichte Augsburgs* (Munich: C.H. Beck, 2005).

[27] See Rosemarie Dietrich, *Die Integration Augsburgs in den bayerischen Staat (1806–1821)* (Sigmaringen: Thorbecke, 1993).

working-class demographics.[28] By 1910, Augsburg's population had surpassed 100,000, nearly doubling over the course of four decades.[29]

The "German Manchester" now found itself torn between two disparate identities: a historic city of monuments and an industrial city of workers. The nineteenth-century influx of rural residents led to the overcrowding of the city's working-class suburbs, where death rates were among the highest in the Kingdom of Bavaria. In 1872, the Augsburg municipal government, dominated by Catholic conservatives but influenced by a powerful minority of middle-class, Protestant liberals, aimed to prevent the spread of disease by building a city-wide sewer system. After the turn of the century, the construction of an extensive streetcar network and the opening of new rail stations allowed for the further integration of working-class suburbs into the city center. Between 1910 and 1916, the city officially incorporated many of these former villages, increasing the population by roughly 40,000. The working-class residents of these suburbs hoped that this expansion would bring about improvements in education, infrastructure, and hygienic conditions, but the ensuing world war, revolution, and depression delayed progress. In densely populated districts like Lechhausen and Oberhausen, infant mortality rates remained high, while tuberculosis and other preventable diseases continued to claim hundreds of victims.[30] In the meantime, Augsburg's working-class population began to vote for the Social Democratic Party of Germany (SPD). In the Reichstag election of 1890, the SPD garnered 21.8 percent of the Augsburg vote; in 1912, they received almost 30 percent, close to the national average. In 1908, the Social Democrats acquired seats on the Augsburg City Council, and their presence continued to grow as the city absorbed working-class suburbs.[31]

The modernization of Augsburg also led to a physical transformation of the city's appearance, especially in the historic center. In the densely-populated Old City, or *Altstadt*, the municipal government presided over

---

[28] Gerhard Hetzer, "Die Industriestadt Augsburg: Eine Sozialgeschichte der Arbeiteropposition," in *Bayern in der NS-Zeit, III: Herrschaft und Gesellschaft im Konflikt, Teil B*, ed. Martin Broszat, Elke Fröhlich, and Anton Grossman (Munich: R. Oldenbourg Verlag, 1981), 2–8.

[29] Zorn, *Augsburg*, 251–258. See also Ilse Fischer, *Industrialisierung, sozialer Konflikt und politische Willensbildung in der Stadtgemeinde. Ein Beitrag zur Sozialgeschichte Augsburgs 1840–1914* (Augsburg: H. Mühlberger, 1977).

[30] Hetzer, "Die Industriestadt Augsburg," 28, 30.

[31] Gerhard Hetzer, "Von der Reichsgründung bis zum Ende der Weimarer Republik 1871–1933," in *Geschichte der Stadt Augsburg*, 568–569, 573–574; Hetzer, "Die Industriestadt Augsburg," 42; Roeck, *Geschichte Augsburgs*, 169, 172–174.

the expansion of old streets and the creation of new ones, as well as the outright elimination of historical fortifications, gates, and narrow alleyways. Inspired by a romantic appreciation for historic architecture, many locals protested the destruction of Augsburg's early modern center. In 1882, the demolition of a row of old houses led to the creation of middle-class organization dedicated to historical preservation. These men were responsible for the subsequent restoration of the eastern façade of the Augsburg City Hall (*Rathaus*), as well as the renovation of the Maximilians-Museum. Founded in 1854 and containing a wealth of historical artifacts, the latter attraction was one of several Augsburg institutions built during the late nineteenth century. A new municipal theater on the western edge of the *Altstadt* opened in 1878, and a large city park in southwestern Augsburg opened during the Industrial Exhibition of 1886.[32]

By the end of the nineteenth century, Augsburg represented a divided metropolitan culture, simultaneously old and new, traditional and progressive. It was at this point that some residents began taking steps to promote municipal tourism. This initiative originated with the middle-class associations, "the real mediators" between the population and the local government before 1918.[33] On December 1, 1891, 141 Augsburg citizens met for the inaugural meeting of the Association for the Improvement of Tourism, the precursor to the Augsburg Tourism Association, or *Verkehrsverein Augsburg* (VVA).[34] The stated objectives of this organization reflected the priorities of middle-class city dwellers, and included the expansion and improvement of rail connections to Augsburg, the preservation of municipal buildings, the distribution of tourist propaganda, and all other efforts that would promote municipal tourism.[35] The tourism association financed its activities with a subsidy from the municipal government, in addition to contributions from its members, which included hotels, breweries, and other businesses, as well as private citizens.[36] The factory-workers who constituted a huge proportion of Augsburg's population were neither represented by the organization, nor

---

[32] Hetzer, "Von der Reichsgründung bis zum Ende der Weimarer Republik," 575–576.

[33] Ibid., 573–574.

[34] Günther Grünsteudel, Günther Hagele, and Rudolf Frankenberger, *Augsburger Stadtlexicon*, 2nd edn., ed. Günther Grünsteudel, Günther Hagele, and Rudolf Frankenberger (Augsburg: Perlach Verlag, 1998), 740.

[35] This information was printed in an article celebrating the fifty-year anniversary of the Augsburg Tourism Association. *Neue Augsburg Zeitung* (Augsburg), November 29, 1941.

[36] StadtAA, 20, 588: "Förderung des Fremdenverkehrs, IV. Band, 1928."

pursued as potential tourists. Considering the middle-class orientation of the tourism industry during the long nineteenth century, this oversight is not surprising. To be fair, some Augsburg workers did travel before World War I, but they did so as members of socialist organizations like the "Friends of Nature," which sought to build working-class solidarity through excursions into the natural environment. This highly politicized form of travel was very different than that endorsed by the middle-class VVA.[37]

At its inception, the Augsburg tourism industry relied exclusively on the city's historical attractions, thereby diverting attention from the working-class suburbs. A locally produced 1900 guidebook called attention to a diversity of sights defined by history, from the architecture of the *Altstadt* to the municipal archive and library. Among the most noteworthy attractions were the Cathedral of Augsburg, the Basilica of Saint Ulrich and Saint Afra, and the famous *Rathaus*, the masterpiece of native son Elias Holl and the most enduring symbol of the city.[38] Indeed, history dominated the fin-de-siècle tourist gaze, and visitors to Augsburg found it easy to overlook the more modern dimensions of the city. Pius Dirr, the director of the Munich City Archive, visited Augsburg in 1909 and observed that the "loud metropolis" had not overshadowed the charm of the *Altstadt*, especially since most of the factories were "banished" to the outskirts of the city.[39] Locals were also enamored with historical Augsburg. In a biographical work, Augsburg native Walter Brecht (younger brother of author Bertolt Brecht) glorified the city's historical monuments, defining them as the "symbols of the imperial city's power and independence." Echoing the tourist propaganda, Brecht raved about the *Rathaus*, "the greatest architectural achievement in German lands since the age of the cathedrals."[40] While the city itself expanded and looked toward the future, locals and visitors remained fixated on the past. Incidentally, this occurred just as the city's economic and demographic growth began to fall behind that of Munich and Nuremberg. An

---

[37] Hetzer, "Die Industriestadt Augsburg," 43; Hachtmann, *Tourismus-Geschichte*, 101–105.

[38] Fr. König's Hofbuchhandlung, Hanau, *Führer durch Augsburg: Kurze Beschreibung der Stadt und ihrer Sehenswürdigkeiten* (Augsburg: Math. Rieger'sche Buchhandlung (A. Himmer), 1900), 3.

[39] Klaus-Jörg Ruhl, *Augsburg in alten und neuen Reisebeschreibungen*, ed. Klaus-Jörg Ruhl (Düsseldorf: Droste Verlag GmbH, 1992), 208.

[40] Walter Brecht, *Unser Leben in Augsburg, Damals: Erinnerungen*, 2nd edn. (Frankfurt am Main: Insel Verlag, 1985), 16–17.

inferiority complex, fueled by talk of stagnation and decline, began to develop.[41]

Tourism offered a way for Augsburg to compete with larger cities like Munich and Nuremberg, but World War I presented challenges for both the Augsburg Tourism Association and the city itself. While the VVA relied on its 2,500-mark subsidy from the municipal government to issue free brochures and guidebooks to wounded and sick soldiers, the city was plagued by food shortages throughout the war, and lost over 3,500 men on the battlefields of the Eastern and Western Fronts.[42] In the meantime, the Augsburg machinery industry received a temporary boost due to an increased demand for armaments, just as the textile industry dismissed roughly half of its workforce.[43] During the final months of the war, the Augsburg Tourism Association maintained that tourism could revitalize the local economy after four years of loss and privation. Consequently, they began urging the municipal government to finance measures that might revitalize this comatose industry. In spite of appeals to the best interests of "our city," the local government was unwilling to offer much support, and remained occupied with the more pressing issues of material shortages, economic destabilization, and growing political unrest.[44]

Political unrest was widespread in Germany at the end of 1918, as material shortages and military defeat fed the fires of revolution throughout the exhausted country.[45] In Munich, a peaceful demonstration at the *Theresienwiese* on November 8 gave way to the seizure of weapons and the occupation of government buildings. In response, King Ludwig III and his family fled the Bavarian capital, ending centuries of Wittelsbach rule. On the following day, Independent Socialist Kurt Eisner created a "revolutionary parliament" and appointed himself provisional president of the Bavarian Republic.[46] News of the revolution in Munich led to

---

[41] Gerhard Hetzer, "Weimarer Republik und Drittes Reich," in *Augsburger Stadtlexicon*, 118.

[42] StadtAA, 34, 291: "Verein zur Hebung des Fremdenverkehrs, Zuschuss, I. Band., 1893–1931."

[43] Roeck, *Geschichte Augsburgs*, 174–175.

[44] StadtAA, 20, 585: "Förderung des Fremdenverkehrs, I. Band, 1917–1925."

[45] Pierre Broué, *The German Revolution, 1917–1923*, trans. John Archer (Boston: Brill, 2005), 139–143.

[46] For more on the Bavarian Revolution, see Allen Mitchell, *Revolution in Bavaria, 1918–1919: The Eisner Regime and the Soviet Republic* (Princeton: Princeton University Press, 1965); Richard Grunberger, *Red Rising in Bavaria* (London: Barker, 1973); Martin Geyer, *Verkehrte Welt: Revolution, Inflation und Moderne: München 1914–1924* (Göttingen: Vandenhoeck & Ruprecht, 1998), 50–129; Bernhard Grau, *Kurt Eisner 1867–1919* (Munich: C.H. Beck, 2000).

FIGURE 8. Postcard featuring the *Rathaus* and central square of Augsburg, undated. Note the streetcar in the lower right corner. From the author's collection.

declarations of solidarity among Augsburg's proletariat, and on November 9, a red flag flew outside the *Rathaus*, as a newly constituted workers' and soldiers' council convened inside. These men were not prepared for the enormous task ahead of them, and the new government proved incapable of dealing with deteriorating economic conditions, a growing unemployment rate, and ongoing material shortages.[47] Frustrations boiled over in late February 1919, when the assassination of Kurt Eisner in Munich triggered protests, violence, and looting in central Augsburg. Enraged soldiers and factory workers targeted government institutions, storming the judicial building, destroying official records, and liberating inmates from the city prison. This unrest resulted in two deaths and numerous injuries, leading the municipal government to declare martial law, while the labor unions responded with a general strike.[48]

On April 3, 1919, a group of radical Augsburg council members met to discuss plans for the creation of a soviet republic, alliances between Bavaria and communist Russia and Hungary, and the nationalization of the Bavarian economy. Three days later, the revolutionary government in Munich approved the Augsburg resolution, and triumphantly proclaimed the birth of the Soviet Republic of Bavaria.[49] Radicalization hastened the demise of the Bavarian Revolution, alienating the moderates and horrifying the conservatives. Shortly after the proclamation of the Soviet Republic, Bavaria's democratically elected premier, SPD politician Johannes Hoffmann, fled to the Franconian town of Bamberg, where he established a government-in-exile and prepared for a military assault on Munich. On April 13, the Augsburg labor unions made a deal with the Hoffmann government, guaranteeing the city's neutrality during the impending offensive against Munich. Seven days later, counter-revolutionary, paramilitary units known as *Freikorps* entered Augsburg, where they met some resistance in working-class neighborhoods outside of the *Altstadt*. Fighting lasted for two days, and claimed forty-four lives.[50] By early May, Augsburg was restored to order, as the distant sound of artillery fire in Munich signaled the final demise of the Bavarian Revolution.[51]

[47] Hetzer, "Von der Reichsgründung bis zum Ende der Weimarer Republik," 580–582.
[48] Merith Niehuss, *Arbeiterschaft in Krieg und Inflation* (Berlin: Walter de Gruyter, 1985), 208–209.
[49] Hetzer, "Von der Reichsgründung bis zum Ende der Weimarer Republik," 582.
[50] Ibid., 582–583.
[51] Roeck, *Geschichte Augsburgs*, 179; Brecht, *Unser Leben in Augsburg*, 323.

The "Bloody Easter" of 1919 had a lasting influence on the tourism industry of Bavaria. In addition to scaring countless visitors away, this violent episode threatened the myths of continuity and stability that framed many Bavarian tourist destinations. The "Bloody Easter" also transformed Augsburg. Its violence led to the creation of a standing military force designed to suppress rebellions, a precaution that existed until early 1922. The radicalization and swift suppression of the revolution also forced the organized labor movement to reconsider its strategies, just as the Augsburg Social Democrats chose to isolate themselves from both the Independent Socialists and the Communists.[52] All of this coincided with the extensive restructuring of the municipal government. The "Self-Government Law" of May 22, 1919, created an independent city council chosen by an expanded electorate that now included women. The SPD may have received the largest percentage of the vote in the national and communal elections of 1919, but the non-socialist parties still held a collective majority in the city council. This strategic coalition of middle-class parties elected Bavarian *Volkspartei* (BVP) politician Kaspar Deutschenbaur as Augsburg's new mayor in 1919.[53] During the next ten years, Deutschenbaur developed a productive partnership with his deputy mayor, Friedrich Ackermann, a successful attorney and member of the SPD.[54] In general, cooperation and compromise characterized the activity of the municipal government throughout the 1920s, allowing them to combat the occasional opposition from the Independent Socialists and the Communists.[55] However, conciliation in city hall did not guarantee peace on the streets, and in early September 1920, a mass demonstration aimed at better and cheaper rations ended in bloodshed, as soldiers fired shots into an unruly mob, killing four workers.[56]

The coalition government of Augsburg certainly faced its share of tribulations after the war. During an August 1919 meeting, items on the city council's agenda included the supply of rations, the naturalization of immigrants, and the supply of water for the suburb of Kriegshaber.[57]

[52] Hetzer, "Weimarer Republik und Drittes Reich," 116–117.
[53] Niehuss, *Arbeiterschaft in Krieg und Inflation*, 200–201.
[54] Roeck, *Geschichte Augsburgs*, 179–180.
[55] Hetzer, "Von der Reichsgründung bis zum Ende der Weimarer Republik," 583–584; Niehuss, *Arbeiterschaft in Krieg und Inflation*, 203–206.
[56] *Augsburger Neueste Nachrichten* (Augsburg), September 1, 1920; Wolfgang Zorn, *Schwaben und Augsburg in der ersten Hälfte des 20. Jahrhunderts* (Munich: Verlag Ernst Vögel, 1976), 11.
[57] *Augsburger Neueste Nachrichten* (Augsburg), August 18, 1919.

This last item confirms that the working-class suburbs continued to force new priorities upon the predominantly middle-class residents of the city center, as the latter now had to contend with the problems of Augsburg's growing proletariat.[58] In addition to dealing with the economic and political aftershocks of war and revolution, the city council also had to improve local roads, expand the sewage system, extend the municipal gas, electricity, and drinking water networks, and reduce the housing shortage. These public work projects were overdue responses to the city's rapid growth, but during the interwar period, they had the additional benefit of combating unemployment.[59] Even with this preoccupation on infrastructure, the coalition government (and Ackermann in particular) managed to make token contributions to Augsburg's cultural life, among them the renovation of the City Theater in 1927. Still, during a period of economic uncertainty, even the most pragmatic cultural projects drew protests from the local community, who often had different priorities.[60] No wonder the middle-class members of the Augsburg Tourism Association had a difficult time convincing the coalition government to increase its financial support of tourism.

Then again, limited funding was just one of several issues that the Augsburg Tourism Association had to contend with after the war. Statewide restrictions on railway travel due to coal shortages lasted until March 1920, seriously limiting the number of potential tourists. Furthermore, the VVA conceded in a June 1920 memo that a large portion of their members had left the association due to the recent "economic upheavals."[61] This robbed the organization of both initiative and additional capital. In 1921, the Augsburg Tourism Association began to receive additional pressure from the nationalist, middle-class newspaper, *Augsburger Neueste Nachrichten*, which insisted that tourism should accomplish higher "cultural, ethnic, hygienic, and social goals," in addition to offering tangible economic benefits for the local community.[62] During a July 1921 meeting with the local Association of Hoteliers, VVA members expressed concern that tourists were passing over Augsburg because they believed that the city's limited lodgings were already full. In response, they decided to distribute flyers refuting this misconception in popular Bavarian destinations like Nuremberg, Würzburg,

---

[58] Hetzer, "Weimarer Republik und Drittes Reich," 118.
[59] Niehuss, *Arbeiterschaft in Krieg und Inflation*, 228–229.
[60] Hetzer, "Von der Reichsgründung bis zum Ende der Weimarer Republik," 586.
[61] StadtAA, 34, 284.
[62] *Augsburger Neueste Nachrichten* (Augsburg), June 25, 1921.

and Oberstdorf, as well as in the passenger trains that were regularly passing through Augsburg. This was part of an "ambitious marketing campaign" that also attempted to bring conventions to Augsburg.[63] By drawing trade fairs, conferences, and corporate meetings to Augsburg, the local tourism association hoped to attract a wider demographic of travelers.

A month after this discussion, the city council confirmed a new interest in municipal tourism by inviting representatives of the Augsburg Tourism Association to a meeting in city hall. During his introductory remarks, Deputy Mayor Friedrich Ackermann admitted that the local community could do more to promote tourism. One idea that he forwarded was the organization of new cultural events, such as concerts offered by the local music academies. Additional suggestions made during the meeting included the improvement of train connections with Munich, the production of a detailed inventory of local accommodations, the recruitment of local high school students as tour guides, and the advertisment of tourist information at the central train station. Moreover, the tourism association could solicit designs for posters as well as guidebook illustrations by organizing a city-wide contest. The meeting concluded with the consensus that the "intensive marketing of Augsburg must begin immediately," especially if the city was to capitalize on the Passion Play in Oberammergau and the German Trade Fair in Munich, both scheduled for 1922.[64]

This new commitment to marketing resulted in the publication of an expanded edition of the *Augsburg Official Guidebook*. At ninety pages long, the 1922 edition was approximately three times the size of the 1921 edition, and it included thirty photographs.[65] Priced at twelve marks, the guidebook was divided into the standard sections, including a short introduction, a brief overview of the city's history, a detailed inventory of sights worth seeing, a description of a "Walk around the City," and finally, a number of recommendations for excursions outside of the city, confirming that nature retained its appeal during the interwar period. The short introduction began by commenting on the duality of the contemporary city, asserting: "Augsburg is rich in historical memories, and in modern times it has grown into one of the foremost commerce and

[63] StadtAA, 34, 284.

[64] *Die Neue Augsburger Zeitung* (Augsburg), August 27, 1921; *Augsburger Neueste Nachrichten* (Augsburg), August 29, 1921.

[65] Verkehrsverein Augsburg, *Amtlicher Führer durch die Stadt Augsburg* (Augsburg: Selbstverlag des Verkehrsvereins Augsburg, 1921).

industry centers of southern Germany."[66] However, aside from a few allusions to contemporary Augsburg, history was the dominant theme of the guidebook, which consistently depicted the city as a microcosm of the larger German nation. For example, the introduction asserted that the city's museums and collections showcased the "larger cultural evolution of Germany," while a list of noteworthy Augsburg buildings and their previous inhabitants featured the artists Hans Holbein the Elder and Younger, Martin Luther, Emperor Maximilian I, Leopold Mozart (father of Wolfgang Amadeus Mozart), and economist Friedrich List.[67] Such passages created a connection between Augsburg's history and a broader German identity, and the inclusion of List in particular pointed to both nineteenth-century industrial growth and German national identity, as the economist was well-known for his theory of "national economics."

The *Official Guidebook*'s brief historical overview made similar connections between Augsburg's past and the larger history of the German people. For example, the guidebook described the Battle of Lechfeld (955) as a definitive moment in "world history," when a united German army reigned victorious over the invading Huns just south of Augsburg. The overview also dedicated special attention to the Renaissance, when Augsburg became "the transit station of commerce between northern Europe, and Italy and the Levant, thereby dominating world trade." It was during this period that Augsburg's most famous citizens, the Fuggers and Welsers, became internationally renowned as the "princes of European businessmen." As the Fuggers gained notoriety for rescuing Holy Roman Emperors from bankruptcy and commissioning the housing settlement known as the Fuggerei (later referred to as "the oldest and even today one of the most admirable attempts to solve the social question"), Bartholomäus Welser armed his own shipping fleet to take Venezuela as "the first German colony." According to this historical overview, the city reached its zenith at the beginning of the seventeenth century, a period defined by the work of local architect Elias Holl, whose masterpiece, the Augsburg *Rathaus*, was still under construction when the Thirty Years War began. After Augsburg's occupation by the army of Gustavus Adolphus (who hoped to transform the city into the center of a

---

[66] StadtAA, 20, 585. *Augsburg Amtlicher Führer (Mit Einem Stadplan und 30 Abbildungen)* (Augsburg: Verlag der Augsburger Buchhändler-Bestellenanstalt e.G.m.b.H., 1922), 1.

[67] Ibid., 1–10.

Swedish-German empire), the city lost its political and economic momentum. It was only after its incorporation into the Kingdom of Bavaria that Augsburg experienced a partial revival, taking a leading role in commerce and industry.[68] In this case, the Augsburg Tourism Association endorsed a Bavarian identity defined by a common economy, and not much more. There was apparently little room for regional particularism between these assertions of local and national pride.

According to the *Official Guidebook*, the history of Augsburg effectively culminated with the end of the Napoleonic Wars, and the years of 1914–1919 were conspicuously if not predictably absent. By eliminating these less triumphant episodes, the publication endorsed what Nietzsche would refer to as a "monumental history" of Augsburg, an uncritical representation of the past meant to inspire.[69] In general, the guidebook offered very little information about the modern city, aside from some statistics about the growing population and a brief reference to factories in the "Walk around the City" section: "In the south stretches the Haunstetter-Street with numerous factories."[70] Thus, the 1922 *Official Guidebook* suggests that the VVA still viewed history as the city's only selling point. Still, it is worth emphasizing that this was a whitewashed history that omitted the modern episodes of political strife and military defeat.

In addition to publishing a new edition of the *Official Guidebook*, the Augsburg Tourism Association took further measures to improve and promote tourism in 1922. In March, they announced a training course for local tour guides. This course would consist of three lectures and two sight-seeing tours, with the first lecture to be held in the historic *Drei Mohren* hotel at the end of the month.[71] This initiative demonstrated that the Augsburg Tourism Association was not only interested in attracting visitors; it also sought to promote awareness and enthusiasm among the local population. At the same time, the VVA experimented with alternative means of marketing. In April, they announced that they were working with a well-known Munich film studio, Cabinet-Film-Gesellschaft, to produce a propaganda film entitled *Augsburg and Its Industry*. This film would advertise Augsburg as both an industrial center and a tourist destination to potential visitors in Germany and abroad. In order to make the film more aesthetically pleasing and interesting, the VVA insisted on

[68] Ibid., 10–15, 61–62.
[69] Nietzsche, *Unfashionable Observations*, 96–100.
[70] *Augsburg Amtlicher Führer* (1922), 79.
[71] *Augsburger Neueste Nachrichten* (Augsburg), March 27, 1922.

filming in historical locations, particularly in the Fuggerei. It also appealed to the municipal government for an additional 20,000 marks for the film's production, a request that was subsequently denied.[72] Despite such setbacks, the film was completed and debuted on July 6, 1922. On the following day, it received a rather negative review in the *Augsburger Neueste Nachrichten*. Although *Augsburg and Its Industry* reportedly featured impressive cinematography that juxtaposed the historical and the modern, its overall effect was diminished by advertisements for local companies and businesses, and extended demonstrations of industrial techniques.[73] In marketing Augsburg as a sight worth seeing, the propaganda film focused too much on its industry, instead of the historical center that defined the city.

In spite of such mixed results, the Augsburg Tourism Association did manage to break new ground during this period, until the hyperinflation of 1922–1923 abruptly stopped its momentum.[74] The devaluing of the mark had a discernible effect on conspicuous consumption in Germany, as both wealthy residents and international visitors used highly valued foreign currency to stock up on luxury goods. During the summer of 1922, Augsburg newspapers reported that "stuffy, middle-class" foreigners speaking English, French, Italian, Dutch, and even Spanish had descended upon the city, where they took advantage of the plummeting exchange rate.[75] Throughout Bavaria, widespread fears that outsiders would consume limited resources bred open animosity and xenophobia, and the residents of Upper Bavaria and Munich in particular acquired a reputation for their poor treatment of foreigners. In Oberammergau, the first post war performance of the Passion Play brought a multitude of foreign tourists in 1922, but it also led to threats of violence and rioting from local miners. Although the performance was uneventful, high prices dissuaded visitors from staying.[76] In 1924, the German-Jewish journalist Kurt Tucholsky compelled travelers to "shun Bavaria," insisting that they would be "more comfortable and safe" in Africa.[77]

---

[72] StadtAA, 34, 290: "Filmaufnahme der Stadt Augsburg, I. Bd., 1921–1931."
[73] *Augsburger Neueste Nachrichten* (Augsburg), July 7, 1922.
[74] See Gerald D. Feldman, *The Great Disorder: Politics, Economics, and Society in the German Inflation, 1914–1924* (New York: Oxford University Press, 1993).
[75] *Augsburger Neueste Nachrichten* (Augsburg), August 12, 1922.
[76] Feldman, "The 'Fremdenplage' in the Weimar Inflation," 643, 645; Waddy, *Oberammergau in the Nazi Era*, 34–35.
[77] *Die Weltbühne* (Berlin), February 7, 1924. For this particular piece, Tucholsky used one of his pen names, Ignaz Wrobel.

This unprecedented local resistance to tourists tarnished Bavaria's reputation, but it only occurred when the financial benefits of tourism were no longer guaranteed. Indeed, tourist locales throughout Bavaria struggled to make ends meet during the early 1920s. This was certainly the case in Bad Reichenhall, where a lack of capital led to the closing of several bathing facilities and hotels, as well as the dissolution of the spa orchestra.[78] The situation was not nearly as serious in Franconian Switzerland, but limited municipal budgets did delay one of the local tourism industry's long-term goals: an improvement of the region's roads that would facilitate automobile travel.[79] In Augsburg, the tourism industry pursued similar long-term goals in spite of economic hardships. Although the Augsburg Tourism Association did manage to convince the municipal government to increase its subsidy to 200,000 marks in September 1923, it still lacked the financial resources to expand marketing.[80] Meanwhile, the number of visitors declined dramatically after the "plague of foreigners" in 1922. Extensive statistics assembled by the VVA confirmed that the number of registered guests dropped from 106,179 to 70,197 between 1921 and 1923. This represents a decrease of over 30 percent, slightly higher than the 25 percent decrease recorded by the Nuremberg tourism industry during the same years.[81] Statistics also confirm that Augsburg, like so many other German cities, attracted mostly domestic visitors, with foreigners constituting only a small percentage of the overall figure.[82] Of the 70,197 guests that registered in 1923, approximately 77 percent came from Bavaria or Prussia alone, while only 7 percent, or 4,487, traveled from abroad.[83] These were not reassuring statistics for the VVA, whose members had only recently begun to revitalize Augsburg's image.

New Directions and Old Habits

In the midst of the hyperinflation in March 1923, the Augsburg Tourism Association appointed a new director: native-born economist Dr. Hans

---

[78] Pfisterer, *Bad Reichenhall in seiner bayerischen Geschichte*, 342–343.

[79] Schottky, *Geschichte des Fränkische-Schweiz-Vereins*, 82.

[80] StadtAA, 34, 284.

[81] StadtAN, Hauptregistrar, 1292: "Hebung des Fremdenverkehrs, sowie Fremdenverkehr überhaupt, 1936–1939, III. Band." *Die Statistik des Fremdenverkehrs (Mitteilungen des Statistischen Amts der Stadt der Reichsparteitage)*, Heft 14 (Nuremberg: Im Auftrage des Oberbürgermeisters der Stadt der Reichsparteitage Nuremberg, Herausgegeben vom Statistischen Amt, 1938), 14–23.

[82] See McElligott, *The German Urban Experience*, 151.

[83] StadtAA, 20, 588.

Alfred Steib. A year beforehand, Steib had assumed control of the newly-formed Augsburg Press Office, among the first of its kind in Germany. It was during his ten years as director of the VVA that the "intensive marketing" of Augsburg really began.[84] With the help of colleagues like architect Thomas Wechs, graphic artist Friedrich Döllgast, and publisher Dr. Benno Filser, Steib mobilized limited resources to promote the city both domestically and internationally as a historically rich but modern metropolis.[85] Although the contemporaneous tourist propaganda continued to focus on the treasures of the *Altstadt*, it also devoted more attention to the modern dimensions of the city. At the end of the decade, Steib was likewise responsible for several new attractions that literally reframed Augsburg's historical space. This careful balancing of old and new identities was a deliberate strategy designed to secure Augsburg's reputation as both a tourist sight and a nationalist site. It was also a response to growing criticism from sources like the *Augsburger Neueste Nachrichten*, which proclaimed in June 1923: "The glorious reminders of the past cannot draw large numbers of visitors on their own if the city does not offer something meaningful from its modern, cultural life."[86] There had to be a harmony between past and present.

Early efforts to create such a balance were evident in the 1924 edition of the *Official Guidebook*. Much of the information in this publication was reprinted from the 1922 edition discussed above, but there were some notable changes. For example, the new guidebook contained a "Foreword" by local author Wilhelm Schäfer, who declared: "What distinguishes Augsburg from the other cities of Germany is precisely this: its old section does not remain superfluous after the city's nineteenth-century rise to prominence, instead, the old city of Augsburg is in fact also the new city of Augsburg."[87] As the city's primary tourist attraction, the historical center was not an anachronism; it was the heart of the modern metropolis. The 1924 *Official Guidebook* also featured new sections on "Sports" and "Industrial Augsburg." While the former revealed a new interest in mass culture, the latter section repeatedly stressed the international reputation of the city's two leading industries: textiles and metalwork. It also turned modern-day unemployment into a selling point, advising "those who seek work in Augsburg" to apply at the various metalworking factories where

---

[84] Grünsteudel, Hagele, and Frankenberger, eds., *Augsburger Stadtlexicon*, 846.
[85] Fritz Weisser, "*. . . wie Augsburg für sich warb.*" *1891–1991* (Augsburg: Helga Vetterle Marketing-Management Werbeagentur GmbH, 1991), 5–6.
[86] *Augsburger Neueste Nachrichten* (Augsburg), June 11, 1923.
[87] StadtAA, 20, 585. *Augsburg Amtlicher Führer* (1924), 5.

"refined tools and machinery" were used to manufacture "products that enjoy an international reputation."[88] The most celebrated of these Augsburg products was the Diesel motor, but Augsburg's industrial output also included beer, paper, furniture, and aircraft.

By going into such detail about industry, this section broke new ground. It even cast factories as potential tourist attractions, announcing that "[t]ours through industrial facilities are arranged by the Tourism Office."[89] Admittedly, a German obsession with the American economic models of rationalization and Fordism had engendered a unique form of industrial tourism in the 1920s, drawing German entrepreneurs, engineers, and students to industrial sites in Chicago, Detroit, and Pittsburgh. Those interested in confronting their own country's "crisis of industrial backwardness" might have been compelled to visit Augsburg's textile or machinery factories, but we have no evidence that they did so.[90] Still, the fact that the Augsburg Tourism Association even extended the offer suggests that the self-definition of the city had evolved.

By 1924, "industrial Augsburg" had become a more prominent feature of the constructed identity of the city, even though visitors remained focused on historical Augsburg. After visiting the city in the early 1920s, Munich resident Thomas Mann praised the overall beauty of Augsburg, its intimacy and "medieval German character," and the friendliness of its inhabitants. He proclaimed: "There may be residents of Augsburg who consider their city's proximity to the much larger Munich as one of the benefits of their place of residence. I belong to those residents of the capital who regard the proximity to Augsburg as one of Munich's countless advantages."[91] Another author, Nazi sympathizer Will Vesper, used the language of romantic infatuation in describing his feelings about Augsburg:

I will also admit, that I am a little prejudiced and partial, like a lover, because I adore Augsburg; I love its gorgeous, old buildings, above all others the noble masterpieces of Elias Holl, which have left their immortal mark on the spirit and character of the city; I love its magnificent, roaring fountains, that have no equal throughout Germany; I love the exciting blue skies over the rooftops and towers, the thunder of the Lech River . . . the pristine and small Fuggerei, the towering, proud churches and the old gates of the city walls . . .[92]

---

[88] Ibid., 39–40.
[89] Ibid., 40–41, 43.
[90] Nolan, *Visions of Modernity*, 22.
[91] Verkehrsverein Augsburg, *Das schöne Augsburg* (Augsburg: Selbstverlag. des Verkehrsvereins Augsburg, 1925), 1.
[92] Ibid., 3.

In 1925, the Augsburg Tourism Association capitalized on such sentiments by publishing an oversized pamphlet entitled "Beautiful Augsburg," which included the endorsements of Mann and Vesper, along with similar passages from art historian Josef Ponten and author Stefan Zweig.[93] These endorsements revealed a fascination with historical Augsburg, but they also helped to locate the city within modern German culture. Furthermore, the fact that some of this praise came from members of Munich's cultural elite made the 1925 publication even stronger in the eyes of the Augsburg Tourism Association. In 1926, its members decided to exploit their city's popularity by trying to convince famous authors and artists to relocate from Munich to Augsburg, where their very presence would transform the city into a center of modern culture. Although this particular strategy failed, the idea alone confirms that the Augsburg Tourism Association was ready to test new waters. In a September 1926 communiqué, representatives of the VVA insisted that new tourist propaganda must place greater emphasis on Augsburg's contributions to the economy and culture of modern Germany. The monuments of the *Altstadt* were no longer adequate, and the local tourism industry needed to utilize every possible selling point to improve the image of its city.[94]

This interest in updating marketing was evident in another initiative: the production of a new travel poster for distribution across Germany. Implementing a plan that had been discussed for years, the Augsburg Tourism Association organized a city-wide contest in 1924, inviting residents to submit designs for the new advertisement, and offering a 400-mark prize for the first place.[95] Although they received sixty-eight submissions from artists throughout the region, the association ultimately chose a 1924 design by Friedrich Döllgast, a close colleague of Hans Alfred Steib. His sleek and eye-catching design, printed on both posters and postcards, featured the simple slogan: "The Old Free Imperial City of Augsburg." Directly above the slogan were two silhouettes of the Augsburg cityscape: the larger silhouette in the background introduced the more recognizable landmarks of the city, while the second silhouette in the foreground depicted a number of nondescript smaller buildings, including church steeples and several smokestacks. Dominating the left-hand side of the poster was a red eagle, perched upon the official symbol of Augsburg, an upright pine cone atop a Corinthian column.[96] Just as

[93] Ibid., 3–4. The travel accounts of Mann, Vesper, and Zweig are also available in Ruhl, ed., *Augsburg in alten und neuen Reisebeschreibungen*, 221–229.
[94] StadtAA, 20, 586: "Förderung des Fremdenverkehrs, II. Band, 1926."
[95] *Augsburger Neueste Nachrichten* (Augsburg), April 9, 1924.
[96] StadtAA, 20, 586.

FIGURE 9. Poster produced by the Augsburg Tourism Association, 1926. Note the inclusion of smokestacks in the foreground. Courtesy of Stadtarchiv Augsburg.

the simple design and limited text reflected new marketing trends, the juxtaposition of the two Augsburg skylines reflected a new commitment to balancing the city's historical and modern identities, even though the former was clearly more prominent than the latter. The sight of factories in the midst of steeples and medieval gates complicated earlier visions of Augsburg, and marked a departure from smokestack-less silhouette of the city that appeared in 1921's *Official Guidebook*.[97]

In general, official and unofficial publications gave more attention to the modern features of Augsburg during the late 1920s. For example, the 1927 *Official Guidebook* listed two "new" attractions within its list of sights: the large dam on the River Lech, completed in 1912 in the "most modern style," and the Western Cemetery, first constructed in 1872 and now equipped with "modern facilities," including a crematorium.[98] By calling attention to these modern facilities, the 1927 Augsburg guidebook

[97] Verkehrsverein Augsburg, *Amtlicher Führer durch die Stadt Augsburg* (1921), 1.

[98] Verkehrsverein Augsburg, *Augsburg: Amtlicher Führer* (Augsburg: Selbstverlag des Verkehrsvereins Augsburg, 1927), 50–51. For more on cremation in modern Germany, see Simone Ameskamp, "Fanning the Flames: Cremation in Late Imperial and Weimar Germany," in *Between Mass Death and Individual Loss: The Place of the Dead in Twentieth-Century Germany*, ed. Alon Confino, Paul Betts, and Dirk Schumann (New York: Berghahn, 2008), 93–103; Monica Black, *Death in Berlin: From Weimar to Divided Germany* (New York: Cambridge University Press, 2010), 41–44.

accentuated the progressive character of the city itself. Other publications advertised modern Augsburg by employing what one scholar has called the "malleable yet consistent discourse about continuity."[99] In a 1926 brochure, Fritz Droop argued that the "unison of order and strength" had elevated Augsburg to economic and political preeminence during the Renaissance, while simultaneously bolstering the status of Germany. This powerful force persisted in modern Augsburg, where "the exhaust of the factories' smokestacks and the noise of a hundred workplaces rise toward the heavens like an oath of resolute action...The spirit of the Fuggers is still awake in this country!"[100] One location where this "spirit" survived was the Fuggerei, the famous social settlement that opened in 1519. In a travelogue first published in 1927, American Robert Medill McBride described the Fuggerei as a "memorial to the wealth and philanthropy of this illustrious family." Yet the settlement was more than a historical monument; it was a living part of contemporary Augsburg: "This miniature village has survived the centuries; it is like a modern spotless town and is occupied by indigent Roman Catholic citizens who enjoy the houses for nominal rents."[101] McBride, like the authors of many guidebooks, emphasized the continuity between the old and new Augsburg.

A 1927 guidebook by Alexander Heilmeyer also connected the historical legacy of Augsburg to its modern-day status as an industrial center, reminding tourists that "alongside this modern, bustling Augsburg, the immortal, 'eternal Augsburg' still stands, with its splendor and its monuments."[102] The 1925 *Trade and Industry Guidebook* issued by the Augsburg Tourism Association emphasized continuity as well, insisting that the "spirit" of Augsburg's most famous merchants of the past lived on in the modern city.[103] Remarkably, this spirit persisted in spite of the unstable economic conditions of the 1920s, just as it seemed to exist independently of the modern-day factory workers, who, like the peasants

---

[99] Koshar, *Germany's Transient Pasts*, 11.

[100] StadtAA, NL Förg, Broschüre "Augsburg die goldene Stadt (Von deutscher Städte Schönheit / Band I)," hg. von Fritz Droop (Augsburg: Im Bärenmeister-Verlag zu Augsburg, 1926), 5, 15–17.

[101] Robert Medill McBride, *Towns and People of Modern Germany* (New York: Robert M. McBride & Company, 1930), 123.

[102] Alexander Heilmeyer, *Augsburg und Bayerisch-Schwaben (Bayerische Reisebücher Band IV)* (Munich: Knorr & Hirth, G.m.b.H., 1927), 30–32.

[103] Verkehrsverein Augsburg, *Führer durch Augsburgs Industrie und Handel* (Augsburg: Selbstverlag des Verkehrsvereins Augsburg, 1925), 5.

of Franconian Switzerland, received little attention in tourist publications. The *Official Guidebook* of 1927, for example, only mentioned the workers once in the five-page section covering "Industrial Augsburg," identifying "the unionized training of the industrial workforce" as one of the reasons why Augsburg's industry was able to overcome the difficulties of recent years.[104] In general, the tourism industry endorsed an apolitical vision of modern Augsburg that eliminated one of its most volatile elements: the proletariat.

Industry and commerce helped to link the historical city of Augsburg with the German present, but it did not provide a wide range of sights worth seeing. Consequently, some tourist publications tried to point visitors to modern attractions that were potentially more enjoyable than a factory visit. Just as a 1926 guidebook produced by the Tourism Association of Munich and Southern Bavaria depicted Augsburg's cultural offerings as evidence of "modern life," VVA guidebooks advertised attractions that were more typical of 1920s mass culture, including various football clubs and at least five movie theatres in the city center.[105] Factories were not the only evidence of modernity available to tourists, and contemporary urban life was a potential attraction as well. Conversely, Augsburg possessed green spaces where visitors could enjoy a respite from the speed and noise of modern life. By identifying this variety of attractions, the tourism industry recognized an expanded clientele. Tourism was now part of a growing mass culture no longer defined by middle-class preoccupation with self-cultivation.

The local tourism industry promoted this revised image of Augsburg throughout Germany. In March 1926, the Augsburg City Council contributed 300 marks for an advertisement in an April issue of the *Leipziger Illustrirte Zeitung*, Germany's longest running illustrated newspaper. The advertisement, which appeared next to a detailed travel piece on Augsburg, contained the standard historical tropes along with an endorsement of Augsburg's "modern theater" and "metropolitan entertainment." Such recommendations complicated Augsburg's profile, suggesting that the city was not only industrially vibrant, but also culturally vibrant. The brief text concluded with a new slogan: "Whoever wants to know Germany,

[104] Verkehrsverein Augsburg, *Augsburg: Amtlicher Führer* (1927), 42–43.

[105] *Südbayern, hrsg. im Auftrage des Landesfremdenverkehrsrates vom Fremdenverkehrsverein München und Bayer. Alpen E.V.* (Munich: Gerber, 1926), 83–84; Verkehrsverein Augsburg, *Augsburg: Amtlicher Führer* (1927), 53–55. Previously known as the Association for the Promotion of Tourism in Munich and the Bavarian Highlands, the Tourism Association of Munich and Southern Bavaria was disbanded and reconstituted under a new name in 1923.

must know the city of Augsburg."[106] This slogan was an appropriation of King Ludwig I's claim that anyone who has not seen Munich "did not know Germany."[107] In both cases, a Bavarian city became a German city, but Augsburg's significance was not based on history alone. The article accompanying the advertisement reaffirmed Augsburg's overlapping identities as a historical site, a modern metropolis, and an industrial hub:

The actual significance of modern Augsburg lies in the areas of industry and commerce. Around the nearly traffic-free, pristinely preserved old city, in which one sees no evidence of industrialization, the principal factories of the textile and machinery industries stand along the banks of the Lech and Wertach... It is fortunate that in the ancient Roman city of Augsburg the image of an important historical center of art is united with that of a modern metropolis and industrial city.[108]

Alongside the advertisement subsidized by the Augsburg Tourism Association, the *Leipziger Illustrirte Zeitung* presented its readers with a balanced, apolitical vision of Augsburg, a city that was simultaneously old and new, but also German.

Nevertheless, tourists continued to favor "immemorial Augsburg," as one travel writer dubbed it.[109] In *Motor Rambles in Central Europe*, Frank Rimington dedicated fourteen pages to Augsburg, which he described as "an attractive old city." Unconcerned with Augsburg's "modern suburbs," the author marveled at the "old-time character" of the historic city, paying special attention to the remodeled *Drei Mohren* hotel, the *Rathaus*, and the Renaissance fountains.[110] Similarly, Frank Schoonmaker endorsed the "ancient town" of Augsburg in his 1930 travelogue, ranking it among "the most interesting towns of Germany." Unlike Rimington, however, Schoonmaker conceded that Augsburg had recently undergone a process of modernization that detracted from the city's overall charm.[111] In general, the traditional tourist view of Augsburg persisted, and was often endorsed by publications like a 1926 North German Lloyd magazine that identified Augsburg, alongside Nuremberg and Rothenburg ob der Tauber, as "towns that stood still."[112] In a 1928 report in the *Neue Pariser Zeitung*, German

---

[106] *Leipziger Illustrirte Zeitung* (Leipzig), April 4, 1926.
[107] The Nuremberg Tourism Association also used a similar slogan. StadtAN, Hauptregistrar, 1269: "Hebung des Fremdenverkehrs Bd. 1, 1903–1922."
[108] *Leipziger Illustrirte Zeitung* (Leipzig), April 4, 1926.
[109] Wilhelm Hausenstein, *Die Welt um München* (Munich: Knorr & Hirth, 1929), 41, 43.
[110] Rimington, *Motor Rambles in Central Europe*, 47–60.
[111] Schoonmaker, *Come With Me Through Germany*, 105–106.
[112] StadtAA, 20, 586.

traveler Albert Bintz described Augsburg as follows: "Here history lives on forever; there is no need for the imagining of the 'back then' of sunken times, because the memory endures, more beautiful and more natural than the weak means of a 'historical film' could ever accomplish."[113] In the eyes of both domestic and foreign visitors, Augsburg's living history was the star attraction, providing solace in a time of political and economic uncertainty. Even locals remained enthusiastic about Augsburg's history. In his 1927 travelogue, Robert Medill McBride recounted how the custodian of the *Rathaus* admitted him into the Golden Hall when it was closed for lunch, and guided him "through the apartments and pointed out the treasures with as much pride as if they been his own property."[114]

Throughout the 1920s, the Augsburg Tourism Association was trapped between the Scylla of the past and the Charybdis of the present; the former had proved incapable of attracting enough tourists, while the latter threatened to negate the one formula that seemed to work. In the end, they chose both. The 1929 edition of the *Augsburg Official Guidebook*, for example, did not rely on the city's traditional persona, but instead endorsed an amalgamation of municipal identities, which appeared as slogans printed on the top and bottom of each page. Some were reminiscent of older marketing, and pointed to the city's illustrious past: "Augsburg's Unique Cityscape is a Mirror of Two Thousand Years" and "Augsburg, the City of the Romans, Reichstage, Renaissance, and Reformation." Other slogans confirmed the city's contemporary economic significance, and even more importantly for the tourist, its accessibility: "The Modern Augsburg: The Industrial Center of Southern Germany – Machinery Factories, Aircraft Works, Textile and Paper Industries," and "Augsburg is a Railway Hub and International Airport."[115] On the other hand, the author conceded that many seasoned travelers had never visited Augsburg, with many preferring to travel straight on to Munich, an odd turn of events considering the fact that Augsburg had already achieved international prestige when the founder of Munich, Henry the Lion, was "still in diapers." To add insult to injury, the author of the guidebook also claimed that Munich had only become a great metropolis as a result of its proximity to Augsburg.[116]

[113] *Neue Pariser Zeitung* (Paris), June 9, 1928.
[114] McBride, *Towns and People of Modern Germany*, 124–125.
[115] Verkehrsverein Augsburg, *Augsburg: Amtlicher Führer, Kleine Ausgabe 1929/30* (Augsburg: Hieronymous Mühlberger, 1929).
[116] Ibid., 3–4.

Although the Augsburg Tourism Association produced a variety of new publications after Steib's appointment, the organization did not limit its efforts to printed propaganda. In July 1924, the organization announced that it was sponsoring a second film about Augsburg, but this time it was a feature film set in the Renaissance. In the wake of the hyperinflation, the local government surprisingly pledged both material and financial support, ultimately contributing 22,500 marks to the film's production, in addition to permitting film crews inside the Golden Hall and other historic locations. The local community contributed to the production of the film as well, with approximately 500 residents volunteering to appear as extras. The film, *Die Galgenbraut*, premiered in November 1924, and was screened in numerous German cities. Although it did achieve the goal of increasing Augsburg's visibility among potential visitors, there were some reservations about the appearance of the historic buildings in the film, with members of the Augsburg Tourism Association believing that certain landmarks were relegated to the background.[117] For some, historical Augsburg was simply not prominent enough.

Later that year, the Augsburg Tourism Association sponsored a marionette theater on an outdoor stage in the city park, where visitors and locals alike could pay 30 cents to watch a performance of "Dr. Johannes Faust."[118] Although this initiative did draw some tourists out of the city center, it was not exactly profitable. In a report to the city council the following year, the VVA confessed that it had lost 10,000 marks in financing the puppet show, and consequently planned to shorten the theater's season to two months the following year.[119] Another initiative that produced mixed results was the "Augsburg Tourism Auto," a twenty-two-seat vehicle that allowed visitors to "comfortably" and "effortlessly" view the attractions of the *Altstadt*. However, these inexpensive tours through the city center did not yield enough profit to pay for the maintenance of the 40 PS-Wagen, forcing the tourism association to use the vehicle for day-trips to regional destinations like Hohenschwangau and Starnberg. This led some locals to suggest that the VVA should change its name to the "Association for the Improvement of Tourism in Other Cities."[120]

One of the ways in which the Augsburg Tourism Association responded to such criticism was by renewing efforts to bring Munich

---

[117] StadtAA, 34, 290; Weisser, "*... wie Augsburg für sich warb." 1891–1991*, 3.
[118] Weisser, "*... wie Augsburg für sich warb." 1891–1991*, 1.
[119] StadtAA, 34, 284.
[120] *Augsburger Neueste Nachrichten* (Augsburg), June 12, 1924, August 12, 1924.

residents to the Swabian capital. In 1925, the VVA was responsible for coordinating a special train, or *Sonderzug*, from Munich to Augsburg. Demonstrating a new interest in attracting day-trippers that was already prevalent among the members of the Franconian Switzerland Association, the Augsburg Tourism Association organized this offer in conjunction with the Oberpollinger department store in Munich.[121] This initiative promised to bring hundreds of Munich residents to Augsburg, drawing the two cities closer together, and introducing a new market to the "City of the German Renaissance." In a communiqué to the city council in March 1925, the Augsburg Tourism Association suggested that the municipal government grant the Munich visitors free admission to the city's various attractions. The city council promptly rejected the idea. This did not prevent the Augsburg Tourism Association from proceeding with its plans, and the *Sonderzug* containing 750 Munich residents arrived in Augsburg during the first week of April. An article in the *Münchner Neuesten Nachrichten* described the trip as a huge success, noting that over 1,200 people had visited Augsburg's *Rathaus* that day. As a result of the intervention of the municipal government, we can assume that all of them had to pay.[122]

During an April 1927 meeting, the members of the Augsburg Tourism Association resolved to take a more "goal-oriented and devoted" interest in the everyday life of the city. If the promotion of travel to Augsburg was the true objective, then the local tourism association resolved to become involved in all matters relating to the appearance, development, and future of the city, as the "living presence" of Augsburg could produce a far greater effect than the printed word.[123] Historical preservation was part of this program, and both the tourism association and the municipal government were committed to improving the overall appearance of the historical city of Augsburg. An article in a September 1926 issue of the "News Service of the Reich Central Office for German Tourism Promotion" commended the city for its extensive restoration of historic buildings. The piece reported that Augsburg's most popular tourist attraction, the *Rathaus*, was currently covered in scaffolding, allowing for "massive repair and renovation work." Local craftsmen had also completed restoration work in the Augsburg Cathedral, returning the "oldest stained glass windows in the world" to their original glory. Finally, private buildings throughout the interior of the *Altstadt* were receiving new coats of

---

[121] See Schottky, *Geschichte des Fränkische-Schweiz-Vereins*, 67.
[122] *Münchner Neueste Nachrichten* (Munich), April 7, 1925.
[123] StadtAA, 20, 587.

paint, "in accordance with their character" and Augsburg's historically "colorful image."[124]

By financing preservation work, the municipal government indirectly promoted tourism by enhancing Augsburg's "living presence," even though renovations for the sake of visitors were not limited to traditional tourist attractions. In the late 1920s, both the Augsburg Tourism Association and the municipal government took an interest in overhauling the appearance of the central train station. As the first "sight" encountered upon arrival in Augsburg, this unattractive building did not exactly impress tourists. In a 1920 editorial in the *München-Augsburger Abendzeitung*, a visitor from Berlin suggested that the city erect a sign that stated: "This building is one of the few unattractive buildings in the city."[125] After years of criticism, the city of Augsburg finally unveiled a new entrance hall to the central train station at the peak of the tourist season in 1926. This did not satisfy the VVA, whose members now urged the city council to turn its attention to the unsightly square in front of the train station.[126] The municipal government proved responsive, and promptly paved the street in front of the train station that summer. In spite of these efforts, the general appearance of the square remained a contentious issue.[127]

Both the diversification of marketing messages and the improvement of the cityscape itself confirm that the local community of Augsburg was more committed to tourism during the latter half of the 1920s. As a result of more stable economic conditions, the municipal government was even able to enlarge its annual subsidy to the Augsburg Tourism Association by 50 percent, increasing the sum from 20,000 marks, the adjusted figure after the hyperinflation, to 30,000.[128] Still not satisfied with the number of visitors, the over 500 members of the Augsburg Tourism Association worked to engineer new attractions. In 1928, a representative of the VVA contacted the Munich office of the General Electricity Company (AEG), inquiring about using spotlights to illuminate historic monuments. Always interested in attracting more visitors, the

---

[124] *Deutsche Verkehrsblätter: Nachrichtendienst der Reichszentrale für Deutsche Verkehrswerbung* (Berlin), September 21, 1926.

[125] StadtAA, 50, 1133: "Erhaltung u. Ausstellung des architektonischen Gesamtbildes der Stadt Augsburg, 1902–1979." *Die München-Augsburger Abendzeitung* (Munich), December 17, 1920.

[126] StadtAA, 50, 1288: "Ausgestaltung des Bahnhofvorplatzes, 1925–1978."

[127] *Augsburger Neueste Nachrichten* (Augsburg), October 28, 1927. See also Andreas Romer, *Willkommen in der Bahnhofstrasse!: Die Entwicklung der Augsburger Bahnhofstrasse und ihre Bedeutung für die Bürger* (Munich: Hampp, 2006).

[128] StadtAA, 34, 284.

tourism association advised the municipal government to organize a "test illumination" of the city's most reliable symbol, the Elias Holl *Rathaus*. After the obligatory debate, all parties involved decided that it would be more reasonable to illuminate the Basilica of Saint Ulrich and Saint Afra. Charging a fee of 200 marks, the AEG conducted a test illumination that summer. The event was a great success, and the local press applauded the spectacle of electric light on one of Augsburg's most recognizable landmarks.[129] Modern technology had literally presented Augsburg's past in a new light.

Another new attraction utilized the double parish of Saint Ulrich and Saint Afra in an entirely different fashion, employing it as a gigantic backdrop instead of casting it directly in the spotlight. In 1928, Hans Alfred Steib took the lead in planning a series of open-air performances in the double parish's large courtyard. A VVA flyer of June 1928 announced that a "mystery play" written by Hugo von Hofmannsthal would be performed in the unique venue every Sunday evening in July and August. Staging the play in this square, where one of the most prominent features of the cityscape was literally part of the performance, was designed to bring out locals as well as the "traveling public."[130] Furthermore, this new addition to the city's list of attractions would help to foster a new municipal identity. With its own annual, cultural event, Augsburg could compete with the other "festival cities" of Bavaria, including Bayreuth, Oberammergau, and Rothenburg ob der Tauber, site of the annual "*Meistertrunk*" performance.[131] The *Official Guidebook* of 1929 confirmed the success of the performances at the Basilica of Saint Ulrich and Saint Afra, which had allegedly established Augsburg's reputation as a "festival city."[132]

Steib hoped to solidify this reputation in 1929 with the construction of a permanent open-air theater at the medieval Red Gate, an idea first suggested by the director of the Munich *Kammerspiele*, Otto Falckenberg. Deputy Mayor Ackermann took a special interest in this project, and helped to secure government support for the construction of the theater. Situated on the southern end of the *Altstadt*, this new venue contained 2,000 seats, and transformed a recognizable portion of the historic city into an impressive stage set. The Open-Air Theater at the Red Gate hosted

[129] StadtAA, 20, 588.
[130] StAA, Regierung von Schwaben (Kammer des Innern), 18 362: "Fremdenverkehr, 1890–1932."
[131] Hagen, *Preservation, Tourism and Nationalism*, 66–79.
[132] Verkehrsverein Augsburg, *Augsburg: Amtlicher Führer, Kleine Ausgabe 1929/30*, 20.

two performances in August 1929: a Munich *Kammerspiele* production of a play by Austrian writer Max Mell and the open-air debut of Beethoven's only opera, *Fidelio*.[133] A 1929 publication issued by the RDV described these performances as a "total success," noting that they had consistently sold out.[134] The 1929 *Official Guidebook* announced that more "festival performances" were planned for 1930 in what was now being referred to as "Germany's largest open-air theater at the historic Red Gate."[135] Later, a traveling exhibition about German open-air theaters featured models of the Augsburg venue, which was praised by stage professionals as the most impressive of its kind in Germany.[136] Foreign visitors also took note of this new attraction, and an article in a June 1932 issue of *The Chicago Tribune: European Edition* promoted the performances at the Red Gate, announcing "Unusually Interesting Program of Music is Offered at Augsburg."[137]

Just as Steib and the Augsburg Tourism Association were overseeing Augsburg's transformation into a "festival city," they were also completing preparations for the 400-year anniversary of the *Confessio Augustana*, one of the most important declarations of the Lutheran faith. Events planned for the summer of 1930, the first of the Great Depression, included a series of musical performances ("From Bach to Beethoven") held in the Golden Hall of the *Rathaus*, as well as a detailed exhibition on the history of the Reformation and Counter-Reformation.[138] The latter was located in the royal chambers of the *Rathaus*, and featured a variety of artifacts from the Reformation era.[139] Additional festivities for the actual anniversary included theater performances, concerts, a parade, and an extensive illumination of the *Altstadt*.[140] The anniversary of the *Confessio Augustana* ensured that 1930 was an important year for Augsburg tourism, while the summer performance of the Passion Play in nearby Oberammergau ensured that a horde of international tourists were not far away.[141]

[133] Zorn, *Augsburg*, 267; Grünsteudel, Hagele, and Frankenberger, eds., *Augsburger Stadtlexicon*, 411

[134] StadtAA, 34, 276: "Förderung des Fremdenverkehrs, V. Band, 1929."

[135] Verkehrsverein Augsburg, *Augsburg: Amtlicher Führer, Kleine Ausgabe 1929/30*, 20.

[136] Weisser, ". . . *wie Augsburg für sich warb.*" 1891–1991, 2.

[137] StadtAA, 34, 303: "Verkehrswerbung im Ausland, I. Band, 1928–1936."

[138] StadtAA, 34, 276.

[139] Eduard Gebele, *Confessio Augustana 1530–1930: Führer durch die Ausstellung, Rathaus Fürstenzimmer* (Augsburg: Buchdruckerei Hieronymous Mühlberger, 1930), 1–2.

[140] See Verkehrsverein Augsburg, *Augsburg Amtlicher Führer, Kleine Ausgabe 1929/1930*.

[141] StadtAA, 34, 276.

In pursuit of these tourists, the members of the Augsburg Tourism Association initiated an unprecedented marketing campaign. They distributed a total of 33,000 brochures in German, English, Danish, and Swedish, in addition to 22,545 posters, 7,900 templates for newspapers, and 3,500 photos.[142] They also reached out to the local community, asking citizens to actively promote tourism, while also advising caution against the citizens of Munich, who were allegedly determined to "divert the expected tourist masses from Augsburg."[143] The Augsburg Tourism Association even oversaw the extensive training of local tour guides, who would receive an official license after six to eight weeks of winter courses.[144] Dedicating both time and money to the 400-year anniversary of the *Confessio Augustana*, the local tourism industry prepared itself for the inevitable flood of tourists.

Superficially, the *Confessio Augustana* celebrations were a success, and the well-attended events were praised by the local press. One article in an August 1930 issue of the *Augsburger Neueste Nachrichten* reported on the visit of 500 Americans who were supposedly very vocal about their "astonishment and admiration" for the "City of the German Renaissance." The mayor even found time to officially greet these Americans, and he made a speech emphasizing the historical connections between America and Germany, the latter now beaten to the ground and "bleeding from a thousand wounds."[145] Later reports indicated that Augsburg was one of the few success stories of the Bavarian tourism industry that year. During an October 1930 meeting of the Tourism Association of Swabia, Hans Alfred Steib (who had established this regional organization in 1926) confirmed that numbers had dropped throughout the region during the previous season, while the figure of overnight visitors in Augsburg had actually increased by 10 percent during the summer months.[146] Had the time and effort finally paid off?

Figures assembled by the Augsburg City Statistics Office confirm that the number of visitors rose slightly in 1930. Overnight visitors increased from 97,387 in 1929 to 103,619 in 1930, an increase of roughly 6 percent. This was a minor improvement from the nearly 4 percent growth between 1928 and 1929. More impressive was the fact that the number of foreign visitors to Augsburg swelled by approximately 40 percent

---

[142] Weisser, "... *wie Augsburg für sich warb.*" *1891–1991*, 12.

[143] StadtAA, 34, 277.

[144] StadtAA, 50, 1287: "Fremdenführerwesen, 1929–1978."

[145] *Augsburg Neueste Nachrichten* (Augsburg), August 4, 1930.

[146] StadtAA, 34, 277.

in 1930, increasing from 6,341 to 8,891. Efforts to draw more tourists to Augsburg had succeeded, but only temporarily. The overall number would drop in 1931, with only 92,938 guests registered. Still, this figure was greater than the number of visitors recorded in 1927 (89,214), and represented a less than 5 percent decrease from 1929. Not bad, but in September 1932 the local press reported that the number of guests had declined again that summer.[147]

Before the Great Depression paralyzed the German tourism industry, Augsburg had witnessed a significant increase in visitors, with the number of registered guests rising by over 10 percent between 1926 and 1929. However, if we compare these statistics with similar data from other Bavarian destinations, then Augsburg's triumph appears less impressive. For example, between 1926 and 1929, the number of registered guests in Nuremberg rose from 218,803 to 288,646, an increase of roughly 30 percent.[148] During the same period, Rothenburg ob der Tauber recorded "especially explosive" growth, with the number of overnight stays increasing by over 100 percent, from 43,036 to 100,053.[149] A 1930 report printed in the *Bayerische Staatszeitung* used the number of overnight stays in Bavarian cities and towns to compile a list of the region's most popular tourist destinations. Augsburg ranked #30, falling behind rural retreats like Berchtesgaden and Füssen, and the recovering spa town of Bad Reichenhall.[150] During the tourist boom of the late 1920s, when economic stabilization and diplomatic rapprochement drew millions of domestic and foreign visitors to Bavaria, Augsburg had failed to distinguish itself as a preeminent tourist destination. The local tourism association faced additional challenges after the Nazi seizure of power in January 1933, but in many ways, it remained caught between past and present, searching for the ideal balance between historical significance and contemporary relevance.

* * *

The objective of attracting visitors to Augsburg was no easy task during the Weimar era. In a 1928 memo, the members of the Augsburg Tourism Association identified several obstacles that were perpetually in their way. First, there was the fact that many local industries did not support tourism, for the basic reason that "tourism brings luxury, luxury

---

[147] StadtAA, 20, 587; StadtAA, 34, 278: "Förderung des Fremdenverkehrs, VIII. Band, 1932–1933."
[148] StadtAN, Hauptregistrar, 1292. *Die Statistik des Fremdenverkehrs*, 14–23.
[149] Hagen, *Preservation, Tourism and Nationalism*, 154.
[150] *Bayerische Staatszeitung* (Munich), January 12, 1931.

creates increased demands, and increased demands lead to higher wages." In other words, tourism threatened to disrupt the status quo among Augsburg's industrial workers. Apparently, leisure travel was not for everyone. Second, there was a general lack of local patriotism among Augsburg's citizens. This meant that the local tourism association had trouble generating enthusiasm among the local populace, who often responded to the VVA's efforts with apathy or even skepticism. Finally, there was the proximity of Munich, the leading tourist destination of Bavaria that boasted a wealth of sights and experiences.[151] In fact, aside from an obscure history of Roman settlement and Dark Ages tribulation, Augsburg could not offer anything that its sister city did not already possess, including factories.[152] In addition to these three obstacles, the local tourism industry also had to contend with the unstable German economy. The postwar recession, hyperinflation, and the Great Depression severely limited the amount of money available for leisure travel, just as material shortages and civil unrest dissuaded international tourists from traveling to Germany.

In spite of these obstacles during the Weimar era, the Augsburg tourism industry pursued more visitors while cultivating a new, progressive image of their city. For example, tourist publications began to place more emphasis on Augsburg's industrial output, often by identifying specific industries and factories in the city. By stressing the industrial might of Augsburg, these publications emphasized the industrial might of Germany at large, demonstrating belief in its interwar resilience while simultaneously ignoring the proletariat and their politics. Tourist propaganda also devoted more attention to the city's modern-day culture, which now ranged from football matches and movies to open-air performances of Beethoven at the Red Gate. In the meantime, guidebooks and brochures reframed the long and colorful history of Augsburg by making numerous connections between past and present. Their selective vision of municipal history minimized conflict and loss, yielding a narrative of consistent greatness that overshadowed contemporary crises. By highlighting the themes of historical continuity, industry, and culture, the tourism industry of Augsburg redefined their city with distinctly German attributes that could inspire the nation.

This was certainly a different rendering of grounded modernity than those on display in Franconian Switzerland and Bad Reichenhall, where modern amenities, technology, and medicine were the dominant icons

---

[151] StadtAA, 34, 284.
[152] StadtAM, Zeitgeschichtliche Sammlung, 116/1: "Fremdenverkehr München bis 1945."

of progress. Augsburg's tourist propaganda highlighted several of these features earlier, but it was only after World War I that it really began to focus on the city's contemporary identity. Thus, the Augsburg Tourism Association developed its own version of grounded modernity, putting visitors in touch with the German past and present. Still, the success of this new direction remains debatable. The tourism industries of Munich and Nuremberg, in contrast, developed much more profitable versions of grounded modernity after 1933 by anchoring contemporary mass politics in selective history and invented traditions. While Augsburg tourist propaganda steered clear of politics throughout the 1920s, subsequent publications in Munich and Nuremberg heralded the triumph of the National Socialists. And while Augsburg struggled to attract visitors throughout the interwar period, Munich and Nuremberg became packed pilgrimage sites for loyal Germans and curious foreigners alike.

5

The Nazified Tourist Culture of Munich and Nuremberg

"Munich, as the center of German tourism and an international travel destination, has summer after summer surpassed other German cities with its high volume of visitors, an accolade which carries the obligation of offering something exceptional during the peak season, as every German should experience their trip to Munich as more than a visit to a picturesque city or beautiful country; it should be an experience to be in the 'Capital of the Movement.' This experience should have an even more powerful effect on the foreigner, because it is in Munich that the spirit of the New Germany visibly advances..."[1]

Munich's Festival Summer 1935
(Distributed by the Munich Tourism Association)

"Atop the Imperial Fortress, one can look out over the old city to the urban sprawl of modern Nuremberg and the grounds of the Reich Party Rallies... a space that, once completed, will possess no rivals. This harmonious juxtaposition of the long-ago and the contemporary, of the spirit and culture of past centuries, and the spirit, culture, and powerful resurgence of the present, can only be found in one place in Germany, and every visitor will return from Nuremberg with unforgettable impressions."[2]

Nuremberg: Brief Guidebook, 1939
(Distributed by the Nuremberg Tourism Association)

After a string of electoral victories for the National Socialists, a group of conservative politicians appointed Adolf Hitler as German chancellor

---

[1] StadtAM, Zeitgeschichtliche Sammlung, 116/1.
[2] BayHStA, Sammlung Varia, 268: "Bayerische Verkehrs- (Fremdenverkehrs-) Vereine."

in January 1933. In the following months, the new *Führer* quickly established the foundations of the Third Reich, a fascist dictatorship that would unleash unprecedented destruction in pursuit of German racial purity and living space. Before engulfing much of Europe in flames, Hitler's regime took an active interest in tourism, which it viewed as a disciplined form of leisure that could reinforce the bonds of the national community. With the creation of the Strength through Joy program, the Nazis fueled the growth of mass tourism by offering new travel opportunities to the working classes. At the same time, Hitler inspired an entirely new variety of tourism that elevated the National Socialist movement and its leader. This new tourist culture was associated with a series of annual events, and it spotlighted a number of neoclassical structures that symbolized the Nazi triumph. Among these sights were the Temples of Honor in Munich and the buildings of the Reich Party Rally Grounds in Nuremberg, tourist attractions that drew thousands of visitors between 1933 and 1939. At these sacred sites, visitors could walk on hallowed ground and come into contact with the monumental history of the "New Germany."[3]

By analyzing the development of this unique tourist culture, the following chapter offers an answer to one of the most pressing questions about the Third Reich: How did Hitler's regime maintain the image of legitimacy after the suspension of democracy? The short answer: Nazis sold themselves well. With propaganda and pageantry, the Nazi party and the Bavarian tourism industry marketed a politically charged version of grounded modernity that used historical material to validate and glorify the rise of the Third Reich. This new historical consciousness led to a substantial re-imagining of two of Bavaria's leading tourist destinations. Munich, the provincial but cosmopolitan "Athens on the Isar," became the "Capital of the National Socialist Movement," one of the most holy sites in the Third Reich. Nuremberg, the "German Reich's Treasure Chest" long adored by romantics, became the "City of the Reich Party Rallies," a congregation point for the National Socialist party and the German people alike. Sights associated with Hitler and the Nazi Party became the defining features of these two Bavarian cities, helping to secure their reputation as German destinations.

---

[3] Throughout this chapter, I alternate between the terms "sights" and "sites," as I view these places as both tourist attractions and national *"lieux de mémoire* . . . material, symbolic, and functional." See Pierre Nora, "Between Memory and History: Les Lieux de Mémoire," *Representations*, no. 26 (Spring 1989): 18–19.

Locally produced tourist propaganda endorsed the Nazi identity of Bavaria's largest cities by detailing the recent history of the National Socialist movement. These publications also made numerous links between contemporary history and select elements of the Bavarian, German, and even Greco-Roman past. Furthermore, the prevalence of pseudo-religious imagery and practices within this tourist culture created a bridge between traditional Christianity and modernity. Such connections between past and present were central to this new version of grounded modernity, which helped to recast an inherently violent political movement as the natural and inevitable outcome of history. For many observers, the incomprehensible became innocuous, if not inspiring. Once considered a liability by the Bavarian tourism industry, the Nazis became one of its most profitable attractions, a veritable commodity available for consumption. By celebrating and selling the Nazi triumph, the Bavarian tourism industry compelled the German nation to move beyond the turmoil and strife of the previous decades and contemplate a glorious future.

Hitler's Bavaria and the People's Community

Within the larger story of tourism in the Third Reich, Bavaria merits special attention because its experiences were both exemplary and exceptional. Like other German tourist regions, Bavaria experienced a state-mandated *Gleichschaltung*, or "coordination," of its commercial tourism industry. For example: in 1933 the Tourism Association of Munich and Southern Bavaria (Bavarian Alps), which had existed for over sixty years, was reconstituted as the State Tourism Association of Munich and Southern Bavaria. This was in line with the Law for the Reich Committee for Tourism, which had established a national organization to coordinate leisure travel throughout the Third Reich.[4] The administrative simplification of *Gleichschaltung* also led to the dissolution of a number of smaller, sub-regional tourism associations that had occupied the space between the local *Vereine* and the newly reorganized state tourism associations supervised by the Reich Committee for Tourism. Among the casualties was the Franconian Switzerland Association, officially dissolved during a meeting in the Streitberg *Kurhaus* in June 1934.[5]

---

[4] StadtAM, Fremdenverkehrsamt, 14: "Verkehrs-Verein-München: Planstellen, Arbeitsgebiet, Errichtung, Gesetzblätte, Zeitungsartikel . . . 1933–1949."
[5] Schottky, *Geschichte des Fränkische-Schweiz-Vereins*, 100.

Like other select German destinations, Bavaria also profitted from the National Socialist leisure program, Strength through Joy. As one of the nation's top tourist destinations before 1933, the region was an obvious choice for KdF excursions. A September 1934 issue of the Nazi newspaper, the *Völkischer Beobachter*, reported that Strength through Joy had brought over 44,000 German tourists to Upper Bavaria during the previous eight months.[6] The following year, special KdF trains began transporting visitors en masse to Garmisch-Partenkirchen, where construction was already underway for the 1936 Winter Olympics.[7] Elsewhere, all inclusive trips to destinations in the Bavarian Alps and Franconian Switzerland helped to rejuvenate local economies and engineer support for the regime.[8] Even operatives of the exiled Social Democratic Party, who regularly discussed Nazi vacation policies in their reports, identified Strength through Joy activities in Bavaria as a "genuinely commendable achievement of National Socialism."[9] Bavaria's star role in this national leisure program helped to integrate the former kingdom into the Third Reich, while simultaneously elevating it above other German regions.

In addition to its experiences with *Gleichschaltung* and Strength through Joy, Bavaria witnessed a rise in defensive nationalism that transformed the marketing of certain tourist attractions, similar to what was already happening on Germany's "bleeding border" with Poland.[10] In the case of the "Bayerische Ostmark," German chauvinism combined with the myth of Czechoslovakian aggression to transform this border region into a "bulwark against the Slavs."[11] After 1933, guidebooks portrayed the "Eastern Marches" in ominously nationalist and militant terms, referring to the historical "colonization" of the "besieged border

[6] *Völkischer Beobachter* (Munich), September 13, 1934.
[7] See Josef Ostler, *Garmisch und Partenkirchen 1870–1935. Ein Olympia-Ort entsteht* (Garmisch-Partenkirchen: Verein für Geschichte, Kunst- und Kulturgeschichte im Landkreis Garmisch-Partenkirchen, 2000); Large, *Nazi Games*, 110–146.
[8] Ian Kershaw, *Popular Opinion and Political Dissent in the Third Reich: Bavaria, 1933–1945*, 2nd edn. (New York: Oxford University Press, 2002), 124, 136.
[9] *Deutschlandberichte der Sozialdemokratischen Partei Deutschlands (SOPADE)* 3, no. 7 (July 1936): A-54.
[10] See Elizabeth Harvey, "Pilgrimages to the 'Bleeding Border': Gender and Rituals of Nationalist Protest in Germany, 1919–39," *Women's History Review* 9, no. 2 (2000): 201–229.
[11] Jörg Haller, "'Die heilige Ostmark': Ostbayern als völkische Kultregion 'Bayerische Ostmark'" *Bayerisches Jahrbuch für Volkskunde* (2000): 63–73.

area," and the "absorption" of the "long sequestered region."[12] Meanwhile, in northern Bavaria, the local tourism industry of Franconian Switzerland discovered that its century-old moniker was now deemed unpatriotic by the Reich Tourism Association, the successor to the Reich Committee for Tourism. In a 1938 communiqué, Bavarian Prime Minister Ludwig Siebert conceded that "foreign" labels for German landscapes were indeed undesirable, but that this particular label had obvious economic significance. To change the name in the middle of the tourist season would hardly be in the interests of the local tourism industry.[13] Franconian Switzerland may have lost its tourism association during the Nazi era, but it managed to keep its profitable moniker.

While Bavaria had much in common with other German tourist regions during the Nazi era, it stood out for one simple reason: its central role in the history of the National Socialist movement. The region contained a number of locations associated with Hitler and the party, including Munich, Nuremberg, Berchtesgaden, and Landsberg am Lech. After 1933, other Bavarian locations grew in stature because of their inclusion in the National Socialist "liturgy of events," a schedule of secular holidays that included the anniversary of the seizure of power on January 30 and the Führer's birthday on April 20.[14] Within Bavaria, Hitler's regular attendance of the Wagner Festival helped to revive the tourism industry of Bayreuth, while the heavily politicized celebration of the "Franconian Days" outside of Ansbach annually drew close to 100,000 visitors.[15] Impressive landscapes, a rich historical legacy, and select images of modernity were common motifs for the marketing of Bavaria long before 1933. The rise of Hitler and the National Socialist Party added another element, and the promoters of regional tourism lost little time in capitalizing on Bavaria's Nazi connections.

In March 1933, a Munich firm issued a dense brochure entitled "Visit Bavaria, the Homeland of Adolf Hitler." Designed for distribution in northern Germany free of charge, the brochure celebrated the fact

---

[12] Herbert Günther, *Franken und die Bayrische Ostmark* (Berlin: Atlantis-Verlag, 1936), 7.

[13] StAN, Regierung von Mittelfranken (Abgabe 1978), 3699.

[14] Norbert Frei, *National Socialist Rule in Germany: The Führer State, 1933–1945*, trans. Simon B. Steyne (Cambridge, MA: Blackwell, 1993), 84.

[15] See Frederic Spotts, *Bayreuth: A History of the Wagner Festival* (New Haven: Yale University Press, 1994), 159–188; Thomas Greif, *Frankens braune Wallfahrt – Der Hesselberg im Dritten Reich* (Ansbach: Selbstverlag des Historischen Vereins für Mittelfranken, 2007).

that the "national uprising" of the German people had begun with the
creation of the Nazi Party in Munich, and consequently, Bavaria's
"national sentiments" were unrivaled. The provincial region was now at
the center of the modern nation. After the requisite sections on Munich
and the Alps (both beloved by the Führer, it noted), the brochure identified several other locations that were now associated with Hitler. Among
them was Braunau am Inn, an Austrian town that had not been part of
Bavaria since 1816, but still had the distinction of being the "birthplace
of the People's Chancellor, Adolf Hitler." The border town of Passau was
similarly redefined as the "city of Adolf Hitler's youth," while Landsberg
am Lech was singled out for its fortress, where Hitler was interned after
the 1923 "Beer Hall Putsch." Berchtesgaden, the Alpine resort town near
Bad Reichenhall, was even re-defined as the rustic retreat of the new chancellor, an attraction that was drawing a "constant stream of pilgrims"
as early as 1933, notes one historian.[16] The guidebook not only invited
northern Germans to visit Bavaria, but also compelled them to travel
to locations sanctified by the very presence of "our" Adolf Hitler, the
messianic unifier of the German people.

This 1933 guidebook offers an early glimpse of the Nazified tourist culture of Bavaria: a highly politicized form of travel that revolved around
sites associated with Hitler and the National Socialist party. The fact
that this particular publication appeared three months before the June
1933 legislation creating the Reich Committee for Tourism corroborates
one of Kristin Semmens' central points about what she refers to as the
"Nazi tourist culture": it was "a spontaneous, usually voluntary reaction to the Nazis' assumption of power."[17] This is a valuable point, but
her distinction between "Nazi" and "normal" tourist cultures prevents
us from appreciating how politicized attractions in Bavaria could redefine the travel experience without completely replacing traditional
tourist cultures. New attractions like the Temples of Honor or the Party
Rally Grounds were at the center of a Nazified tourist culture that presented the Third Reich as the natural extension of centuries of history.

Historical continuity was a dominant theme of the Nazified tourist
culture, even though it was a selective continuity that omitted divisive

---

[16] StadtAA, Bestand 34, 278: "Förderung des Fremdenverkehrs, VIII. Band, 1932–1933."
   For more on Berchtesgaden, see Ian Kershaw, *The "Hitler Myth": Image and Reality
   in the Third Reich* (New York: Oxford University Press, 1987), 60; Ulrich Chaussy
   and Christoph Püschner, *Nachbar Hitler. Führerkult und Heimatzerstörung am Obersalzberg,* 6th edn. (Berlin: C. Links, 2007).
[17] Semmens, *Seeing Hitler's Germany,* 42.

episodes like the Thirty Years War and the Revolutions of 1918–1919. By passing over these periods of conflict, the tourism industry promoted a vision of a harmonious German nation that endured into the present day. This vision corresponded well with official propaganda. In his 1938 work, *The Myth of the Twentieth Century*, Nazi ideologue Alfred Rosenberg argued that history was more than scholarly reconstruction or retroactive glorification of forgotten deeds; it was a means of elevating the racial community in the present day. While lambasting the detrimental influence that the Jewish race had on the Nordic people of central Europe, Rosenberg insisted that the German *Volk* was destined to lose its course if its bonds with the past were severed.[18] The Nazis worked to ensure that these ties remained intact. With propaganda and pageantry, Hitler and his followers compelled the members of the German nation to overcome recent trauma and racial degeneration by reconnecting with a monumental history full of heroes and triumphs. While many German historians now agree that the Third Reich was not simply a backward-looking, antimodern anomaly, but rather "the quintessential manifestation of modernity," it is clear that a strong historical consciousness was central to the Nazi worldview.[19]

This historical consciousness facilitated a perception of continuity between past and present in modern Germany. Annual Nazi events held at major tourist attractions in Munich and Nuremberg accomplished something similar through their use of Christian motifs. Several scholars have noted parallels between Nazi rituals and Catholic traditions, with some suggesting that the Catholic backgrounds of high-ranking Nazis like Hitler, Hermann Göring, and Joseph Goebbels might have played a role.[20] Recent scholarship has confirmed that Catholics played a major part in the early Nazi movement, influencing its ideology and providing crucial support during its formative years. This relationship was more or less over by 1925, but the Catholic influence was discernible in the pseudo-religious character of the Nazi festival culture, "a sort of hollow residue of

[18] Alfred Rosenberg, *Der Mythus des 20. Jahrhundert: Eine Wertung des seelisch-geistigen Gestaltenkämpfe unserer Zeit* (Munich: Hoheneichen-Verlag, 1938), 678, 684.

[19] Mark Roseman, "National Socialism and the End of Modernity," AHR Forum: "Historians and the Question of 'Modernity,'" *American Historical Review* 116, no. 3 (June 2011): 690.

[20] George Mosse, *The Nationalization of the Masses: Political Symbolism and Mass Movements in Germany from the Napoleonic Wars through the Third Reich* (New York: H. Fertig, 1975), 80; Jay Baird, *To Die for Germany: Heroes in the Nazi Pantheon* (Bloomington: Indiana University Press, 1990), 54; Robert S. Wistrich, *Weekend in Munich: Art, Propaganda, and Terror in the Third Reich* (London: Pavilion, 1995), 43.

the liturgical performativity of the earlier Catholic orientation."[21] While scholars continue to debate whether National Socialism was a secular "political religion" or a form of "religious politics," my research indicates that the pseudo-religious pageantry of the Third Reich, like so many other invented traditions, helped to establish the illusion of continuity between past and present.[22]

Continuity, both historical and cultural, implied unity, and the impression of unity helped to legitimize the National Socialist regime. During the past two decades, scholarship on the Third Reich has shifted away from a preoccupation with dissatisfaction or resistance to a new concentration on consent and the legitimacy of the Nazi dictatorship.[23] Especially useful is the work of Peter Fritzsche, who has explained the appeal of the "people's community," or *Volksgemeinschaft*, by focusing on "the realm of ideas and loyalties." Refuting the claim that the Treaty of Versailles and interwar economic crises led to the rise of the Nazi party, Fritzsche argues that the German people desired a new Reich founded upon ethnic nationalism and social reform. While previous governments had proved incapable of satisfying such desires, the National Socialist movement proposed "a program of cultural and social regeneration premised on the superordination of the nation and the Volk."[24] After Hitler's political triumph in January 1933, the idea of the *Volksgemeinschaft* was no longer a distant memory; it was an enticing reality that "dazzled disillusioned Germans."[25]

Admittedly, the idea of a *Volksgemeinschaft* could take many forms in Nazi Germany, ranging from a people's community grounded in an

---

[21] Derek Hastings, *Catholicism and the Roots of Nazism: Religious Identity and National Socialism* (New York: Oxford University Press, 2010), 4, 14–15.

[22] Hobsbawm, "Introduction: Inventing Traditions," 2. For more on "political religion," see Michael Burleigh, *The Third Reich: A New History* (London: Macmillan, 2000), 10; Philippe Burrin, "Political Religion: The Relevance of a Concept," *History and Memory* 9 (Fall 1997): 321–349. For more on National Socialism and its "religious politics," see Richard Steigmann-Gall, *The Holy Reich: Nazi Conceptions of Christianity, 1919–1945* (New York: Cambridge University Press, 2003).

[23] Examples of this earlier historiography include Kershaw, *Popular Opinion and Political Dissent in the Third Reich* and the six volumes of *Bayern in der NS Zeit*, edited by Martin Broszat. More recent works exemplifying the latter trend include Robert Gellately, *Backing Hitler: Consent and Coercion in Nazi Germany* (New York: Oxford University Press, 2001); Götz Aly, *Hitler's Beneficiaries: Plunder, Racial War, and the Nazi Welfare State*, trans. Jefferson Chase (New York: Metropolitan Books, 2005).

[24] Peter Fritzsche, *Germans into Nazis* (Cambridge, MA: Harvard University Press, 1998), 7, 235.

[25] Fritz Stern, *Dreams and Delusions: National Socialism in the Drama of the German Past* (New York: Vintage Books, 1989), 149.

idealized past, to a national community rooted in nature, or, more specifically, the primordial German forest.[26] What Fritzche and others have confirmed is that we should not dismiss the concept of the *Volksgemeinschaft*, however articulated, as mere propaganda. To do so would be to overlook the true nature of propaganda in the Third Reich, which actually did more to "confirm" attitudes than to "convert" them. Historian David Welch argues that official Nazi propaganda often appealed to "the rational elements in human nature," reinforcing "existing trends and beliefs" instead of creating new ones. One of these preexisting beliefs was the notion of a people's community grounded in an "idealized past."[27] Again, the Nazi dictatorship did not manufacture the idea of the *Volksgemeinschaft*, it simply mobilized it.[28] Moreover, it was not only official propaganda that endorsed the idea of the people's community, and thousands of citizens made "grassroots propaganda" at the local and regional levels.[29] This category included countless producers of tourist propaganda, who, in spite of the *Gleichschaltung* of the travel industry, rarely received specific orders on what to publish. Largely without coercion, these propagandists developed their own visions of *Volksgemeinschaft*, promoting a unified and historically grounded community that marked a departure from the impersonal and egotistical society described by Tönnies, Weber, and other cultural critics.

In Brown Bavaria, the regional tourism industry responded to popular demand by marketing modern-day pilgrimage sites that united and inspired the members of the *Volksgemeinschaft*.[30] We now know that nationalism motivated many regional and national tourism industries during the interwar period, leading them to promote certain sights and experiences that could draw citizens together as a nation. However, inclusion cannot occur without a certain amount of exclusion, and nationalism

---

[26] See Michael Imort, "'Planting a Forest Tall and Straight Like the German Volk': Visualizing the Volksgemeinschaft through Advertising in German Forestry Journals, 1933–1945," in *Selling Modernity*, 102–126.

[27] Welch, *The Third Reich: Politics and Propaganda*, 5, 9, 60–61.

[28] For a similar point, see Kershaw, *The "Hitler Myth,"* 4.

[29] Randall L. Bytwerk, "Grassroots Propaganda in the Third Reich: The Reich Ring for National Socialist Propaganda and Public Enlightenment," *German Studies Review* 33, no. 1 (February 2010): 95; Richard Evans, *The Third Reich in Power, 1933–1939* (New York: Penguin Group, 2005), 137–140.

[30] For more on the similarities between modern leisure travel and the tradition of pilgrimage, see Lloyd, *Battlefield Tourism*, 13–19; John F. Sears, *Sacred Places: American Tourist Attractions in the Nineteenth Century* (Amherst: University of Massachusetts Press, 1998), 5–7.

often relies on the premise of alterity, positioning "us" against "them." As Sigmund Freud noted in 1930's *Civilization and Its Discontents*: "It is always possible to bind together a considerable number of people in love, so long as there are other people left over to receive the manifestations of their aggressiveness."[31] This was certainly the case in the Third Reich, where a pseudo-scientific racism inspired by social Darwinism determined who was a part of the New Germany, and who was an alien threat. Among the latter group, German Jews experienced state-mandated discrimination as early as 1933, as they were gradually but systematically excluded from the political, economic, and cultural life of the nation.[32]

Nazi antisemitism certainly had an impact on German tourism, but this impact was neither immediate nor uniform. While some tourist locales embraced the party line, others proved reluctant to abandon their carefully cultivated reputations of hospitality. In Bavaria, many smaller communities did demonstrate hostility toward Jewish guests. For example, the local historical association of Rothenburg ob der Tauber placed four antisemitic "warning plaques" at the town's medieval gates, informing visitors that they were entering a racially pure German place where enemies of the Aryan race were unwelcome.[33] The Franconian tourist destinations of Ansbach and Dinkelsbühl posted similar signs announcing: "Jews are not wanted here."[34] In Upper Bavaria, allegedly amicable relationships between Jewish visitors and Catholic hosts in Oberammergau did not stop municipal authorities from endorsing a number of antisemitic measures, including the boycott of Jewish businesses and a law barring Jews from using the new swimming complex.[35] Antisemitism also impacted business in Bavarian health resorts, where Aryanization tended to proceed more slowly than it did in the seaside resorts of northern Germany. In Bad Tölz, local Nazis began targeting a Jewish-owned hotel in 1935, eventually leading to the mass exodus of the resort's approximately 350 Jewish guests. One year later, the hotel owner sold to an

---

[31] Sigmund Freud, *Civilization and Its Discontents*, trans. James Strachey (New York: W.W. Norton & Company, 2010), 98.

[32] For more on racial exclusion, see Michael Wildt, *Hitler's Volksgemeinschaft and the Dynamics of Racial Exclusion: Violence Against Jews in Provincial Germany, 1919–1939*, trans. Bernard Heise (New York: Berghahn, 2012).

[33] Hagen, *Preservation, Tourism and Nationalism*, 211–216.

[34] StadtAN, Hauptregistrar, 1286: "Verkehrsverband Nordbayern e.V., Bd. 2, 1933–1934."

[35] Waddy, *Oberammergau in the Nazi Era*, 182–186.

Aryan innkeeper, and Jews were officially barred from entering the spa town. In larger, internationally renowned health resorts like Bad Kissingen and Bad Reichenhall, the local tourism industry refused to implement antisemitic measures for fear of alienating Jewish guests.[36] Initially, the Reich Tourism Association proved unwilling to enforce such measures, but this all changed when State Minister Hermann Esser issued new provisions after the 1936 Olympics. From this point onward, Jews were only allowed to sojourn in spas that already possessed a "Jewish infrastructure." In Bavaria, this meant the "state baths" of Kissingen, Brückenau, and Reichenhall, where a veritable system of apartheid confined Jewish guests to pre-approved hotels and spa facilities, thus preventing them from "polluting" the air and water enjoyed by other tourists.[37] Still, Bad Reichenhall was not exactly "*judenfrei*," and it remained one of the few tourist destinations in Germany where Jews were legally allowed to vacation.[38]

The municipal authorities of Munich and Nuremberg had their own approaches to antisemitism, reflecting various political, ideological, and ultimately economic concerns. While the city of Munich hesitated to jeopardize its *Gemütlichkeit*-based, cosmopolitan character, the city of Nuremberg never denied its reputation as a center of German nationalism and antisemitism. However, even in the latter case, discrimination was not publicized in tourist propaganda, and racism was extremely subtle. In general, tourism relies on the dynamic of inclusion, as it seeks to sell its attractions to the greatest number of visitors. Consequently, some local tourism industries in Bavaria tended to mask the uglier implications of *Volksgemeinschaft*. Open discrimination may have been feasible in smaller towns like Rothenburg and Oberammergau, but it was not part of the carefully constructed image of Germany's great cities.

The Nazi regime attached special significance to five cities in particular, the so-called Führer cities. There was Berlin, imperial capital and the new center of "Germania"; Hamburg, "Gateway to the World" and center of international trade; Linz, Hitler's hometown and a burgeoning cultural center; Nuremberg, former Imperial Free City and site of the Reich Party Rallies; and finally, Munich, "Capital of the Movement" and longtime

---

[36] Bajohr, *Bäder-Antisemitismus im 19. und 20. Jahrhundert*, 127–135; Lang, "Jüdische Kurtradition und Bäderantisemitismus in Bad Reichenhall," 148.

[37] Bajohr, *Bäder-Antisemitismus im 19. und 20. Jahrhundert*, 127–135; Lang, *Geschichte von Bad Reichenhall*, 752–760.

[38] Lang, "Jüdische Kurtradition und Bäderantisemitismus in Bad Reichenhall," 148–149.

headquarters of the party.[39] After 1933, a 1,000-mark tariff discouraged German tourists from traveling to Austria, and consequently, Linz did not figure prominently in the tourist propaganda before the annexation of Austria in 1938.[40] Meanwhile, the other cities were marketed as the symbolic centers of Hitler's Germany. A 1937 publication by the Reich Railway Office for German Travel addressed all four under the title "German Capitals: Munich, Nuremberg, Berlin, Hamburg," offering valuable insight into how these urban centers were marketed during the Third Reich. In the case of Berlin, the brochure briefly covered the short history of the city before dedicating attention to its modern-day significance: "In recent years Berlin has increasingly become the spiritual, economic, and above all, political center of strength in Germany. All the essential elements of the New Germany are united before the visitors' eyes in the capital: politics and economics, science and art, commerce and trade . . . "[41] Such marketing emphasized the political and "spiritual" triumph of the Nazis, diverting attention from the decadence and depravity that had defined Berlin during the Weimar years.[42] Similarly, the brochure advertised Hamburg as unequivocally modern, casting the former Hanseatic city as a progressive and bustling metropolis that retained its economic might into the twentieth century. Decidedly cosmopolitan, Hamburg may have lacked traditional tourist attractions, but it was home to countless scientific and cultural institutions, as well as the notorious *Reeperbahn*, the "haven of pleasure."[43]

The brochure's descriptions of the Bavarian cities of Munich and Nuremberg adopted a somewhat different tone. Munich was characterized as "the heart of Germany," and alongside the decidedly modern Berlin, tangible evidence of the "internal wealth" of the nation and the "diversity of the German tribes." Munich was modern, but it had additional selling points, including its charming Bavarian culture, *Gemütlichkeit*, and colorful past (even though it was not much older than Berlin). Nuremberg, on the other hand, was depicted as the medieval city

[39] Eckart Dietzfelbinger and Gerhard Liedtke, *Nürnberg – Ort der Massen: Das Reichsparteitagsgelände – Vorgeschichte und schwieriges Erbe* (Berlin: Christoph Links, 2004), 32.

[40] Hachtmann, *Tourismus-Geschichte*, 134–137.

[41] HAT, Sachkatalog, D061/00/937/DEU: *Deutsche Hauptstädte: München, Nürnberg, Berlin, Hamburg* (Berlin: Deutsches Propagande-Atelier, 1937).

[42] A similar logic influenced Nazi plans to transform Berlin. See Large, *Berlin*, 255, 300.

[43] HAT, Sachkatalog, D061/00/937/DEU: *Deutsche Hauptstädte: München, Nürnberg, Berlin, Hamburg*.

of Albrecht Dürer and the Mastersingers, renowned for its hand-crafted toys and gingerbread. In fact, the brochure pointed to Nuremberg's historical identity as the reason behind its transformation into "The City of the Reich Party Rallies," claiming that the annual celebration forged a link between "yesterday and today, from the praiseworthy and empowering past to the living and energetic resurgence of the New Germany."[44] Such visions of grounded modernity reinforced the notion of *Volksgemeinschaft*, uniting the German people in the name of a common culture and history, while obscuring the fact that the new nation was actually built upon selective memory and racism.

The Capital of the Movement

Compared to the Roman-settled Bad Reichenhall or Augsburg, Munich was a relatively young city. Founded in 1158 near a settlement of Benedictine monks on the Isar River, Munich was located along the profitable salt trading route, and quickly grew into an important fortified city. It became the capital of Bavaria in 1506, and later served as an important center of the Counter-Reformation. After Napoleon transformed the Duchy of Bavaria into a kingdom in 1806, Munich served as the royal capital and the architectural centerpiece of the realm. Its stock rose even further after the re-location of the state university from Landshut to Munich in 1826, and the opening of a rail connection in 1839. After German Unification in 1871, the empire's third largest city acquired a status as a center of high arts and folk culture, equally renowned for its museums and concerts as it was for its beer halls and popular festivals.

Tourists found no shortage of sights worth seeing in the "Athens on the Isar." The *Altstadt* was the location of many of these attractions, including the iconic onion-domed towers of the gothic "Cathedral of our Blessed Lady" (*Frauenkirche*), as well as the largest downtown palace in Germany, the Wittelsbach *Residenz*. Another popular attraction was the beer hall known as the *Hofbräuhaus*, first established during the sixteenth century as the court brewery of brown beer. Outside the walls of the *Altstadt* were a number of internationally renowned museums centered around the *Königsplatz*, or "King's Square." While the Ludwig I-commissioned Glyptothek possessed a collection of sculptures from ancient Greece and Rome, the nearby Pinakothek contained paintings from European masters like Raphael, Rembrandt, and Rubens. Munich

---

44 Ibid.

also contained a variety of privately owned galleries, leading travelogue writer Olive Colton to declare: "All roads in Munich lead to a gallery, and art reigns supreme."[45]

Fin-de-siècle tourist propaganda celebrated this wealth of attractions, in addition to stressing that modern Munich remained a warm and inviting destination. The 1907 guidebook, *Our Bavarian Land*, proudly proclaimed: "Today Munich is a city of half a million residents. But in spite of the growth of its tourism, it remains the city of rest and relaxation, the city of friendliness and informality."[46] An 1899 "Illustrated Hotel Tourist Guide" urged visitors not to overlook the city's famous "art industry," but more importantly, not to forget about the world-renowned beer, which could be enjoyed in any number of inviting locales, where the "straightforward and open character of Munich's residents" was on display.[47] In numerous regards, this was a city of dichotomies, defined by the twin pillars of high and low culture, refinement and merriment, Rembrandt and *Weißbier*. Historian David Clay Large identifies additional contradictions in prewar Munich, a city that harbored the avant-garde tendencies of the *Blaue Reiter* and *Jugendstil*, as well as the antimodern, antisemitic, and *völkisch* sentiments of men like Julius Friedrich Lehmann. In several regards, Munich simultaneously embraced and rejected "metropolitan modernity," just as it attracted those in search of a more grounded version of the present.[48]

World War I and its revolutionary aftermath inaugurated a period of crisis for Munich's tourism industry. As was the case in Augsburg, bloodshed marked the end of socialist experimentation in the Bavarian capital, as the arrival of counterrevolutionary forces led to 600 deaths over the course of two days, and the summary executions of dozens more during the first week of May 1919.[49] In 1926, the Association for the Promotion of Tourism in Munich and the Bavarian Highlands reported that many travelers still believed that Munich was a dangerous place where they might find themselves caught in the middle of political street-fighting.[50] That very same year, an article in the local nationalist

---

[45] Olive A. Colton, *Rambles Abroad* (Toledo: The Franklin Printing & Engraving Co., 1904), 143.
[46] Platz, *Unser Bayerland*, 5.
[47] StadtAM, Zeitgeschichtliche Sammlung, 116/1.
[48] David Clay Large, *Where Ghosts Walked: Munich's Road to the Third Reich* (New York: W.W. Norton & Company, 1997), 3–42.
[49] Geyer, *Verkehrte Welt*, 50–129.
[50] StadtAM, Fremdenverkehrsamt, 7: "Verkehrswerbung, Reichszentrale, 1925–1928."

newspaper, *Münchner Neueste Nachrichten*, lamented: "Unfortunately, Munich can no longer count on its beauty, art, and hospitality to attract visitors. The tourist no longer feels at ease with us, and only uses the city as a transit point; the influx of visitors is steadily decreasing."[51] To make matters worse, the currency crisis had wreaked havoc on the hospitality industry, with a glass of beer costing up to 150 billion marks in November 1923. Although the hyperinflation initially brought an invasion of tourists, "flaunting their hard currency," locals tended to respond with excessively high prices and xenophobia, not the *Gemütlichkeit* promised by tourist propaganda.[52] Unprecedentedly, Munich residents rejected tourists, and economic hardships were to blame.

The ramifications of the 1929 stock market crash only complicated efforts to improve Munich's image. The municipal government's annual subsidy for advertisement within Germany decreased from 55,000 to 35,000 marks in 1931, sparking a crisis mentality among tourism advocates. Some of these individuals were responsible for the creation of organizations like the "Emergency Group for the Advancement of Domestic Tourism," an association whose very name betrayed the heightened nationalism of the interwar period.[53] A January 1932 issue of the *Bayerische Staatszeitung* announced a "sharp decline" in tourism during the previous season, noting that the number of overnight guests had decreased by 21.4 percent from 1930 to 1931, falling from 857,765 to 674,256. The number of foreign guests had dropped even more dramatically, falling 32 percent from 186,281 to 125,786.[54] Some observers attributed this decline to the political turmoil of the Weimar era, with several journalists blaming the National Socialists in particular. In addition to scaring away tourists with their periodic displays of violence, Bavarian Nazis adopted a decidedly anti-tourism stance in the summer of 1931. In response to alleged police harassment, Munich City Councilman and Nazi party member Hermann Esser announced that his party planned to "spoil" tourism in the Bavarian capital. Citing similar complaints, the Nazi party periodical, the *Völkischer Herold*, compelled its readers to avoid vacations in "Roman-ruled Bavaria," which had recently acquired a "frightening character." The local tourism industry and its

[51] *Münchener Neueste Nachrichten* (Munich), March 24, 1926.
[52] Large, *Where Ghosts Walked*, 159–160; Feldman, "The 'Fremdenplage' in the Weimar Inflation," 643; Geyer, *Verkehrte Welt*, 184.
[53] StAM, Polizeidirektion München, Vereinsakten, 5999: "Notgemeinschaft zur Förderung der Inlandreisen, 1931–1935."
[54] *Bayerische Staatszeitung* (Munich), January 24, 1932.

supporters took these threats very seriously, equating Esser's comments with "treason."[55]

In the end, the National Socialists did not spoil tourism in the Bavarian capital; they helped to save it. When the Munich tourism industry rebounded in 1933, it was a result of both the slow resurgence of the German economy and the sacralization of several sites associated with Adolf Hitler and the rise of the Nazi Party. That latter story began in 1913, when the struggling Austrian painter first arrived in Munich.[56] The conservative tendencies and carnival mood of the Bavarian capital connected with young Hitler, who later wrote in *Mein Kampf*: " . . . there was the heartfelt love which seized me for this city more than for any other place that I knew, almost from the first hour of my sojourn there. A German city! What a difference from Vienna!"[57] Upon the outbreak of World War I, Hitler was among the thousands of Munich citizens that participated in a massive patriotic demonstration on Munich's *Odeonsplatz* in front of the neoclassical *Feldherrnhalle*. Shortly thereafter, the young Austrian enlisted and headed for the Western Front. Four years later, a wounded but decorated corporal, Hitler returned to a city he barely recognized.[58]

In the political turmoil of postwar Munich, Hitler became a spy for the *Reichswehr*, and infiltrated the fledgling German Workers' Party, led by the antisemitic and anticommunist Anton Drexler.[59] Recognizing an affinity for the party's ideology, Hitler quickly became their star speaker, and even helped to draft the party program of the newly renamed National Socialist German Workers' Party in 1920.[60] By July 1921, he had replaced Drexler as the party's leader. During these early years, Hitler gained the loyalty of men who followed him throughout his career, including Hermann Göring, Julius Streicher, and Hermann Esser. He also secured the patronage of some elite figures, among them, General

[55] *Münchener Post* (Munich), July 21, 1931.
[56] Ian Kershaw, *Hitler, 1889–1936: Hubris* (New York: W.W. Norton & Company, 1998), 68, 81–82.
[57] Adolf Hitler, *Mein Kampf*, trans. Ralph Manheim (New York: Houghton Mifflin Company, 1999), 126. See J. Trygve Has-Ellison, "Nobles, Modernism, and the Culture of fin-de-siècle Munich," *German History* 26, no. 1 (January 2008): 1–23.
[58] Kershaw, *Hitler, 1889–1936: Hubris*, 89–90, 109.
[59] Large, *Where Ghosts Walked*, 128–129. See also Anton Joachimsthaler, *Hitlers Weg begann in München 1913–1923* (Munich: Herbig, 2000), 177–319.
[60] Kershaw, *Hitler, 1889–1936: Hubris*, 140–145; Hans Zöberlin, "München, die Stadt der Bewegung," *Das Bayerland. Illustrierte Wochenschrift für Bayerns Volk und Land* (October 1934), 589–590.

Erich Ludendorff, the symbolic leader of Germany's radical nationalist Right.[61]

It was Hitler's choice to capitalize on his association with Ludendorff that led to the failed revolution of 1923, a seminal event for the Nazified tourist culture of Munich. Using Ludendorff as a front, Hitler organized a putsch attempt modeled after Mussolini's "March on Rome." On the evening of November 8, 1923, Hitler and an armed entourage interrupted a mass meeting in the banquet hall of the *Bürgerbräukeller* beer hall. After silencing the crowd by firing his pistol at the ceiling, Hitler announced the beginning of the "national revolution." The following morning, Hitler, Ludendorff, and roughly 2,000 armed and somewhat hung-over men marched toward the Bavarian Ministry of War. On the road between the Wittelsbach *Residenz* and the *Feldherrnhalle*, they confronted one hundred armed policemen. After a brief exchange of fire, four police officers and fourteen insurgents lay dead, with two more of the latter group mortally wounded.[62] An injured Hitler managed to escape, but was subsequently arrested for high treason, and brought before a specially organized "People's Court" in Munich. The trial was a spectacle. Although Hitler received a sentence of five years in prison, he served only nine months.[63]

The coup attempt had been a fiasco, but it endowed Munich with indisputable symbolic capital that raised its stock as a tourist attraction. In the meantime, Hitler's brief incarceration in the fortress of Landsberg am Lech had brought the party's momentum to a standstill, but it was hardly enough to stamp it out entirely. A 1938 independently published guidebook on Munich described the party's rebirth, in English, as follows:

Yet though its source was for a time buried by a force beneath the debris its strength was not spent. Like some primeval power of the earth it burst forth again to the light of day. The free hands of the movement worked untiringly. On February 27th, 1925, Adolf Hitler could issue his summons in the Bürgerbräu-Keller to refound the National Socialist German Workers' Party under the motto: The Future of Germany and our Movement. And now the movement took its irresistible and unwavering course over Munich, Bavaria, all Germany... Yet Munich's fame will endure as the source and stronghold of the Movement – the

---

[61] Kershaw, *Hitler, 1889–1936: Hubris*, 149, 160–165, 186–190, 194–195; Andreas Heusler, *Das Braune Haus: Wie München zur "Hauptstadt der Bewegung" wurde* (Munich: Deutsche Verlags-Anstalt, 2008), 80–90.

[62] Kershaw, *Hitler, 1889–1936: Hubris*, 206–212. See also Harold J. Gordon, *Hitler and the Beer Hall Putsch* (Princeton, NJ: Princeton University Press, 1972), 270–409.

[63] Richard Evans, *The Coming of the Third Reich* (New York: Penguin Group, 2004), 195–196.

Movement, which as the leader promised, has indeed become identical with the future of Germany.[64]

Munich, "source and stronghold of the Movement," was effectively cast as the site of the party's Passion and Resurrection. In reality, the city lost much of its political significance during the years between 1923 and 1933, as the Nazi party focused on electioneering across Germany, and the majority of Munich's population proved unreceptive to the Nazi ideology.[65] However, after the seizure of power, Munich acquired a nearly unrivaled status in Hitler's Germany, a standing bolstered by frequent political festivals and visits by foreign dignitaries like Mussolini.[66]

In July 1935, Hitler officially designated Munich as the "Capital of the Movement," a title that carried serious political and cultural weight. Berlin may have been the political capital of Nazi Germany, but Munich remained the administrative center of the National Socialist Party, and was inextricably associated with the Führer.[67] The new title also branded the Bavarian capital as undeniably "German," thus obscuring any remnants of Bavarian particularism. But Munich was not only the city where the National Socialist Party had been founded; it was one of the first places where blood had been spilt for the New Germany, as Hitler often claimed.[68] Tourist propaganda employed similar language, with obvious religious overtones. A 1935 brochure issued by the Munich Tourism Association declared: "Munich is the Capital of the Movement. Here the spirit of the young nation became flesh and blood; here the first martyrs of the new empire fell."[69] In other words, Munich was the sacred birthplace of the Third Reich. Sanctioning this new identity, city officials commissioned a new municipal coat of arms, with the Bavarian lion now replaced by the iconography of the Third Reich: the eagle and the swastika.[70] Foreign observers also took note of this transformation. A July 1934 issue of *The New York Times* reported that Munich, "more

[64] Theodor Trautwein, *Guide Book for Munich, the Capital of the National Socialist Movement, Its Environs, and the Royal Castles* (Munich: Bergverlag Rudolf Rother, 1938), 19–20. This guidebook was also printed in German, containing relatively identical text.

[65] Heusler, *Das Braune Haus*, 117, 121–126.

[66] Elizabeth Angermair and Ulrike Haerendel, *Inszenierter Alltag: "Volksgemeinschaft" im nationalsozialistischen München, 1933–1945* (Munich: Hugendubel, 1993), 14.

[67] Helmut M. Hanko, "Kommunalpolitik in der 'Hauptstadt der Bewegung' 1933–1935. Zwischen 'revolutionärer' Umgestaltung und Verwaltungskontinuität," in *Bayern in der NS-Zeit, III: Herrschaft und Gesellschaft im Konflikt, Teil B*, 408.

[68] Heusler, *Das Braune Haus*, 203, 210.

[69] StadtAM, Zeitgeschichtliche Sammlung, 116/1.

[70] Large, *Where Ghosts Walked*, 231.

virulent in its faith than any other German center, save perhaps Nuremberg," was being "groomed to be a political and cultural south German
capital."[71]

This process began in 1933 when the Nazi regime erected a small
memorial tablet on the eastern side of the *Feldherrnhalle*. This *Mahnmal*, under the constant supervision of two SS men, commemorated
the 1923 putsch attempt by glorifying the sacrifice of the sixteen fallen
putschists. The tablet read: "The *Feldherrnhalle* is bound for all times
with the names of the men who gave their lives on November 9, 1923
for the movement and the rebirth of Germany."[72] The location of the
memorial alongside the *Feldherrnhalle* allowed for another connection
to a national past. Commissioned by Ludwig I, the *Feldherrnhalle* was a
monument to past military victories, and contained bronze statues of the
generals Johann Tilly and Karl Philip von Wrede, heroes, respectively,
of the Thirty Years War and Napoleonic Wars. The central bronze figure, depicting the goddess Bavaria, was added after the German Wars of
Unification, and was flanked by two lions, symbols of the former kingdom. It was a fortunate coincidence, then, that the 1923 putsch came to
a bloody end in the shadow of this nineteenth-century monument, as it
meant that the Nazi martyrs were venerated alongside the military heroes
of the Bavarian past. Different strands of regional and national history
were united in a common space of collective remembrance, even though
propaganda rarely provided details about the two generals, especially the
fact that Tilly fought against fellow Germans, and was notorious for the
Sack of Magdeburg. Visitors also neglected historical specifics, and travelogue author Georg Lang praised the location of the Nazi memorial near
statues of two generals "who had once written history with blood and
sword."[73]

Local tourist propaganda also acknowledged the new status of the
Feldherrnhalle, ranking the monument among the city's most important
sights while drawing vague connections between the German past and
present. For example, a 1938 guidebook published by the independent
Trautwein firm proclaimed:

This fine, yet solemn structure contains the statues of Bavarian generals and a
monument in honour of the great deeds of the old Bavarian army... On the east
side of the Feldherrn-Halle (Residenz-Strasse) the Mahnmal (Memorial Tablet)

---

[71] *The New York Times* (New York), July 1, 1934.

[72] Semmens, *Seeing Hitler's Germany*, 53. Semmens' translation.

[73] Georg Lang, *Im Auto zwischen München und Rom* (Bielefeld: Deutschen Heimatverlag
Ernst Gieseking, 1938), 8.

reminds us of an event of fateful importance for the New Germany. Here, on November 9, 1923, many of her best sons sank wounded and dying to the ground, the Leader, too, among them. The Mahnmal is dedicated to their memory and to the memory of all who died for the New Germany.[74]

This treatment of the landmark linked the "great deeds of the old Bavarian army" with the memory of the Beer Hall Putsch, grounding the New Germany in the process. Propaganda integrated recent history into the larger trajectory of the German nation *and* the architectural cityscape of the Bavarian capital. The *Feldherrnhalle* provided a crucial link between past and present, and photographs and paintings of the memorial on its eastern side became a standard addition to brochures and guidebooks, as well as a popular subject of picture postcards. An undated brochure issued by the Munich Tourism Association even used an image of the memorial for the cover of its brochure, "München."[75] What was once just another stop in Munich's long list of attractions was now a national shrine, the location where the "German eagle had commenced its flight toward the sun," as Georg Lang put it.[76] A 1935 Baedeker guide reported that tourists and residents alike were expected to perform the "German greeting" – the outstretched right arm – as they passed the memorial beside the *Feldherrnhalle*.[77] While one historian has argued that "the Hitler greeting" helped to create a sense of community among those that practiced the custom, one traveler noted that visitors could easily pass the *Feldherrnhalle* memorial without saluting, "and the Black Guards will not shoot you or even appear to notice you."[78]

In spite of occasional indifference, the Nazi regime insisted upon the reverent treatment of its fallen heroes. A German cult of heroism and sacrifice existed long before the rise of the Third Reich, but the Nazis transformed older traditions into unprecedented propaganda spectacles.[79] This cult of "national sacrifice" united and rejuvenated the people's

---

[74] Trautwein, *Guide Book for Munich*, 66. The word *Mahnmal* appears in bold in the guide.

[75] BayHStA, Sammlung Varia, 268; BWA, Bildpostkarten, 120: "München: Feldherrnhalle" (dated 25 September 1938).

[76] Lang, *Im Auto zwischen München und Rom*, 8.

[77] Karl Baedeker, *München und Südbayern Handbuch für Reisende* (Leipzig: Karl Baedeker, 1935), 15, 25.

[78] Evans, *The Third Reich in Power*, 123; John Alfred Cole, *Just Back From Germany* (London: Faber and Faber Ltd., 1938), 129.

[79] See Karen Hagemann, "German Heroes: The Cult of the Death for the Fatherland in 19th Century Germany," in *Masculinities in Politics and War: Gendering Modern History*, ed. Stefan Dudink, Karen Hagemann, and John Tosh (New York: Palgrave, 2004), 116–134; George Mosse, *Fallen Soldiers: Reshaping the Memory of the World Wars* (New York: Oxford University Press, 1990), 70–106.

community, "turning defeat and setback into victory and triumph."[80] The fallen putschists honored at the *Feldherrnhalle* acquired the status of mythological figures during the Third Reich, and their sacrifice was commemorated through an elaborate, state ceremony every November until 1939. The first commemoration of the putsch in 1933 concluded nine months of celebration following Hitler's appointment as chancellor, and it drew over 50,000 visitors to Munich.[81] Other festive occasions, such as the May Day celebrations in Berlin, or the Harvest Thanksgiving in Lower Saxony, paled in comparison to the extensive pageantry of the November commemoration, which Hitler reportedly took a personal interest in organizing.[82] On the morning of November 8, all of Munich was adorned with swastika flags and banners, many of them provided by the citizens themselves. The local government effectively shut the city down, closing retail stores and forbidding the use of motor vehicles in certain neighborhoods. The festivities officially began with a performance of Richard Wagner's *Lohengrin*, and concluded with the solemn, commemorative march from the *Bürgerbräukeller* to the *Feldherrnhalle*, complete with the remaining "Old Guard" and the cherished "*Blutfahne*," the Nazi banner stained with the blood of fallen putschists.[83] By retracing the route of the sixteen martyrs, the Nazi party developed something akin to its own stations of the cross. Moreover, the vaguely religious motifs that defined the Munich ceremony helped to sanctify the space on which it was celebrated.

This sacred space was expanded with the completion of the open-air Temples of Honor (*Ehrentempel*) in 1935. Located at the eastern edge of the *Königsplatz*, the monuments completed Ludwig I's neoclassical forum, "unfinished" for "hundreds of years," according to one guidebook.[84] They were designed by Hitler's favorite architect, Paul Ludwig Troost, who shared the Führer's love of neoclassical architecture.[85]

[80] Smith, *The Cultural Foundations of Nations*, 151.

[81] *Münchener Neueste Nachrichten* (Munich), November 9, 1933.

[82] Baird, *To Die for Germany*, 49. See also Bernd Sösemann, "Appell unter der Erntekrone: Das Reichserntedankfest in der nationalsozialistischen Diktatur," *Jahrbuch für Kommunikationsgeschichte* 2 (2000): 113–156.

[83] Baird, *To Die for Germany*, 50–51.

[84] HAT, Sachkatalog, D061/00/936/BRO: *Passing Through Germany*, 10th edn. (Berlin: Terramare Office, 1936), 82.

[85] See Karl Arndt, "Paul Ludwig Troost als Leitfigur der nationalsozialistischen Repräsentationsarchitektur," in *Bürokratie und Kult. Das Parteizentrum der NSDAP am Königsplatz in München. Teil 1: Geschichte und Rezeption*, ed. Iris Lauterbach (Munich: Deutscher Kunstverlag, 1995) 147–156; Kershaw, *Hitler, 1889–1936: Hubris*, 82–83.

In Hitler's case, affinity for the neoclassical style could not be reduced to mere aesthetics; he was drawn to ancient Greece and Rome for ideological reasons. He admired the imperial Romans for their militarism, their obsession with social order, and their political hierarchy ruled by a man with almost god-like status. In *Mein Kampf*, Hitler referred to Roman history as "the best mentor, not only for today, but probably for all time."[86] Conversely, he viewed the ancient Greeks as the "racial ancestors" of the German *Volk*, and he admired classical Sparta in particular as "the clearest example in history of a city-state based on race." Thus Hitler hoped that neoclassical architecture would establish connections with historical antiquity while also demonstrating how the Third Reich could surpass the achievements of both the Greek city-states and the Roman Empire.[87]

Hitler was drawn to classical antiquity, but he was not interested in "purity of style." Instead, he sought to create new architectural forms that would become historical in their own right. The design of the Temples of Honor displayed the unique synthesis of neoclassicism and functionalism that became the trademark of Nazi monumental architecture. Serving as the final resting place of the martyrs of November 1923, the monument consisted of two square atria, each supported by a series of freestanding pillars without classical capitals. With no superfluous ornamentation, the sixteen iron-ore tombs sat in plain view, serving, in the words of one local newspaper, as "immortal guardians of the Holy Empire of all Germans."[88] With these twin monuments acting as its new entrance, the *Königsplatz* became the final station during the annual commemoration of the 1923 putsch, which climaxed with the "Führer's lonely walk" to each of the open temples, and his silent reverence before the tombs of martyrs.[89] Afterwards, the names of the fallen heroes were read aloud. At the sound of each name, the uniformed members of the audience responded with a resounding "Here," proclaiming a connection with one another and the fallen members of the people's community.[90]

Both guidebooks and tourists praised the Temples of Honor. In an independently published guidebook, Alexander Heilmeyer claimed:

---

[86] Hitler, *Mein Kampf*, 423.
[87] Alexander Scobie, *Hitler's State Architecture: The Impact of Classical Antiquity* (University Park: Pennsylvania State University Press, 1990), 2–5, 13–14.
[88] *Münchener Neueste Nachrichten* (Munich), November 9, 1935; Scobie, *Hitler's State Architecture*, 16, 40, 56–64.
[89] Frei, *National Socialist Rule in Germany*, 84.
[90] Heusler, *Das Braune Haus*, 205.

No member of our people's community will be able to visit this square in the future without taking note of the martyrs of the movement, whose memory is also honored by the memorial on the eastern side of the *Feldherrnhalle* near the *Residenz*. And thus these two Temples of Honor will become a site of worship and consecration in the historical consciousness of present as well as future generations.[91]

Heilmeyer used religious language in describing Munich's new monuments, but noticeably, only discussed their impact on members of the people's community, employing the dynamic of inclusion as well as exclusion. Although occasionally overlooked, foreign travelers also testified to the spiritual character of the site. In a 1938 account, English novelist John Alfred Cole discussed the "extraordinary effect of the place," describing the Temples of Honor as more impressive than the London Cenotaph or the Tomb of the Unknown Soldier in Paris. He reported that "pilgrims" constantly flocked to the shrine: "They may come as laughing coach-loads of tourists, or happy family parties out on a trip, but as they draw near their demeanor changes, they mount the steps slowly and quietly, look for a minute or more at the coffins below, give the Nazi salute and then slowly make their way to the other shrine."[92] Similarly, English author and tourist Charles W. Domville described the square as a "place of pilgrimage for all patriotic Germans," who walked "with bared heads up the broad stone steps from which one looks down upon the sacred slabs of marble."[93] The local *Münchener Zeitung* corroborated such impressions, reporting on the thousands of visitors from throughout the Reich that annually "made the pilgrimage" to the sarcophagi of the sixteen martyrs.[94]

As a sacred site and the new focal point of the *Königsplatz*, the Temples of Honor were not the only addition planned for this particular part of the Capital of the Movement. Before his death in 1934, Troost restored the interior of the nearby "Brown House," which had served as the Nazi Party headquarters since 1930.[95] In a 1936 publication, a travel writer described this building as "the symbol of Nazi dominance in Germany,"

---

[91] HAT, Sachkatalog, D061/09/01/938/HEI: Alexander Heilmeyer, "Die Bauten des Dritten Reiches," in *Reiseland Südbayern*, ed. Paul Wolfrum (Munich: Verlag Knorr & Hirth, 1938), 65.
[92] Cole, *Just Back From Germany*, 124–126.
[93] Charles W. Domville, *This is Germany* (London: Seeley Service & Co. Ltd., 1939), 251–254.
[94] *Münchener Zeitung* (Munich), November 10, 1938.
[95] Heusler, *Das Braune Haus*, 127–169.

where "[b]ronze eagles and swastikas adorn the walls and predominate on the floors and carpets."[96] Troost was also responsible for the blueprints of two additional buildings on the *Königsplatz*. The *Führerbau*, christened during Mussolini's 1937 visit to Munich, contained offices, a massive auditorium, and even a restaurant in the basement.[97] The administrative building (*Verwaltungsbau*), which was connected to the *Führerbau* via an underground tunnel, housed the offices of the Reich Treasury along with an extensive index of party members.[98] With their vaguely classical façades and colonnaded porches, these twin constructions completed a ring of monumental architecture on the *Königsplatz* that included the nineteenth-century landmarks of the *Glyptothek* and the *Propyläen*.[99] Even Goebbels, who had never been fond of Munich, admitted in his diary that the buildings were "indescribably beautiful," adding: "Here the Führer has translated his will into stone."[100] Alexander Heilmeyer claimed that every step closer to the twin party buildings revealed further evidence of the structures' architectural merit, demonstrating that modern buildings could boldly reflect the "spirit of classical Antiquity" without merely reproducing archaic designs.[101] These Nazi buildings established a link with the past, but they also signified improvement over Greco-Roman classicism and nineteenth-century neoclassicism. Nevertheless, a 1937 report from the exiled SPD speculated that the average citizen of Munich had "no appreciation for the architectural addiction of the Führer."[102]

Officially, the *Königsplatz* in Munich was more than an administrative center for the Nazi Party; it was "a sacred cult center" for a "political community of faith."[103] After 1933, the lawn between Ludwig

---

[96] I. Burrows, *The Intelligent Traveler's Guide to Germany* (New York: Knight Publications, 1936), 53.

[97] Baedeker, *München und Südbayern Handbuch für Reisende*, 32.

[98] Ulrike Grambitter, "Vom 'Parteiheim' in der Brienner Straße zu den Monumentalbauten am 'Königlichen Platz': Das Parteizentrum der NSDAP am Königsplatz in München," in *Bürokratie und Kult. Das Parteizentrum der NSDAP am Königsplatz*, 74.

[99] Lang, *Im Auto zwischen München und Rom*, 8.

[100] Joseph Goebbels, *Die Tagebücher von Joseph Goebbels: Teil I, Aufzeichnungen 1924–1941; Band 3/I, April 1934-Februar 1936*, ed. Elke Fröhlich (New York: K.G. Saur, 2006), 278.

[101] HAT, Sachkatalog, D061/09/01/938/HEI: Heilmeyer, "Die Bauten des Dritten Reiches," 65–66.

[102] *Deutschlandberichte der Sozialdemokratischen Partei Deutschlands (SOPADE)* 4, no. 8 (August 1937): A-9.

[103] Arndt, "Paul Ludwig Troost als Leitfigur der nationalsozialistischen Repräsentationsarchitektur," 150; Scobie, *Hitler's State Architecture*, 63.

l's monuments was paved over with over 20,000 square meters of granite, and was equipped with eighteen permanent lanterns, as well as an extensive network of underground electrical cables that could be used for additional lighting and amplification. The new *Königsplatz* could accommodate over 50,000 people, and was utilized during the November celebrations and the festivities surrounding the "Day of German Art."[104] An English-language brochure issued by the Munich Tourism Association characterized the *Königsplatz* as "the national sanctuary of the German People." A photo adjacent to this description showed pedestrians leisurely strolling through the newly remodeled square, offering a somewhat depoliticized depiction of the Munich attraction.[105] Even when the square was not the site of mass ceremonies, it still drew visitors.

For residents and tourists alike, the Temples of Honor and the other Nazi buildings of the *Königsplatz* served as examples of the New Munich, in addition to somewhat shifting the symbolic nucleus of the Bavarian capital slightly northwest. A postcard printed by August Lengauer, a local Munich firm, showcased the magnitude of the *"Königlicher Platz,"* a new title that diverted attention from the actual Bavarian king who oversaw the square's initial construction.[106] The postcard featured a painted, black-and-white aerial view of the square from the west, with the *Propyläen* in the foreground, Ludwig's museums on either side, and the Temples of Honor and the Party Buildings figuring prominently at the top. The towers of the *Altstadt* are barely recognizable in the background, although the twin domes of the *Frauenkirche* are discernible in the upper right corner.[107] While the recent additions to the city dominate this particular view, the remote past of Munich is literally and figuratively positioned in the background, but hardly omitted. Serving as the backdrop for the new "Party Center," the *Altstadt* remained connected with the New Munich celebrated in the Nazified tourist culture.

The *Königsplatz* was the most ambitious example of the architectural transformation of Munich, but it was just one element of a larger vision. Although the city was not slated for the massive reconstruction planned for Berlin, Hitler did hope to underscore Munich's cultural and

[104] Hans Lehmbruch, "ACROPOLIS GERMANIAE. Der Königsplatz – Forum der NSDAP," in *Bürokratie und Kult. Das Parteizentrum der NSDAP am Königsplatz*, 20–24, 36.

[105] BayHStA, Sammlung Varia, 268.

[106] Heusler, *Das Braune Haus*, 227.

[107] BWA, Bildpostkarten, 64: "München, Hauptstadt der Bewegung: Königlicher Platz" (Munich: A. Lengauer, undated).

FIGURE 10. Postcard featuring the Königsplatz in Munich, 1930s. Note the towers of the *Altstadt* in the upper right corner. From the author's collection.

historical significance with a new Opera House and a museum dedicated to contemporary history.[108] There were also plans to construct a number of large skyscrapers near Munich's central train station, with one of them containing a KdF hotel.[109] While these plans were destined to remain on the drawing board, several additional architectural projects were completed before 1939. Among them was the expansion of the bridge between the *Bürgerbräukeller* and the *Feldherrnhalle*, which had apparently grown too narrow for the annual November procession.[110] Other projects were more destructive in nature, namely the demolition of a number of monuments commemorating the revolutionaries of 1918–1919, as well as several Munich synagogues.[111] Both actions erased evidence of the Bolshevik-Jewish menace from the historic cityscape. The

[108] HAT, Sachkatalog, D061/00/937/DEU: *Deutsche Hauptstädte: München, Nürnberg, Berlin, Hamburg*; *Münchener Neueste Nachrichten* (Munich), November 9, 1935. For more on the extensive plans for Berlin, see Stephen Helmer, *Hitler's Berlin: The Speer Plans for Reshaping the Central City* (Ann Arbor: University of Michigan Research Press, 1985).

[109] Large, *Where Ghosts Walked*, 280–281.

[110] StadtAM, Fremdenverkehrsamt, 14; Hanko, "Kommunalpolitik in der 'Hauptstadt der Bewegung' 1933–1935," 438–439.

[111] Gavriel D. Rosenfeld, "Monuments and the Politics of Memory: Commemorating Kurt Eisner and the Bavarian Revolutions of 1918–1919 in Postwar Munich," *Central European History* 30, no. 2 (1997): 229–233; Heusler, *Das Braune Haus*, 243–245.

limited urban renewal of Munich therefore assisted in the codification of an official and selective version of the past that suited the needs of the present regime.

Still, the elimination of the Jewish presence in Munich was not immediately apparent to tourists. For example, Grieben's 1934 guidebook on the *Bavarian Highland* advertised three "Jewish ritual" restaurants within the city, demonstrating that Nazi antisemitism did not instantaneously transform tourist propaganda.[112] In Munich, local authorities initially hesitated to implement anti-Jewish economic policies as they feared that such measures might scare away foreign tourists, or at least give the wrong impression about Germany.[113] If international tourism was a means of earning revenue and combating negative stereotypes, then Munich would serve as a cultural representative of the Third Reich, reassuring foreign tourists that allegations of militarism and antisemitic violence were unfounded. David Clay Large has concluded that foreigners were by and large fooled, and Munich's "indefatigable festival culture and apparent joie de vivre were therefore an effective cover for the ugly realities of Nazi policy."[114] Foreign tourists were largely unburdened with the knowledge that antisemitism had played a role in Munich politics since the turn of the century.[115] Unlike the local inhabitants, they were also largely unaware of the existence of Nazi Germany's first concentration camp, located a mere sixteen kilometers outside of the city near the town of Dachau.[116]

The tourist profile of the New Munich relied on a positive depiction of the National Socialist movement, but it also relied on the city's reputation as the capital of German art.[117] Hitler demonstrated his commitment to

---

[112] HAT, Sachkatalog, GRI-63/BAY. HOCHLAND-38 . . . D061/09/01: Griebens Reiseführer [Firm], *Bayerisches Hochland mit München und Allgäu*, 38th edn. (Berlin: Grieben-Verlag, 1934), 30.

[113] Large, *Where Ghosts Walked*, 248.

[114] Ibid., 276–277.

[115] Heusler, *Das Braune Haus*, 66–70.

[116] See Harold Marcuse, *Legacies of Dachau: The Uses and Abuses of a Concentration Camp, 1933–2001* (New York: Cambridge University Press, 2001), 21, 28–29; Sybille Steinbacher, "Das eine und das andere Dachau: Die Stadt und ihr Konzentrationslager," in *Das Konzentrationslager Dachau: Geschichte und Wirkung nationalsozialistischer Repression*, ed. Wolfgang Benz and Angelika Königseder (Berlin: Metropol, 2008), 43–52; Sybille Steinbacher, *Dachau. Die Stadt und das Konzentrationslager in der NS-Zeit. Die Untersuchung einer Nachbarschaft*, 2nd edn. (Frankfurt am Main: Peter Lang, 1994).

[117] Karl Arndt, "Die Münchener Architekturszene 1933/34 als ästhetisch-politisches Konfliktfeld," in *Bayern in der NS-Zeit, III: Herrschaft und Gesellschaft im Konflikt, Teil B*, 445–446.

FIGURE 11. Postcard featuring the House of German Art in Munich, 1930s. From the author's collection.

both Munich and German culture when he laid the foundation stone for the House of German Art on October 15, 1933. Located at the southern end of the English Garden, the city's newest attraction would serve as a temple of true German art, not the decadent experimentation of the Weimar era. It was based on plans created by Troost before his death in 1934, and was a synthesis of neoclassicism and functionalism: a symmetrical, rectangular building with a wide porch surrounded by columns without capitals. The emphasis was not on height, but on length and width, and the House of German Art was designed to blend in with its surroundings, achieving harmony with Munich's green lung.[118] Subsequent tourist publications showered praise upon the museum, describing it as a "magnificent temple of art," and, in spite of its vaguely Greco-Roman design, as a "truly German building, a monumental expression of the mighty cultural will of the Third Reich."[119]

The House of German Art officially opened on July 18, 1937, an occasion commemorated with the "Day of German Art." The centerpiece of the newest Nazi festival was the exhibition of "Great German Art," which featured canvases and sculptures by relatively unknown artists. Their work was inspired by nineteenth-century romanticism and realism, and their subject matter included a large number of landscapes, portraits,

---

[118] Ibid., 457–462, 475.
[119] Trautwein, *Guide Book for Munich*, 73.

and still-lifes.[120] Taken as a whole, these selections were meant to prove that the German race could produce outstanding and "pure" pieces of art long after the achievements of Lukas Cranach and Albrecht Dürer. During his speech on the museum's opening day, Hitler declared: "I know, therefore, that when the *Volk* passes through these galleries it will recognize in me its own spokesman and counselor… it will draw a sigh of relief and joyously express its agreement with this purification of art."[121] Although official statistics recorded 400,000 visitors during the 1937 exhibition, the expansive galleries of Munich's new museum were often relatively empty, suggesting that the Führer's enthusiasm was not shared.[122] In contrast, the "Degenerate Art Exhibition" organized by Goebbels' Propaganda Ministry made quite a stir. Opening one day after the exhibition at the House of German Art in 1937, and featuring works by artists like Wassily Kandinsky, Max Ernst, and Pablo Picasso, this counter-exhibition attracted over two million visitors in Munich, and later traveled to eleven other cities in Germany and Austria.[123]

Aside from the exhibition, the Day of German Art (eventually three days) featured more egalitarian attractions outside of the traditionally bourgeois confines of the museum. One of these was the "Two Thousands Years of German Culture" parade: a procession of lavish floats that offered a "chronological narrative of German achievement from a Nazi perspective."[124] This parade began with mythology and ended with modernity, with individual floats depicting the Nibelungen legend, Emperor Friedrich Barbarossa, "The World of Richard Wagner," and several examples of the "monumental architecture of the Führer." Furthermore, the parade route itself was anchored in local history, as it passed some of Munich's most well-known tourist attractions, including the *Feldherrnhalle*, the *Königsplatz*, the *Frauenkirche*, and the Wittelsbach *Residenz*.[125] Historian Joshua Hagen has recently suggested that

[120] Arndt, "Die Münchener Architekturszene 1933/34," 451–453.
[121] Benjamin Sax and Dieter Kuntz, eds, *Inside Hitler's Germany: A Documentary History of Life in the Third Reich* (Lexington, MA: D.C. Heath & Company, 1992), 224–232.
[122] Large, *Where Ghosts Walked*, 263.
[123] Wistrich, *Weekend in Munich*, 64. See also Neil Levi, "'Judge for Yourselves!' – The 'Degenerate Art' Exhibition as Political Spectacle," *October* 85 (Summer 1998): 41–64.
[124] Joshua Hagen, "Parades, Public Space, and Propaganda: The Nazi Culture Parades in Munich," *Geografiska Annaler* 90, no. 4 (2008): 349. See also Stefan Schweizer, "*Unserer Weltanschauung sichtbaren Ausdruck geben": Nationalsozialistische Geschichtsbilder in historischen Festzügen zum "Tag der Deutschen Kunst"* (Göttingen: Wallstein, 2007).
[125] From the official 1937 program for the parade, entitled: "Zweitausend Jahre Deutsche Kultur: Der Festzug am Tag der Deutschen Kunst 1937 in München." StAM,

the impact of the parade was limited by Munich's existing spatial layout and the incomprehensible historical exposition, but the sheer spectacle of the public display was undeniable.[126] After witnessing the 1937 event, even representatives of the exiled SPD were forced to admit that their expectations had been "surpassed."[127]

By the summer of 1939, the Day of German Art was one of the most important occasions on the Nazi festival calendar. The three-day event drew thousands of visitors to Munich, with 100,000 arriving by car, and over 70,000 arriving by rail.[128] In addition to the art exhibition and the historical parade, the program included performances of Mozart and Wagner operas, as well as music and dancing at the "Classic Old-Munich Summer Celebration" in the English Garden.[129] While performances of classical music confirmed the preeminence of German *Kultur*, informal celebrations in Munich's city park linked the Third Reich with elements of local culture and identity. The new Nazi festival was not for the museum crowd alone; it was available to all members of the people's community.[130] The regime sought to guarantee the egalitarian character of the festival not only by refusing to charge admission to many of the events, but also by directing several KdF trains full of working-class tourists to the Capital of the Movement.[131]

Even with its many new attractions, Hitler's favorite city was still the location of the Oktoberfest and the *Hofbräuhaus*, the unpretentious city where past and present blended together, where "old traditions" and "eternal youth" lived harmoniously side by side.[132] The Bavarian capital may have been the symbolic heart of the Nazi movement, but it was also the site of a traditional tourist culture revolving around refinement and merriment. Visiting Munich in 1935, W.E.B. DuBois described it chiefly as "a city of theater, of music, of marvelous old buildings, and of beer."[133] A

Verwaltung der staatlicher Schlösser, Gärten, und Seen (SGSV), 1468: "Durchführung des Tages der Deutschen Kunst im Englischen Garten, 1937–1940."

[126] Hagen, "Parades, Public Space, and Propaganda," 349–367.

[127] *Deutschlandberichte der Sozialdemokratischen Partei Deutschlands (SOPADE)* 4, no. 8 (August 1937): A-9.

[128] Hagen, "Parades, Public Space, and Propaganda," 360.

[129] StAM, Verwaltung der staatlicher Schlösser, Gärten, und Seen (SGSV), 1468.

[130] Frei, *National Socialist Rule in Germany*, 84; Arndt, "Die Münchener Architekturszene 1933/34," 450.

[131] *Münchener Neueste Nachrichten* (Munich), July 4, 1937, July 15, 1937.

[132] As stated in a 1937 issue of the locally published Anglo-German journal, *München*. StdAM, Zeitgeschichtliche Sammlung, 116/1.

[133] Oliver Lubrich, ed. *Travels in the Reich, 1933–1945: Foreign Authors Report from Germany*, trans. Kenneth Norcott, Sonia Wichtmann, and Dean Krouk (Chicago: University of Chicago Press, 2010), 142.

series of publications issued by the Munich Tourism Association in 1938 and 1939 characterized Munich as "The City of Art and Joy of Life," a metropolis of charming contradictions and a tourist destination rich in German art, Bavarian culture, and beautiful landscapes.[134] These layers of identity coexisted with each other in a larger package that blended past and present, local and national identity, and high and low culture.

Nevertheless, even traditional features of Munich's tourist culture acquired a more pronounced Nazi character during the six years before World War II. In the case of the annual Oktoberfest, the regime took measures to transform the quintessentially Bavarian festival into an *"urdeutsches Volksfest"* available to all members of the people's community.[135] One new tradition designed to broaden the appeal of the event was the annual exhibition of riding and jousting performed by SS horsemen.[136] Meanwhile, Oktoberfest souvenirs began to feature combinations of Bavarian and Nazi iconography, just as Nazi banners replaced the standard blue and white colors of Bavaria that usually lined the fairground.[137] The Nazification of the Oktoberfest peaked in 1938, when in the wake of the *Anschluss* and in the midst of the Sudeten Crisis it was extended an additional week and rechristened as the "Greater German Folk Festival."[138] Attractions that had once represented a decidedly traditional tourist culture became Nazi spectacles, founded upon the perceived unity between the party, the people, and the past.

Did the Nazification of Munich's tourist culture have an impact on the number of visitors? Statistics assembled by the Munich Tourism Association during this period verify that the Bavarian capital enjoyed increased popularity among tourists. Between the years of 1932 and 1936, the number of overnight visitors during the summer season increased by 73 percent, rising from 395,273 to 681,809. Between 1932 and 1934 alone, the number of German visitors increased by 35 percent, with the figure climbing from 325,502 to 441,041. Conversely, the number of foreign visitors declined between 1932 and 1933, but rose steadily afterwards,

---

[134] StadtAM, Zeitgeschichtliche Sammlung, 116/1. Two publications issued in 1938 and 1939, respectively, featured this title: "München: Die Stadt der Kunst und der Lebensfreude."

[135] *Münchener Zeitung* (Munich), September 18, 1935.

[136] Reported in the "Vergnügungs-Anzeiger: Bayerischer Fremdenführer," September 28, 1935. StadtAM, Zeitgeschichtliche Sammlung, 116/1.

[137] Large, *Where Ghosts Walked*, 275–276; BWA, Bildpostkarten, 302. "Gruβ vom Oktoberfest" (Munich: Emil Köhn, Kunstverlag, undated).

[138] Semmens, *Seeing Hitler's Germany*, 65. See also Florian Nagy and Johann C. Bentele, *Oktoberfest. Zwischen Tradition und Moderne* (Munich: München Verlag, 2007), 28–33.

confirming that the New Munich appealed to non-Germans as well.[139]
These statistics point to a remarkable recovery of Munich's tourism industry, especially in light of Christine Keitz's conclusion that the overall
number of overnight guests in Germany only rose between 10 and 15
percent during the Nazi era.[140] A revival of the Munich tourism industry
was apparent, reflecting the impact of the city's new status.

Instead of obscuring or lamenting this new status, local tourist propaganda celebrated it. The sights associated with Hitler and the rise of
the Nazi party became the dominant symbols of the city. For example, a 1937 map printed by the firm "Munich Visitor Tours" only contained pictures of "modern Munich," including images of the *Königsplatz*
with the Temples of Honor and Brown House, the House of German
Art, the World War I monument, the *Feldherrnhalle*, and the German
Museum.[141] An undated brochure entitled "Munich" offered an itinerary
for an ideal seven-day stay in the Capital of the Movement, recommending the *Pinakothek*, the Brown House, and the *Feldherrnhalle* as the most
important sights to visit.[142] This recommendation indirectly confirmed
Munich's artistic reputation, as well as its contemporary significance
within the Third Reich. Then again, not every tourist publication dwelled
on the city's Nazi connections. For example, a 1936 guidebook entitled
All Over Upper Bavaria dedicated its Munich section to a discussion of
the city's historic architecture. In fact, the guidebook only mentioned the
Nazi connection in the foreword, placing the cultural policies of the Third
Reich within the larger context of foreign contributions to Munich's artistic scene.[143] This was a noteworthy exception that confirms that the local
tourism industry was not limited to a single marketing formula mandated
by the state.

The City of the Reich Party Rallies

Like Munich, the Franconian city of Nuremberg also enjoyed a privileged
status within the Third Reich. While its well-preserved medieval core had

[139] StadtAM, Fremdenverkehrsamt, 14. "Summer" ran from April to September, "Winter"
ran from October to March.
[140] Keitz, *Reisen als Leitbild*, 214.
[141] StadtAM, Zeitgeschichtliche Sammlung, 116/1.
[142] HAT, Prospekte, D061/09/01/A-Z/.-45: "München" (Munich: Herausgegeben vom
Landesverkehrs-verband München-Südbayern (Bayer. und Allgäuer Alpen), Haupt-
bahnhof Nordbau, undated).
[143] HAT, Sachkatalog, D061/09/01/936/GUE: Erich Günther, *Kreuz und quer durch Oberbayern. Ein kultureller Führer für Reisende und Heimatfreunde* (Ulm-Donau: Verlag
Dr. Karl Höhn, 1936), 1–2.

made it a popular destination long before 1933, its transformation into the "City of the Reich Party Rallies" provided another dimension to the tourist experience. Perhaps even more so than Munich, Nuremberg became a place where the history of the *Volksgemeinschaft* was on display alongside the modern-day "Triumph of the Will." The spectacle of the Reich Party Rally annually drew thousands of visitors to the historic city, while the monumental structures of the rally grounds, both complete and incomplete, became tourist attractions that legitimized the Nazi claim to greatness.

Nuremberg's historical legacy was especially rich. Founded in the eleventh century, it became one of the most important cities of the Holy Roman Empire, especially after the Golden Bull of 1356 decreed that every Holy Roman Emperor must hold his first Imperial Diet in the free city of Nuremberg. As the "unofficial capital of the Reich," the city enjoyed 300 years of political significance and economic affluence, and was the center of the German Renaissance. By the time of the Napoleonic Wars, a weaker Nuremberg had become part of the new Kingdom of Bavaria, just as its star began to rise among German romantics. Like Franconian Switzerland, Nuremberg seemed to represent a "simpler world" free of modern anxieties.[144] The "Pearl of Medieval Cities" played a prominent role in Ludwig Tieck's and Wilhelm Heinrich Wackenroder's 1798 novel, *Franz Sternbald's Wanderings*, in addition to serving as the backdrop for E.T.A. Hoffmann's 1816 short story, "The Nutcracker and the Mouse-King." Nuremberg was also unique in that it had never been associated with the particularism that characterized Upper Bavaria and Munich. In his account of Nuremberg as modern Germany's "imaginary capital," scholar Stephen Brockmann argues that the city "had always seen its fate as intimately connected to the fate of the German whole. Nuremberg was indeed a synecdoche for Germany itself."[145] Such sentiments helped to shape the marketing of the medieval city, especially during the Nazi era.

At the beginning of twentieth century, numerous publications described a visit to Nuremberg as a journey into the German past. Published in 1900, Grieben's *Guidebook to Nuremberg and its Environs* claimed that an evening stroll through the city's medieval gates and

---

144 Hermann Glaser, "Um eine Stadt von innen bietend: Historische Stadt und kulturelle Aneignung," in *Die Alte Stadt: Denkmal oder Lebensraum?*, ed. Cord Meckseper and Harald Siebenmorgen (Göttingen: Vandenhoeck & Ruprecht, 1985), 11.
145 Stephen Brockmann, *Nuremberg: The Imaginary Capital* (New York: Camden House, 2006), 179–180.

winding alleyways was like being propelled into a past century: "Nowhere else in Germany can we find a city in which the history of our people and their great deeds is so vividly captured as in Nuremberg... Every stone here tells us of history, every house is its very own, so perfectly German."[146] Indeed, Nuremberg's primary tourist attraction around the turn of the century was its general medieval character, with one tourist sarcastically noting: "Anything made here since 1500 is considered hopelessly modern."[147] Among the most popular attractions were the historic buildings of the *Altstadt*, including the Imperial Fortress, the gothic churches of St. Sebald and St. Lorenz, and the Hangman's Tower and Bridge along the Pegnitz River. Ernst Platz's 1907 guidebook praised the architectural landmarks of the "German Reich's Treasure Chest," which also contained priceless works of art from masters such as Peter Vischer, Adam Kraft, Lukas Cranach, and Albrecht Dürer.[148] Other publications noted that the city was the home of the legendary Hans Sachs, the shoemaker, poet, and Meistersinger, immortalized in Richard Wagner's opera, *The Mastersingers of Nuremberg.*[149]

Nuremberg's identity as the "German Reich's Treasure Chest" began to change after World War I, when the local tourism industry was handicapped by recession, inflation, and a damaged international reputation.[150] A 1929 guidebook published by the Tourism Association of Northern Bavaria placed heavy emphasis on "the Nuremberg of the present," offering details on the city's public transportation and local factories before even mentioning Albrecht Dürer. The guidebook's author, August Sieghart, argued that modern Nuremberg was much more than a historical site: "today the city stands as a symbol for German skill, German industriousness, and German efficiency... The State of Bavaria ranks Nuremberg ahead of all others as *the greatest and most important center of industry and commerce*, whose products have always been highly sought after on the international market."[151] Some tourist destinations

---

[146] Griebens (Firm), *Führer durch Nürnberg und Umgebungen* (Berlin: Griebens Reisebücher, 1900), 17–19.

[147] Colton, *Rambles Abroad*, 169.

[148] Platz, *Unser Bayerland*, 30.

[149] Colton, *Rambles Abroad*, 171; StadtAN, Hauptregistrar, 1269: "Hebung des Fremdenverkehrs Bd. 1, 1903–1922."

[150] See Gesa Büchert, "Förderer des Fremdenverkehrs: Der Verkehrsverein Nürnberg von den Anfängen bis zum Zweiten Weltkrieg," *Mitteilungen des Vereins für Geschichte der Stadt Nürnberg* 92 (2005): 382–385.

[151] August Sieghart, *Nordbayern: Ein Führer durch seine Schönheiten* (Nuremberg: Verkehrsverband Nordbayern, 1929), 8–9.

were marketed as places of rest and relaxation. Nuremberg, like inter-war Augsburg, was now being marketed as a place of work.[152] Still, publications continued to balance contemporary relevance with historical significance. For example, a 1930 brochure issued by the Tourism Association of Northern Bavaria listed the medieval sights of the *Altstadt*, as well as the Transportation Museum, the Nuremberg Stadium, the Zoological Park, and even "schools of all varieties." This publication portrayed Nuremberg as a unique city that had preserved its medieval core in spite of its evolution into a modern industrial center.[153]

This new marketing direction proved incapable of reversing alarming trends in Nuremberg. Heavily advertised festivities commemorating the 400th anniversary of Albrecht Dürer's death in 1928 brought over 280,000 visitors to the city, but the number of overnight guests plummeted in the following years, dropping by 30 percent between 1930 and 1932.[154] Nuremberg tourism rebounded after 1933, but like Munich, the city's reemergence as a leading tourist destination was closely related to the triumph of National Socialism.[155] Long before Hitler arrived in Munich, Protestant Franconia was a hotbed of German nationalism and antisemitism.[156] The Franconian city of Nuremberg was also home to Julius Streicher, member of the Nazi "Old Guard," and the editor of the notorious antisemitic newspaper *Der Stürmer*.[157] As a result, Franconia and Nuremberg in particular became fertile ground for the National Socialist movement, especially after Hitler's imprisonment and the subsequent Upper Bavarian ban on the party in 1923.[158]

Partially as a result of its prominence during this transitional period, Nuremberg was chosen to host the Nazi Party Rally in 1927. Only a tram ride away from the *Altstadt*, the rally was held at the expansive Luitpold Meadow in southeastern Nuremberg, but it failed to raise interest in the movement. Two years later, the second Nuremberg party rally amounted

---

[152] For more on the nineteenth-century industrialization of Nuremberg, see Charlotte Bühl-Gramer, *Nürnberg, 1850 bis 1892: Stadtentwicklung, Kommunalpolitik und Stadtverwaltung im Zeichen von Industrialisierung und Urbanisierung* (Nuremberg: Stadtarchiv, 2003).

[153] StadtAN, Hauptregistrar, 1285: "Verkehrsverband Nordbayern e.V., Bd. 1, 1927–32."

[154] Büchert, "Der Verkehrsverein Nürnberg," 389–394.

[155] Dieter Wuttke, *Nuremberg: Focal Point of German Culture and History* (Bamberg: Stefan Wendel, 1988), 12.

[156] Evans, *The Coming of the Third Reich*, 188.

[157] See Randall L. Bytwerk, *Julius Streicher: Editor of the Notorious Anti-Semitic Newspaper Der Stürmer* (New York: Cooper Square Press, 2001).

[158] Dietzfelbinger and Liedtke, *Nürnberg – Ort der Massen*, 23–24.

to "a far bigger and more grandiose spectacle," showcasing a more confident party, and drawing an estimated 40,000 visitors to the city.[159] However, the 1929 rally also featured the sort of political violence that had already tainted some Bavarian tourist destinations. Clashes between Nazis and leftist opponents, many of them occurring at locales frequented by Communists, resulted in multiple brawls, stabbings, and ultimately two deaths.[160] Ten days after the conclusion of the party rally, the city council engaged in a two-hour debate about whether or not Nuremberg should allow the Nazis to return, with Social Democrats emphasizing that the party rally had tarnished the honor of their city and damaged its reputation as a tourist destination.[161] The city council subsequently prohibited the National Socialist party from convening in the city, sparking protests from locals who had benefited financially from the influx of visitors.[162] At this point, the Nazis appeared to be both a threat and an asset to the local tourism industry.

Hitler and the National Socialists returned to Nuremberg in August 1933, bringing greater numbers and proclaiming a "Victory of Faith." No longer was the rally a "celebration of the party," it was now a veritable "celebration of the nation," and an opportunity for the people's community to connect with the Nazi regime.[163] Distancing themselves from their predecessors, the new Nuremberg City Council proposed that their city would be the permanent site of the Reich Party Rally, and Hitler obliged. While some historians have argued that this decision was based on the city's central location, its vast expanses of open land, and the presence of a sympathetic police chief along with a strong Nazi contingent, Stephen Brockmann insists that a much more important factor was the city's layered historical significance.[164] Not only had Nuremberg provided a home to the Nazi party during a period of transition and uncertainty, it also allowed the movement to connect its own history with the greater political and cultural legacy of the city.[165] The previously cited 1937 brochure on "German Capitals" was quite clear on this connection: "The Führer's decision to make Nuremberg the City of the Reich Party

---

[159] Kershaw, *Hitler, 1889–1936: Hubris*, 293, 310.

[160] *Nordbayerische Zeitung* (Nuremberg), August 5, 1929.

[161] Ibid. August 14, 1929.

[162] Dietzfelbinger and Liedtke, *Nürnberg – Ort der Massen*, 27.

[163] Here I am utilizing two of Bernd Sösemann's categories of Nazi festivals, the third being "*traditionelle Feste.*" See Sösemann, "Appell unter der Erntekrone," 115.

[164] Brockmann, *Nuremberg*, 133–140.

[165] Dietzfelbinger and Liedtke, *Nürnberg – Ort der Massen*, 66.

Rallies had a deep rationale behind it. Nuremberg is the embodiment of German history, with both its splendor as well as the reminders of its tragic downfall."[166] Hitler's decision was potentially based on other factors too, for example, his well-documented admiration for the region of Franconia and his passion for Richard Wagner, who had paid homage to medieval Nuremberg with his famous opera.[167] Regardless of what led to Hitler's decision, one thing is certain: Nuremberg's history was central to its new identity as the "City of the Reich Party Rallies." As was the case with Munich, the Nazis built upon a preexisting municipal identity, augmenting and omitting where necessary. The subsequent marketing of the city revolved around historical continuity, with the buildings of the Reich Party Rally representing the culmination of a long tradition of German industry and culture.

The popularity of the Reich Party Rally as both a political spectacle and a tourist attraction grew substantially after 1933.[168] The event typically drew over half a million visitors, filling Nuremberg with party members and civilians of all ages, and temporarily making it one of the most populated cities in the Third Reich.[169] The city itself was lavishly decorated for the event, and many of Nuremberg's most famous landmarks, including the town hall and the Albrecht Dürer House, were adorned with garlands, golden wreaths, and ribbons, as well as countless banners emblazoned with the iconography of the Imperial Free City and the Third Reich.[170] An early highlight of the festivities was the "Day of Greeting," when Hitler arrived by plane, and was driven into the center of the *Altstadt*, where he was received by the local government in front of Nuremberg's medieval town hall on the newly renamed *Adolf-Hitler-Platz*.[171] The opening sequence of Leni Riefenstahl's film, *Triumph of*

[166] HAT, Sachkatalog, D061/00/937/DEU: *Deutsche Hauptstädte: München, Nürnberg, Berlin, Hamburg.*

[167] In his 1934 autobiographical work, *With Hitler on the Road to Power*, Reich press chief Dr. Otto Dietrich noted that Hitler commonly referred to Franconia as "the most German of all landscapes." Quoted in an undated press release from the Nuremberg Tourism Association. StadtAN, Hauptregistrar, 1286.

[168] See Josef Henke, "Die Reichsparteitage der NSDAP in Nürnberg 1933–1938. – Planung, Organisation, Propaganda," in *Aus der Arbeit des Bundesarchivs*, ed. Heinz Boberbach and Hans Booms (Boppard am Rhein: Harald Boldt Verlag, 1977), 398–422.

[169] Brockmann, *Nuremberg*, 152; Dietzfelbinger and Liedtke, *Nürnberg – Ort der Massen*, 68–69.

[170] StadtAN, Zweckverband Reichsparteitag, 1102: "Reichsparteitag 1936 Stadtschmückung, 1 Fasz."

[171] Peter Reichel, "Culture and Politics in Nazi Germany," trans. Dorothea Blumenberg, in *Political Culture in Germany*, ed. Dirk Berg-Schlosser and Ralf Rytlewski (New York: St. Martin's Press, 1993). 63.

the Will, captures this procession well: narrating Hitler's drive through historic Nuremberg, the camera repeatedly cuts from his smiling face, to the jubilant crowd, to various monuments of the city's illustrious past, from the Imperial Castle to the "Beautiful Fountain."[172]

Events like the "Day of Greeting" exposed German citizens to the medieval center of Nuremberg, but they also promised proximity to the Führer himself. Hitler certainly played a prominent role in the Nazi festivals of Munich, but he was central to the proceedings in Nuremberg, where he effectively "towered over the party."[173] Those in attendance were eager to see the charismatic leader who had become synonymous with the New Germany. Even if they only caught a glimpse of Hitler, or heard his voice projected through a loudspeaker, they felt united. Hitler reinforced this perception, proclaiming at the 1936 party rally: "Not all of you can see me, and I cannot see all of you. But I feel you, and you feel me!"[174] Many visitors shared his enthusiasm. An inscription on the back of a "Reichsparteitag 1937" postcard noted that "the Führer had been seen many times," leading the author to exclaim: "I would have never thought that such a thing existed."[175] Visiting Nuremberg in 1938, Scottish writer A.P. Laurie recounted the reaction of an Austrian woman upon seeing Hitler in person: "[S]he was silent, her eyes filled with tears. She turned to me and said in English, 'I have never seen the Führer before – I think my heart is breaking'."[176] Such reactions confirm the tangible power of the "Hitler myth," which united many Germans in their adoration of the new savior.

After the "Day of Greeting," the Reich Party Rally climaxed with an elaborate ceremony at the "Hall of Honor" in the Luitpold Meadow. Nazi pageantry effectively transformed this monument to World War I casualties into another shrine for the sixteen martyrs of the Beer Hall Putsch. In Nuremberg, the Party honored these men through a pseudo-religious ritual, with the *Blutfahne* once again serving as the object of veneration. Each year, new members of the SS and SA watched as the blood-stained relic was rededicated and touched with new Nazi standards.[177] Before

[172] *Triumph des Willens*, dir. Leni Riefenstahl, 120 min., Synapse Films, 2001, DVD. For more on *Triumph of the Will*, see David Welch, *Propaganda and the German Cinema, 1933–1945*, 2nd edn. (New York: I.B. Tauris, 2001), 125–133; Brockmann, *Nuremberg*, 190–200.
[173] Kershaw, *The "Hitler Myth,"* 69.
[174] Quoted in Levi, "'Judge for Yourselves!,'" 54.
[175] StadtAN, Postkarten, 1428: "Festpostkarte zum Reichsparteitag" (1937).
[176] A.P. Laurie, *The Case for Germany: A Study of Modern Germany* (Berlin: Internationaler Verlag, 1939), 40.
[177] Dietzfelbinger and Liedtke, *Nürnberg – Ort der Massen*, 30, 45–46.

a monument dedicated to the fallen soldiers of a past war, in a structure commissioned by Luitpold, former Prince Regent of Bavaria, the Nazis commemorated their past, and framed it with myths of heroism and rebirth. Such rituals allowed the Nazi regime to gather disparate threads of the German past and weave them into a single, comprehensible narrative leading to the Third Reich, "the culmination and salvation of two millennia of German history."[178] Witnessing these events firsthand in 1934, American journalist William Shirer commented in his diary: "I'm beginning to comprehend, I think, some of the reasons for Hitler's astounding success. Borrowing a chapter from the Roman church, he is restoring pageantry and color and mysticism to the drab lives of twentieth-century Germans."[179] Still, it is worth noting that the Reich Party Rally was not dedicated exclusively to symbolically loaded rituals; it also featured sports competitions, musical performances, and even the largest fireworks display in Germany.[180] In other words, it was a manifestation of mass culture just as much as it was a means of consecrating the people's community.[181]

Tourist publications confirmed the significance of Nuremberg's new status as the "City of the Reich Party Rallies" by listing it among the city's various titles. An advertisement in an August 1934 issue of the *Neue Leipziger Zeitung* insisted that every German must become acquainted with Nuremberg, "The German Reich's Treasure Chest, the City of the Mastersingers, and the Reich Party Rallies."[182] These claims did not contradict one another; they coexisted, and complemented one another. Other publications employed similar combinations. The twelfth edition of the *Nuremberg Official Guidebook*, for example, featured the simple slogan: "City of the Mastersingers and Reich Party Rallies."[183] A 1938 brochure issued by the State Tourism Association of Nuremberg and Northern Bavaria used the same tagline, praising the coexistence of the "immortal Nuremberg of the German romantics and German history"

---

178 Wistrich, *Weekend in Munich*, 82.
179 William L. Shirer, *Berlin Diary: The Journal of a Foreign Correspondent, 1934–1941* (New York: Alfred A. Knopf, 1941), 18.
180 Reichel, "Culture and Politics in Nazi Germany," 63–65.
181 Frei, *National Socialist Rule in Germany*, 83.
182 StadtAN, Hauptregistrar, 1270: "Hebung des Fremdenverkehrs, sowie Fremdenverkehr überhaupt, 1923–1935, II. Band." *Neue Leipziger Zeitung* (Leipzig), July 8, 1934.
183 HAT, Sachkatalog, D061/09/02/934/NUE: *Nürnberg. Des Deutschen Reiches Schatzkästlein: Offizieller Führer*, 12th edn. (Nuremberg: Rudolf Kern Druckerei G.m.b.H., 1934), 4.

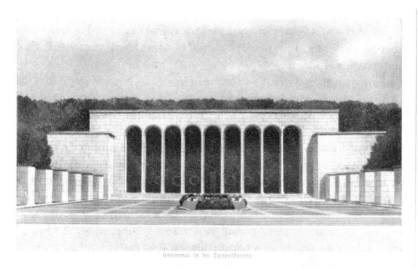

FIGURE 12. Postcard featuring the Luitpold Arena in Nuremberg, 1930s. From the author's collection.

and the new Nuremberg of the "Reich Party Rallies."[184] Past and present remained balanced in the marketing of Nuremberg, but now the Reich Party Rally Grounds replaced factories and trade schools as the dominant symbol of the city's modernity. Conversely, the "Nuremberg of the German romantics and German history" was never clearly defined.

Nuremberg's Nazi identity significantly changed the outlook of the local tourism industry. Nuremberg mayor and tourism advocate, Willy Liebel, proclaimed in a 1935 speech that the city's recent transformation into the "City of the Reich Party Rallies" had captured the attention of Germany and the world, in addition to instilling pride in the local population. Consequently, it was the duty of the local population to assist in "the cultivation of tourism," encouraging future visits by ensuring the satisfaction of each guest. According to Liebel, this was a "political undertaking of the greatest consequence and importance."[185] Such enthusiasm overshadowed any concerns that Nuremberg's associations with National Socialism might scare off international visitors. In fact,

---

[184] BayHStA, Sammlung Varia, 268. "Nürnberg: Die Stadt der Meistersinger/Die Stadt der Reichsparteitage," Landes-Fremdenverkehrs-Verband Nürnberg und Nordbayern mit Bayer. Ostmark e.V., 1938.

[185] StadtAN, Hauptregistrar, 1290: "Fremdenverkehrsverein Nürnberg und Umgebung, Band 2, 1928–1937."

the Nuremberg Tourism Association predicted in January 1934 that the city's identity as "a center of National Socialism in general and the struggle against the Jews in particular" would become an attractive feature for the international tourist.[186]

Did antisemitism actually attract foreigners to Nuremberg? It is difficult to say, but the local tourism industry clearly did not dodge the issue. In a 1934 memo, the director of the State Tourism Association of Franconia praised the region's commitment to fighting the "Jewish plague," and advised local communities to post signs that announced that Jews were not welcome. Such measures might temporarily impede the growth of tourism, he noted, but once the "truth about the Jewish question" was revealed, then Franconia would be commended for its unyielding antisemitism, and cities like Nuremberg would attract a multitude of "national comrades" and "racially conscious" foreigners.[187] One year later, a report by the Nuremberg Tourism Association refuted speculation that the city's antisemitic reputation was a liability by pointing to an increase in visitors since 1933.[188] Representatives of the tourism industry neither rejected nor downplayed Nuremberg's antisemitic reputation in internal memos, but they rarely stressed it in tourist propaganda, presumably for fear of alienating international tourists. One exception can be found in a brochure issued by the Nuremberg Tourism Association in 1939, that is, after the violence of "The Night of Broken Glass." The brochure boldly stated: "The healthy national and racial instincts that reside in the Franks ensured Nuremberg's transformation into a stronghold of National Socialism, even before other cities had heard Adolf Hitler's call."[189] Although it evokes the racial component of the *Volksgemeinschaft*, this passage still stressed inclusion over exclusion. Still, it did so nearly four years after the Nuremberg Laws passed at the 1935 "Party Rally of Freedom" authorized exclusion by depriving Jews of their legal status.[190]

For many visitors, it was the spectacle of the Reich Party Rally that defined contemporary Nuremberg, not the "national and racial instincts" of the Franks. As the number of visitors grew each year, it became obvious that the grounds around the Luitpold Meadow were inadequate, both

[186] StadtAN, Hauptregistrar, 1286.
[187] Ibid.
[188] StadtAN, Hauptregistrar, 1290.
[189] BayHStA, Sammlung Varia, 268. "Nürnberg: Kurzführer," Herausgeber: Verkehrsverein Nürnberg e.V., 8.39.
[190] Brockmann, *Nuremberg*, 153.

logistically and symbolically. As a result, Hitler and his associates developed plans for a complex of buildings and parade grounds that would rival the forum of ancient Rome. By 1939, Nuremberg was the largest building site in the world.[191] The buildings of the Reich Party Rally Grounds were the Third Reich's most ambitious architectural project, exuding a "supra-temporal megalomania . . . appropriate to the Nazi leadership's ideological and political self-image."[192] Hitler had always understood architecture primarily as a "statement of power," and the buildings of the Reich Party Rally Grounds, like the new buildings in Munich, were designed to legitimize the new regime.[193] As symbolic representations of the nation, these buildings would reflect the weight of recent German history, as well as the sheer magnitude of the Third Reich.[194] In terms of design, the buildings echoed the Nazi architecture of Munich, but Troost's successor, Albert Speer, took his predecessor's style to new extremes, developing a sort of "hyperthyroid neoclassicism."[195] In his postwar memoirs, he justified his bloated designs by stating that the Nuremberg structures were designed "to emphasize the insignificance of the individual engulfed in the architectural vastness of a state building."[196]

The new structures of the Party Rally Grounds included, in order and degree of completion, the Luitpold Arena, the Zeppelin Field, the Congress Hall, and the German Stadium. The Luitpold Arena was built near the preexisting Hall of Honor in the Luitpold Meadow in 1933. Its grandstands enclosed an area of over 80,000 square meters, which could accomodate up to 150,000 participants. The main grandstand could seat 500 dignitaries, and was flanked on each end by bronze eagles standing seven meters tall.[197] The next building completed was the massive Zeppelin Field, an open-air arena that would serve as the congregation point of the National Socialist leadership and a drill field for *Wehrmacht* and Labor Force units. Surrounded by grandstands that could seat up to

[191] Wuttke, *Nuremberg: Focal Point of German Culture and History*, 12. See also Rudy Koshar, *From Monuments to Traces: Artifacts of German Memory, 1870–1990* (Berkeley: University of California Press, 2000), 133.

[192] Frei, *National Socialist Rule in Germany*, 197.

[193] Evans, *The Coming of the Third Reich*, 163; Angermair and Haerendel, *Inszenierter Alltag*, 21.

[194] Brockmann, *Nuremberg*, 149.

[195] Large, *Berlin*, 315.

[196] Albert Speer, *Inside the Third Reich: Memoirs*, trans. Richard and Clara Winston (New York: Macmillan, 1970), 19, 40.

[197] These figures were reported by a local guidebook in 1934. HAT, Sachkatalog, D061/09/02/934/NUE: *Nürnberg. Des Deutschen Reiches Schatzkästlein*, 67–68.

FIGURE 13. Postcard featuring the Zeppelin Field in Nuremberg, 1930s. From the author's collection.

70,000 people, the Zeppelin Field was dominated by a main grandstand that rose seventeen meters above the ground. With its wide steps and long colonnade, the *Zeppelinhaupttribüne* mirrored the Pergamon Altar, conveniently located in Berlin since 1910. Unlike the Hellenistic original, however, this structure's ornamentation was limited to a colossal swastika above the speaker's rostrum, and a massive stone eagle.

The third massive structure built for the Reich Party Rallies was the Congress Hall, or "New Nazi Congress Palace," designed not by Albert Speer, but by Nuremberg architects Ludwig and Franz Ruff. Construction began in 1935, but was incomplete at the start of the war. Featuring a rounded façade with three tiers of arches, the Congress Hall had its classical precedent in the Roman Colosseum.[198] A local tourism publication boasted: "upon completion, this new building will cover an area of 45,000 square meters, the big congress room will seat 60,000 men and two smaller rooms 5,500 and 2,000, not to mention many other side rooms."[199] As impressive as this incomplete structure was, it paled in

[198] Paul B. Jaskot, *The Architecture of Oppression: The SS, Forced Labor and the Nazi Monumental Building Economy* (New York: Routledge, 2000), 53.

[199] StadtAN, Hauptregistrar, 1292: "Hebung des Fremdenverkehrs, sowie Fremdenverkehr überhaupt, 1936–1939, III. Band."

comparison to Speer's ambitious plans for the world's largest stadium, the German Stadium, which was to be used for the sports spectacles of the rallies.[200] With its horseshoe design, its huge barrel-vaulted sub-structures, and arcaded façade, the massive structure was inspired by the Circus Maximus in Rome and the stadium of Herodes Atticus outside of Athens. Had it actually been completed, this "symbol of German sport" would have dwarfed its classical forerunners, standing at a height of 90 meters and seating up to 405,000 people.[201] Construction began in 1937 when the Führer laid the cornerstone, but was halted abruptly in 1939 after the invasion of Poland.[202]

Although they were ostensibly built for the Nazi party, the structures of the Reich Party Rally Grounds made an impact on all kinds of visitors. One of them was John Baker White, an invited guest of the German government. In his 1938 travelogue, White could not mask his admiration for the monumental architecture. His description of the Zeppelin Field registered his awe:

A vast green field some four times the size of the Wembley Stadium, with a broad asphalt track running across one side of it. Surrounding it on all four sides, save for three wide entrances, white stone stands, surmounted on one side by a long colonnade in the Grecian style, flanked with two bowls of living fire and capped in the centre with a huge swastika wreathed in gold . . . Waving above the stands a forest of national flags. Such is the Zeppelin field at Nürnberg, the main parade ground of National Socialism.[203]

Similarly, an October 1937 edition of *The Washington Post* praised the "huge stone grandstand surrounding the Zeppelin meadow," in which German people honored the achievements of the Führer and his party.[204] Visitors were also struck by the incomplete buildings, and White reported that plans were already underway for an even more colossal structure: "[A]lthough the Zeppelin Field stands hold 180,000 the new stadium now being built will contain 400,000!"[205] As "statements of power" and concrete representations of a resurgent Germany grounded in historical styles, the architecture of the Reich Party Rally Grounds did not fail to impress, even though it was clearly incomplete.

---

[200] Jaskot, *The Architecture of Oppression,* 57.
[201] See Wilhem Lotz, "Das Deutsche Stadion in Nürnberg," *Kunst und Volk* 5 (1937): 257–259.
[202] Jaskot, *The Architecture of Oppression,* 59–61.
[203] John Baker White, *Dover-Nürnberg Return* (London: Burrup, Mathieson, 1938), 23–24.
[204] *The Washington Post* (Washington), October 10, 1937.
[205] White, *Dover-Nürnberg Return,* 33.

Local and national tourist propaganda hailed the Reich Party Rally Grounds as full of sights worth seeing, while simultaneously incorporating them into the preexisting tourist landscape. As early as 1934, the Nuremberg Tourism Association printed 100,000 copies of a brochure detailing the plans for the Reich Party Rally Grounds, while the official guidebook of the city began featuring the grounds in its list of tourist attractions.[206] In 1937, an English-language brochure produced by the Official Bavarian Travel Bureau praised the city's blending of "tradition and old German culture" with the "new life and struggles of the present times," acknowledging Nuremberg's medieval charm and industrial might before moving on to the rally grounds:

Having seen and enjoyed all the sights of the great past of Nuremberg one ought to pay a visit also to the sites of our modern times... No visitor should fail to see the gigantic Parade Ground with the Memorial to our soldiers who fell in the Great War. Out there between the picturesque "Dutzendteiche" (Dozen Lakes) and the Zoological Garden amid extensive green lawns a tremendous piece of ground is being prepared to make room for the great assemblages and festivals of the German Nation, such as nowhere else may be found.[207]

Great, gigantic, tremendous – these were the words that the tourism industry used to market the Reich Party Rally Grounds to both Germans and foreigners. This language of immensity was also recognizable in a short guide issued by the Nuremberg Tourism Association in August 1939, which described the architecture as "an expression of a new artistic and cultural spirit that will leave its mark on the following centuries."[208] Picture postcards also showcased the sheer size of these new structures, with one example depicting a scale model of the German Stadium, complete with details on its planned dimensions.[209] Like the "German Art" on display in Munich, the architecture of the Reich Party Rally Grounds was a symbol of a triumphant German culture grounded in the past.

While the Reich Party Rally drew large numbers of visitors to Nuremberg in September, the grounds attracted tourists year-round. As early as 1935, the Nuremberg Tourism Association reported that visitors were requesting tours of the rally grounds. Shortly thereafter, the organization began offering official tours, conducted along prearranged routes

[206] Büchert, "Der Verkehrsverein Nürnberg," 400–401.
[207] Brochure was entitled "1937 Nuremberg: Excursions and Sightseeing Program." BWA, Amtliches Bayerisches Reisebüro (F 14), 6: "abr-Zweigstelle Nürnberg, 1935–1939."
[208] BayHStA, Sammlung Varia, 268.
[209] StadtAN, Bildpostkarten, 5198: "Nürnberg 'Deutsches Stadion'" (Fürth i. Bayern: Verlag Ludwig Riffelmacher, undated).

with carefully chosen local guides.[210] A November 1936 issue of the *Nürnberger Zeitung* announced that 3,283 European tourists had visited the Reich Party Rally Grounds in August, and another 1,763 had toured the grounds in October. The article also conceded that the "approximate number of guests who visited outside of the tour is difficult to calculate."[211] This last concern was quickly alleviated by two new policies: tours of the Reich Party Rally Grounds were only available through officially licensed guides, and entrance to the grounds was otherwise forbidden.[212] Furthermore, the official tours were only offered a few times per day (three times a day on weekdays, four times a day on Saturday, and five times a day on Sunday).[213] An undated brochure issued by Nuremberg Tourism Association, entitled "The Answers to the Most Important Questions during your Nuremberg Visit," advertised "tours in sightseeing wagons" as well as "tours by foot," with groups of *Wehrmacht*, Hitler Youth, SS, and SA members receiving reduced rates, alongside KdF vacationers.[214]

Whether touring the grounds by foot or by car, the tourist was likely to hear the same details, as there was a standardized script prepared by the Special Association for the Reich Party Rally. This text mirrored the tourist propaganda of the period, describing the buildings of the rally grounds with a mathematical language of immensity, even if the figures themselves were not always consistent. Numbers aside, the text of the official tour also called attention to the political significance and sheer spectacle of the Reich Party Rallies. For example, when describing the main grandstands of the Zeppelin Field, the text strayed from the facts to offer qualitative commentary:

The Führer gives his speeches from the central tribune. The many banners of the Movement, the guests of honor, and the representatives of party and state also find their places here. All of this combines with the fully-seated grandstands and assembled formations to produce the impression of a determination, as well as sights of such magnitude, spirit, and magnificence that words simply cannot describe.[215]

---

[210] StadtAN, Zweckverband Reichsparteitag, 337: "Führungen im Reichsparteitags-gelände – Fremdenrundfahrten, 1935–1943."
[211] *Die Nürnberger Zeitung* (Nuremberg), November 23, 1936.
[212] StadtAN, Zweckverband Reichsparteitag, 337.
[213] StadtAN, Zweckverband Reichsparteitag, 338: "Führungen im Reichsparteitags-gelände – Handakt des ZRN, 1936–1943."
[214] BayHStA, Sammlung Varia, 268.
[215] StadtAN, Zweckverband Reichsparteitag, 337.

Even without the fully seated grandstands and the assembled formations, a tour of the Reich Party Rally Grounds was sold as an unforgettable experience. A 1936 issue of *Der Fremdenverkehr*, the "official organ" of the Reich Committee for Tourism, described one of these official tours in "A Morning in the Reich Party Rally Grounds." Impressed with the scope as well as the public nature of these buildings ("National Socialist Germany has nothing to hide"), the author concluded: "Even those who have looked upon these buildings only once, with their proportions so difficult to comprehend, will never forget their prominence." The author characterized the grounds as the "cathedral of National Socialism," evoking the religious language that was so common within the Nazified tourist culture.[216]

This glowing account of the tour suggested that the buildings of the Reich Party Rally Grounds were no average tourist attractions; they were historic representations of a revived national consciousness. Still, some visitors complained that the Reich Party Rally Grounds were overshadowing other Nuremberg attractions. In 1936, English tourist Madeline Kent noticed that the galleries of the Germanic National Museum were largely empty. Speculating on where all the tourists had gone, she concluded that they had been duped by the official propaganda: "They are then driven round the walls of Nuremberg... and so out beyond the city to the immense stadiums for the Party Congress, each one vaster than the last, more uncannily pagan in design, more thickly studded with giant swastikas in concrete and gilded eagles."[217] Even a critic of the Nazi regime like Kent had to comment on the magnitude of the Reich Party Rally Grounds.

Whether they visited during the rally itself or during another time of the year, tourists to Nuremberg were presented with a city where the past and present intersected and pointed toward a glorious future for Germany. A 1938 guide published by the Nuremberg Tourism Association distinguished the city as the "living embodiment of German history," where every year at the Reich Party Rally "new currents of national energy and enthusiasm" originated and subsequently spread across the German fatherland.[218] A 1937 English-language brochure proclaimed:

[216] *Der Fremdenverkehr: Reichsorgan für den deutschen Fremdenverkehr* (Berlin), August 8, 1936.
[217] Madeleine Kent, *I Married a German* (New York: Harper & Brothers, 1939), 328.
[218] BayHStA, Sammlung Varia, 268.

In no other city in Germany are tradition and old German culture as harmonically blended with the new life and struggles of the present times as here in Nuremberg. He who visits Nuremberg for the first time, even though it be only for a short stay, will undoubtedly as soon as he enters the town be impressed by the imposing developments of the present, amidst the many signs that bear witness to a great and glorious past.[219]

Whether directed at domestic or international visitors, tourist propaganda consistently invoked historical significance and contemporary relevance in its marketing of Nuremberg. Picture postcards achieved a similar effect. One card in particular featured a painted image depicting three layers of decidedly German iconography. In the foreground, three German soldiers march with Nazi flags. Behind them stands one of the massive bronze eagles of the Luitpold Arena, while the swastika banners of the Reich Party Rally Grounds are visible to their left. In the distance, the Imperial Fortress looms, with the traditional standards of the Free City hanging from the foremost tower.[220] This postcard accomplished with images what so many other examples of tourist propaganda attempted with words: the integration of Nuremberg's twin identities as the historical, "unofficial capital of the Holy Roman Empire" and the modern "City of the Reich Party Rallies."

This new version of grounded modernity helped to make the abstract concept of Germany more tangible by linking it to a historically significant location. For Germans in particular, this engagement with history helped to overcome the sense of discontinuity and rupture that defined the interwar period. An exhibition at the Germanic National Museum that coincided with the 1937 party rally sought to accomplish this quite overtly. Organized by Alfred Rosenberg's Fighting League for German Culture, the exhibition was entitled "Nuremberg, the German City: From the City of the Imperial Diets to the City of the Reich Party Rallies." With various displays, it highlighted the historical continuities between the early modern assemblies and the modern-day rallies in order to substantiate the Third Reich's claim that it was the ideological heir to the First Reich. Moreover, the official guidebook of the exhibit explicitly linked the fate of Nuremberg to the fate of the German nation, arguing that when the Reich was strong, Nuremberg was strong, and when the Reich was divided, Nuremberg was divided.[221] After immersing themselves in

---

[219] BWA, Amtliches Bayerisches Reisebüro (F 14), 6.
[220] StadtAN, Postkarten, 5196: "Reichsparteitag Nürnberg" (Munich: Photo-Hoffman, undated).
[221] Brockmann, *Nuremberg*, 176, 179.

FIGURE 14. Postcard for the City of the Reich Party Rallies, 1930s. Courtesy of Stadtarchiv Nürnberg.

German history at the museum, visitors could witness history firsthand at the nearby rally grounds.[222]

The Reich Party Rally transformed the tourist profile of Nuremberg, and statistics reflected the event's impact. An article in a March 1934 issue of the *Abendblatt/Münchener Telegrammzeitung* reported that the 1933 Reich Party Rally brought "345,872 visitors to Nuremberg, roughly 150,000 more than the standard tourism could deliver."[223] An annual report issued by the Nuremberg Tourism Association in 1934 confirmed a 20 percent increase in visitors during the 1933 season (April 1, 1933 – March 31, 1934), but also stressed that the roughly 346,000 Reich Party Rally participants could not be classified as normal tourists, since most of them had to remain on the rally grounds.[224] In 1938, the Statistics Office of the City of the Reich Party Rallies published more extensive data on Nuremberg tourism. In general, the statistics reflected a remarkable increase in the number of overnight visitors in Nuremberg, which rose from roughly 200,000 in 1932 to over 500,000 in 1938. Unsurprisingly, the month of September always posted large numbers, with over 21,000 new visitors in 1933, and over 75,000 in 1938, roughly 14 percent of the annual amount. Furthermore, these figures did not include the number of participants in the Reich Party Rally, which were tallied separately. Statistics indicating the nationality of visitors are likewise revealing, as the number of international tourists visiting Nuremberg nearly tripled between 1932 and 1938. A closer look at the year of 1937 reveals that the greatest number of international tourists to Nuremberg traveled from Great Britain and Ireland (13,566), the United States of America (10,684), Austria (8,157), Czechoslovakia (6,129), and Denmark (5,340). However, the events of 1938, including the annexation of Austria and the November pogrom, appeared to have an adverse effect on international tourism, as that year's overall figure of visitors did not register the growth of previous years.[225] Still, these statistics prove that National Socialist Nuremberg was a popular destination among both German tourists and international visitors, both eager to behold the spectacle of the Third Reich and the alternative modernity that it represented.

* * *

In 1934, a former member of the *Freikorps* and a longtime Nazi supporter named Josef Mayr became mayor of Augsburg. While in office, he was

---

[222] Semmens, *Seeing Hitler's Germany*, 67.
[223] *Abendblatt/Münchener Telegrammzeitung* (Munich), March 7, 1934.
[224] StadtAN, Hauptregistrar, 1290.
[225] StadtAN, Hauptregistrar, 1292. *Die Statistik des Fremdenverkehrs*, 14–23, 24, 31–36.

determined to increase the visibility of Augsburg as both a tourist sight and a nationalist site.[226] The Augsburg Zoo, which opened on June 16, 1937, would accomplish both of these objectives. Munich and Nuremberg had opened their own zoological parks in 1911 and 1912 respectively, but a local lobby group in Augsburg had been unsuccessful in its attempts to create a similar institution in Bavaria's third largest city. After 1933, this group finally received the support of the municipal government, which assumed financial responsibility for the construction of a zoological park on eighteen hectares of land in the Siebentischwald, a large forest south of Augsburg. In order to distinguish this zoo from its Bavarian rivals, the local government decided to give the facility "a modern look." In this case, "modern" meant overtly nationalist. "The Park of the German Animal World" was a tribute to the biological roots of the nation, and it featured indigenous German animals in a relatively undisturbed natural setting. The presence of rare and endangered species such as elk, lynx, and bison proved to be a popular draw, and the Augsburg Zoo welcomed approximately 100,000 visitors during its first nine months.[227] A 1941 brochure edited by the mayor praised the success of the zoo's first four years, insisting that the "first German animal park" had accomplished something tremendous: it had recreated a natural world that was once common in "Greater Germany."[228] Defined as a true "homeland zoo" (*Heimattiergarten*), the Augsburg institution not only reacquainted the nation with its origins, it added a modern attraction to Augsburg's inventory of sights, which had remained relatively static since 1930.

Like the new tourist attractions of Munich and Nuremberg, the Augsburg Zoo established a link between a premodern age and modern times. However, this celebration of natural history was not nearly as popular as the celebration of political history, and unlike the neoclassical monuments of Munich and Nuremberg, the Augsburg Zoo did not completely redefine the city's tourist culture. While it is tempting to interpret the Nazified tourist culture of Munich and Nuremberg as an unprecedented

---

[226] Bernhard Gotto, *Nationalsozialistische Kommunalpolitik: Administrative Normalität und Systemstabilisierung durch die Augsburger Stadtverwaltung, 1933–1945* (Munich: R. Oldenbourg Verlag, 2006), 261–264.

[227] *Fünf Jahre Aufbau der Stadt Augsburg: Ein Rechenschaftsbericht über die Jahre 1933–1937, Textband* (Augsburg: Herausgegeben vom Oberbürgermeister der Gauhauptstadt Augsburg, 1938), 217.

[228] StadtAA NL, Broschüre "Der Augsburger Tiergarten und seine Ausgestaltung zum Deutschen Naturkundepark," hg. vom Oberbürgermeister der Gauhauptstadt Augsburg (Augsburg, 1941), 3–5, 9.

development that signaled a dramatic aberration from that which preceded and followed it, this form of tourism actually represented one
more phase in an ongoing process rather than an abrupt volte face. Just
as the Nazi dictatorship's efforts to extend vacationing opportunities
to the masses represented a new chapter in the continuing rise of mass
tourism, the marketing of the Nazified tourist culture in Bavaria represented another example of the local tourism industry's attempts to com-
bine the themes of history and modernity within the constructed image
of the locality. This was an instance of continuity, not rupture.

Tourism, and specifically the propaganda that surrounded it, must be
examined as an integral part of the larger story of Nazi Germany. As
a historical topic, it sheds invaluable light on the subjects of cultural
diplomacy, racism, and most importantly, the construction of the loyal
Volksgemeinschaft. While earlier works have focused on the Strength
through Joy program or provided an overview of tourism throughout
Hitler's Germany, this chapter has utilized the case studies of Munich
and Nuremberg to investigate the appeal of the Third Reich. It is now
clear that the tourist cultures of Bavaria's largest cities became thoroughly
Nazified after 1933, as attractions like the Temples of Honor and the
Reich Party Rally Grounds became the definitive features of each city's
tourist profile without completely eradicating the preexisting tourist culture. In the wake of the economic crises of the Weimar era, the tourism
industry quickly realized that National Socialism sold well.

The undeniable popularity of the sights of Brown Bavaria confirms that
there was something appealing about National Socialism, both inside and
outside of Germany. However, tourist propaganda presented a whitewashed Third Reich that was largely devoid of the corruption, coercion,
and racism that defined everyday life for many of its citizens. Looking
past potentially disappointing realities, the tourism industry marketed a
nation that was united by history, culture, and a common cause in the
present. In the end, the balancing of past and present that had been the
modus operandi of the Bavarian tourism industry for decades had its
ultimate expression under the Nazis, who used the language of grounded
modernity to frame their past triumphs and validate their contemporary
crusades.

Epilogue

By concluding the previous chapter with the fateful year of 1939, I do not mean to imply that the outbreak of World War II marked a complete caesura in the larger story of German tourism. On the contrary, a surprising amount of continuity characterized the activity of the German tourism industry during the early years of the war. The situation was very different than it had been in 1914, as travel was no longer understood as a middle-class luxury, but as an entitlement and a necessity.[1] Furthermore, the Nazi dictatorship maintained that tourism served an important ideological function in the midst of war, as it boosted morale among the broader population. Promising rest and rejuvenation, leisure travel would keep the people's community strong, united, and committed to the war effort.[2] The government's commitment to tourism was confirmed at a February 1940 meeting, when Hermann Esser announced to seventy representatives of the German travel industry: "It is the will of the Führer that the work of tourism continues."[3] In Bavaria, the tourism industry proceeded with business as usual, and organizations like the Administration of State Castles, Gardens, and Lakes ensured both the government and visitors that their attractions would remain open throughout the war.[4] At

---

[1] Keitz, *Reisen als Leitbild*, 247.
[2] Semmens, *Seeing Hitler's Germany*, 154–157.
[3] BArch, Reichskanzlei, R 43-II/768A: "Verkehrswesen, Hebung des Fremdenverkehrs, Band 4, 1940–1944."
[4] BayHStA, Verwaltung der staatl. Schlösser, Gärten und Seen, 406: "Schloßbesichtigungen, besonders der Residenz München mit Schatzkammer und Reicher Kapelle – Generalia, Bd. 6, 1939–1952."

the same time, local newspapers insisted that the tourism industry would not succumb to the same problems that had paralyzed it during World War I.[5]

In spite of such promises and efforts, the German tourism industry did face serious obstacles during the war. The government may have recognized the ideological significance of tourism, but they also had to prioritize the war effort. As a result, they reluctantly took measures to regulate leisure travel. This began as early as 1940, when the German Reich Railway abolished special fares in order to free trains for military use. After this measure failed to stop civilians from riding the trains, the authorities took more extreme measures to prevent unnecessary travel, even threatening violators with internment in concentration camps.[6] The military appropriation of trains as well as buses meant that Strength through Joy package tours were no longer feasible, just as the closing of international borders led to a dramatic decrease in international travel.[7] At home, the government sought to curb the demand for domestic travel by ordering the regional tourism industries to stop producing propaganda, a measure that would also preserve precious paper resources.[8] In November 1941, Esser passed a resolution that denied vacations of over four weeks to anyone who was not a soldier, a member of a soldier's immediate family, or an employee of a "war-essential industry."[9] This was only the first of many decrees that limited the length of vacations in wartime Germany. In spite of these efforts, many local communities chose to ignore the new rules, and tourism continued to flourish in certain locations. In Rothenburg ob der Tauber, for example, the number of visitors remained relatively high through 1944.[10]

Commercial tourism thrived in many locales during the early years of the war, but the Battle of Stalingrad marked a real turning point in the history of German leisure travel. After the winter of 1943, military setbacks, air raids, and the renewed practice of total war made tourism

[5] *Münchener Neueste Nachrichten* (Munich), January 21, 1941. A February 1941 issue of *Der Fremdenverkehr* made similar claims. *Der Fremdenverkehr: Reichsorgan für den deutschen Fremdenverkehr* (Berlin), February 1, 1941.

[6] *Völkischer Beobachter* (Munich), March 23, 1942.

[7] Baranowski, *Strength Through Joy*, 199–201.

[8] Semmens, *Seeing Hitler's Germany*, 158–160.

[9] StAN, Regierung von Mittelfranken (Abgabe 1978), 3700: "Lenkung des Fremdenverkehrs im Kriege, 1941–1944." In November 1943, civilians injured in bombing raids were added to the list of prioritized vacationers. StadtAN, Hauptregistrar, 1301: "Lenkung des Fremdenverkehrs im Kriege, 1942–1944."

[10] Hagen, *Preservation, Tourism and Nationalism*, 217.

inconceivable for most Germans.[11] At the conclusion of the war, the tourism industry was one of the most incapacitated sectors of the German economy, and its infrastructure and most of its attractions lay in ruins.[12] Allied air raids, which left 7 million Germans homeless and approximately 600,000 dead, had devastated tourist hubs like Berlin, Dresden, and Munich.[13] In contrast to the cities, which lost 60–95 percent of their preexisting architecture, health resorts were relatively unscathed by Allied bombers. In the American zone of occupation, which included Hesse, Baden-Württemberg, and Bavaria, spa towns and climatic health resorts boasted damage rates of less than 5 percent.[14] One exception was Bad Reichenhall, which was the target of an American air raid on April 25, 1945. Close to a thousand bombs left considerable portions of the modern spa town in ruins, in addition to claiming at least 215 lives.[15]

Even relatively undisturbed tourist destinations had to contend with another consequence of the Second World War: the multitude of German expellees from the East. The 1945 Potsdam Agreement dictated that the 12 million ethnic Germans living in Eastern Europe would be "humanely transferred" to occupied Germany. By the end of 1945, Bavaria was crowded with over one million refugees. The newly founded State Secretariat for Refugee Affairs was responsible for housing these displaced people, and oversaw the construction of 1,153 camps, spending 23 million marks in the process.[16] This proved insufficient, and the bureau struggled to accommodate the nearly two million refugees that resided in Bavaria by early 1950. Many of the expellees relocated to urban centers: 69,000 dwelt in Munich, 21,600 in Nuremberg, and 19,200 in Augsburg, a figure that constituted 10.5 percent of the city's overall population.[17]

[11] Semmens, *Seeing Hitler's Germany*, 155, 174, 186.
[12] Alexander Wilde, "Zwischen Zusammenbruch und Währungsreform. Fremdenverkehr in den westlichen Besatzungszonen," in *Goldstrand und Teutonengrill: Kultur- und Sozialgeschichte des Tourismus in Deutschland 1945 bis 1989*, ed. Hasso Spode (Berlin: Verlag für universitäre Kommunikation, 1996), 87.
[13] Koshar, *Germany's Transient Pasts*, 200; W.G. Sebald, *On the Natural History of Destruction*, trans. Anthea Bell (New York: Modern Library, 2004), 3–4.
[14] Wilde, "Fremdenverkehr in den westlichen Besatzungszonen," 87.
[15] Lang, *Geschichte von Bad Reichenhall*, 782.
[16] Brenda Melendy, "Expellees on Strike: Competing Victimization Discourses and the Dachau Refugee Camp Protest Movement, 1948–1949," *German Studies Review* 28, no. 1 (February 2005): 109–110. See also Karin Pohl, *Zwischen Integration und Isolation: Zur kulturellen Dimension der Vertriebenenpolitik in Bayern (1945–1975)* (Munich: Iudicium, 2009).
[17] Jeffry Diefendorf, *In the Wake of War: The Reconstruction of German Cities after World War II* (New York: Oxford University Press, 1993), 128.

Other refugees descended upon rural communities, often to the detriment of local economies. In places like Franconian Switzerland, refugees impeded the revival of the tourism industry by filling hotels and inns. A 1947 memo from the Tourism Association of Nuremberg and Northern Bavaria reported that the villages of Streitberg, Muggendorf, and Gößweinstein were infested with refugees. Gößweinstein was allegedly so packed that it could not accommodate another single person.[18]

Insufficient accommodations were one of the greatest obstacles confronted by the German tourism industry after World War II. In 1946, Bavaria could offer only 10 percent of the guest rooms that were available before the war.[19] In 1947, it was reported that over half of the guest beds in the American zone were reserved for refugees or members of the occupying army, while only one third were available for tourists.[20] In a 1948 statement, the Christian Social Union of Bavaria (CSU), the postwar successor to the Bavarian *Volkspartei*, politicized the issue, claiming that the regional tourism industry had been "dismantled" by the "allocation of tourism facilities to occupation forces and refugees."[21] This represents just one instance of a broader trend: Germans blaming the victorious Allies for their postwar hardships.

Aside from room shortages, the Bavarian tourism industry also grappled with the limits of postwar transportation, most obviously in the case of the German railway, which was still handicapped by structural damage and energy shortages. In more ways than one, tourism had become more difficult. In spite of that, many people did travel during the early postwar years. In addition to the millions of expellees seeking refuge in cities and villages across western Germany, many crisscrossed the country in search of missing relatives and friends, while thousands more traveled in pursuit of supplies.[22] Germans also traveled to the devastated cities in order to tour the piles of rubble. Unlike the "romantic ruins" tourism of the nineteenth century, this was not exactly pleasurable travel. Instead, it was a means of processing recent developments, as Germans familiarized

---

[18] BayHStA, Ministerium für Wirtschaft und Verkehr, 26435: "Förderung des Fremdenverkehrs in der Fränkischen Schweiz, 1947–1953."

[19] Keitz, *Reisen als Leitbild*, 266.

[20] Wilde, "Fremdenverkehr in den westlichen Besatzungszonen," 88.

[21] BayHStA, Ministerium für Wirtschaft und Verkehr, 26233: "Fremdenverkehr, allgemein, Bd. 1, 1946–1948, 2. Teil."

[22] Keitz, *Reisen als Leitbild*, 258–259; Alex Schildt, "'Die kostbarsten Wochen des Jahres'. Urlaubtourismus der Westdeutschen (1945–1970)," in *Goldstrand und Teutonengrill*, 69–70.

themselves with "the scope of destruction and the status of rebuilding efforts."[23]

The very notion of leisure travel remained incomprehensible for most Germans during the immediate postwar period. This did not, however, dissuade the tourism industry from attempting to rebuild. In some cases, efforts began just weeks after the German defeat. In July 1945, representatives of Lower Saxony's tourism industry appealed to the British for permission to create a new tourism association. The occupying forces hesitated, but eventually sanctioned the new organization in March 1946, four months after the first postwar tourism association was founded in Baden. By early 1947, thirteen tourism associations were in operation in the Rhineland, Westphalia, Württemberg, and Bavaria. In due course, they all joined the German League of Tourist Associations and Spas, which met for the first time in June 1946.[24] At the local level, organizations like the Tourism Association of Munich initially focused on practical tasks like finding accommodations for evacuees, reconstructing hotels, and assisting the Bavarian Red Cross in their efforts to locate missing people.[25] During the early postwar years, promoting leisure travel in Germany and abroad did not rank high among their priorities.

Things began to turn around for the German tourism industry in 1948. The introduction of the *Deutsche Mark* halted inflation and inaugurated an era of economic revival for western Germany. The subsequent "economic miracle" (*Wirtschaftswunder*) of the 1950s ensured a level of stability that ultimately allowed many Germans to plan vacations in advance.[26] For travel agencies offering package tours, this meant a sudden increase in business.[27] In the meantime, postwar legislation helped to "re-normalize" the idea of the vacation, as the governments of the individual German states passed laws guaranteeing at least twelve paid vacation days for all workers.[28] Naturally, some tourist regions recovered more quickly than others. Bavaria, for example, became the "undisputed

---

[23] Koshar, *German Travel Cultures*, 182–1833.

[24] Alon Confino, *Germany as a Culture of Remembrance: Promises and Limits of Writing History* (Chapel Hill: University of North Carolina Press, 2006), 214–215, 243; Koshar, *German Travel Cultures*, 173; Wilde, "Fremdenverkehr in den westlichen Besatzungszonen," 95–96.

[25] StadtAM, Fremdenverkehrsamt, 14.

[26] See Wilde, "Fremdenverkehr in den westlichen Besatzungszonen," 93.

[27] See Christopher M. Kopper, "The Breakthrough of the Package Tour in Germany after 1945," *Journal of Tourism History* 1, no. 1 (March 2009): 67–92.

[28] Keitz, *Reisen als Leitbild*, 263–264, 268.

center of travel" after 1950, and was eventually responsible for a third of all overnight stays in Germany.[29]

The reconstruction of the German tourism industry coincided with the reconstruction of German cities. Although one scholar has argued that the reconstruction of these urban centers "prohibited any look backwards... pointing the population exclusively towards the future and enjoining on it silence about the past," this was clearly not the case.[30] Yes, reconstruction permitted Germans to move beyond recent horrors and establish the foundations of a new Germany, but it did not necessitate a total liquidation of the nation's past. On the contrary, the restoration and reconstruction of historic buildings promoted a vague appreciation of the past without dwelling on specific historical events. This helped to ground the uprooted German people, who understood reconstruction as a means of returning to normality.[31]

In Bavaria's largest cities, reconstruction promoted a selective appreciation of the past while simultaneously diverting attention from the architectural impact of the Third Reich. Reconstruction proceeded rather rapidly in Munich and Nuremberg, but the rebuilding of Augsburg's historic center, which had been destroyed during an air raid in February 1944, dragged on for close to a decade.[32] This did not prevent the tourism industry from continuing to market the Bavarian city as a worthwhile destination. A 1949 brochure reported that Augsburg's city center had finally been cleared of rubble, while the restoration of its Renaissance landmarks was ongoing.[33] In Nuremberg, over 80 percent of the *Altstadt* had been destroyed during an air raid in January 1945. One building that survived was the modern Palace of Justice, which served as the venue of the International Military Tribunal, the first and only international trial of Nazi war criminals. In preparation for the event, General George Patton ordered 15,000 German prisoners of war to clear the city streets of rubble.[34] Shortly thereafter, the reconstruction of the *Altstadt* commenced. Municipal authorities were not preoccupied with restoring every historic building, but were determined to recreate the

---

[29] Hagen, *Preservation, Tourism and Nationalism*, 244; Koshar, *German Travel Cultures*, 173; Schildt, "Urlaubtourismus der Westdeutschen," 70.

[30] Sebald, *On the Natural History of Destruction*, 7.

[31] Koshar, *Germany's Transient Pasts*, 207, 242.

[32] Roeck, *Geschichte Augsburgs*, 186–187, 190.

[33] StAM, Kurverwaltung Bad Reichenhall, 267: "Bücher, Zeitschriften, Reklame, 1906–1955."

[34] Brockmann, *Nuremberg*, 237–238.

medieval ambience that had defined the city in the eyes of tourists. They were largely successful in this regard. Years later, British travel writer Gary Hogg wrote the following about postwar Nuremberg:

The most ancient parts of the city did indeed suffer disastrously in an air raid which it seems hard to justify on any grounds whatsoever; but the extensive restoration, not only of the great churches and public buildings but of more humble structures, has been carried out lovingly and skillfully, and it often takes an expert's eye to spot where the new has been married to the old.[35]

Reconstruction was not comprehensive in Nuremberg, but it did manage to resurrect the city's general medieval character.[36]

Historic buildings were also on display in the largely undamaged Reich Party Rally Grounds, although they were not advertised as tourist attractions. During the military occupation, American forces utilized the rally grounds as a base of operations; the former SS barracks housed American soldiers, while the wide thoroughfare dividing the grounds became a runway. The American army even staged military parades in the massive Zeppelin Field, inviting residents of Nuremberg to attend.[37] Aside from the symbolic destruction of the oversized swastika on the central tribune of the Zeppelin Field, the Americans did not alter the preexisting architecture.[38] The municipal government of Nuremberg also put the rally grounds to practical use. They converted the Luitpold Arena back into a city park, while another portion of the grounds served as a refugee camp before being transformed into a new suburb known as Langwasser. In 1950, the city of Nuremberg even celebrated its 900th anniversary with a ceremony in the unfinished Congress Hall.[39] In all of these cases, there was little interest in the historical significance of the rally grounds.[40]

The city of Munich also had to deal with a complicated past in the midst of reconstruction. Between 1945 and 1950, the Bavarian government committed 30 million marks to eighteen restoration projects in the capital city.[41] With the help of the Catholic Church and various

---

[35] Gary Hogg, *Bavarian Journey* (London: R. Hale, 1958), 18.
[36] Diefendorf, *In the Wake of War*, 87.
[37] Brockmann, *Nuremberg*, 220, 257–258.
[38] Paul Jaskot, "The Reich Party Rally Grounds Revisited: The Nazi Past in Postwar Nuremberg," in *Beyond Berlin: Twelve German Cities Confront the Nazi Past*, ed. Gavriel Rosenfeld and Paul Jaskot (Ann Arbor: University of Michigan Press, 2008): 147–148.
[39] Brockmann, *Nuremberg*, 257; Koshar, *Germany's Transient Pasts*, 209.
[40] See Jaskot, "The Reich Party Rally Grounds Revisited"; Neil Gregor, *Haunted City: Nuremberg and the Nazi Past* (New Haven: Yale University Press, 2008).
[41] See Hagen, *Preservation, Tourism and Nationalism*, 227.

private donors, the government rebuilt and repaired neoclassical and baroque exteriors, while updating the interiors of many historic buildings. The American authorities supported this historical restoration, but they were also responsible for the destruction of several Nazi-era buildings, including the Temples of Honor in the *Königsplatz*.[42] Other architectural reminders of the Third Reich were put to new use. For example, the *Führerbau* was reborn as the *Amerika Haus*, an institution dedicated to the promotion of American culture in occupied Germany. In the meantime, the adjoining administrative building became a sorting center for artwork looted by the Nazis. Across town, the House of German Art was transformed into an American recreation center, complete with a basketball court.[43]

In general, the citizens of postwar Munich and Nuremberg were eager to forget about their Nazi past, and there was little interest in acknowledging the historical significance of sites like the Party Rally Grounds or the House of German Art.[44] The Bavarian tourism industry was also eager to forget, and during the immediate postwar period, they tended to overlook reminders of the Nazi past in favor of timeless landscapes, provincial traditions, and Wittelsbach kitsch. In fact, it was during the postwar period that the tourism industry finally began to market Bavaria as a single tourist destination, with numerous groups (including smaller sub-regional organizations like the Tourism Association for Munich and Upper Bavaria) producing tourist propaganda that covered the combined region.[45] These postwar publications tended to offer a somewhat nostalgic vision of the German region, with one guidebook compelling visitors to become acquainted with the "hospitable and jovial manners" of this "land of farmers."[46] Another publication marketed the unified region

---

[42] Diefendorf, *In the Wake of War*, 74, 91, 94.

[43] Large, *Where Ghosts Walked*, 351–352; HAT, Sachkatalog, Do61/00/952/TEN: *Ten Days in Germany* (Munich: Universitäts-buchdruckerei Dr. C. Wolf & Sohn, 1952), 38.

[44] See Gavriel Rosenfeld, *Munich and Memory: Architecture, Monuments, and the Legacy of the Third Reich* (Berkeley: University of California Press, 2000), 6, 8–9.

[45] A few examples include HAT, Prospekte, Do61/09/00//45–80: *Come to Bavaria: A Travelling Companion of the Bayerische Vereinsbank* (Munich: Offseitdruck Karl Knörzer, 1954); HAT, Sachkatalog, Do61/09/00/955/FOI: Walter Foitzick and Fritz Busse, *Bayern: Erlebt und Gesehen* (Munich: F. Bruckmann, 1955). The Regional Tourism Association of Bavaria and the Tourism Association for Munich and Upper Bavaria were also responsible for an undated brochure simply entitled "Bayern." StadtAM, Zeitgeschichtliche Sammlung, 117/2: "Fremdenverkehrs-Verband München-Oberbayern, 1950–1974."

[46] HAT, Sachkatalog, Do61/09/01/949/BRA: Carl Braun, *Handbuch für Oberbayern/ Vacation Guide to Upper-Bavaria* (Munich: Carl Braun, 1949), 5.

as a romantic land of history and enduring traditions, asking potential tourists: "Are you looking for the country of the leather pants and the beer-mug, a country with old customs, beautiful costumes, folks dancing and yodeling – THEN VISIT BAVARIA!"[47] For a nation burdened by the recent past and beleaguered by the present, Bavarian tourism provided a much-needed escape from the modern world. While tourist publications produced by the American authorities developed their own version of grounded modernity, balancing an appreciation for historical Bavaria with praise for German industry and engineering, the local tourism industry seemed less concerned with the modern world than it had once been.[48]

***

Historians tend to avoid making sweeping generalizations about a particular epoch, nation, or historical phenomenon. In some cases, however, such generalizations still seem appropriate. For example: The German nation experienced unprecedented political, social, economic, and cultural upheaval during the nineteenth and twentieth centuries. To be fair, modern history in general has been defined by conflict and revolutions, broadly defined, and in this sense, the history of Germany is exemplary. Since the era of the Napoleonic Wars, this part of central Europe has experienced industrialization and urbanization, unification and re-unification, numerous political revolutions and military occupations, while the German people have been at the center of two world wars and genocide. This is a story of progress and regression, triumph and terror, hope and despair. While many historians have insisted on the peculiarities of Germany's "special path," the nation's history could be viewed as a paradigm of modernity at large, showcasing its most remarkable achievements, contradictions, and failures.

Many scholars have also discussed Bavaria in terms of singularity, either dismissing the German region as a provincial backwater or singling it out as a stronghold of regional particularism. In either case, there is the implicit designation of the "antimodern." This has prevented us from appreciating how Bavaria is exemplary of Germany itself, and therefore, quintessentially modern. During the Napoleonic Wars, Bavaria coped with military occupation and heavy casualties on battlefields in central Europe and Russia. The government pursued political modernization at home and *Realpolitik* abroad, and was rewarded with new territories,

---

[47] HAT, Prospekte, D061/09/00//45–80: *Come to Bavaria*, no page numbers included.
[48] For an example of the American marketing of Bavaria, see *Information Bulletin: Magazine of the U.S. Military Government in Germany* (Munich), February 8, 1949.

including portions of Swabia and Franconia. In less than thirty years, Bavaria doubled in size, while its population increased threefold. Over the course of the long nineteenth century, the new kingdom experienced a gradual industrialization that complicated the historical identities of cities like Augsburg and Nuremberg. After German unification, urban populations swelled as a result of the influx of rural migrants, just as the Bavarian state struggled to retain vestiges of independence within the federalist system of Imperial Germany. During World War I, thousands of Bavarian residents volunteered for military service, while many on the home-front dedicated themselves to charity in the name of the *Volksgemeinschaft*. The region, like the rest of Germany, dealt with material shortages and political unrest during the latter half of the war. In 1918, revolution erupted in Munich and Augsburg, and the fires it kindled burned long after the socialist visions in northern Germany were violently compromised. During the interwar period, a politically polarized Bavaria served as the birthplace of National Socialism, a decidedly modern political movement that dramatically altered the history of Germany and the world at large.

Progress sowed many seeds of discontent in Bavaria and Germany; industrialization led to the atomization of society and the creation of a politically conscious proletariat, while urbanization produced new health concerns and fueled a longing for natural landscapes. The rise of the nation-state had the potential to unite people across social, confessional, and regional divides, but it also led to World War I, which produced a rupture in the historical consciousness of the German people. Tourism in Bavaria promised antidotes to each of these problems. It offered access to natural landscapes where travelers were safe from the noise, traffic, and stress of urban life. It catered to a new health consciousness by granting access to the healing power of mountain air, water, and even the terrain itself. During the interwar period, an ostensibly egalitarian tourism functioned as a means of compensation and distraction for industrial workers. It also helped to conceal class differences by propagating the illusion of a people's community united by a common past and culture. While it is difficult to ascertain whether or not the tourism industry actually achieved any of this, the promises were extraordinary. Although tourism was often marketed as an escape from modern life, it was actually more of a therapy, creating a space for collective reflection where visitors and visited alike could come to terms with life in a post-traditional world.

As a modernism in its own right, tourism led to a massive remapping of Bavaria in several regards. First, this new Bavaria was characterized by a sense of perpetuity. Destinations like Franconian Switzerland and Bad Reichenhall were defined by their natural landscapes, which seemed to exist outside of time. These locations appealed to the allegedly primordial bond between the German people and the untamed wilderness, but they became especially appealing in the wake of nineteenth-century urbanization. Assertions of timelessness were also recognizable in the Bavarian tourism industry's treatment of history. Guidebooks and brochures often focused on ahistorical forces that transcended particular eras and geographical boundaries, such as the ambiguous "industrial spirit" of Augsburg. These enduring forces survived into modern Germany, establishing a sense of continuity between past and present. However, this myth of continuity could not function without certain omissions in the historical record. Divisive episodes like the Austro-Prussian War of 1866 and the German Revolutions of 1918–1919 rarely received attention. Continuity was contingent on unity, just as timelessness was contingent on forgetfulness.

The Bavarian tourism industry provided access to the foundations of modern society in the form of timeless landscapes and historic cityscapes, but these sites also contained evidence of modernization. Tourist propaganda did not obscure this fact; it celebrated it, and in this manner, helped to re-map Bavaria as a modern place. In Franconian Switzerland, guidebooks and brochures emphasized the rural region's distance from the city, while also advertising modern accommodations at local inns, as well as new technologies like the telegraph and the railroad. In Bad Reichenhall, tourist propaganda glorified the timeless mountain landscape just as it praised the progressive treatments available within the spa facilities, as well as the "modern look" of the town itself. During the 1920s, tourist publications in Augsburg continued to focus on the historic *Altstadt* while dedicating more attention to the modern dimensions of the city, including its factories and urban culture. After 1933, the marketing of Munich and Nuremberg continued to endorse the traditional sights, but it devoted more space to the neoclassical structures associated with the Führer and the new regime. The language of these publications revealed an enthusiasm for forms of technological and urban modernity that coexisted with a neo-romantic infatuation with the natural environment and the national past. In other words, pre-modern nostalgia was compatible with a positive experience of modernity.

By integrating contemporary history, technology, and politics into its constructed image of Bavaria, the tourism industry cast a positive light on the present. Throughout this book, I have referred to this alternative rendering of modernity as grounded modernity, a marketable vision that relied on the balancing of tradition and progress, nature and technology, and historical significance and contemporary relevance. Although the Bavarian tourism industry never employed the term grounded modernity, there was a remarkable consistency to the tourist propaganda, which consistently juxtaposed the "old" with the "new." This idea is reminiscent of Herf's "reactionary modernism," but grounded modernity was a much more flexible and widespread idea. It celebrated nature, tradition, and history alongside technology, experimental medicine, city planning, mass culture, and popular political movements. Furthermore, grounded modernity was not always articulated in explicitly nationalist terms, like reactionary modernism. Countless sights and experiences defined this synthetic vision of modernity, and yet they all had an aura of authenticity that appealed to disillusioned city-dwellers from Germany and abroad.

Tourism branded Bavaria as simultaneously timeless and modern, and during the interwar period, "German" became part of the marketing formula. In the case of Bad Reichenhall, this process began during World War I, when the language of nationalism abruptly replaced the language of cosmopolitanism. In Augsburg, Munich, and Nuremberg, tourist propaganda became increasingly nationalist after 1918. Guidebooks and brochures defined local sights in explicitly German terms, and highlighted the importance of each city within the modern nation. Still, it would be a mistake to conclude that tourist propaganda was always cosmopolitan before World War I, and exclusively nationalist thereafter, as there were several exceptions. For example, an 1876 guidebook defined Franconian Switzerland as one of "the natural wonders of our German Fatherland" and "a precious pearl of the German *Heimat*." Conversely, a 1936 guidebook on Munich promoted the image of a cosmopolitan metropolis with an artistic scene defined by the contributions of foreigners. Nevertheless, the general tone of tourist propaganda did shift during the interwar period, reflecting a new nationalist consciousness fueled by the experiences of war and defeat, as well as the ideology of National Socialism.

In many ways, tourism led to a massive remapping of Bavaria. It raised the profile of many locations while rendering others invisible. Previously secluded destinations like Franconian Switzerland and Bad Reichenhall acquired spots on the new tourist map of Bavaria, while the city of Augsburg struggled to secure a place. Tourism also transformed city maps by spotlighting the architectural symbols of civic identity. On a larger scale, tourism impacted regional and national boundaries. At the end of the nineteenth century, Bad Reichenhall became part of a unified Alpine tourist region that included both German and Austrian destinations. During the 1930s, the new status of Munich and Nuremberg helped to transform Bavaria into the symbolic center of the Third Reich, blurring the boundaries between the region and the rest of the nation.

This last point returns us to the subject of regionalism. Although I have employed the region as a category of historical analysis, I have not addressed Bavarian regionalism for a single reason: before 1945, tourist propaganda rarely referred to a unified regional identity. Instead, they engaged with a multiplicity of identities. In articulating what made a particular destination unique and worthy of a visit, publications seldom employed the "Bavarian" label, preferring categories like natural, romantic, timeless, traditional, historic, modern, progressive, German, and even Franconian or Swabian. Admittedly, Munich was something of an exception. As the region's premier tourist destination since the nineteenth century, Munich became a symbol of Bavarian culture and *Gemütlichkeit*, but this was coupled with its reputation as an international city of art. Furthermore, its popularity made it the bane of local tourism industries across Bavaria, which sought to achieve Munich's success while also distinguishing their localities from the Bavarian capital. Resistance to a collective Bavarian identity was also recognizable in the historical overviews of Augsburg and Nuremberg tourist propaganda, which focused on all the great things that had happened when each city was part of the Holy Roman Empire, long before the creation of the Kingdom of Bavaria. During the 1920s, the Augsburg Tourism Association conceded that a shared Bavarian identity did exist, but this identity was defined by a common economy, and not much more.

Bavaria was a political and administrative unit, but it was also a region of localities. Tourism did not fortify a regional consciousness; it simply reflected regional fragmentation. Still, this did not rule out the emergence of a national consciousness. The Germans were a people who loved many regions, but in spite of this (or maybe even because of this), they were one people. At least, that is what the tourist propaganda encouraged visitors to believe. While other scholars have argued that the glorification of local communities was an effective building block of German nationalism, this book has shown how the promotion of tourism could also function as a "common denominator" between the concrete locality and the abstract nation. In Bavaria, there was an obvious connection between selling community and imagining community, even though the "region" itself was rarely part of this equation.

This work has shed light on the development of collective identities in modern Germany, but that has not been its primary goal. More significantly, it has contributed to the ongoing debate about the nature of modern consciousness in Germany. Throughout the preceding five chapters, I have discounted the myth of German (and Bavarian) exceptionalism, and specifically, the idea that German culture was somehow opposed to modernity. By demonstrating how local tourism industries across Bavaria deployed the language of grounded modernity, this book has confirmed that neo-romantic sentiments were not always explicitly reactionary, and that the acceptance of modernity did not preclude pre-modern sensibilities. In conclusion, it is clearly not helpful to think in terms of "modern" versus "anti-modern." We should appreciate the ways in which Germans combined these different currents of thought, developing visions of a better modernity that could profitably appeal to domestic and international visitors. This latter point suggests that the experience of German modernization was not unique, and that the therapy offered by the German tourism industry was not culturally specific. In fact, the marketing of tourist destinations in Britain and France reveals similar visions of grounded modernity, suggesting that non-Germans also sought authenticity in an increasingly unfamiliar world.[49]

After considering the various connections between the marketing of tourism in Bavaria and the experience of modernity in Germany, I want to return to one simple point: tourism is much more than pure escapism. The tourist often runs *away* from something, but he or she also runs *toward* something. Regardless of whether the objective is rejuvenation or self-cultivation, the tourist travels to sanctified places that offer more than breathing space. In an earlier chapter, this book identified the religious pilgrimage as an important form of proto-tourism. The last chapter identified similarities between Christian pilgrimages and the Nazified tourist culture of Munich and Nuremberg. Although there are important differences between these forms of travel, there is something to be gained from viewing the tourist as a modern-day pilgrim. Anthropologists Victor and Edith Turner made a similar point when they asserted that "a tourist is half a pilgrim, if a pilgrim is half a tourist. Even when people

---

[49] See Grenier, *Tourism and Identity in Scotland*; Young, "Of Pardons, Loss, and Longing."

bury themselves in anonymous crowds on beaches, they are seeking an almost sacred, often symbolic, mode of communitas, generally unavailable to them in the structured life of the office, the shop floor, or mine."[50] Pilgrims travel in pursuit of penance or out of a desire to witness the extraordinary. They also travel to sites of memory that promise greater proximity to the sacred, or a richer experience of it. Similarly, tourists seek spiritual redemption and temporary access to the mystical "Beyond," as Siegfried Kracauer put it. Like pilgrims, many tourists travel in search of a cure, seeking treatment for a variety of ailments, ranging from pulmonary disorders to the more modern complaint of neurasthenia. More importantly, both pilgrims and tourists travel in search of an authenticity that eludes them in their real lives. This authenticity might only be a vision, a feeling, a fleeting moment, but it recenters the traveler, who returns with a new perspective on the world. In the end, travel is not only about getting away, it is also about coming home.

---

[50] Victor Turner and Edith Turner, *Image and Pilgrimage in Christian Culture* (New York: Columbia University Press, 1978), 20.

Bibliography

1. Archival Material

Bayerisches Hauptstaatsarchiv, Munich (BayHStA)

Ministerium für Wirtschaft und Verkehr (MWi)
    26233, Fremdenverkehr, allgemein, Bd. 1, 1946–1948, 2. Teil
    26435, Förderung des Fremdenverkehrs in der Fränkischen Schweiz, 1947–
    1953
Sammlung Varia
    267, Deutsche Verkehrs- (Fremdenverkehrs-) Vereine
    268, Bayerische Verkehrs- (Fremdenverkehrs-) Vereine
Verwaltung der staatl. Schlösser, Gärten und Seen
    406, Schloßbesichtigungen, Generalia, Bd. 6, 1939–1952

Bayerisches Wirtschaftsarchiv, Munich (BWA)

Amtliches Bayerisches Reisebüro (F 14)
    6, abr-Zweigstelle Nürnberg, 1935–1939
Bildpostkarten
    64, 120, 302
Industrie- und Handelskammer für München und Oberbayern (K 001)
    39/2, Fremdenverkehr in Bayern, Juni 1922–1928

Bundesarchiv, Abteilung R, Berlin (BArch)

Reichskanzlei (R43)
    R43-II / 768a, Verkehrswesen, Hebung des Fremdenverkehrs, Band 4, 1940–
    1944

Historisches Archiv zum Tourismus, Freie Universität
Berlin (HAT)

Prospekte
D060/00/-33/RDV/-33/RDV/3/Verkehrsbücher, Reichsbahnzentrale für Deutsche Verkehrswerbung, -1933
D061/09/01/A-Z/.-45, Südbayern, -1945
D061/09/01/00//-45, Südbayern, -1945
Sachkatalog
BRU-65/BAYERN-12...D061/09: *Bruckmanns Bayerisches Hochland mit Salzburg und angrenzendem Tirol*, 1907
GEU-207/SALZKAMMERGUT-6...A26: *Geuthers Salzkammergut und Salzburg*, 1913
GRI-63/BAY. HOCHLAND-38...D061/09/01: *Griebens Bayerisches Hochland mit München und Allgäu*, 1934
D061/00/936/BRO: *Passing Through Germany*, 1936
D061/00/937/DEU: *Deutsche Hauptstädte: München, Nürnberg, Berlin, Hamburg*, 1937
D061/00/952/TEN: *Ten Days in Germany*, 1952
D061/09/00/955/FOI: *Bayern: Erlebt und Gesehen*, 1955
D061/09/00//45-80: *Come to Bavaria: A Travelling Companion of the Bayerische Vereinsbank*, 1954
D061/09/01/915/VER: *München, Die Kurorte, Sommerfrischen und Gaststätten im Bayerischen Hochland. Kriegsausgabe*, 1915
D061/09/01/936/GUE: *Kreuz und quer durch Oberbayern. Ein kultureller Führer für Reisende und Heimatfreunde*, 1936
D061/09/01/938/HEI: *Reiseland Südbayern*, 1938
D061/09/01/949/BRA: *Handbuch für Oberbayern/Vacation Guide to Upper-Bavaria*, 1949
D061/09/02/934/NUE: *Nürnberg. Des Deutschen Reiches Schatzkästlein: Offizieller Führer*, 1934
Zeitschriften
072, Mitteilungen des Vereins zur Förderung des Fremdenverkehrs in München und im bayrischen Hochland (e.V.), 1907–1920

Staatsarchiv Augsburg (StAA)

Regierung von Schwaben (Kammer des Innern)
18 362, Fremdenverkehr, 1890–1932

Stadtarchiv Augsburg (StadtAA)

NL Förg
Broschüre "Der Augsburger Tiergarten und seine Ausgestaltung zum Deutschen Naturkundepark," hg. vom Oberbürgermeister der Gauhauptstadt Augsburg, Augsburg o.D. [1941]

Broschüre "Augsburg die goldene Stadt (Von deutscher Städte Schönheit / Band 1)," hg. von Fritz Droop, Augsburg [1926]

Überlieferungen aus verschiedenen städtischen Aktengebieten

20 / 585, Förderung des Fremdenverkehrs, I. Band, 1917–1925
20 / 586, Förderung des Fremdenverkehrs, II. Band, 1926
20 / 587, Förderung des Fremdenverkehrs, III. Band, 1927
20 / 588, Förderung des Fremdenverkehrs, IV. Band, 1928
25 / 105, Förderung des Fremdenverkehrs, VII. Band, 1931
34 / 276, Förderung des Fremdenverkehrs, V. Band, 1929
34 / 277, Förderung des Fremdenverkehrs, VI. Band, 1930
34 / 278, Förderung des Fremdenverkehrs, VIII. Band, 1932–1933
34 / 290, Filmaufnahme der Stadt Augsburg, I. Bd., 1921–1931
34 / 291, Verein zur Hebung des Fremdenverkehrs, Zuschuss, I. Band., 1893–1931
34 / 303, Verkehrswerbung im Ausland, I. Band, 1928–1936
50 / 1133, Erhaltung u. Ausstellung des architektonischen Gesamtbildes der Stadt Augsburg, 1902–1979
50 / 1287, Fremdenführerwesen, 1929–1978
50 / 1288, Ausgestaltung des Bahnhofvorplatzes, 1925–1978

Staatsarchiv Bamberg (StAB)

Regierung von Oberfranken

1978, Fremdenwesen, Hebung des Fremdenverkehrs, Nordbayerischer Verkehrsverein, 1891–1920

Staatsarchiv München (StAM)

Kurverwaltung Bad Reichenhall

7, Amtsgeschäfte des Badeskommisars, 1861–1937
8, Kirchen- und Religionssachen, 1873–1938
23, Landesverein zur Hebung des Fremdenverkehrs, 1890–1896
24, Münchner Fremdenverkehrsverein, 1903–1928
32, Bund deutscher Verkehrsvereine und Reichszentrale für deutsche Verkehrswerbung, 1913–1931
242, Literatur und Pressestimmen, 1884–1908
247, Fonds zur Errichtung eines Sängerheimes in Bad Reichenhall, 1911–1919
248, 1.Weltkrieg, 1914–1918, 1914–1920
249, Vergünstigungen für Kriegsteilnehmer des 1. Weltkriegs, 1914–1922
251, Gemüseanbau im Kurgarten während des 1. Weltkriegs, 1917–1918
256, Allgemeiner Charakter des Kurortes, 1890–1936
265, Bücher, Zeitschriften, Reklame, 1900–1955
267, Bücher, Zeitschriften, Reklame, 1906–1955
269, Bücher, Zeitschriften, Reklame, 1910–1956

273, Badeprospekte, 1901–1934
276, Das Wochenblatt "Der Untersberg," 1914
286, Fremdenverkehr, 1854–1936
288, Fremdenverkehr, 1898–1937, 1951
836, Errichtung und Betrieb eines Militär-Erholungsheimes in Bad Reichenhall, 1911–1932
838, Bäderfürsorge für Kriegsteilnehmer, 1915–1919
Polizeidirektion München
5999, Notgemeinschaft zur Förderung der Inlandreisen, 1931–1935
SGSV (Verwaltung der staatlicher Schlösser, Gärten, und Seen)
1468, Durchführung des Tages der Deutschen Kunst im Englischen Garten, 1937–1940

Stadtarchiv München (StadtAM)

Fremdenverkehrsamt
7, Verkehrswerbung, Reichszentrale, 1925–1928
12, Landesfremdenverkehrsrat, Bayerischer: Berichte, 1911–1920
14, Verkehrs-Verein-München: Planstellen, Arbeitsgebiet, Errichtung, Gesetzblätter, Zeitungsartikel... 1933–1949
Zeitgeschichtliche Sammlung
116/1, Fremdenverkehr München bis 1945
117/1, Fremdenverkehr Oberbayern, vor 1945
117/2, Fremdenverkehrs-Verband München-Oberbayern, 1950–1974
Zeitungsausschnitte
339, Fremdenverkehr, allg., 1930–1949

Staatsarchiv Nürnberg (StAN)

Regierung von Mittelfranken
3699, Landesfremdenverkehrsrat, 1933–1952
3700, Lenkung des Fremdenverkehrs im Kriege, 1941–1944

Stadtarchiv Nürnberg (StadtAN)

Hauptregistrar (C7/I)
1269, Hebung des Fremdenverkehrs, Band 1, 1903–1922
1270, Hebung des Fremdenverkehrs, Band 2, 1923–1935
1285, Verkehrsverband Nordbayern e.V., Bd. 1, 1927–1932
1286, Verkehrsverband Nordbayern e.V., Bd. 2, 1933–1934
1290, Fremdenverkehrsverein Nürnberg und Umgebung, Band 2, 1928–1937
1292, Hebung des Fremdenverkehrs, sowie Fremdenverkehr überhaupt, Band 3, 1936–1939
1301, Lenkung des Fremdenverkehrs im Kriege, 1943–1944
Postkarten (A5)
1428, 5196, 5198

Zweckverband Reichsparteitag (C32)
337, Führungen im Reichsparteitagsgelände – Fremdenrundfahrten, 1935–1943
338, Führungen im Reichsparteitagsgelände – Handakt des ZRN, 1936–1941
1102, Reichsparteitag 1936 Stadtschmückung, 1 Fasz.

2. Guidebooks and Brochures

Alexander, Bruno. *Bad Reichenhall als klimatischer Kurort*. Munich: Verlag der Ärztlichen Rundschau Otto Gmelin, 1911.

Bernard, Julius. *Reisehandbuch für das Königreich Bayern und die angrenzenden Länderstriche, besonders Tyrol und Salzkammergut mit besonderer Rücksicht auf Geschichte, Topographie, Handel und Gewerbe*. Stuttgart: Paul Gauger, 1868.

Bühler, Adolf. *Fremden-Führer durch Bad Reichenhall, Berchtesgaden, Salzburg und Lofer*. Bad Reichenhall: H. Bühler, 1915.

———. *Bad Reichenhall und seine Umgebungen*, 6th edn. Bad Reichenhall: Verlag von Paul Brunnquell, 1869.

———. *Führer durch Bad Reichenhall, Salzburg & Berchtesgaden*, 21st edn. Bad Reichenhall: H. Bühler, 1900.

Burrows, I. *The Intelligent Traveler's Guide to Germany*. New York: Knight Publications, 1936.

Das Königliche Kurhaus in Bad Reichenhall: Denkschrift zur Feier der Eröffnung. Munich: Baugeschäft Heilmann & Littman, 1900.

Der Neue Fremdenführer durch Wiesbaden, Langenschwalbach, Schlangenbad und Umgebungen. Wiesbaden: A Menne Nachfolger, 1913.

Die Fränkische Schweiz, das Schwabachthal und die Gräfenberger Umgebung. Erlangen: Th. Bläsings Universitäts-Buchhandlung, 1895.

Die Fränkische Schweiz, das Schwabachthal und die Gräfenberger Umgebung, Unter besonderer Berücksichtigung der Radfahrtouren. Erlangen: Th. Bläsings Universitäts-Buchhandlung, 1898.

Die Fränkische Schweiz und die Kur-Anstalt zur Streitberg: Ein treuer Führer für Reisende und ärztlicher Rathgeber für Kurgäste nebst Naturgeschichte der Fränkischen Schweiz. Erlangen: Verlag von Andreas Deichert, 1889.

Dittmar, Franz. *400 Ausflüge in die Umgegend von Nürnberg und Fürth, in das Pegnitztal, in die Altdorfer Gegend, in das Rednitz- und Altmühlgebiet und in die Fränkische Schweiz*. Nuremberg: Tümmel, 1897.

Ende, Friedrich. *Praktischer Führer durch die Fränkische Schweiz (mit ausführlicher Orientierungs-Karte)*. Nuremberg: Selbstverlag von Friedr. Ende and Erh. Kolb, 1894.

———. *Vollständiger Führer durch die ganze Fränkische Schweiz und Teile der Oberpfalz*. Nuremberg: Selbstverlag von Friedr. Ende, 1895.

Esper, Johann Friedrich. *Ausführliche Nachricht von neuentdeckten Zoolithen unbekannter vierfüssiger Thiere und denen sie enthaltenden, so wie verschiedenen andern denkwürdigen Grüften der Obergebürgischen Lande der Marggrafthums Bayreuth*. Nuremberg: G.W. Knorrs Erben, 1774.

Fick, Johann Christian. *Historisch-topographisch-statistische Beschreibung von Erlangen und dessen Gegend mit Anweisungen und Regeln für Studirende.* Erlangen: J.J. Palm, 1812.

Fr. König's Hofbuchhandlung, Hanau (Firm). *Führer durch Augsburg: Kurze Beschreibung der Stadt und ihrer Sehenswürdigkeiten.* Augsburg: Math. Rieger'sche Buchhandlung (A. Himmer), 1900.

Führer durch die Fränkische Schweiz, Mit Wegweiser durch das Schwabachthal von Erlangen nach Gräfenberg und die sog. Hersbrucker Schweiz. Erlangen: Verlag von Andreas Deichert, 1887.

Gebele, Eduard. *Confessio Augustana 1530–1930: Führer durch die Ausstellung, Rathaus Fürstenzimmer.* Augsburg: Buchdruckerei Hieronymous Mühlberger, 1930.

Grieben's Reise-Bibliothek (Firm). *Das Fichtelgebirge und die Fränkische Schweiz. Mit besonderer Berücksichtigung von Bamberg und Bayreuth,* 5th edn. Berlin: Verlag von Alber Goldschmidt, 1876.

———. *Führer durch Nürnberg und Umgebungen.* Berlin: Griebens Reisebücher, 1900.

Günther, Herbert. *Franken und die bayrische Ostmark.* Berlin: Atlantis-Verlag, 1936.

Heilmeyer, Alexander. *Augsburg und Bayerisch-Schwaben (Bayerische Reisebücher Band IV).* Munich: Knorr, 1927.

Heller, Joseph. *Muggendorf und seine Umgebung oder die fränkische Schweiz: Ein Handbuch.* Bamberg: J.C. Dresch, 1829.

Karl Baedeker (Firm). *München und Südbayern.* Leipzig: Karl Baedeker, 1935.

———. *Südbayern, Tirol, Salzburg, usw.* Leipzig: Karl Baedeker, 1908.

Kleiner Führer durch die Fränkische Schweiz, sowie Wegweiser durch das Schwabachtal von Erlangen nach Gräfenberg und die sogenannte Herbrucker Schweiz. Erlangen: Th. Bläsings Universitäts-Buchhandlung, 1891.

Körber, Philipp von. *Illustrirter Fremdenführer durch die fränkische Schweiz und das Fichtelgebirg, Bamberg, Bayreuth, Erlangen und Coburg.* Bamberg: Verlag der Buchner'schen Buchhandlung, 1858.

Kurverein e.V. Bad Reichenhall. *Bad Reichenhall: Illustrierter Badprospekt des Kurortes.* Munich: Alphons Bruckmann, 1904.

———. *Bad Reichenhall: Illustrierter Badprospekt des Kurortes.* Bad Reichenhall: M. Zugschwerdts Nachf., 1911.

Leo Woerl (Firm). *Führer durch Bad Reichenhall und Umgebung.* Leipzig: Woerl's Reisebücherverlag, 1904.

———. *Führer durch Mittelfranken, die Hersbrücker und Fränkische Schweiz.* Würzburg: Verlag von Leo Woerl, 1890.

———. *Führer durch Oberfranken.* Würzburg: Verlag von Leo Woerl, 1891.

Merers Reisebücher (Firm). *Süd-Deutschland.* Leipzig: Bibliographisches Institut, 1905.

Murray, John. *A Handbook for Travellers to the Continent,* 2nd edn. London: John Murray and Son, 1838.

Platz, Ernst. *Unser Bayerland, hrsg. Vom Verein zur Förderung des Fremdenverkehrs in München und im bayerischen Hochland.* Munich: Gerber, 1907.

Reiselsberger, Jakob. *Die Kleine Schweiz, oder Einladung zur Reise nach Streiberg, Muggendorf, Weischenfeld und deren Umgebungen.* Weischenfeld: Selbstverlag des Verfassers, 1820.

Scheurer, Hans. *Führer durch den Chiemgau.* Prien am Chiemsee: Josef Schlichter, 1908.

Schmidt, Caesar. *Illustrirtes Wanderbuch für Südbayern und Salzkammergut.* Zürich: Verlag von Caesar Schmidt, 1892.

Schnars, Carl Wilhelm. *Wild's Führer durch Baden-Baden und Umgebung.* Baden-Baden: Verlag der C. WILD'schen Hof-Buchhandlung, 1903.

Schuster, Anton. *Kleiner Führer durch die Fränkische Schweiz.* Bamberg: Reindl, 1891.

Sieghart, August. *Nordbayern: Ein Führer durch seine Schönheiten.* Nuremberg: Verkehrsverband Nordbayern, 1929.

Südbayern, hrsg. im Auftrage des Landesfremdenverkehrsrates vom Fremdenverkehrsverein München und Bayer. Alpen E.V. Munich: Gerber, 1926.

Trautwein, Theodor. *Das Bairische Hochland mit dem Allgäu, das angrenzende Tirol und Salzburg nebst Salzkammergut,* 6th edn. Augsburg: Lampart, 1893.

——. *Führer durch München, der Hauptstadt der Bewegung und Umgebung nebst den Königsschlössern.* Munich: Bergverlag Rudolf Rother, 1938.

——. *Guide Book for Munich, the Capital of the National Socialist Movement, Its Environs, and the Royal Castles.* Munich: Bergverlag Rudolf Rother, 1938.

Verkehrsverein Augsburg. *Amtlicher Führer durch die Stadt Augsburg.* Augsburg: Selbstverlag des Verkehrsvereins Augsburg, 1921.

——. *Augsburg: Amtlicher Führer.* Augsburg: Selbstverlag des Verkehrsvereins Augsburg, 1927.

——. *Augsburg: Amtlicher Führer, Kleine Ausgabe 1929/30.* Augsburg: Hieronymous Mühlberger, 1929.

——. *Das schöne Augsburg.* Augsburg: Selbstverlag des Verkehrsvereins Augsburg, 1925.

——. *Führer durch Augsburgs Industrie und Handel.* Augsburg: Selbstverlag des Verkehrsvereins Augsburg, 1925.

Wiedemann, Fritz. *Führer durch Bad Reichenhall und Umgebung mit Berchtesgaden und Salzburg.* Bad Reichenhall: M. Zugschwerdts Nachfolger, 1915.

3. Additional Primary Sources

Adam, Thomas, and Gisela Mettele, eds. *Two Boston Brahmins in Goethe's Germany: The Travel Journals of Anna and George Ticknor.* Lanham, MD: Lexington Books, 2009.

Barry, R. Milner. *Bayreuth and Franconian Switzerland.* London: S. Sonnenschein, Lowrey & Co., 1887.

Baudelaire, Charles. *Selected Writings on Art and Literature.* Translated by P.E. Charvet. New York: Penguin Books, 1992.

Benjamin, Walter. *Illuminations.* Translated by Harry Zohn. New York: Schocken Books, 1969.

Brecht, Walter. *Unser Leben in Augsburg, Damals: Erinnerungen,* 2nd edn. Frankfurt am Main: Insel Verlag, 1985.

Cole, John Alfred. *Just Back From Germany*. London: Faber and Faber Ltd., 1938.

Colton, Olive A. *Rambles Abroad*. Toledo: The Franklin Printing & Engraving Co., 1904.

Domville, Charles W. *This is Germany*. London: Seeley Service & Co. Ltd., 1939.

Dostoyevsky, Fyodor. *The Gambler*. Translated by Constance Garnett. New York: Dover Publications, 1996.

Forbes, John. *Sight-Seeing in Germany and the Tyrol in the Autumn of 1855*. London: Smith, Elder, and Co., Cornhill, 1856.

Franck, Harry. *Vagabonding through Changing Germany*. New York: Harry & Brothers Publishers, 1920.

Fraprie, Frank Roy. *Little Pilgrimages Among Bavarian Inns*. Boston: L.C. Page & Company, 1906.

Freud, Sigmund. *Civilization and Its Discontents*. Translated by James Strachey. New York: W.W. Norton & Company, 2010.

Fünf Jahre Aufbau der Stadt Augsburg: Ein Rechenschaftsbericht über die Jahre 1933–1937, Textband. Augsburg: Herausgegeben vom Oberbürgermeister der Gauhauptstadt Augsburg, 1938.

Goebbels, Joseph. *Die Tagebücher von Joseph Goebbels: Teil I, Aufzeichungen 1924–1941; Band 3/I, April 1934-Februar 1936*. Edited by Elke Fröhlich. New York: K.G. Saur, 2006.

Hausenstein, Wilhelm. *Die Welt um München*. Munich: Knorr & Hirth, 1929.

Heeringen, Gustav von. *Wanderungen durch Franken*. Leipzig: G. Wigand, 1840.

Heygate, John. *Motor Tramp*. London: Jonathan Cape, 1935.

Hitler, Adolf. *Mein Kampf*. Translated by Ralph Manheim. New York: Houghton Mifflin Company, 1999.

Hogg, Gary. *Bavarian Journey*. London: R. Hale, 1958.

Kahl, Werner. *Der deutsche Arbeiter reist!* Berlin: Deutscher Verlag, 1940.

Kent, Madeleine. *I Married a German*. New York: Harper & Brothers, 1939.

Koch-Neuses, Adam. *Die Romantik der Fränkischen Schweiz*. Forchheim: F.A. Streit, 1890.

Kracauer, Siegfried. *The Mass Ornament: Weimar Essays*. Translated by Thomas Y. Levin. Cambridge, MA: Harvard University Press, 1995.

———. *The Salaried Masses: Duty and Distraction in Weimar German*. Translated by Quinton Hoare. New York: Verso, 1998.

Krauss, Maximilian. *Fünfundzwanzig Jahre Fremdenverkehr: Werkstatterinnerungen und Grundlagen*. Munich: Gerber, 1929.

Lang, Georg. *Im Auto zwischen München und Rom*. Bielefeld: Deutschen Heimatverlag Ernst Gieseking, 1938.

Laurie, A.P. *The Case for Germany: A Study of Modern Germany*. Berlin: Internationaler Verlag, 1939.

Lin, Jan, and Christopher Mele, eds. *The Urban Sociology Reader*. New York: Routledge, 2013.

Lotz, Wilhelm. "Das Deutsche Stadion in Nürnberg." *Kunst und Volk* 5 (1937): 256–259.

Lubrich, Oliver, ed. *Travels in the Reich, 1933–1945: Foreign Authors Report from Germany*. Translated by Kenneth Norcott, Sonia Wichtmann, and Dean Krouk. Chicago: University of Chicago Press, 2010.

Mann, Thomas. *The Magic Mountain*. Translated by John E. Woods. New York: Vintage International, 1995.

McBride, Robert Medill. *Towns and People of Modern Germany*. New York: Robert M. McBride & Company, 1930.

Moser, Adolf. *Die wirtschaftliche und finanzielle Bedeutung des bayerischen Fremdenverkehrs für Land und Gemeinden*. Munich: Fremdenverkehrsverband München und bayrische Alpen, 1927.

Nietzsche, Friedrich. *Unfashionable Observations*. Translated by Richard T. Gray. Stanford: Stanford University Press, 1995.

Nordau, Max. *Degeneration*. Lincoln: University of Nebraska Press, 1968.

Packard, Horace. "Bad Reichenhall: A Health Resort of Southern Germany." *The Boston Medical and Surgical Journal* 165, no. 1 (September 1911): 487–488.

Riehl, Wilhelm Heinrich. *Die Naturgeschichte des Volkes als Grundlage einer deutschen Sozial-Politik*. Vol. I, Land und Leute, 2nd edn. Stuttgart: J.G. Cotta, 1861.

Rilke, Rainer Maria. *The Selected Poetry of Rainer Maria Rilke*. Translated by Stephen Mitchell. New York: Vintage International, 1989.

Rimington, Frank C. *Motor Rambles in Central Europe: Some Descriptions and Some Reflections*. New York: Houghton Mifflin Company, 1927.

Rosenberg, Alfred. *Der Mythus des 20. Jahrhundert: Eine Wertung des seelisch-geistigen Gestaltenkämpfe unserer Zeit*. Munich: Hoheneichen-Verlag, 1938.

Rousseau, Jean-Jacques. *Emile, or On Education*. Translated by Allan Bloom. New York: Basic Books, 1979.

———. *Julie, or the New Heloise: Letters of Two Lovers Who Live in a Small Town at the Foot of the Alps*. Translated by Philip Stewart and Jean Vaché. Hanover, NH: University Press of New England, 1997.

Rudorff, Ernst. "Ueber das Verhältniss des modernen Lebens zur Natur." *Preussische Jahrbücher* 45 (1880): 261–276.

Ruggles, Henry. *Germany Seen Without Spectacles, or Random Sketches of Various Subjects Penned from Different Standpoints in the Empire*. Boston: Lee and Shepard, 1883.

Ruhl, Klaus-Jörg, ed. *Augsburg in alten und neuen Reisebeschreibungen*. Düsseldorf: Droste Verlag GmbH, 1992.

Sax, Benjamin, and Dieter Kuntz, eds. *Inside Hitler's Germany: A Documentary History of Life in the Third Reich*. Lexington, MA: D.C. Heath & Company, 1992.

Schoonmaker, Frank. *Come With Me Through Germany*. New York: Robert M. McBride & Company, 1930.

Schwartz, Philip, ed. *Bayern im Lichte seiner hundertjährigen Statistik*. Munich: J. Lindauersche Universitäts-Buchhandlung, 1933.

Shelley, Mary Wollstonecraft. *Rambles in Germany and Italy in 1840, 1842, and 1843*. London: Edward Morton, 1844.

Shirer, William L. *Berlin Diary: The Journal of a Foreign Correspondent, 1934–1941.* New York: Alfred A. Knopf, 1941.

Sopwith, Thomas. *Three Weeks in Central Europe. Notes of an Excursion, Including the Cities of Treves, Nuremberg, Leipzig, Dresden, Freiberg, and Berlin.* London: Willis, Sotheran, and Co., 1869.

Speer, Albert. *Inside the Third Reich: Memoirs.* Translated by Richard and Clara Winston. New York: Macmillan, 1970.

Spencer, Edmund. *Sketches of Germany and the Germans, With a Glance at Poland, Hungary, and Switzerland in 1834, 1835, and 1836,* 2 vols. London: Whitaker & Co., 1836.

Steub, Ludwig. *Wanderungen im bayerischen Gebirge.* Munich: G.A. Fleischmann's Buchhandlung, 1862.

Stoddard, Lothrop. *Into the Darkness: Nazi Germany Today.* New York: Duell, Sloan & Pearce, 1940.

Strahan, Lisbeth Gooch Séguin. *Walks in Bavaria: An Autumn in the Country of the Passion-Play.* London: Alexander Strahan, 1884.

Taylor, Bayard. *At Home and Abroad: A Sketchbook of Life, Scenery, and Men.* New York: G.N. Putnam, 1862.

Taylor, Charles. *A Historical Tour in Franconia, in the Summer of 1852.* London: Longman & Co., 1852.

Tieck, Ludwig, und Wilhelm Heinrich Wackenroder. *Die Pfingstreise von 1793 durch die Fränkische Schweiz, den Frankenwald und das Fichtelgebirge.* Helmbrechts: Wilhelm Saalfrank, 1970.

Tönnies, Ferdinand. *Community and Society.* Translated by Charles P. Loomis. New York: Dover Publications, 2002.

Tucker, Robert, ed. *The Marx-Engels Reader.* New York: Norton, 1972.

Twain, Mark. *A Tramp Abroad.* New York: Oxford University Press, 1996.

Weber, Max. *The Protestant Ethic and the "Spirit" of Capitalism and Other Writings.* Translated by Peter Baehr and Gordon C. Wells. New York: Penguin Books, 2002.

White, John Baker. *Dover-Nürnberg Return.* London: Burrup, Mathieson, 1938.

Whitling, Henry John. *Pictures of Nuremberg and Rambles in the Hills and Valleys of Franconia.* London: R. Bentley, 1850.

Wolfinger, Viktor. *Ergebnisse einer Schulreise durch die Fränkische Schweiz. Festgestellt aus freien Schüleraufsätzen.* Nuremberg: Verlag der Friedrich Kornschen Buchhandlung, 1908.

4. German-Language Periodicals

Abendblatt/Münchener Telegrammzeitung

Amtliche Fremdenliste für Bad Reichenhall

Amts-Blatt für die kgl. Bezirksämter Forchheim & Ebermannstadt sowie für die kgl. Stadt Forchheim

Augsburger Neueste Nachrichten

Bayerische Staatszeitung

Bayerisch Land und Volk: Offizielles Organ des Landesverbandes zur Hebung des Fremdenverkehrs in Bayern

Das Bayerland. Illustrierte Wochenschrift für Bayerns Volk und Land
Deutsche Verkehrsblätter: Nachrichtendienst der Reichszentrale für Deutsche Verkehrswerbung
Deutschlandberichte der Sozialdemokratischen Partei Deutschlands (SOPADE)
Dresdner Anzeiger
Der Fremdenverkehr: Reichsorgan für den deutschen Fremdenverkehr
Illustrirte Zeitung
München-Augsburger Abendzeitung
Münchner Neueste Nachrichten
Münchener Post
Münchener Zeitung
Neue Augsburg Zeitung
Neue Leipziger Zeitung
Neue Pariser Zeitung
Neues Münchener Tagblatt
Nordbayerische Zeitung
Nürnberger Zeitung
Reichenhaller Grenzbote
Der Untersberg: Bad Reichenhaller Wochenblatt
Völkischer Beobachter
Die Weltbühne
Wiener Hausfrau-Zeitung: Organ für hauswirtschaftliche Interessen

5. English-Language Periodicals

The Boston Medical and Surgical Journal
The Chicago Tribune
Harper's New Monthly
Information Bulletin: Magazine of the U.S. Military Government in Germany
The Ladies' Repository: A Monthly Periodical Devoted to Literature and Religion
The New York Times
The Traveller
The Washington Post

6. Secondary Sources

Aitchison, Cara, Nicole E. Macleod, and Stephen J. Shaw. *Leisure and Tourism Landscapes: Social and Cultural Geographies.* New York: Routledge, 2000.

Aly, Götz. *Hitler's Beneficiaries: Plunder, Racial War, and the Nazi Welfare State.* Translated by Jefferson Chase. New York: Metropolitan Books, 2005.

Anderson, Benedict. *Imagined Communities: Reflections on the Origin and Spread of Nationalism.* New York: Verso, 1991.

Anderson, Susan C., and Bruce H. Tabb, eds. *Water, Leisure and Culture: European Historical Perspectives.* New York: Berg, 2002.

Angermair, Elizabeth, and Ulrike Haerendel. *Inszenierter Alltag: "Volksgemeinschaft"im nationalsozialistischen München, 1933–1945*. Munich: Hugendubel, 1993.

Applegate, Celia. "A Europe of Regions." AHR Forum: "Bringing Regionalism back to History," *American Historical Review* 104, no. 4 (October 1999): 1157–1182.

———. *A Nation of Provincials: The German Idea of Heimat*. Berkeley: University of California Press, 1990.

Bacon, William. "The Rise of the German and the Demise of the English Spa Industry: A Critical Analysis of Business Success and Failure." *Leisure Studies* 16 (1997): 173–187.

Baird, Jay. *To Die For Germany: Heroes in the Nazi Pantheon*. Bloomington: Indiana University Press, 1990.

Bajohr, Frank. *"Unser Hotel ist judenfrei": Bäder-Antisemitismus im 19. und 20. Jahrhundert*. Frankfurt am Main: Fischer, 2003.

Baranowski, Shelley. *Strength Through Joy: Consumerism and Mass Tourism in the Third Reich*. New York: Cambridge University Press, 2004.

Baranowski, Shelley, and Ellen Furlough, eds. *Being Elsewhere: Tourism, Consumer Culture, and Identity in Modern Europe and North America*. Ann Arbor: University of Michigan Press, 2001.

Barker, Mary L. "Traditional Landscape and Mass Tourism in the Alps." *Geographical Review* 72, no. 4 (October 1982): 395–415.

Barlösius, Eva. *Naturgemässe Lebensführung: Zur Geschichte der Lebensreform um die Jahrhundertwende*. Frankfurt am Main: Campus Verlag, 1997.

Bausinger, Hermann, Klaus Beyrer, and Gottfried Korff, eds. *Reisekultur: Von der Pilgerfahrt zum modernen Tourismus*. Munich: Oscar Beck, 1991.

Bayly, C.A. *The Birth of the Modern World, 1780–1914*. Malden, MA: Blackwell, 2004.

Becher, Ursula A.J. *Geschichte des modernen Lebensstils. Essen-Wohnen-Freizeit-Reisen*. Munich: C.H. Beck, 1990.

Beer, Helmut. *Grüße aus Nürnberg 3, Nürnberg in Ansichtskarten um 1900 – "Lebendige Altstadt."* Nuremberg: W. Tümmels Buchdruckerei und Verlag GmbH, 1994.

Beiser, Frederic C. *The Romantic Imperative: The Concept of Early German Romanticism*. Cambridge, MA: Harvard University Press, 2003.

Bendix, Regina. "Moral Integrity in Costumed Identity: Negotiating 'National Costume' in 19th Century Bavaria." *The Journal of American Folklore* 111, no. 440 (Spring 1998): 133–145.

Benz, Wolfgang, and Angelika Königseder, eds. *Das Konzentrationslager Dachau: Geschichte und Wirkung nationalsozialistischer Repression*. Berlin: Metropol, 2008.

Berman, Marshall. *All That Is Solid Melts Into Air: The Experience of Modernity*. New York: Penguin Books, 1988.

Bernard, Paul P. *The Rush to the Alps: The Evolution of Vacationing in Switzerland*. New York: Columbia University Press, 1978.

Bhabha, Homi K., ed. *Nation and Narration*. New York: Routledge, 1990.

Bitz, Matthias. *Badewesen in Südwestdeutschland 1550 bis 1840: Zum Wandel von Gesellschaft und Architektur.* Idstein: Schulz-Kirchner, 1989.

Black, Jeremy. *The British and the Grand Tour.* Dover, NH: Croom Helm, 1985.

Black, Monica. *Death in Berlin: From Weimar to Divided Germany.* New York: Cambridge University Press, 2010.

Blackbourn, David. *The Conquest of Nature: Water, Landscape, and the Making of Modern Germany.* London: Jonathan Cape, 2006.

———. "Fashionable Spa Towns in Nineteenth-Century Europe." In *Water, Leisure, and Culture,* ed. Susan C. Anderson and Bruce H. Tabb, 9–22. New York: Berg, 2002.

———. *The Long Nineteenth Century: A History of Germany, 1780–1918.* New York: Oxford University Press, 1998.

———, and Geoff Eley. *The Peculiarities of German History: Bourgeois Society and Politics in Nineteenth-Century Germany.* New York: Oxford University Press, 1984.

———, and James Retallack, eds. *Localism, Landscape, and the Ambiguities of Place: German-Speaking Central Europe, 1860–1930.* Toronto: University of Toronto Press, 2007.

Blechman, Max, ed. *Revolutionary Romanticism.* San Francisco: City Light Books, 1999.

Blessing, Werner K. "The Cult of Monarchy, Political Loyalty, and the Workers' Movement in Imperial Germany." *Journal of Contemporary History* 13, no. 2 (April 1978): 357–375.

Borsay, Peter, Gunther Hirschfelder, and Ruth E. Mohrmann, eds. *New Directions in Urban History: Aspects of European Art, Health, Tourism and Leisure since the Enlightenment.* Münster: Waxmann, 2000.

Bothe, Rolf, ed. *Kurstädte in Deutschland: Zur Geschichte einer Baugattung.* Berlin: Fröhlich & Kaufmann, 1984.

Botzenhart, Christof. *Die Regierungstätigkeit König Ludwig II. von Bayern: "ein Schattenkönig ohne Macht will ich nicht sein".* Munich: C.H. Beck, 2004.

Bourassa, Stephen C. *The Aesthetics of Landscape.* London: Belhaven Press, 1991.

Bourdieu, Pierre. *Distinction: A Social Critique of Taste.* Translated by Richard Nice. Cambridge, MA: Harvard University Press, 1984.

Bradley, Ian. *Water Music: Music Making in the Spas of Europe and North America.* New York: Oxford University Press, 2010.

Breckman, Warren G. "Disciplining Consumption: The Debate about Luxury in Wilhelmine Germany, 1890–1914." *Journal of Social History* 24, no. 3 (Spring 1991): 485–505.

Brennan, Michael G., ed. *The Origins of the Grand Tour: The Travels of Robert Montagu, Lord Mandeville (1649–1654), William Hammond (1655–1658), Banaster Maynard (1660–1663).* London: The Hakluyt Society, 2004.

Brilli, Attilio. *Als Reisen eine Kunst war. Vom Beginn des modernen Tourismus: Die 'Grand Tour'.* Translated by Annette Kopetzki. Berlin: Klaus Wagenbach, 2012.

Brockmann, Stephen. *Nuremberg: The Imaginary Capital.* New York: Camden House, 2006.

Broszat, Martin, Elke Fröhlich, and Anton Grossman, eds. *Bayern in der NS-Zeit, III: Herrschaft und Gesellschaft im Konflikt, Teil B*. Munich: Oldenbourg, 1981.

Broué, Pierre. *The German Revolution, 1917–1923*. Translated by John Archer. Boston: Brill, 2005.

Bruford, W.H. *The German Tradition of Self-Cultivation: 'Bildung' from Humboldt to Thomas Mann*. New York: Cambridge University Press, 1975.

Büchert, Gesa. "Förderer des Fremdenverkehrs: Der Verkehrsverein Nürnberg von den Anfängen bis zum Zweiten Weltkrieg." *Mitteilungen des Vereins für Geschichte der Stadt Nürnberg* 92 (2005): 343–414.

Bühl-Gramer, Charlotte. *Nürnberg, 1850 bis 1892: Stadtentwicklung, Kommunalpolitik und Stadtverwaltung im Zeichen von Industrialisierung und Urbanisierung*. Nuremberg: Stadtarchiv, 2003.

Burleigh, Michael. *The Third Reich: A New History*. London: Macmillan, 2000.

Burrin, Philippe. "Political Religion: The Relevance of a Concept," *History and Memory* 9 (Fall 1997): 321–349.

Buzard, James. *The Beaten Track: European Tourism, Literature, and the Ways to Culture, 1800–1918*. New York: Oxford University Press, 1993.

Bytwerk, Randall L. "Grassroots Propaganda in the Third Reich: The Reich Ring for National Socialist Propaganda and Public Enlightenment." *German Studies Review* 33, no. 1 (February 2010): 93–118.

———. *Julius Streicher: Editor of the Notorious Anti-Semitic Newspaper Der Stürmer*. New York: Cooper Square Press, 2001.

Casson, Lionel. *Travel in the Ancient World*. Baltimore: Johns Hopkins University Press, 1994.

Chaussy, Ulrich, and Christoph Püschner. *Nachbar Hitler. Führerkult und Heimatzerstörung am Obersalzberg*, 6th edn. Berlin: C. Links, 2007.

Chickering, Roger. *Great War and Urban Life in Germany: Freiburg, 1914–1918*. New York: Cambridge University Press, 2007.

Cioc, Mark. *The Rhine: An Eco-Biography, 1815–2000*. Seattle: University of Washington Press, 2002.

Confino, Alon. *Germany as a Culture of Remembrance: Promises and Limits of Writing History*. Chapel Hill: University of North Carolina Press, 2006.

———. *The Nation as a Local Metaphor: Württemberg, Imperial Germany, and National Memory, 1871–1918*. Chapel Hill: University of North Carolina Press, 1997.

———, Paul Betts, and Dirk Schumann, eds. *Between Mass Death and Individual Loss: The Place of the Dead in Twentieth-Century Germany*. New York: Berghahn, 2008.

———, and Rudy Koshar. "Régimes of Consumer Culture: New Narratives in Twentieth-Century German History." *German History* 19, no. 2 (June 2001): 135–161.

Cowan, Michael. *Cult of the Will: Nervousness and German Modernity*. University Park, PA: Pennsylvania State University Press, 2008.

Crane, Susan. *Collecting and Historical Consciousness in Early Nineteenth-Century Germany*. Ithaca: Cornell University Press, 2000.

Cross, Gary. *Time and Money: The Making of Consumer Culture*. London: Routledge, 1993.

Crouch, David, and Nina Lübbren, eds. *Visual Culture and Tourism*. New York: Berg, 2003.

Dahrendorf, Ralf. *Gesellschaft und Demokratie in Deutschland*. Munich: R. Piper, 1968.

De Grazia, Victoria. *The Culture of Consent: Mass Organization of Leisure in Fascist Italy*. New York: Cambridge University Press, 1981.

Denning, Andrew. "Alpine Modern: Central European Skiing and the Vernacularization of Cultural Modernism, 1900–1939." *Central European History* 46, no. 4 (December 2013): 850–890.

———. *Skiing into Modernity: A Cultural and Environmental History*. Oakland: University of California Press, 2015.

Dickinson, Edward. "Altitude and Whiteness: Germanizing the Alps and Alpinizing the Germans, 1875–1935." *German Studies Review* 33, no. 3 (October 2010): 579–602.

Diefendorf, Jeffry. *In the Wake of War: The Reconstruction of German Cities after World War II*. New York: Oxford University Press, 1993.

Dietrich, Rosemarie. *Die Integration Augsburgs in den bayerischen Staat (1806–1821)*. Sigmaringen: Thorbecke, 1993.

Dietzfelbinger, Eckart, and Gerhard Liedtke. *Nürnberg – Ort der Massen: Das Reichsparteitagsgelände – Vorgeschichte und schwieriges Erbe*. Berlin: Christoph Links, 2004.

Dipper, Christof, ed. *Strukturwandel einer Region: Der Odenwald im Zeitalter der Industrialisierung*. Darmstadt: Technische Universität Darmstadt, 2000.

Enzensberger, Hans Magnus. "A Theory of Tourism." Translated by Gerd Gemünden and Kenn Johnson. *New German Critique*, no. 68 (Spring-Summer 1996): 117–135.

Evans, Richard. *The Coming of the Third Reich*. New York: Penguin Group, 2004.

———. *Death in Hamburg: Society and Politics in the Cholera Years*. New York: Oxford University Press, 1987.

———. *The Third Reich in Power, 1933–1939*. New York: Penguin Group, 2005.

Feldman, Gerald D. *The Great Disorder: Politics, Economics, and Society in the German Inflation, 1914–1924*. New York: Oxford University Press, 1993.

———. "Welcome to Germany? The 'Fremdenplage' in the Weimar Inflation." In *Geschichte als Aufgabe. Festschrift für Otto Büsch*, ed. Wilhelm Treue, 629–649. Berlin: Colloquium, 1988.

Fischer, Ilse. *Industrialisierung, sozialer Konflikt und politische Willensbildung in der Stadtgemeinde. Ein Beitrag zur Sozialgeschichte Augsburgs 1840–1914*. Augsburg: H. Mühlberger, 1977.

Ford, Caroline. *Creating the Nation in Provincial France: Religion and Political Identity in Brittany*. Princeton: Princeton University Press, 1993.

Foucault, Michel. *The Birth of the Clinic: An Archaeology of Medical Perception*. Translated by A.M. Sheridan. New York: Routledge, 2003.

Frank, Alison F. "The Air Cure Town: Commodifying Mountain Air in Alpine Central Europe." *Central European History* 45, no. 2 (June 2012): 185–207.

_____. "The Pleasant and the Useful: Pilgrimage and Tourism in Habsburg Mariazell." *Austrian History Yearbook* 40 (2009): 157–182.

Frei, Norbert. *National Socialist Rule in Germany: The Führer State 1933–1945*. Translated by Simon B. Steyne. Cambridge, MA: Blackwell, 1993.

Freller, Thomas. *Adlige auf Tour: Die Erfindung der Bildungsreise*. Ostfildern: Thorbecke, 2007.

Fritzsche, Peter. *Germans into Nazis*. Cambridge, MA: Harvard University Press, 1998.

_____. *Stranded in the Present: Modern Time and the Melancholy of History*. New York: Harvard University Press, 2004.

Frohn, Hans-Werner, and Friedmann Schmoll, eds. *Natur und Staat: Staatlicher Naturschutz in Deutschland 1906–2006*. Münster: Landwirtschaftsverlag, 2006.

Fuhs, Burkhard. *Mondäne Orte einer vornehmen Gesellschaft. Kultur und Geschichte der Kurstädte, 1700–1900*. Hildesheim: Olms, 1992.

Furlough, Ellen. "Making Mass Vacations: Tourism and Consumer Culture in France, 1930s to 1970s." *Comparative Studies in Society and History* 40, no. 2 (April 1998): 247–286.

Fussell, Paul, ed. *The Norton Book of Travel*. New York: W.W. Norton & Company, 1987.

Gall, Lothar. *Bürgertum in Deutschland*. Berlin: Siedler, 1989.

Geisthövel, Alexa, and Habbo Knoch, eds. *Orte der Moderne: Erfahrungswelten des 19. und 20. Jahrhunderts*. New York: Campus, 2005.

Gellately, Robert. *Backing Hitler: Consent and Coercion in Nazi Germany*. New York: Oxford University Press, 2001.

Geppert, Alexander C.T., Uffa Jensen, and Jörn Weinhold, eds. *Ortsgespräche: Raum und Kommunikation im 19. und 20. Jahrhundert*. Bielefeld: Transcript, 2005.

Geyer, Martin. *Verkehrte Welt: Revolution, Inflation und Moderne: München 1914–1924*. Göttingen: Vandenhoeck & Ruprecht, 1998.

Glaser, Hermann. "Um eine Stadt von innen bietend: Historische Stadt und kulturelle Aneignung." In *Die Alte Stadt: Denkmal oder Lebensraum?*, ed. Cord Meckseper and Harald Siebenmorgen. Göttingen: Vandenhoeck & Ruprecht, 1985.

Gordon, Harold J. *Hitler and the Beer Hall Putsch*. Princeton, NJ: Princeton University Press, 1972.

Gorsuch, Anne E., and Diane P. Koenker, eds. *Turizm: The Russian and East European Tourist under Capitalism and Socialism*. Ithaca, NY: Cornell University Press, 2006.

Götsch, Silke. "Sommerfrische: Zur Etablierung einer Gegenwelt am Ende des 19. Jahrhunderts." *Schweizerisches Archiv für Volkskunde* 98, no. 1 (2002): 9–15.

Gottlieb, Günther, ed. *Geschichte der Stadt Augsburg: Von der Römerzeit bis zur Gegenwart*. Stuttgart: Konrad Theiss Verlag, 1984.

Gotto, Bernhard. *Nationalsozialistische Kommunalpolitik: Administrative Normälitat und Systemstabilisierung durch die Augsburger Stadtverwaltung, 1933–1945*. Munich: R. Oldenbourg Verlag, 2006.

Grau, Bernhard. *Kurt Eisner 1867–1919*. Munich: C.H. Beck, 2000.

Green, Abigail. *Fatherlands: State-Building and Nationhood in Nineteenth Century Germany*. New York: Cambridge University Press, 2001.

Gregor, Neil. *Haunted City: Nuremberg and the Nazi Past*. New Haven: Yale University Press, 2008.

Greif, Thomas. *Frankens braune Wallfahrt – Der Hesselberg im Dritten Reich*. Ansbach: Selbstverlag des Historischen Vereins für Mittelfranken, 2007.

Grenier, Katherine Haldane. *Tourism and Identity in Scotland, 1770–1914: Creating Caledonia*. Burlington, VT: Ashgate, 2005.

Grunberger, Richard. *Red Rising in Bavaria*. London: Barker, 1973.

Grünsteudel, Günther, Günther Hagele, and Rudolf Frankenberger, eds. *Augsburger Stadtlexicon*, 2nd edn. Augsburg: Perlach Verlag, 1998.

Hachtmann, Rüdiger. *Tourismus-Geschichte*. Göttingen: Vandenhoeck & Ruprecht, 2007.

Hagemann, Karen. "German Heroes: The Cult of the Death for the Fatherland in 19th Century Germany." In *Masculinities in Politics and War: Gendering Modern History*, ed. Stefan Dudink, Karen Hagemann, and John Tosh, 116–134. New York: Palgrave, 2004.

Hagen, Joshua. "The Most German of Towns: Creating an Ideal Nazi Community in Rothenburg ob der Tauber." *Annals of the Association of American Geographers* 94, no. 1 (March 2004): 207–227.

———. "Parades, Public Space, and Propaganda: The Nazi Culture Parades in Munich." *Geografiska Annaler* 90, no. 4 (2008): 349–367.

———. *Preservation, Tourism and Nationalism: The Jewel of the German Past*. Burlington: Ashgate, 2006.

Hagen, William. "Master Narratives beyond Postmodernity: Germany's 'Separate Path' in Historiographical-Philosophical Light." *German Studies Review* 30, no. 1 (February 2007): 1–32.

Haller, Jörg. "'Die heilige Ostmark': Ostbayern als völkische Kultregion 'Bayerische Ostmark.'" *Bayerisches Jahrbuch für Volkskunde* (2000): 63–73.

Hanisch, Manfred. *"Für Fürst und Vaterland": Legitimationsstiftung in Bayern zwischen Revolution von 1848 und deutscher Einheit*. Munich: R. Oldenbourg, 1991.

Hansen, Peter H. "Albert Smith, the Alpine Club, and the Invention of Mountaineering in Mid-Victorian Britain." *Journal of British Studies* 34, no. 3 (July 1995): 300–324.

Harrington, Anne. *Reenchanted Science: Holism in German Culture from Wilhelm II to Hitler*. Princeton: Princeton University Press, 1996.

Harvey, Elizabeth. "Pilgrimages to the 'Bleeding Border': Gender and Rituals of Nationalist Protest in Germany, 1919–39." *Women's History Review* 9, no. 2 (2000): 201–229.

Has-Ellison, J. Trygve. "Nobles, Modernism, and the Culture of *fin-de-siècle* Munich." *German History* 26, no. 1 (January 2008): 1–23.

Hastings, Derek. *Catholicism and the Roots of Nazism: Religious Identity and National Socialism*. New York: Oxford University Press, 2010.

Hau, Michael. *The Cult of Health and Beauty in Germany: A Social History, 1890–1930*. Chicago: University of Chicago Press, 2003.

Helmer, Stephen. *Hitler's Berlin: The Speer Plans for Reshaping the Central City.* Ann Arbor: University of Michigan Research Press, 1985.

Henke, Josef. "Die Reichsparteitage der NSDAP in Nürnberg 1933–1938. – Planung, Organisation, Propaganda." In *Aus der Arbeit des Bundesarchivs*, ed. Heinz Boberbach and Hans Booms, 398–422. Boppard am Rhein: Harald Boldt Verlag, 1977.

Herf, Jeffrey. *Reactionary Modernism: Technology, Culture, and Politics in Weimar and the Third Reich.* New York: Cambridge University Press, 1984.

Heusler, Andreas. *Das Braune Haus: Wie München zur "Hauptstadt der Bewegung" wurde.* Munich: Deutsche Verlags-Anstalt, 2008.

Hobsbawm, E.J., and Terence Ranger, eds. *The Invention of Tradition.* New York: Cambridge University Press, 1983.

Hoenicke Moore, Michaela. *Know Your Enemy: The American Debate on Nazism, 1933–1945.* New York: Cambridge University Press, 2010.

Hölzl, Richard. "Nature Preservation in the Age of Classical Modernity: The Landesausschuss für Naturpflege and the Bund Naturschutz in Bavaria, 1905–1933." *Bulletin of the German Historical Institute, Washington D.C.*, Supplement 3: "From *Heimat* to *Umwelt*: New Perspectives on German Environmental History" (2006): 27–52.

Howind, Sascha. *Die Illusion eines guten Lebens: Kraft durch Freude und nationalsozialistische Sozialpropaganda.* Frankfurt am Main: Peter Lang, 2013.

Hulme, Peter, and Ted Youngs, eds. *The Cambridge Companion to Travel Writing.* New York: Cambridge University Press, 2002.

Jackson, James. *Migration and Urbanization in the Ruhr Valley, 1821–1914.* Atlantic Highlands, NJ: Humanities Press, 1997.

Jaskot, Paul B. *The Architecture of Oppression: The SS, Forced Labor and the Nazi Monumental Building Economy.* New York: Routledge, 2000.

Joachimsthaler, Anton. *Hitlers Weg begann in München 1913–1923.* Munich: Herbig, 2000.

Johnson, Eric A. *Urbanization and Crime: Germany 1871–1914.* New York: Cambridge University Press, 1995.

Judson, Pieter M. *Guardians of the Nation: Activists on the Language Frontiers of Imperial Austria.* Cambridge, MA: Harvard University Press, 2006.

Kaes, Anton. *Shell Shock Cinema: Weimar Culture and the Wounds of War.* Princeton: Princeton University Press, 2009.

Kapczynski, Jennifer M. *The German Patient: Crisis and Recovery in Postwar Culture.* Ann Arbor: University of Michigan Press, 2008.

Kehl, Patrick. "Der Aufstieg der NSDAP in Augsburg – eine Wahlanalyse." In *Nationalsozialismus in Bayerisch-Schwaben*, ed. Andreas Wirsching, 57–88. Ostfildern: Thorbecke, 2004.

Keitz, Christine. "Die Anfänge des modernen Massentourismus in der Weimarer Republik." *Archiv für Sozialgeschichte* 33 (1993): 179–209.

———. *Reisen als Leitbild: Die Entstehung des modernen Massentourismus in Deutschland.* Munich: Deutscher Taschenbuch Verlag, 1997.

Kennedy, Katharine D. "Regionalism and Nationalism in South German History Lessons, 1871–1914." *German Studies Review* 12, no. 1 (February 1989): 11–33.

Kershaw, Ian. *Hitler, 1889–1936: Hubris.* New York: W.W. Norton & Company, 1998.

———. *The "Hitler Myth": Image and Reality in the Third Reich.* New York: Oxford University Press, 1987.

———. *Popular Opinion and Political Dissent in the Third Reich, Bavaria 1933–1945,* 2nd edn. New York: Oxford University Press, 2002.

Killen, Andreas. *Berlin Electropolis: Shock, Nerves, and German Modernity.* Berkeley: University of California Press, 2006.

Kocka, Jürgen, *Das lange 19. Jahrhundert. Arbeit, Nation und bürgerliche Gesellschaft.* Stuttgart: Klett-Cotta, 2001.

———. "German History Before Hitler: The Debate about the German Sonderweg." *Journal of Contemporary History* 23, no. 1 (January 1988): 3–16.

———, ed. *Bürger und Bürgerlichkeit im 19. Jahrhundert.* Göttingen: Vandenhoeck & Ruprecht, 1987.

———, and Allan Mitchell, eds. *Bourgeois Society in Nineteenth-Century Europe.* Providence: Berg, 1993.

Kolb, Eberhard. *The Weimar Republic,* 2nd edn. Translated by P.S. Falla and R.J. Park. New York: Routledge, 2005.

Kopper, Christopher M. "The Breakthrough of the Package Tour in Germany after 1945." *Journal of Tourism History* 1, no. 1 (March 2009): 67–92.

Koshar, Rudy. *From Monuments to Traces: Artifacts of German Memory, 1870–1990.* Berkeley: University of California Press, 2000.

———. *German Travel Cultures.* Oxford: Berg, 2000.

———. *Germany's Transient Pasts: Preservation and National Memory in the Twentieth Century.* Chapel Hill: University of North Carolina Press, 1998.

———. "'What Ought to Be Seen': Tourists' Guidebooks and National Identities in Modern Germany and Europe." *Journal of Contemporary History* 33, no. 3 (July 1998): 323–340.

———, ed. *Histories of Leisure.* Oxford: Berg, 2002.

Kniesche, Thomas W., and Stephen Brockmann, eds. *Dancing on the Volcano: Essays on the Culture of the Weimar Republic.* Columbia, SC: Camden, 1994.

Kraus, Andreas. *Geschichte Bayerns: Von den Anfängen bis zur Gegenwart,* 3rd edn. Munich: Beck, 2004.

Krotz, Larry. *Tourists: How Our Fastest Growing Industry Is Changing the World.* Boston: Faber and Faber, 1996.

Kühnert, Reinhold. "Badereisen im 18. Jahrhundert – Sozialleben zur Zeit der Aufklärung." *Journal für Geschichte* 1 (1987): 16–21.

———. *Urbanität auf dem Lande: Badereisen nach Pyrmont im 18. Jahrhundert.* Göttingen: Vandenhoeck & Ruprecht, 1984.

Kuprian, Hermann J.W., and Oswald Überegger, eds. *Der Erste Welkrieg im Alpenraum. Erfahrung, Deutung, Errinnerung.* Innsbruck: Wagner, 2006.

Kurlansky, Mark. *Salt: A World History.* New York: Penguin Books, 2003.

Küster, Hansjörg. "Die Entdeckung der Lüneburger Heide als 'schöne Natur.'" *Themenportal Europäische Geschichte* (2010), www.europa.clio-online.de/2010/Article=429 (accessed October 20, 2010).

———. *Schöne Aussichten. Kleine Geschichte der Landschaft.* Munich: C.H. Beck, 2009.

Lang, Johannes. *Geschichte von Bad Reichenhall*. Neustadt an der Aisch: Verlag PH.C.W. Schmidt, 2009.

_____. "Vom 'Judenbad' zum 'judenfreien' Staatsbad: Jüdische Kurtradition und Bäderantisemitismus in Bad Reichenhall." *Jahrbuch des Nürnberger Instituts für NS-Forschung und jüdische Geschichte des 20. Jahrhunderts* (2014): 135–151.

Large, David Clay. *Berlin*. Basic Books: New York, 2000.

_____. *Nazi Games: The Olympics of 1936*. New York: W.W. Norton & Company, 2007.

_____. *Where Ghosts Walked: Munich's Road to the Third Reich*. New York: W.W. Norton & Company, 1997.

Lauterbach, Iris, ed. *Bürokratie und Kult. Das Parteizentrum der NSDAP am Königsplatz in München. Teil 1: Geschichte und Rezeption*. Munich: Deutscher Kunstverlag, 1995.

Lee, W.R. *Population Growth, Economic Development and Social Change in Bavaria, 1750–1850*. New York: Arno Press, 1977.

Leed, Eric J. *The Mind of the Traveler: From Gilgamesh to Global Tourism*. New York: Basic Books, 1991.

Lees, Andrew. "Critics of Urban Society in Germany, 1854–1914." *Journal of the History of Ideas* 40, no. 1 (January-March 1979): 61–83.

_____. *Cities, Sin, and Social Reform in Imperial Germany*. Ann Arbor: University of Michigan Press, 2002.

Lees, Andrew, and Lynn Hollen Lees. *Cities and the Making of Modern Europe, 1750–1914*. New York: Cambridge University Press, 2007.

Leibetseder, Mathis. *Die Kavalierstour. Adlige Erziehungsreisen im 17. und 18. Jahrhundert*. Cologne: Böhlau, 2004.

Leinberger, Karl. *Der Fremdenverkehr in Bad Reichenhall, seine Grundlagen, seine Entwicklung und seine Wirkungen*. Bad Reichenhall, 1923.

Lekan, Thomas. *Imagining the Nation in Nature: Landscape Preservation and German Identity, 1885–1945*. Cambridge, MA: Harvard University Press, 2004.

_____. "A 'Noble Prospect': Tourism, *Heimat*, and Conservation on the Rhine, 1880–1914." *The Journal of Modern History* 81, no. 4 (December 2009): 824–858.

_____, and Thomas Zeller, eds. *Germany's Nature: Cultural Landscapes and Environmental History*. New Brunswick, NJ: Rutgers University Press, 2005.

Lempa, Heikki. *Beyond the Gymnasium: Educating the Middle-Class Bodies in Classical Germany*. Lanham, MD: Lexington Books, 2007.

_____. "The Spa: Emotional Economy and Social Classes in Nineteenth-Century Pyrmont." *Central European History* 35, no. 1 (2002): 37–73.

Lenger, Friedrich, ed. *Towards an Urban Nation: Germany since 1780*. New York: Berg, 2002.

Leonardi, Andrea, and Hans Heiss, eds. *Tourismus und Entwicklung im Alpenraum 18.-20. Jahrhundert*. Innsbruck: Studien, 2003.

Lepovitz, Helen Waddy. "Gateway to the Mountains: Tourism and Positive Deindustrialization in the Bavarian Alps." *German History* 7 (1989): 293–318.

————. "Pilgrims, Patients, and Painters: The Formation of a Tourist Culture in Bavaria." *Historical Reflections/Reflexions Historiques* 18, no. 1 (1992): 121–145.

Lerner, Paul Frederick. *Hysterical Men: War, Psychiatry, and the Politics of Trauma in Germany, 1890–1930*. New York: Cornell University Press, 2003.

Le Roy Ladurie, Emmanuel. *The Beggar and the Professor: A Sixteenth Century Family Saga*. Translated by Arthur Goldhammer. Chicago: University of Chicago Press, 1997.

Levi, Neil. "'Judge for Yourselves!'–The 'Degenerate Art' Exhibition as Political Spectacle." *October* 85 (Summer 1998): 41–64.

Littlewood, Ian. *Sultry Climates: Travel and Sex*. Cambridge, MA: Da Capo, 2002.

Lloyd, David W. *Battlefield Tourism: Pilgrimage and the Commemoration of the Great War in Britain, Australia, and Canada, 1919–1939*. New York: Berg, 1998.

Löfgren, Orvar. *On Holiday: A History of Vacationing*. Berkeley: University of California Press, 1999.

Lorenz, Chris. "Beyond Good and Evil? The German Empire of 1871 and Modern German Historiography." *Journal of Contemporary History* 30, no. 4 (October 1995): 729–765.

Löwy, Michael, and Robert Sayre. *Romanticism Against the Tide of Modernity*. Translated by Catherine Porter. Durham: Duke University Press, 2001.

Maase, Kaspar. *Grenzenloses Vergnügen: Der Aufstieg der Massenkultur, 1850–1970*. Frankfurt am Main: Fischer, 1997.

MacCannell, Dean. *The Tourist: A New Theory of the Leisure Class*. New York: Schocken Books, 1976.

Mackaman, Douglas Peter. *Leisure Settings: Bourgeois Culture, Medicine, and the Spa in Modern France*. Chicago: University of Chicago Press, 1998.

Mann, Golo. *Ludwig I. von Bayern*. Frankfurt am Main: Fischer Taschenbuch Verlag, 1999.

Marcuse, Harold. *Legacies of Dachau: The Uses and Abuses of a Concentration Camp, 1933–2001*. New York: Cambridge University Press, 2001.

Matheus, Michael, ed. *Badeorte und Bäderreisen in Antike, Mittelalter und Neuzeit*. Stuttgart: Franz Steiner, 2001.

Mauch, Christof, ed. *Nature in German History*. New York: Berghahn, 2004.

Mayr, Norbert Joseph. "Particularism in Bavaria: State Policy and the Public Sentiment, 1806–1906." Ph.D. diss., University of North Carolina, Chapel Hill, 1988.

McElligott, Anthony. *The German Urban Experience, 1900–1945*. New York: Routledge, 2001.

McIntosh, Christopher. *Ludwig II of Bavaria: The Swan King*. New York: I.B. Tauris, 1997.

Melendy, Brenda. "Expellees on Strike: Competing Victimization Discourses and the Dachau Refugee Camp Protest Movement, 1948–1949." *German Studies Review* 28, no. 1 (February 2005): 107–125.

Menges, Günter. *Wachstum und Konjunktur des deutschen Fremdenverkehrs 1913 bis 1956.* Frankfurt am Main: Kommissionsverlag Waldemar Kramer, 1959.

Mierzejewski, Alfred C. "The German National Railway Company, 1924–1932: Between Private and Public Enterprise." *The Business History Review* 67, no. 3 (Autumn 1993): 406–438.

Mitchell, Allan. "A Real Foreign Country: Bavarian Particularism in Imperial Germany, 1870–1918." *Francia* 7 (1979): 587–596.

————. *Revolution in Bavaria, 1918–1919: The Eisner Regime and the Soviet Republic.* (Princeton: Princeton University Press, 1965.

Morton, Marsha. "German Romanticism: The Search for 'A Quiet Place.'" *Art Institute of Chicago Museum Studies* 28, no. 1 (2002): 8–23, 106–107.

Mosse, George. *Fallen Soldiers: Reshaping the Memory of the World Wars.* New York: Oxford University Press, 1990.

————. *The Nationalization of the Masses: Political Symbolism and Mass Movements in Germany from the Napoleonic Wars through the Third Reich.* New York: H. Fertig, 1975.

Murdock, Caitlin. "Tourist Landscapes and Regional Identities in Saxony, 1878–1938." *Central European History* 40, no. 4 (December 2007): 589–621.

Nagy, Florian, and Johann C. Bentele. *Oktoberfest. Zwischen Tradition und Moderne.* Munich: München Verlag, 2007.

Niehuss, Merith. *Arbeiterschaft in Krieg und Inflation.* Berlin: Walter de Gruyter, 1985.

Nipperdey, Thomas. *Deutsche Geschichte, 1800–1866: Bürgerwelt und starker Staat.* Munich: C.H. Beck, 1983.

————. *Deutsche Geschichte, 1866–1918, Erster Band: Arbeitswelt und Bürgergeist.* Munich: C.H. Beck, 1990.

Nolan, Mary. *Visions of Modernity: American Business and the Modernization of Germany.* New York: Oxford University Press, 1994.

Nora, Pierre. "Between Memory and History: Les Lieux de Mémoire." *Representations,* no. 26 (Spring 1989): 7–24.

Nowack, Thilo. "Rhein, Romantik, Reisen. Der Ausflugs- und Erholungsreiseverkehr im Mittelrheintal im Kontext gesellschaftlichen Wandels (1890 bis 1970)." Ph.D. diss., Rheinische Friedrich-Wilhelms-Universität, Bonn, 2006.

Ostler, Josef. *Garmisch und Partenkirchen 1870–1935. Ein Olympia-Ort entsteht.* Garmisch-Partenkirchen: Verein für Geschichte, Kunst- und Kulturgeschichte im Landkreis Garmisch-Partenkirchen, 2000.

Penny, Glenn. "Fashioning Local Identities in an Age of Nation-Building: Museums, Cosmopolitan Visions, and Intra-German Competition." *German History* 17, no. 4 (1999): 489–505.

Peukert, Detlev. *The Weimar Republic: The Crisis of Classical Modernity.* Translated by Richard Deveson. New York: Hill and Wang, 1992.

Pfisterer, Herbert. *Bad Reichenhall in seiner bayerischen Geschichte,* 2nd edn. Munich: Motor+Touristik-Verlag, 1988.

Phillips, Denise. "Friends of Nature: Urban Sociability and Regional Natural History in Dresden, 1800–1850." *Osiris* 18 (2003): 43–59.

Planert, Ute. "From Collaboration to Resistance: Politics, Experience, and Memory of the Revolutionary and Napoleonic Wars in Southern Germany." *Central European History* 39, no. 4 (December 2006): 676–705.

Pohl, Karin. *Zwischen Integration und Isolation: Zur kulturellen Dimension der Vertriebenspolitik in Bayern (1945–1975).* Munich: Iudicium, 2009.

Porter, Roy, ed. *The Cambridge History of Medicine.* New York: Cambridge University Press, 2006.

Porter, Roy, and Mikuláš Teich, eds. *Romanticism in National Context.* New York: Cambridge University Press, 1988.

Pratt, Mary Louise. *Imperial Eyes: Travel Writing and Transculturation,* 2nd edn. New York: Routledge, 2008.

Prein, Philipp. *Bürgerliches Reisen im 19. Jahrhundert: Freizeit, Kommunikation und soziale Grenzen.* Münster: Lit, 2005.

Pretzel, Ulrich. *Die Literaturform Reiseführer im 19. und 20. Jahrhundert: Untersuchungen am Beispiel des Rheins.* Frankfurt a.M.: Peter Lang Verlag, 1995.

Proctor, Robert N. *The Nazi War on Cancer.* Princeton: Princeton University Press, 1999.

Putschögl, Monika. "Am Anfang stand Ruhpolding." *Die Zeit* 27 (Hamburg), 1 July 1999, 49–50.

Radkau, Joachim. *Das Zeitalter der Nervosität: Deutschland zwischen Bismarck und Hitler.* Munich: Hanser, 1998.

———. *Nature and Power: A Global History of the Environment.* Translated by Thomas Dunlap. New York: Cambridge University Press, 2008.

Reichel, Peter. "Culture and Politics in Nazi Germany." Translated by Dorothea Blumenberg. In *Political Culture in Germany,* ed. Dirk Berg-Schlosser and Ralf Rytlewski, 60–77. New York: St. Martin's Press, 1993.

Repp, Kevin. *Reformers, Critics, and the Paths of German Modernity: Anti-Politics and the Search for Alternatives, 1890–1914.* Cambridge, MA: Harvard University Press, 2000.

Retallack, James, ed. *Imperial Germany, 1871–1918.* New York: Oxford University Press, 2010.

———, ed. *Saxony in German History: Culture, Society, and Politics, 1830–1933.* Ann Arbor: University of Michigan Press, 2000.

Reulecke, Jurgen. *Geschichte der Urbanisierung in Deutschland.* Frankfurt am Main: Suhrkamp, 1985.

———. "Vom blauen Montag zum Arbeiterurlaub: Vorgeschichte und Entstehung des Erholungsurlaubs für Arbeiter vor dem Ersten Weltkrieg." *Archiv für Sozialgeschichte* 16 (1976): 205–248.

Roeck, Bernd. *Geschichte Augsburgs.* Munich: C.H. Beck, 2005.

Rohkrämer, Thomas. "Antimodernism, Reactionary Modernism and National Socialism: Technocratic Tendencies in Germany, 1890–1945," *Contemporary European History* 8, no. 1 (March 1999): 29–50.

———. *Eine andere Moderne? Zivilisationskritik, Natur und Technik in Deutschland, 1880–1930.* Paderborn: Schöningh, 1999.

Rollins, William. *A Greener Vision of Home: Cultural Politics and Environmental Reform in the German Heimatschutz Movement, 1904–1918.* Ann Arbor: University of Michigan Press, 1997.

Romer, Andreas. *Willkommen in der Bahnhofstrasse!: Die Entwicklung der Augsburger Bahnhofstrasse und ihre Bedeutung für die Bürger.* Munich: Hampp, 2006.

Roseman, Mark. "National Socialism and the End of Modernity." AHR Forum: "Historians and the Question of 'Modernity'." *American Historical Review* 116, no. 3 (June 2011): 688–701.

Rosenfeld, Gavriel D. "Monuments and the Politics of Memory: Commemorating Kurt Eisner and the Bavarian Revolutions of 1918–1919 in Postwar Munich." *Central European History* 30, no. 2 (1997): 221–251.

_____. *Munich and Memory: Architecture, Monuments, and the Legacy of the Third Reich.* Berkeley: University of California Press, 2000.

_____, and Paul B. Jaskot, eds. *Beyond Berlin: Twelve German Cities Confront the Nazi Past.* Ann Arbor: University of Michigan Press, 2008.

Ross, Chad. *Naked Germany: Health, Race, and the Nation.* New York: Berg, 2005.

Rothman, Hal K. *Devil's Bargains: Tourism in the Twentieth-Century American West.* Lawrence, KS: University Press of Kansas, 1998.

Sachse, Carola, Tilla Siegel, Hasso Spode, and Wolfgang Spohn. *Angst, Belohnung, Zucht und Ordnung: Herrschaftsmechanismen im Nationalsozialismus.* Opladen: Westdeutscher Verlag Gmbh, 1982.

Saldern, Adelheid von. *The Challenges of Modernity: German Social and Cultural Studies, 1890–1960.* Translated by Bruce Little. Ann Arbor: University of Michigan Press, 2002.

Schäfer, Martin. *Maximillian II.: König von Bayern.* Munich: W. Heyne, 1989.

Schama, Simon. *Landscape and Memory.* New York: Vintage Books, 1996.

Schivelbusch, Wolfgang. *The Railway Journey: The Industrialization of Time and Space in the 19th Century.* Berkeley: University of California Press, 1987.

Schmid, Alois, ed. *Das Neue Bayern. Von 1800 bis zur Gegenwart. Zweiter Teilband: Innere Entwicklung und kulturelles Leben.* Munich: C.H. Beck, 2007.

Schottky, Lilly. *Geschichte des Fränkische-Schweiz-Vereins, und andere heimatkundliche Beiträge.* Erlangen: Palm & Enke, 1989.

Schwartz, Eric. "Waldeinsamkeit: Subjective Ambivalence in German Romanticism." *International Journal of the Humanities* 5, no. 4 (November 2007): 201–209.

Schwarz, Angela. "British Visitors to National Socialist Germany: In a Familiar or in a Foreign Country?" *Journal of Contemporary History* 28, no. 3 (July 1993): 487–509.

_____. *Die Reise ins Dritte Reich: Britische Augenzeugen im nationalsozialistischen Deutschland (1933–39).* Göttingen: Vandenhoeck & Ruprecht, 1993.

Schweizer, Stefan. *"Unserer Weltanschauung sichtbaren Ausdruck geben": Nationalsozialistische Geschichtsbilder in historischen Festzügen zum "Tag der Deutschen Kunst".* Göttingen: Wallstein, 2007.

Scobie, Alexander. *Hitler's State Architecture: The Impact of Classical Antiquity.* University Park: Pennsylvania State University Press, 1990.

Sears, John F. *Sacred Places: American Tourist Attractions in the Nineteenth Century.* New York: Oxford University Press, 1989.

Sebald, W.G. *On the Natural History of Destruction*. Translated by Anthea Bell. New York: Modern Library, 2004.

Semmel, Stuart. "Reading the Tangible Past: British Tourism, Collecting, and Memory after Waterloo," *Representations*, no. 69 (Winter 2000): 9–37.

Semmens, Kristin. *Seeing Hitler's Germany: Tourism in the Third Reich*. New York: Palgrave Macmillan, 2005.

Sheehan, James J. "What is German History? Reflections on the Role of the Nation in German History and Historiography." *Journal of Modern History* 53, no. 1 (March 1981): 1–23.

Simon, Petra, and Margit Behren. *Badekur und Kurbad: Bauten in deutschen Bädern 1780–1920*. Munich: Diederichs, 1988.

Smith, Anthony D. *The Cultural Foundations of Nations: Hierarchy, Covenant and Republic*. Oxford: John Wiley and Sons, 2008.

Sneeringer, Julia. "'Assembly Line of Joys': Touring Hamburg's Red Light District, 1949–1966." *Central European History* 42, no. 1 (March 2009): 65–96.

Solnit, Rebecca. *Wanderlust: A History of Walking*. New York: Viking, 2000.

Sommer, Hermann. *Zur Kur nach Ems: Ein Beitrag zur Geschichte der Badereise von 1830 bis 1914*. Stuttgart: Steiner, 1999.

Sorkin, David. "Wilhelm von Humboldt: The Theory and Practice of Self-Formation (Bildung), 1791–1810." *Journal of the History of Ideas* 44, no. 1 (Jan.–Mar. 1983): 55–73.

Sösemann, Bernd. "Appell unter der Erntekrone: Das Reichserntedankfest in der nationalsozialistischen Diktatur." *Jahrbuch für Kommunikationsgeschichte* 2 (2000): 113–156.

Sperber, Jonathan. "Bürger, Bürgertum, Bürgerlichkeit, Bürgerliche Gesellschaft: Studies of the German (Upper) Middle Class and Its Sociocultural World." *The Journal of Modern History* 69, no. 2 (June 1997): 271–297.

Spode, Hasso. "Fordism, Mass Tourism and the Third Reich: The "Strength through Joy" Seaside Resort as an Index Fossil." *Journal of Social History* 38, no. 1 (Autumn 2004): 127–155.

_____. *Wie die Deutschen "Reiseweltmeister" wurden: Eine Einführung in die Tourismusgeschichte*. Erfurt: Landeszentrale für politische Bildung Thüringen, 2003.

_____, ed. *Goldstrand und Teutonengrill: Kultur- und Sozialgeschichte des Tourismus in Deutschland 1945 bis 1989*. Berlin: Verlag für universitäre Kommunikation, 1996.

Spotts, Frederic. *Bayreuth: A History of the Wagner Festival*. New Haven: Yale University Press, 1994.

Spree, Reinhard. *Soziale Ungleichheit vor Krankheit und Tod: Zur Sozialgeschichte des Gesundheitsbereichs im Deutschen Kaiserreich*. Göttingen: Vandenhoeck & Ruprecht, 1981.

Städtler, Hans-Wolfgang, ed. *Das Heilbad Bad Reichenhall im 19. und 20. Jahrhundert: Festschrift anläßlich des 100-jährigen Jubiläums der Baderhebung 1890–1990*. Bad Reichenhall, 1990.

Steigmann-Gall, Richard. *The Holy Reich: Nazi Conceptions of Christianity, 1919-1945*. New York: Cambridge University Press, 2003.

Steinbacher, Sybille. *Dachau. Die Stadt und das Konzentrationslager in der NS-Zeit. Die Untersuchung einer Nachbarschaft,* 2nd edn. Frankfurt am Main: Peter Lang, 1994.

Steinhauser, Monika. "Das europäische Modebad des 19. Jahrhunderts. Baden-Baden, eine Residenz des Glücks." In *Die deutsche Stadt im 19. Jahrhundert. Stadtplanung und Baugestaltung im industriellen Zeitalter,* ed. Ludwig Grote, 95–128. Munich: Prestel, 1974.

Stern, Fritz. *Dreams and Delusions: National Socialism in the Drama of the German Past.* New York: Vintage Books, 1989.

Sterzl, Anton, and Emil Bauer. *Fränkische Schweiz: Gesichter und Kräfte einer Landschaft.* Bamberg: St. Otto Verlag, 1969.

Storm, Eric. "Regionalism in History, 1890–1945: The Cultural Approach." *European History Quarterly* 33, no. 2 (2003): 251–265.

Sumption, Jonathan. *The Age of Pilgrimage: The Medieval Journey to God.* Mahwah, NJ: Paulist Press, 2003.

Swett, Pamela E., S. Jonathan Wiesen, and Jonathan R. Zatlin, eds. *Selling Modernity: Advertising in Twentieth-Century Germany.* Durham: Duke University Press, 2007.

Timothy, Dallen J., and Daniel H. Olsen, eds. *Tourism, Religion and Spiritual Journeys.* New York: Routledge, 2006.

Towner, John. *An Historical Geography of Recreation and Tourism in the Western World, 1540–1940.* New York: John Wiley & Sons, 1996.

Treml, Manfred, ed. *Geschichte des modernen Bayern: Königreich und Freistaat,* 3rd edn. Munich: Bayerische Landeszentrale für Politische Bildungsarbeit, 2006.

Triendl-Zadoff, Miriam. *Nächstes Jahr in Marienbad. Gegenwelten jüdischer Kulturen der Moderne.* Göttingen: Vandenhoeck & Ruprecht, 2007.

Turner, Victor, and Edith Turner. *Image and Pilgrimage in Christian Culture.* New York: Columbia University Press, 1978.

Umbach, Maiken. *German Cities and Bourgeois Modernism, 1890–1924.* New York: Oxford University Press, 2009.

———. "Memory and Historicism: Reading between the Lines of the Built Environment, Germany c. 1900." *Representations* 88, no. 1 (Fall 2004): 26–54.

Urry, John. *The Tourist Gaze,* 2nd edn. London: Sage Publications, 2002.

Verhey, Jeffrey. *The Spirit of 1914: Militarism, Myth, and Mobilization in Germany.* New York: Cambridge University Press, 2000.

Vogel, Hubert. *Geschichte von Bad Reichenhall.* Munich: Verlag des Historischen Vereins von Oberbayern, 1971.

Voit, Gustave, Brigitte Kaulich, and Walter Rüfer. *Vom Land im Gebirg zur Fränkischen Schweiz: Eine Landschaft wird entdeckt.* Erlangen: Palm & Enke, 1992.

Volkmann, H.J. *Das touristische Image Augsburgs: Eine Studie.* Augsburg: Selbstverlag des Lehrstühls für Didaktik der Geographie der Universität Augsburg, 1985.

Waddy, Helena. *Oberammergau in the Nazi Era: The Fate of a Catholic Village in Hitler's Germany.* New York: Oxford University Press, 2010.

Ward, Janet. *Weimar Surfaces: Urban Visual Culture in 1920s Germany*. Berkeley: University of California Press, 2001.

Wearing, Steven, Deborah Stevenson, and Tamara Young. *Tourist Cultures: Identity, Place and the Traveller*. London: Sage, 2010.

Webb, Diana. *Medieval European Pilgrimage, c.700–c.1500*. New York: Palgrave, 2002.

Wehler, Hans-Ulrich. *The German Empire, 1871–1918*. Translated by Kim Traynor. Dover, NH: Berg Publishers, 1985.

Weichlein, Siegfried. *Nation und Region: Integrationsprozesse in Bismarckreich*. Düsseldorf: Droste, 2004.

Weindling, Paul. *Health, Race, and German Politics between National Unification and Nazism, 1870–1945*. New York: Cambridge University Press, 1989.

Weisser, Fritz. *"...wie Augsburg für sich warb." 1891–1991*. Augsburg: Helga Vetterle Marketing-Management Werbeagentur GmbH, 1991.

Weitz, Eric. *Weimar Germany: Promise and Tragedy*. Princeton: Princeton University Press, 2007.

Welch, David. *Propaganda and the German Cinema, 1933–1945*, 2nd edn. New York: I.B. Tauris, 2001.

————. *The Third Reich: Politics and Propaganda*, 2nd edn. New York: Routledge, 2007.

Widdig, Bernd. *Culture and Inflation in Weimar Germany*. Berkeley: University of California Press, 2001.

Wiesen, S. Jonathan. *Creating the Nazi Marketplace: Commerce and Consumption in the Third Reich*. New York: Cambridge University Press, 2011.

Wildt, Michael. *Hitler's Volksgemeinschaft and the Dynamics of Racial Exclusion: Violence Against Jews in Provincial Germany, 1919–1939*. Translated by Bernard Heise. New York: Berghahn, 2012.

Williams, John Alexander. *Turning to Nature in Germany: Hiking, Nudism, and Conservation, 1900–1940*. Stanford: Stanford University Press, 2007.

Williams, Raymond. *The Country and the City*. New York: Oxford University Press, 1973.

Winter, Jay, and Jean-Louis Robert. *Capital Cities at War: Paris, London, Berlin 1914–1919*. New York: Cambridge University Press, 1997.

Wistrich, Robert S. *Weekend in Munich: Art, Propaganda, and Terror in the Third Reich*. London: Pavilion, 1995.

Withey, Lynne. *Grand Tours and Cook's Tours: A History of Leisure Travel, 1750–1915*. New York: William Morrow and Company, 1997.

Wuttke, Dieter. *Nuremberg: Focal Point of German Culture and History*. Bamberg: Stefan Wendel, 1988.

Wysocki, Josef. *Leben im Berchtesgadener Land, 1800–1990*. Bad Reichenhall: Sparkasse Berchtesgadener Land, 1991.

Young, Patrick. "Of Pardons, Loss, and Longing: The Tourist's Pursuit of Originality in Brittany, 1890–1935." *French Historical Studies* 30, no. 2 (2007): 269–304.

Zeller, Thomas. *Driving Germany: The Landscape of the German Autobahn, 1930–1970*. Translated by Thomas Dunlap. New York: Berghahn, 2007.

Ziemann, Benjamin. *War Experiences in Rural Germany, 1914–1923.* Translated by Alex Skinner. New York: Berg, 2007.

Ziolkowski, Theodore. *Vorboten der Moderne: Eine Kulturgeschichte der Frühromantik.* Stuttgart: Klett-Cotta, 2006.

Zorn, Wolfgang. *Augsburg: Geschichte einer deutschen Stadt.* Augsburg: Mühlberger, 1972.

_____. *Schwaben und Augsburg in der ersten Hälfte des 20. Jahrhunderts.* Munich: Verlag Ernst Vögel, 1976.

Index